Understanding Tolstoy

$\mathscr{U}$NDERSTANDING
$\mathscr{T}$OLSTOY

ANDREW D. KAUFMAN

 THE OHIO STATE UNIVERSITY PRESS / COLUMBUS

Library of Congress Cataloging-in-Publication Data
Kaufman, Andrew, 1969–
 Understanding Tolstoy / Andrew D. Kaufman.
     p. cm.
 Includes bibliographical references and index.
 ISBN 978-0-8142-1164-9 (cloth : alk. paper)—ISBN 978-0-8142-9263-1 (cd)
 1. Tolstoy, Leo, graf, 1828–1910—Criticism and interpretation. I. Title.
 PG3410.K376 2011
 891.73'3—dc23
                              2011017303

Cover design by Juliet Williams
Text design by Juliet Williams
Type set in Adobe Sabon
Printed by Thomson-Shore, Inc.

9   8   7   6   5   4   3   2   1

To Mom and Dad, who gave me the possibility
Aida, who instilled the passion
and
Corinne, who showed me the path

contents

illustrations

acknowledgments

Tolstoy liked to quote the words of Father Zossima in *The Brothers Karamazov:* "Everything, like an ocean, everything flows and comes into contact—you touch in one place, and at the other end of the world it reverberates." During my twenty-year journey with Tolstoy, many people have touched me professionally and personally, and their influence can be felt in ways both subtle and profound on every page of this book.

Understanding Tolstoy evolved in part out of my quest to relay Tolstoy's artistic genius in a way that my students would find compelling and personally relevant. I am grateful to the University of Virginia for the opportunity and financial assistance that have allowed me both to research and to write this book, as well as experiment with new methods of teaching Tolstoy and Russian literature.

In particular, I am grateful to the Office of the Vice President and Provost for a Teaching and Research Fellowship as well as an Academic Community Engagement Faculty Fellow grant; the Youth-NEX Center in the Curry School of Education for a research grant; and the Teaching Resource Center for a Learning Assessment grant. The Slavic Department gave me the opportunity to teach talented, committed undergraduate and graduate students, whose provocative questions and insights pushed my thinking in new directions.

I thank Richard Gustafson for his professional generosity and thoughtful comments on earlier drafts of this book, as well as Donna Orwin for her scholarly counsel and support of my work. Hugh McClean and Irwin Weil offered thorough feedback after a careful reading of the manuscript, and their many insights helped me to sharpen my ideas and avoid mistakes.

My friend and mentor Pyotr Palievsky read and commented on the entire manuscript and arranged for my first professional visit to the Gorky Institute of World Literature in Moscow. Other colleagues at the Gorky Institute—Sergei Bocharov, Marina Shcherbakova, and Aleksandr Gulin— also lent me valuable support.

I thank Galina Alekseeva of the Tolstoy Museum and Estate in Yasnaya Polyana for her scholarly counsel and for reading and commenting on the manuscript, and Vladimir Tolstoy for inviting me to present my scholarship in the place where his great grandfather lived and wrote.

Joseph Frank and Lazar Fleishman at Stanford University offered invaluable feedback on earlier drafts of this book and taught me to stay true to the text and to trust my own critical instincts. Gregory Freidin, Monika Greenleaf, and Stephen Moeller-Sally offered encouragement and scholarly advice during the writing of my doctoral dissertation, out of which this book grew.

I am indebted to Aida Borisovna Abuashvili-Lominadze of Moscow State University. I met Aida while I was an exchange student at Moscow State in 1990. Aida helped me to see, hear, and touch Tolstoy's characters and ideas all around me. Her deep love of Tolstoy, her dedication to her students, and her spiritual courage in the face of adversity remain an inspiration to me.

Dr. James Billington, author of the classic that first sparked my fascination with all things Russian, took the time to read my work, meet with me, and share his encyclopedic knowledge. Dana Gioia gave me a platform in which to share my love of Tolstoy with a wider audience, and George Steiner took the time to read and comment on my work.

I thank my agent, Rob McQuilkin, a consummate professional who has unfailingly steered me in all the right directions. I also thank Albert Small for his support of me and my career for many years, as well as Tom Friedman for kindly assisting my entrée in the book publishing world.

I am indebted to my good friend Sharon Leiter, who read every word of the manuscript and with her sensitive poet's ear helped me to transform a somewhat clunky doctoral dissertation into a book that even she would enjoy reading. John Gray, a gifted listener and a great friend, has supported me for many years and helped me to connect more deeply with Tolstoy's truth as well as my own.

I thank Sandy Crooms, Maggie Diehl, Juliet Williams, and the other editorial staff at The Ohio State University Press for their detailed copy-editing as well as the care, creativity, and professionalism with which they transformed the manuscript into a beautiful book.

My brothers Greg, Bob, and Mike have supported and encouraged me both personally and professionally. Mike, a fellow academic, has become one my closest colleagues, giving generously of himself intellectually and spiritually.

I am deeply grateful to my parents, who first suggested that I start studying Russian almost twenty-five years ago and who, to my good fortune, have been able to witness, in good health and with unfailing love, the many twists and turns of my long Tolstoyan journey that they helped to spark.

Perhaps nobody has experienced the everyday significance of that journey over the past several years more fully than my wife, Corinne. Through her eyes I have learned to see not only Tolstoy but myself more clearly and completely. Everyday Corinne teaches me by example the wisdom of Prince Andrei's words in *War and Peace:* "Everything, everything I understand, I understand only because I love."

$\mathcal{W}$HY ANOTHER BOOK ABOUT TOLSTOY?

For twenty years Tolstoy has stood at the center of my academic life—the compelling focus of my research, teaching, and public lecturing. Yet, it was only recently that I came to a startling realization: in all that has been written about the greatest Russian novelist, there is no one book that might help contemporary readers understand the writer's insight into the timeless question "What is living for?"[1] And yet the need for such a guide, in the twenty-first century, with all its moral complexities, terrors, and opportunities, has never been so compelling.

This book introduces readers to the ways in which Tolstoy, through a series of questing, unforgettable characters, grapples with essential human questions in his art. It not only helps readers understand the characters, themes, and artistry of Tolstoy's major novels and novellas. It introduces them more generally to Tolstoy and his time, while demonstrating how his wisdom is strikingly relevant today.

Tolstoy's art begins and ends with the most basic questions: Who am I? Why am I here? How should I live? But his answers to these questions do not come in the form of prepackaged life lessons, such as we turn to today in self-help books and how-to guides to happiness. Tolstoy's infinitely rich art offers a very different path. Like many great teachers of life—from Socrates, whom Tolstoy admired, to Gandhi, whom he influenced—Tolstoy urges us to engage the world with our complete being, and to seek out answers on our own, never settling for pat formulas or the borrowed ideas of others. For Tolstoy the road to truth begins with unceasing examination of the self, and the path to transcendence starts with a total immersion in the here-and-now.

Given the close connection between Tolstoy's writing and his own such quest, it is no coincidence that most of the searching heroes in his fiction are direct reflections of his own spiritual struggles. This book tells the story of those struggles as they unfold in each of his major characters, as well as in Tolstoy himself. It describes both the philosophical dimension of that quest and how Tolstoy brings it to life through his art. It guides readers through what the novelist called the "endless labyrinth of linkages" in his fiction, in which his meaning and his method are inseparably connected, and his sense of the wholeness of the universe is pervasive. The goal of this book is neither more nor less than to inspire readers to rediscover the enduring power and humanity of great literature.

Tolstoy once wrote: "Man is flowing. In him there are all possibilities: he was stupid, now he is clever; he was evil, now he is good, and the other way around. In this is the greatness of man."[2] These lines, written in 1898, when Tolstoy was seventy, express the author's lifelong belief in the ultimate integrity and goodness of the human spirit. Nowhere is Tolstoy's sense of man's greatness more powerfully expressed than in his four major novels: his little-known work, *The Cossacks* (1863); his panoramic masterpieces, *War and Peace* (1863–69) and *Anna Karenina* (1873–76); and his ideological novel, *Resurrection* (1899); as well as in his two major novellas, *The Death of Ivan Ilyich* (1886) and *Hadji-Murat* (1904). In these works, characters search and suffer, struggle and err, and hit any number of dead ends. Yet they also experience some of the most beautiful moments of transcendent bliss in all of world literature. These frustrated characters each have a capacity for growth and exaltation, despite the many obstacles life throws their way. By following a Tolstoyan character through the peaks and valleys of his or her tumultuous journey, we gain a fuller appreciation not only of the character's richness but also of our own.

To offer just one example, Dmitry Olenin, the young hero of *The Cossacks,* searches passionately for a more authentic way of living and a more just society. He expresses the longing of an entire generation of young Russians, who were frustrated by the moral indifference of an autocratic government as well as the spiritual emptiness of the intellectual elite. Yet Olenin's story transcends his time and place. His quest for a simpler life, close to nature, is mirrored in the experiences of other generations of idealistic youth. Olenin's turning to "natural" life is reminiscent of the hippie communes and back-to-the-earth movements of the 1960s and 1970s in this country, a trend that persists among a small but determined minority of idealists today. In a world threatened by ecological disaster, the question of how to preserve what is precious in nature while honoring the best "civilized" values has acquired a new urgency.

Olenin also voices the longing of our own young contemporaries, who are uninspired by either the promise of American ideological dominance in the world or the vacuity of postmodernist culture. Whether their passion be environmental sustainability, social justice in inner-city Detroit, or human rights in Darfur, young Americans today are increasingly responsive to patterns of social injustice and upheaval on a global scale. Like Olenin, they are looking for a moral compass in an age of relativism and for a unifying ideal in a seemingly broken world. What Tolstoy offers in *The Cossacks* is neither an ideology nor a social movement, but the vivid artistic rendering of one young man, descending to the depths of his being, and confronting his most fundamental yearnings, doubts, and beliefs in his quest for a way to live.

Some readers might wonder whether attempting to discuss Tolstoy's major literary texts, his biography, historical intellectual context, *and* contemporary relevance might be trying to do too much in a single book. I grappled with this question during every stage of writing, beginning with the book's earliest conception as a doctoral dissertation at Stanford. Yet every time I returned to Tolstoy's art I repeatedly found confirmation of the validity of such an approach in the texts themselves.

At the core of Tolstoy's worldview is a fundamental belief in the wholeness of the human person in relation to the totality of the circumstances that make up his or her life. To speak about any one element of Tolstoy's vision of the human struggle in isolation from the others is, in my view, to offer a fragmented, and therefore distorted, view of both the writer and his art. I wanted to write a book that reconstructs, rather than deconstructs Tolstoy—a book that mirrors the very internal unity of Tolstoy's trajectory as a man and artist. No matter where one immerses oneself in the Tolstoyan ocean, the water is essentially the same everywhere, although the current might be smoother in some places, the waves bigger in others.

Of course, no book can capture the whole truth about a writer or his art, as Tolstoy understood and frequently discussed in his notebooks and diaries. As a novelist, however, he also believed it was possible for a creative writer to select just the right details with the proper emphasis and focus in order to capture the "essence" of the object of description. I have tried to apply Tolstoy's insight into the art of fiction-writing to literary criticism, by selecting key characters and scenes and interweaving them with carefully chosen details from his life and times, in order to convey the "essence" of the writer's vision.

Because I wanted to find the right balance between coverage and readability, I was forced to make the difficult decision of excluding several important works from my discussion. I chose to focus on *The Cossacks* rather than the trilogy *Childhood, Boyhood,* and *Youth* (1852–57), because the major themes, autobiographical concerns, and artistic techniques of the early Tolstoy are fully present in *The Cossacks*. In addition, there is also already one very good book in English that deals substantially with the trilogy, but there are no good introductions to *The Cossacks*.[3] I felt that it was important to fill this lacuna in my book.

My reason for excluding *The Kreutzer Sonata* (1889) from the book is that the themes of passion, adultery, and the breakdown of family and social structures that were so important to Tolstoy in his middle career are fully addressed in *Anna Karenina*. *The Kreutzer Sonata* is a more controversial and openly polemical work, but it is also much narrower in its philosophical and artistic conception. The genius of *Anna Karenina* is that it offers a profound vision of the deep interconnectedness of many different people, places, and the social and spiritual problems of modern life. The novel comprises a brilliant "labyrinth of linkages," whereas *The Kreutzer Sonata* is more like a furious, if fascinating, tirade. It adds little to our understanding of Tolstoy's worldview that a deep reading of *Anna Karenina* cannot provide.

As for Tolstoy's nonfictional essays and treatises, I do not treat them in depth for two reasons. First, the ideas expressed in the essays are already present in the fiction, especially from the later period. I do devote some space to connections between the ideas in Tolstoy's nonfictional writings and the older writer's artistic and spiritual quest. But—and here is the second reason for the exclusion—a major premise of this book is that the essence of Tolstoy's worldview is contained most fully and powerfully in his great artistic texts, in which image, word, and idea are inextricably linked.

In his own life Tolstoy failed to live up to many of the ideas and ideals he systematically outlines in his nonfictional writings, and he describes these failings through his fictional characters. This fascinating contradiction between his stated beliefs and the reality of his and his character's lives has led some scholars to conclude that Tolstoy was a great artist, but a bad thinker. I have come to a slightly different conclusion: Tolstoy's best works of art, while certainly undergirded by his ideas, ultimately subsume them into a richer and more nuanced vision of life than could possibly be contained in his—or any writer's—analytical writing. I am persuaded that in order to appreciate the full depth and complexity of Tolstoy's world-view, one must focus on the art first, not the essays.

Regarding the contemporary references that appear throughout the book, I have included them because they reinforce the intellectual and spiritual foundation on which the entire book rests: my firm belief that Tolstoy speaks to us *now,* in the twenty-first century, and can help us engage the social and spiritual issues of our time more honestly, directly, and courageously than we otherwise might have.

Beyond this, my teaching and speaking experience has confirmed that these references assist many readers in navigating through the writer's vast and sometimes complicated terrain by providing concrete, identifiable markers from a world more familiar to them. They help readers to see more clearly the relationship between Tolstoy's issues and the concerns of today, and prod them to reflect more deeply about the relevance of Tol-stoy's art to their own lives. I have found this particularly valuable for students and other nonspecialists, and hope that scholars will find it useful and provocative, as well.

At a time when much contemporary academic literary scholarship insists that literature embodies the inevitability of human differences, stemming from irreconcilable cultural and social worldviews, my own teaching experiences both inside and outside of academia have suggested otherwise. Tolstoy's fiction has demonstrated its unique capacity to facilitate communication and deepen spiritual connections among readers from very different worlds in a way that has only strengthened my belief in the transcendent power of great literature.

Nowhere has my belief in the universal relevance of Tolstoy's art been more gratifyingly confirmed than in workshops and classes I have conducted about *The Death of Ivan Ilyich* for prison inmates and incarcerated youth in Virginia. Ivan Ilyich, a careerist judge living in Russia in the 1880s, could not be more removed socially, economically, and culturally from the world inhabited by these readers. Yet over and over again this novella, which casts a pitiless light on life's meaning in the face of death, has struck a powerful chord in them.

As I travel the country, speaking about Tolstoy to college and university faculty and students, high school teachers and students, professionals, prison inmates, and juvenile offenders, one thing has become clear to me: readers of all ages and from many different walks of life want to understand how great literature can help them live more authentically, fully, and happily in these difficult times. They want an author who can enlighten and inspire them, a writer who can guide them in their own search for meaning, and with whom they can identify personally. That is the Tolstoy I offer readers in this book.

Taken individually and collectively, Tolstoy's works reflect the vast geography of the writer's own consciousness, forever alternating between a sober awareness of what man is and an inspiring vision of what he might become. The portrait of Tolstoy that emerges in this book is of a vital, searching human being who continually grows and surprises us, yet is driven by a single, unchanging quest for truth. By presenting Tolstoy's universal relevance in these terms, *Understanding Tolstoy* offers a guide to readers entering Tolstoy's world for the first time or the tenth, and invites them, while there, to grapple alongside him and his characters with the most fundamental questions of their humanity.

one

$\mathcal{T}$HE LITTLE GREEN STICK AND THE LOST HOUSE

Tolstoy's Journey as Man and Artist

We begin the story of the writer's spiritual journey in the place from which he drew his deepest inspiration and in which his extraordinary life came full circle. Yasnaya Polyana—or "clear glade"—is the 1000-acre estate lying 130 miles southwest of Moscow, where Tolstoy was born in 1828, spent sixty of his eighty-two years, and was buried in 1910. Tolstoy considered Yasnaya Polyana his home in every sense of the word. It was his dominion, his refuge, his touchstone. "Without my Yasnaya," he said, "I cannot imagine my Russia and my relationship to her."[1]

Today Yasnaya Polyana continues to inspire visitors from around the world. As you wander along the maple-, linden-, and birch-lined paths between the heavily forested ravines, and through the meadows, extending beyond the horizon, with their richly scented bouquets of wildflowers, your consciousness alters. Time slows at Yasnaya Polyana, awareness sharpens, and the sense of human possibility expands. You begin to appreciate here—not only with your mind, but with your entire being—that mysterious grandeur of the universe that Tolstoy himself felt so deeply, and that emanates from the pages of his great novels. For, not unlike Yasnaya Polyana itself, each Tolstoyan novel is a world unto itself: buzzing with diverse life, moving with the pulse of time, yet unmistakably timeless and whole. "If the world could write," said Isaac Babel, the Russian Soviet author, "it would write like Tolstoy."[2]

Strolling along one of the main dirt paths at Yasnaya Polyana, you feel the forest growing thicker and the air cooler. Only the light rustling of the leaves of ash and birch trees and the occasional trilling of the sparrows and crickets can be heard. You approach the end of the path on the edge of the forest, and to your right is a small mound of grass, which appears to be growing out of the dusty earth pathway that surrounds it on all sides. This mound, adorned by a bouquet of freshly picked wildflowers and lit by a few rays of sun that have broken through the trees, is Tolstoy's gravesite. It stands there unobtrusively, on the edge of the ravine, without a headstone, without a sign, just as Tolstoy requested.

This is the spot where, as a little boy, Tolstoy and his brother, Nikolai, discovered a little green stick, on which, they believed, was inscribed the secret to universal happiness. When he was in his seventies, Tolstoy wrote in his *Recollections* (1902): "And just as I believed then, that there is a little green stick, on which is written the secret that will destroy all evil in people, and give them great blessings, so now I believe that such a truth exists and that it will be revealed to people and will give them what it promises."[3]

When Tolstoy left home in the middle of the night at the age of eighty-two, presumably to escape to the Caucasus, or possibly to a monastery, he was still searching for that universal truth, for the secret of the little green stick. His gravesite is just where he wanted it to be—on the spot where his quest for life's ultimate purpose began, in a moment of childlike innocence.

If the gravesite represents Tolstoy's lifelong quest for perfection, then there is another landmark at Yasnaya Polyana that points to the writer's intimate familiarity with the inglorious realities of everyday life. This landmark is situated, appropriately, not in the quiet beauty of nature's embrace, but in the main section of the estate, where today, just as in Tolstoy's day, the buzz of activity and the pulse of time can be felt. Visitors from all over the world come and go along the main path. A scholar and an artist amble slowly and converse. A stable hand waters a horse, while a carpenter repairs a broken door. Vehicles can be heard from the main thoroughfare in the distance.

In this section of Yasnaya Polyana, lying in between the Volkonsky house, and the main house, where Tolstoy lived, is a small stretch of land on which lies an unkempt garden. At your feet, nestled among the weeds in the garden, is a barely visible, weather-worn stone, not more than thirty centimeters high. On this stone are etched the words "Here stood the house in which L. N. Tolstoy was born." To his enormous chagrin, Tolstoy was forced to sell that house when he was twenty-six in order to pay off a substantial debt he incurred after one of his frequent gambling binges while he was serving as a young soldier in the Caucasus. "I'm so disgusted with myself that I'd like to forget about my existence," he wrote in his diary on the day it happened.[4]

And yet less than two weeks later he wrote in his diary: "Played cards again and lost another 200 rubles. I can't promise to stop."[5] His gambling sprees continued, as did his merrymaking, his drinking binges, his womanizing, and his laziness. The young libertine drank deeply of the cup of life. He indulged in all manner of sensual stimulation, including an ongoing affair with the peasant Aksynya Bazykina, who bore him an illegitimate child. Tolstoy chastised himself bitterly for his behavior, but his carnal nature continued to torment him. "I must have a woman," he wrote in his diary when he was twenty-five. "Sensuality doesn't give me a moment's peace."[6] And again four years later: "Sensuality torments me; laziness again, boredom and sadness. Everything seems stupid. The ideal is unattainable; I've already ruined myself."[7]

The unattainable ideal, the ruined self—these are not the images one usually associates with the later bearded sage, who preached abstinence from alcohol, advocated celibacy in and out of marriage, founded a religion, and inspired Mahatma Gandhi. And yet Tolstoy would not be Tolstoy were it not for the union of and constant tension between both dimensions—his intense spirituality and his passionate, carnal nature. These are the yin and the yang of his rich, complex personality. And these are the deeply human aspects of the writer, with whom every reader can identify.

The little green stick and the lost house—two quintessentially Tolstoyan images—embody the writer's personal hell and his hope for mankind, his pursuit of perfection and his paradise lost. Not 500 meters separate these two landmarks, yet Tolstoy's entire lifetime was spent negotiating a path between them. Constantly bedeviled by inner turmoil, Tolstoy strove for a perfection of himself and of the world that he knew he could never quite achieve.

The beginning of this drama is well documented in his early diaries, which paint the portrait of an intensely self-conscious young man, whose overfondness for the bottle, women, and cards is matched only by an unshakable faith in his own moral perfectibility. In his libertine lifestyle and moral bravado, the young Count Tolstoy was not so different from other young men of the aristocratic class. What *was* different about him was the combination of an intensely introspective and analytical nature with his passionate search for a higher purpose. "O God!" he wrote when he was stationed at Sevastopol, "[H]elp me on my way, not for the satisfaction of my worthless aims, but for the attainment of the great, eternal aim of existence, unknown to me but of which I am aware."[8]

Two years earlier, when he was twenty-five, Tolstoy wrote in his diary: "Once and for all I must get used to the idea that I'm an exception; that I'm either in advance of my age or that I'm one of those incongruous, unaccommodating natures that are never satisfied." Tolstoy wrote these words after a scuffle with a fellow officer, who accused him of vanity. If Tolstoy's entry is any indication, the officer's assessment might well have been right: "For a long time I deceived myself in imagining I had friends—people who understood me. Nonsense! I've never met a man who was as morally good as me, or who was willing to believe that I can't remember one instance in my life when I wasn't attracted by the good, and wasn't prepared to sacrifice everything for it."[9]

However, as Tolstoy knew all too well, there were days—many of them—in which the young profligate was attracted by what he considered bad. He monitored his behavior by resuming his teenage practice of writing down daily rules of conduct à la Benjamin Franklin, and then grading himself the next day. Apparently, his grades remained low: "It's absurd that having started writing rules at fifteen, I should still be writing them at thirty, without having trusted in, or followed a single one, but still for some reason believing in them and wanting them."[10]

Painfully aware of the vast distance between who he was and who he wanted to become, Tolstoy admitted: "One must first of all get a proper understanding of oneself and one's defects and try to remedy them, and not set oneself the aim of perfection, which is not only impossible to attain from the low point at which I stand, but the mere conception of which destroys the hope of the possibility of attaining it."[11]

Not only did Tolstoy's awareness of the gap between reality and his ideal of perfection apply to his personal development; it also extended to his observations of society and the role he felt called to play in it. At nineteen he confesses that "I would be the unhappiest of men if I could not find a purpose for my life—a purpose both general and useful. . . . So now my whole life will be a constant and active striving to achieve this one purpose."[12] Ten years later, after much inner struggle with self-indulgence and egoism, Tolstoy writes: "Work, a modest reputation, money. What for? Material enjoyment—again, what for? There will soon be eternal night. I keep thinking I'll die soon."[13] In these words we hear the murmurings of a theme that would resound in Tolstoy's writing following his spiritual crisis and conversion twenty-two years later—the problem of how human beings should live correctly given that they will eventually die. How can I live a life, he asked, whose meaning inevitable death cannot destroy?

After his incomplete studies at Kazan University, Tolstoy returned to Yasnaya Polyana in his early twenties to try his hand at useful activity. He tried to free his peasants and implement agricultural reform on his estate. His peasants mistrusted the intentions of their naïve and idealistic master, and Tolstoy quickly realized that he had neither the patience nor the talent for practical affairs. He discovered what Nekhliudov in *A Landowner's Morning* (1856) and Pierre in *War and Peace* (1863–69) come to understand, after they try to implement similar reforms on their estates—that the road to failure is often paved with the noblest intentions.

Tolstoy's difficulties with agricultural reform become a metaphor for the challenges of self-perfection: "It's the same as it was with my estate, my studies, literature, and life. With my estate I wanted to achieve perfection and forgot that first of all it's necessary to correct all the imperfections, of which there are too many. I wanted to prepare the fields, but I had nothing to sow and fertilize them with."[14]

Still, Tolstoy would continue to try to prepare the fields—internally and externally. The self-improvement efforts continued apace, and his faith in an ideal of social perfection inspired him to begin a school for peasant children on his estate when he was thirty-one. In the same year he traveled to Europe to study educational systems and teaching methods, which he could apply to his school. With the notable exception of his meeting with the German novelist Berthold Auerbach, Tolstoy was disappointed with what he found there. In one school he visits "order prevails . . . but it lacks life, I'm afraid." Another is a "[v]ery stupid school, showing what institutions imposed from above can lead to." In yet another school—a "prayer for the king, beatings, everything by heart, frightened and morally deformed children."[15]

The inadequacies of the German teaching methods are manifestations of a more basic problem Tolstoy discovers in Europe—its self-righteous faith in the gods of reason and progress, which mask the deep-seated injustices of Western civilization. "Whoever said to anybody that progress is good?" Tolstoy wrote a month before he left for Europe.[16] A year after he returned he would write again: "The idea of the folly of progress haunts me."[17] During an earlier trip to Europe in 1857 Tolstoy witnessed an execution in France. "When I saw how the head was severed from the body and heard one thing and another as it fell into the box," he would later write in his *Confession* (1884), "I understood, not with my intellect but with my whole being, that no theories of rationality of existence or of progress could justify such an act."[18]

Tolstoy's rejection of the Western ideals of civilization and progress as solutions to his quest for perfection had begun, in fact, much earlier in his life under the influence of the writings of the French philosopher Jean Jacques Rousseau (1712–78), whom he "worshipped" as a young man. Rousseau's critique of modern civilization and his belief in the inherent goodness of untutored nature left a deep imprint on Tolstoy's art and thought. His celebration of the "noble savage" in his fiction, from *The Cossacks* (1863) to *Hadji-Murat* (1904), as well as much of his later assault against the injustices of the state, the institution of serfdom, the Russian Orthodox Church, modern medicine, education, marriage, and sexual mores all derive, in part, from Rousseau's intellectual influence.

And yet the very civilization that Tolstoy so passionately rebuked was also the source of his aristocratic privilege and comfort. He himself sensed this contradiction, and it became more pronounced as he grew older and more intent on exposing the contradictions and injustices of Russian society and of his own life. For the time being, however, the aristocratic comfort that would later fill him with guilt provided the writer with the structure and security he would need to embark on one of the greatest creative journeys of his life—the writing of *War and Peace* between 1863 and 1869.

Tolstoy's marriage to Sofya Andreevna Behrs in 1862, when he was thirty-four, marks the temporary cessation of the spiritual battles that raged in the young writer during his twenties and early thirties. Tolstoy's life now became a round of seemingly constant, joyous, and productive activity. In addition to his intensive work on *War and Peace,* he read voraciously in the classics of world literature and philosophy. He met regularly with leading thinkers and writers of his day to discuss his ongoing work. He was continually occupied by the daily demands of his estate, including pig-farming, horse-breeding, and harvesting of the crops. He sculpted, played the piano, and developed a passion for beekeeping. In his correspondence and diaries of this period Tolstoy frequently described married life as a salvation from his earlier depravity. He spoke of Sofya Andreevna, who famously copied drafts of *War and Peace* by hand multiple times, in glowing terms.

The thirteen children whom Sofya Andreevna bore Tolstoy over the next twenty-five years were an enormous source of happiness to him, despite the tragic loss of five of them. The scenes of family happiness in the Rostov home in *War and Peace* were inspired by Tolstoy's own life during this period. The sudden death of the young Petya Rostov in the novel is a creative distillation of the writer's personal encounter with the tragedy that he knew existed alongside the joys of his life. For fifteen years that tragic reality was a muted presence in Tolstoy's fundamentally joyous worldview.

But in 1878 during the writing of the final part of *Anna Karenina* (1873–76), when Tolstoy was fifty, the darkness that always hovered in the background moved to the foreground. "At first I began having moments of bewilderment, when my life would come to a halt, as if I did not know how to live or what to do," the author described in his *Confession*, finished four years later in 1882 and first published in Switzerland in 1884. "I would lose my presence of mind and fall into a state of depression. But this passed, and I continued to live as before. Then the moments of bewilderment recurred more frequently, and they always took the same form. Whenever my life came to a halt, the question would arise: Why? And what next?"[19]

These questions, which filled the pages of the young Tolstoy's diaries, took center stage in his life once again. Only now he grappled with them with a life-or-death urgency. No longer a young man searching for his place in the world, Tolstoy was a grown man with firmly planted roots in the soil of life. Married with seven children, he was a dedicated farmer, pedagogue, and internationally celebrated author. Yet these roots appeared to him to be decayed. The solid foundation upon which the past sixteen years of his life had rested seemed to be fatally cracked, as the fact of his mortality presented itself to him in all of its stark force:

> My question, the question that had brought me to the edge of suicide when I was fifty years old, was the simplest question lying in the soul of every human being, from a silly child to the wisest of the elders, the question without which life is impossible, such was the way I felt about the matter. The question is this: What will come of what I do today and tomorrow? What will come of my entire life?
>
> Expressed differently, the question may be: Why should I live? Why should I wish for anything or do anything? Or to put it still differently: Is there any meaning in my life that will not be destroyed by my inevitably approaching death?[20]

Tolstoy turned for answers to science and philosophy, but none of their solutions satisfied him. The experimental sciences could teach him how life functions, philosophy what life has meant to others, but neither told him why he was alive and how he should live. Tolstoy lost hope that science and philosophy could provide him with the answers he sought, or even help him ask the right questions.

Institutionalized religion, which he tried for a while after his crisis, also failed to provide him with answers, for it was riddled with inconsistency and falsehood. Similar to some fundamentalist preachers today who claim God's grace only for a select few, "[t]he members of the Orthodox Church regarded as heretics everyone who did not profess the same beliefs as they, just as the Catholics and others viewed the members of the Orthodox Church as heretics."[21] When Tolstoy looked to members of his own aristocratic class, he found no help there either: "I saw only people who did not understand the problem, people who understood it but drowned in their intoxication with life, people who understood it and put an end to life, and people who understood it but out of weakness continued to live a life of despair."[22]

Moreover, Tolstoy could no longer bear the burden of his conventionally "successful" life, which he now believed he had achieved at great moral cost by blindly following the dictates of upper-class society. He describes his early years in this way:

> I cannot think of those years without horror, loathing and heartache. I killed men in war and challenged men to duels in order to kill them. I lost at cards, consumed the labor of the peasants, sentenced them to punishments, lived loosely, and deceived people. Lying, robbery, adultery of all kinds, drunkenness, violence, murder—there was no crime I did not commit, and in spite of that people praised my conduct and my contemporaries considered and consider me to be a comparatively moral man . . .
>
> Thus I lived for ten years.[23]

Even his decision to become a writer, Tolstoy claims, was motivated by "vanity, self-interest, and pride," as was his desire to teach people about progress "without myself knowing what I was teaching."[24] He describes his path from the debauched young man of the world to the self-righteous social reformer to the self-satisfied family man who replaced a "striving for personal perfection" with a "striving for what was best for my family and me."[25] And so, he asks himself in one of the most poignant passages in his *Confession:*

> What, indeed, had I done in all my thirty years of conscious life? Not

only had I failed to live my life for the sake of all, but I had not even lived it for myself. I had lived as a parasite, and once I asked myself why I had lived, the answer I received was: for nothing. If the meaning of human life lies in the way it is lived, then how could I, who had spent thirty years not living life but ruining it for myself and others, receive any reply other than this, that my life was meaningless and evil? It was indeed meaningless and evil.[26]

Distinguished Tolstoy biographer Ernest J. Simmons has described *Confession* as "one of the noblest and most courageous utterances of man."[27] It is beyond doubt the most important document for an understanding of the direction that Tolstoy's spiritual journey would take for the remainder of his life. Severe, critical, and intense, *Confession* marks the beginning of the dominant strain in Tolstoy's later art and thought: his ongoing self-flagellation for his spiritual failures, as well as his condemnation of almost all man-made institutions in modern society for their failure to respond to man's deepest need—to create a life of meaning and purpose in the face of death. For the next twenty years Tolstoy would dedicate his artistic talents to the writing of didactic fiction, ideological treatises, and moralistic stories for the people. At the same time he tried to live in accordance with the spiritual principle of universal love, which, beginning with *Confession,* he associated increasingly with the inborn faith of the Russian peasantry.

There is a charming poignancy to the images of the older Tolstoy in bast boots mowing in the fields with his peasants. Yet, it is hard to view without irony his frequent injunctions to live a life of self-abnegation, delivered to an audience of family and prominent friends, who are enjoying an elaborate meal in the luxurious dining rooms at Yasnaya Polyana and in his home in Moscow. This comedy acquired a tragic dimension in Tolstoy's increasing sense of alienation and his repeated efforts to abandon his home because of irreconcilable differences with his family and his wife over fundamental questions of lifestyle, finances, and the raising of the children. When he left home in the middle of the night in October 1910, it would be for the last time. His final attempt to find a life free of what he considered to be falsehood and moral compromise ended ten days later, when he died of pneumonia in the little railroad station at Astapovo on November 7, 1910.

When viewed in its entirety, Tolstoy's spiritual journey, like that of every human being, is full of irreconcilable paradoxes. Yet, like that of his searching characters, the story of his life is filled with the spirit of human pathos and possibility. Indeed, if there is a unifying principle in Tolstoy's life and art, it is an overarching vision of man as finite and flawed, yet ennobled by a great and striving spirit. The little green stick and the lost house—unflinching realism and fierce idealism—are the two inseparable landmarks on Tolstoy's path as a man and an artist. The story of this journey in the life of every human being is the fundamental subject and the unifying theme of Tolstoy's great works. In the pages that follow we will take that journey to the center of Tolstoy's world—and our own. Before embarking, however, it will be helpful to examine Tolstoy's own journey toward determining the goals and methods of his art.

two

"THE HERO OF MY TALE IS TRUTH"

Tolstoy's consuming passions—whether social questions or writing—were fired by spiritual impulses rather than professional ambition. Unlike his well-known contemporaries Ivan Turgenev and Ivan Goncharov, he never aspired primarily to be a professional man of letters. Fiction-writing was his way of exploring the workings of his own soul—his plumb line for sounding the depths of the human experience. In everything he wrote, Tolstoy was, first and foremost, a teacher of life, a spiritual seeker, a moral philosopher "through images," as the nineteenth-century Russian philosopher V. V. Rozanov called him.[1] He measured his worth as a writer by what he contributed, not to literature, but to life.[2]

Each one of Tolstoy's novels—*The Cossacks* (1863), *War and Peace* (1863–69), *Anna Karenina* (1873–76), and *Resurrection* (1899), and each novella, *The Death of Ivan Ilyich* (1886) and *Hadji-Murat* (1904)— embodies his lifelong striving to capture the truths of human nature as they manifest themselves in the ever-changing details of everyday life. Among modern writers, perhaps only Tolstoy would dare to write, without a tinge of irony: "The hero of my tale—whom I love with all the power of my soul, whom I have tried to portray in all its beauty, who has been, is, and always will be beautiful—is Truth."[3] The "Truth" contained in a Tolstoyan work is neither the truth of the little green stick nor that of the lost house, but a larger, synthetic truth that encompasses both the ideal and the real.

Tolstoy's major characters drink from a deep cup. The depths of confusion, hurt, and loss they experience are equaled by the heights of their blissful moments: Olenin's sublime sense of inner wholeness while lying in a stag's lair (*The Cossacks*), Pierre's sudden revelation that he is in love as he watches the comet of 1812 soar across the nighttime sky (*War and Peace*), Levin's terrified rapture during the birth of his first child and his ecstasy while mowing in the field with his peasants (*Anna Karenina*). Each of these frustrated characters has an intense inner vitality, a capacity for continual growth and exaltation, despite the many obstacles life throws his way. If, as Artistotle said, "art not only imitates nature, but also completes its deficiencies," then for Tolstoy that completion can be felt in the elusive sense of perfection and wholeness that his characters momentarily glimpse.

One of Tolstoy's strongest weapons in his search for life's overarching truth is the literary technique of psychological analysis, which he first developed in his diaries, and used with great poetic force in his fiction. The same analytical prowess that allowed him to dissect his own soul with excruciating honesty also permitted him to divine the hidden depths and heights of his characters' inner lives. This ability to see ordinary life in all its intricacy allowed Tolstoy to create a fictional world far more convincing than that of his Romantic predecessors, who wrote about beauty in metaphysical abstractions and inspired clichés.

Tolstoy's first critics immediately noticed his unusual analytical gift. The contemporary critic Pavel Annenkov said in an 1856 article that Tolstoy's literary genius lay in the fact that he wrote with the analytical precision of a scientist, while at the same time capturing the vital poetry of life.[4] Another of Tolstoy's contemporaries, the French critic Eugène-Melchior de Vogüé, marveled at the writer's unique combination of analytical rigor with deep spirituality, when he described Tolstoy as "a queer combination of the brain of an English chemist with the soul of an Indian Buddhist."[5]

To a degree unique in world literature, almost all of Tolstoy's searching heroes are direct reflections of the writer's private spiritual quest. Nikolenka Irtenev, the narrator of *Childhood* (1852), would become the first in a long line of autobiographical heroes, or better, "auto-psychological" heroes, a term coined by the well-known Soviet critic Lidiia Ginzburg.[6] She emphasizes the strong spiritual affinities between the author and his heroes, even if the biographical correspondence is not always precise. Dmitry Olenin in *The Cossacks,* Pierre Bezukhov in *War and Peace,* Konstantin Levin in *Anna Karenina,* and Butler in *Hadji-Murat* are taken directly from Tolstoy's own life circumstances.

Most of Tolstoy's searching protagonists find happiness in a balanced, mature view of the world as a place where joy and tragedy, meaningful moral choice and providential design, are present in equal measure. Prince Andrei, the sole tragic hero in *War and Peace,* is unable to reconcile his noble ideals with reality. But if Andrei himself fails to achieve inner harmony, his death helps complete the circle of other characters' evolution by creating the possibility for Pierre's spiritual resurrection and marriage to Natasha. Anna Karenina, too, is a tragic heroine. Still, the novel named after her ends not with her death but with the growth of Levin's and Kitty's family in the countryside. The final note in Tolstoy's novels is always one of optimism and the assertion of life's continuity.

The searching characters from Tolstoy's earlier works begin by looking for life's ultimate truth *out there,* in some vaguely perceived distant perfection. According to the Russian saying, "It's pleasant for me to be where I am not." But those who are successful in their quest eventually discover that the ideal exists *right here, right now,* in the concrete, imperfect realities of everyday life. This is especially true in Tolstoy's first two novels, *The Cossacks* and *War and Peace,* where the real and the ideal exist in harmonious balance.

But Tolstoy's truth becomes more elusive and difficult to attain as his work evolves. By the time we get to *The Death of Ivan Ilyich,* Tolstoy's ultimate good seems only a distant, superimposed ideal. If for Pierre in *War and Peace* "God is here, right here, everywhere," then Levin in *Anna Karenina* will find God only in nature and his family, in faith and the hard moral choices he must make. Ivan Ilyich and Dmitry Nekhkliudov, in *Resurrection,* will find God only after a long process of internal cleansing and repentance. They must first confront the truth of their sinful lives and the society that encouraged it, and only then can they embrace the moral commandments necessary for self-transformation.

Tolstoy's final novella-masterpiece, *Hadji-Murat,* completed in 1904 and published posthumously, tells the story of Russia's imperial expansion into the Caucasus and colonization of Chechnya—a subject as topical today as in Tolstoy's time. But the work transcends social commentary to become a supreme artistic meditation on the struggle between good and evil. *Hadji-Murat* stirs readers through powerful understatement and lifelike description, and by arousing sympathy for the Chechen freedom-fighter Hadji-Murat, whose innate goodness and personal heroism are juxtaposed with the spiritual bankruptcy of Russian imperial society.

In *Hadji-Murat* Tolstoy himself becomes the ultimate searcher. Like his own characters, who continually discover, reject, and then rediscover truths about themselves and their world, Tolstoy weaves together the images, themes, literary techniques, and biographical facts of a lifetime. In his swan song and "summary epic," as one scholar has called the work, the writer, now in his seventies, takes us back not only to the Caucasus of his youth, but also to the epic spirit of *War and Peace*.[7] But *Hadji-Murat* is more than a repetition of an earlier artistic vision. It subsumes the past into an entirely new creation. The tragic-comedic sensibility and exuberant spirit of the young author of *The Cossacks* and *War and Peace* are now expanded into the sublimely tragic vision of an author nearing death.

If Pushkin's *Evgenii Onegin* (1831) is Russia's great experimental "novel in verse," then *Hadji-Murat* is its crowning poem in prose. The aura of legend, of "mythical epic," as Harold Bloom called it, reverberates through the grime and grit of everyday reality.[8] The novella unites the tragic and the sublime, the serious and the satirical, in a highly compressed epic framework, while remaining painstakingly true to historical facts, which Tolstoy gleaned from his study of 172 sources. The result is a poetic realism that is unprecedented in Tolstoy or any other Russian writer.

All of Tolstoy's novels and novellas—even the openly ideological *Resurrection*—offer a transcendent vision while never eschewing life's rough edges and gaps, or the ebb and flow of the ordinary. Seen through the narrator's transformative lens, daily reality itself acquires transcendent meaning. Each moment is shown to be both finite and possessed of infinite possibility, both irreducibly distinct and an integral component in the tapestry of human life. The smallest detail takes on larger spiritual significance when seen in the context of the artistic fabric of which it is a part.

ARTIST AND CRITIC:
THE "ENDLESS LABYRINTH OF LINKAGES"

In 1876 Tolstoy wrote to his close personal friend the philosopher and literary critic Nikolai Strakhov: "For art criticism we need people who would show the senselessness of looking for ideas in a work of art, but who instead would continually guide readers in that endless labyrinth of linkages that makes up the stuff of art, and bring them to the laws that serve as the foundation for those linkages."[9] Even in a career as varied as Tolstoy's, these words are perhaps the best single expression of the writer's lifelong artistic and philosophical credo. Tolstoy had a fundamental belief in the wholeness of the universe and in art's unique capacity to capture that wholeness. In our postmodernist climate, these beliefs will strike many as both naïve and passé.

In Tolstoy's time, too, the position was unique. In fact, his credo was, in part, a reaction against the radical Russian intelligentsia, who were dominant in Russian social thought in the latter half of the nineteenth century, and who approached literature in precisely the way that Tolstoy opposed. Influential literary critics, such as Nikolai Dobroliubov in his essay "What Is Oblomovitis?" (1860) on Ivan Goncharov's novel *Oblomov* (1859), and Dmitry Pisarev in his essay "Bazarov" (1862) about Ivan Turgenev's novel *Fathers and Sons* (1862), read literature as if it were a mere documentary snapshot of contemporary social conditions. On the basis of that snapshot, they extracted a single idea—that the current social order has produced a breed of starry-eyed aristocratic lazybones (Dobroliubov), or that practical, steely-eyed empiricists are the only hope for Russia's future (Pisarev). Each went on to use that one idea to further his own ideological agenda.

This way of reading—reducing a work of art to a statement of ideology rather than seeing it as a complex and organically unified vision of life—was anathema to Tolstoy. He believed that it stemmed from the vulgar utilitarianism and antispiritualism characteristic of the radical intelligentsia. In their worldview, the spiritual strivings that are fundamental to Tolstoy's conception of man become irrelevant. The radicals also mocked Tolstoy's faith in the power of the artist to transcend the limits of ordinary consciousness in order to discover a higher, purposeful order.

Tolstoy was not alone in his distaste for the radical intelligentsia. His contemporary Ivan Turgenev referred to Pisarev and Dobroliubov as the "snake and the rattlesnake."[10] And Nikolai Strakhov, who was one of the foremost practitioners of the so-called organic criticism, frequently expressed to Tolstoy his rejection of the radicals' belief that science can replace morality, religion, and literature in providing answers to man's ultimate questions.[11] Strakhov and Tolstoy both believed that insight into human life required an "organic," suprarational kind of thinking, which is beyond the reach of scientific reasoning, but attainable by the creative artist.

At least this was what Tolstoy believed *some* of the time. After his spiritual crisis and conversion in 1878, his views as a literary critic seem to have been written by someone else altogether. In his well-known theoretical treatise "What is Art?" published in 1897, Tolstoy writes about art in just the manner he condemned in his letter to Strakhov. He offers a rigid theorem about two categories of art: "good art" and "bad art." "Good art," he argues, "infects" its recipients with "good," moral, Christian ideals. "Bad art" lacks this Christian underpinning. It infects for the sake of infection alone. It only titillates the senses and thus reinforces the spiritually bankrupt status quo of modern secular life. Rather than encouraging spiritual communion, secular art maintains and even intensifies the separation of human beings from one another and from God.

Tolstoy's narrow definition of art in "What is Art?" leads the writer to the preposterous conclusion that his own *War and Peace* and *Anna Karenina,* Shakespeare's plays, and all of Beethoven fail to infect audiences with "good" Christian feelings, and are therefore to be relegated to history's trash heap of "bad art." Not surprisingly, then, the openly didactic and illustrative fiction of Tolstoy's later years transforms the all-encompassing vision of life in his earlier novels into a narrowly moralistic one. We need only consider the works of late didactic fiction, such as "How Much Land Does a Man Need?" (1886), "God Sees the Truth but Waits" (1872), and "Alyosha the Pot" (1905), to recognize the contrast between the circumscribed, hortatory worldview of the artist-as-preacher and the immense, life-embracing vision of the creator of *War and Peace.*

The earlier artist is, as Henry James aptly called him, "a reflector as vast as a natural lake; a monster harnessed to his great subject—all of life!"[12] The author of the later didactic fiction and moral treatises is more like a fixed, furious warning beacon, a preacher harnessed to his bully pulpit. True, such works of late fiction as *The Death of Ivan Ilych* (1886) and "Master and Man" (1895) astound readers with their compact intensity. But they do not "force people to love life in all its innumerable, inexhaustible manifestations," as Tolstoy, in an 1865 letter to the novelist P. D. Boborykin, said art should do.[13]

In these later masterpieces of tendentious fiction, Tolstoy does not celebrate life's holism for its own sake, as he does in his earlier works. He does not discover in an imperfect world a higher poetic truth. Rather, he extracts from the world clear moral maxims. The beginning of this tendency can be felt at the end of *Anna Karenina,* more distinctly in *The Death of Ivan Ilych,* and most intensely in *Resurrection.*

The later Tolstoy sometimes diminishes the very complexity that makes the quest of the characters of his earlier novels so engrossing to readers. The early, searching characters constantly strive for a perfection they can never quite achieve, for a truth that never presents itself to them in clear, rigid formulations. They live in a fictional world in which it is impossible to proclaim a single religious, moral, or intellectual truth as the novel's ultimate "meaning." How, after all, can we extract a moral or religious idea—or any idea—from *War and Peace,* that supramoral, pantheistic meditation on the beauty of *everything* life offers?

In the novels he wrote before *Resurrection,* Tolstoy illuminates the endless process by which human beings strive, as the author himself did, to construct from the parts a vision of the whole, a vision of the ideal amidst the real.[14] The truth contained in *The Cossacks, War and Peace,* and the first seven parts of *Anna Karenina* is always shifting and unfolding, like the complex beauty of a diamond that refracts light viewed from multiple perspectives into a rainbow of gorgeous colors. And at the same time, like a diamond, each novel consists of the same solid, organically unified material.

The Cossacks and *War and Peace* pulsate with lifelike dynamism, like the vibrating, shimmering ball of Pierre's dream. *Anna Karenina* is an architecturally tight novel, recreating the sense of entrapment felt by many of the characters themselves, who are forced to find their path in a new world that has been suddenly foisted upon them. If *The Cossacks* and *War and Peace* celebrate their young characters' quest to embrace the fullness of life, and *Anna Karenina* describes their search for a system of values that can give meaning to human life in a society that is crumbling socially and spiritually, then *The Death of Ivan Ilyich* and *Resurrection* describe the individual's tortuous journey back to spiritual health in a world that has already fallen.

Ivan allegorically poses the question that Tolstoy asked directly in his *Confession:* "Is there any meaning in my life that will not be destroyed by my inevitably approaching death?"[15] In this harrowing and humane novella, Tolstoy presents his answer in the metaphorical Passion of the title character: only by vigorously casting off the internalized falsehoods of modern society can an individual find the divine spark within and reestablish his connection with the human family.

Resurrection communicates this same point by piercing readers' hearts and stirring their moral imagination with the sharp sword of documentary truth. In this, his most ideological novel, Tolstoy brilliantly combines tendentiousness with astounding psychological realism. The author's moral position is absolutely clear on every page, and yet the portrait of Russian society in spiritual decay is so truthfully and fully developed that the moral solutions offered at the end do not seem too extreme an antidote. Part journalism, part preaching, *Resurrection* nevertheless remains art of the highest order. Unlike many of Tolstoy's later publicist essays and religious treatises, *Resurrection* represents a brilliant synthesis of the ideologue and the artist—a unique achievement that distinguishes Tolstoy from any other Russian writer.

TOLSTOY'S REALISM AND HIS READERS

John Paul Sartre said that the "technique of the novel always refers us back to the metaphysics of the novelist."[16] In other words, what an author imagines the world to be is inextricably linked with *how* the author presents that world to his reader. In a Dostoevskian novel, for example, the cramped, often overheated, internal spaces of the modern city are the backdrop for the seething battle between the forces of good and evil in the characters' psyches. Dostoevsky's frequent description of oppressive interior spaces, the intense, dramatic dialogues among characters, and the extended, rambling monologues by internally split characters often teeter on the verge of hallucination. Through his literary technique, Dostoevsky evokes the psychological intensity and moral desperation of a world pressing down relentlessly on the human spirit. Only through extreme acts of self-sacrifice and spiritual repentance can fallen man hope to regain his wholeness.

If, for Dostoevsky, man is a seething cauldron of conflicting impulses in a hostile universe, then for Tolstoy man is born good, whole, and spiritually free. He need only cast off the internalized falsehoods of modern society in order to return to his original state of natural goodness. Unlike Dostoevsky's novels, which emphasize the psychological crises, cracks, and explosions of the human soul, Tolstoy's novels depict the norms and continuities of human behavior by means of grand narratives that expand slowly over time and against the backdrop of vast natural tableaus. In Tolstoy's novels one hears both the noisy march of time and the quiet grandeur of eternity.

Each Tolstoyan novel is a penetrating photograph of the details of life in a specific time and place, as well as a transformative lens through which a particular moment in Russian history becomes a window into universal human experience. "One can't help loving people: they are all—*we* are all—so pitiable," Tolstoy wrote a few years before he embarked on *War and Peace*.[17] Indeed, "we" is the subject of his epic masterpiece, which the critic Nikolai Strakhov rightly described as "[a] complete picture of the things in which men set their happiness and greatness, their sorrow and their shame."[18]

In fact, it might be said that "we" is the subject of all of Tolstoy's art. The universality of human experience is fundamental to Tolstoy's worldview. From the very first, he sought to develop a literary technique that would best present the complex makeup of every individual and the truths common to all human beings. The writer's method evolved directly from his metaphysics.

When he was only twenty-four, Tolstoy wrote of the necessity of creating full-blooded characters with whom readers can identify: "For readers to sympathize with a hero, they must be able to recognize in him their weaknesses as much as their virtues."[19] In the same year Tolstoy wrote of the importance of combining "in one image all [of a character's] features, both moral and physical. . . . From a collection of shortcomings one can sometimes form such an intangible but fascinating character that it inspires love."[20] Toward the end of his life, in *Resurrection*, Tolstoy would write: "Human beings are like rivers: the water is one and the same in all of them. . . . Every man bears within him the germs of every human quality, and now manifests one, now another, and frequently is quite unlike himself, while still remaining the same man."[21]

Tolstoy's "realist" technique, then, points to his metaphysics—what we might call a highly individualized universality. His art expresses a vision of life in which every detail, like every human being, is fully fleshed out and intrinsically significant, and at the same time a reflection of a larger whole. Perhaps our sense that Tolstoy's fictional world so closely resembles our own stems from the fact that we recognize in his art a truth about the nature of our own lives: that life both depends on us and happens in spite of us, that it consists both of the unique, unrepeatable details of everyday experience and of vast, impersonal forces. Tolstoy's novels combine the personal and the impersonal, the individual and the universal, in a way that Tolstoy the man, wavering in his own lifetime between intense egoism and radical self-renunciation, never could.

In this book we will move back and forth between the part and the whole, the details and the overarching vision. The world's grand Truth, Tolstoy believed, is grasped by carefully and lovingly observing the color of every blade of grass, the timbre of a sparrow's song, the texture of a baby's skin, the temperature of the breeze on a hot summer day. The author labored over every detail, sometimes rewriting his novels eight, nine, even ten times or more.

Tolstoy's novels reward readers with an expanded sense of self and a deepened appreciation of things that once passed unnoticed or unexamined. That kind of reading requires sustained effort and patience. As soon as readers become comfortable in Tolstoy's world, the author jolts them out of their complacency, in the same way that ever-changing reality challenges characters' firm convictions and conclusions. Tolstoy's characters have revelations only when they move beyond their conventional formulations, let go of their egoistic demands of the world, and embrace life in its infinite splendor.

Readers of Tolstoy can have revelations, too, if they let go of their preconceived notions about what literature is or ought to be. No writer exposed lies more vehemently; none celebrates human possibility more triumphantly. By accepting the challenge of seeking the beautiful simplicity of his vision within the complex, detailed fullness of Tolstoy's art, they will enrich their own life connection. In our age of fast-food psychology and sound-byte social commentary, reading Tolstoy can be a rare but important exercise in deep thinking, deep feeling, and clear seeing. In the letter to P. D. Boborykin quoted earlier, Tolstoy continues:

> The goal of the artist is not to solve a question irrefutably, but to force people to love life in all its innumerable, inexhaustible manifestations. If I were told I could write a novel in which I should set forth the apparently correct attitudes towards all social questions, I would not devote even two hours of work to such a novel, but if I were told that what I shall write will be read in twenty years by the children of today and that they will weep and smile over it and will fall in love with life, I would devote all my life and all my strength to it.[22]

Tolstoy would indeed devote nearly eight years of his life to his first novel, *The Cossacks*. In that work he resolves no social questions, but instead takes us on a transformative journey to the luxuriant Caucasus, and into the expansive mind and heart of his first major searcher, Dmitry Olenin.

three

$\int$EEKING AUTHENTICITY IN AN ALIENATED AGE

Olenin and *The Cossacks*

When Tolstoy published *The Cossacks* in 1862, both the Caucasus as a geographical region and the Cossacks as a community were already culturally and emotionally laden themes in nineteenth-century Russian literature. The Caucasus was a favorite venue for Romantic writers to celebrate their love of exotic cultures and places. In the expansive nature of the south they found a welcome contrast to the constricted civilized culture of the northern Russian cities. At the heart of this tradition was the myth of the vital, free Cossacks, which had been firmly established in the Russian cultural imagination through the writings of Pushkin and Bestuzhev-Marlinksy, as well as in Gogol's *Taras Bul'ba* (1835), before Tolstoy entered literature in the 1850s.

Among the earliest and most famous works of Russian literature dealing with this theme were Pushkin's and Lermontov's narrative poems "The Gypsies" (1824) and "Izmail-Bey" (1832), respectively. Both of these works, as well as Tolstoy's personal experiences as a soldier in the Caucasus, were influential in the writer's creation of *The Cossacks*. Tolstoy's initial work on the novel took place at a time when he was fascinated by the romantic image of the Caucasus as a land of spiritual freedom and poetic inspiration. He called it "that wild region in which two such completely opposite things as war and freedom are so strangely and poetically blended."[1]

In Tolstoy's hands, the Caucasian tale became a different animal altogether. On one level, it debunks the Romantic treatment of the Caucasus, highlighting both the comedy and the tragedy of attempting to communicate across cultures. The "civilized" man's encounter with a "primitive" world, rather than opening vast horizons before him, only forces him to confront impassible barriers, both within himself and in the brave new world he seeks to enter.

But if *The Cossacks* were only a parody of the romantic myth of the exiled European among savages, it hardly would have prompted Turgenev to call it "the masterpiece of Tolstoy and the whole of Russian fiction."[2] Nor would it have done justice to Tolstoy's very real enthrallment to the spiritual essence of the Caucasus, without which he most likely would not have written his novel in the first place. Tolstoy's creative genius was an affirmative, synthesizing one. He was less interested in razing a building than in constructing a new one, or re-enlivening an outworn, inadequate structure with his transforming vision.[3]

If Tolstoy debunks certain thematic and linguistic aspects of the literary Caucasus, he does so only in order to resurrect that region for his readers and inject it with fresh artistic vigor. His "rewriting" of the Caucasian tale, then, lies not merely in demystifying his hero's romanticized perceptions of the region, but in penetrating his hero's inner world, with all its idealistic strivings and contradictions. Tolstoy's emphasis is as much—or more—on the inner landscape, the spiritual life of the hero, as on the geographical region.[4] In its artistic exploration of the universal problems of truth, morality, and existential meaning, *The Cossacks* becomes a rich universe of artistic thought.[5] For Tolstoy's contemporaries, however, the work was an anachronism. We can understand their reaction if we examine the impassioned political and intellectual debates of the times.

THE SEARCHING SPIRIT OF THE TIMES

The crushing Russian loss in the Crimean War of 1854–56, which Tolstoy immortalized in his *Sevastopol Tales,* was not only a moral defeat for Russians. It also became the impetus for the government's reevaluation of its political, social, and economic agenda. These events coincided with the death of the oppressive Nicholas I in 1855, and the ascension of his son, Alexander II, who implemented the Great Reforms, beginning with the Emancipation of the Serfs in 1861. With the rise of the radical

Russian intelligentsia, the reformist movement took on a more militant coloration. This generation of young intellectuals, steeped in the natural sciences and in the theories of French Utopian socialism, advocated an ideologically inflexible reform agenda which insisted that all of human life and society could be explained—and therefore improved—by relying on the principles of science and reason alone. For some of these radical thinkers, such as Nikolai Chernyshevsky and Nikolai Dobroliubov, a lukewarm commitment to reform was unacceptable, and they regarded Alexander II's Great Reforms as too little, too late. Nothing short of a commitment to violent revolution would satisfy them. A passion for ideas was in the air, and could be felt in all aspects of Russian intellectual life. Alexander Herzen, one of the era's leading liberal thinkers and the founder of the journal *The Bell*, which helped to bring about the emancipation of the serfs, wrote in 1851: "The storm is approaching, it is impossible to be mistaken about that. The Revolutionaries and Reactionaries are at one about that. All men's heads are going round; a weighty question of life and death lies heavy on men's heads."[6]

Given this historical context, it is hardly surprising that many of Tolstoy's contemporaries, who praised the artistic quality of *The Cossacks*, considered its general theme of the superiority of natural man to civilized man to be superficial and irrelevant to the concerns of the time. A reviewer in *The Contemporary* wrote: "*The Cossacks* is no more advanced than those Byronic works of Russian literature in which the hero sets out to find peace and oblivion in lands where the cliffs hide in the clouds and where people are as free as eagles. . . . But what may been attractive and timely in the 1820s smells of anachronism in the 1860s."[7]

Persuasive as it might have seemed to Tolstoy's contemporaries, this view overlooks just how deeply aware Tolstoy was of the literary and social issues of his day, and how intently he was searching for a voice amid the myriad competing ideologies in that radicalized era. It was precisely because of Tolstoy's sensitivity to his intellectual environment that the writer felt compelled to make what scholar Boris Eikhenbaum called a "strategic retreat" from literature, in order to develop his own views and literary voice, which were not in accord with any of the ideological positions then in circulation.[8] When he returned to literature in the early 1860s, he had solidified his ideological position. He was neither a liberal nor a progressive, but an "archaist," who advocated traditional values and paradigms, and who sought to make them applicable to contemporary reality. He believed in universal truths and objective laws of life and nature, characteristic of the moral philosophy of the eighteenth century, and he directed those beliefs against the various theorizers and ideological extremists of both camps in his time.

Tolstoy's conception was of a life both more organic and more fluid than any liberal or conservative ideology could embrace. So when Olenin comments that "'the people live as nature lives: they die, are born, unite, and more are born—they fight, eat, and drink, rejoice and die, without any restrictions but those that nature imposes on sun and grass, on animal and tree,'" he is giving voice to Tolstoy's own belief system, which emphasized the continuum of life and the universality of the laws of nature (190, 26).[9] This rebuttal of the theories offered by the liberals and the conservatives of his era was perhaps too subtle to be heard amid the noisy ideological extremism.

Beyond these polemics, Tolstoy engaged in another kind of debate at this period in his life, one focused on the more inward search for existential meaning in his own life. Like his hero Olenin, he was embroiled in what Robert Jackson has characterized as an acute internal battle between Homeric and Christian ethics.[10] In 1857 he was torn by his simultaneous attraction to two works whose philosophical outlooks represented the poles of his own divided vision of life: *The Iliad*, with its celebration of heroism, the ecstasy of violence, and its supramoral acceptance of the plenitude of life, and the Gospels, with their articulation of a divinely mandated morality.[11] This extended struggle may partially explain why the writer labored over *The Cossacks* in fits and starts for nearly ten years, from 1852 to 1862.[12] It certainly explains the novel's strong philosophical bent, which appeared to many of Tolstoy's contemporaries as a throwback to the era of the 1830s and 1840s in Russia, when abstract philosophizing was a cultural norm among artists and intellectuals.

And yet, in a fundamental sense, Olenin is a quintessential representative of the age in which he was conceived. In his incessant quest for a more authentic way of living, we hear the many voices of Tolstoy's contemporaries, young and old, who were themselves passionately searching for a more just society. In Olenin's inability to find a spiritual home in either Russia or among the Cossacks, we sense the feelings of uprootedness experienced by an entire generation of Russians, who attempted to make sense of the vast social changes sweeping through their society. Olenin's quest for existential significance thus embodies the very searching spirit of the era in which he was conceived, even if his quest does not directly address the specific concerns and terms of debate in Russia of the 1850s and 1860s. Tolstoy has created a novel and a character who are both completely of their time—and timeless.

The artistic richness of *The Cossacks* lies partly in its capacity to combine two contradictory attitudes toward life: an unflinching sense of the immutable nature of things, on the one hand, and a recognition that human beings do have the capacity to shape their own destiny, on the other.[13] Tolstoy does not claim primacy for one or the other of these two realms, but instead combines both into a synthetic artistic vision.[14] Nowhere is this vision more clearly, if subtly, communicated than in the description of Olenin's spiritual journey, each stage of which reveals a unique aspect of his enlightenment.

". . . I AM BEGINNING A NEW LIFE"

As the novel begins, the young aristocrat Olenin, having just broken off a love affair, is preparing to leave for the Caucasus. "'I don't want to defend myself,'" Olenin says to his two acquaintances at his farewell dinner in a Moscow restaurant, "'but I should like you at least to understand me as I understand myself, and not look at the matter superficially'" (86, 1). Olenin goes on attempting to justify himself, but the reader begins to sense that what was supposed to be a conversation between Olenin and his colleagues is, in fact, an internal debate within Olenin himself: "'Why shouldn't one love? Because love doesn't come. . . . No, to be loved is a misfortune.'" A moment later, admitting that he deceived himself about being in love, Olenin asks himself: "'Am I to blame for my inability? What was I to do?'" (86, 1). Olenin continues aloud: "'Ah well! What's the use of talking? I've made an awful mess of life! But anyhow it's all over now; you are quite right. And I feel that I am beginning a new life.'" To which one acquaintance responds: "'Which you will again make a mess of'" (87, 1). By the novel's end the reader realizes that the words "which you will again make a mess of" do contain at least as much truth about Olenin's fate as the hero's own stated promise of self-renewal.

Olenin thus becomes the object of irony on the part of both his interlocutors and the narrator, at the very moment when he most wishes to be taken seriously. There is a touch of artistic cruelty in this; but there is an equally strong sense of artistic liberation. The irony affords a degree of playfulness and comic relief at the same time that the novel begins to reveal a weightier, more tragic truth about the hero's life: that in his attempts to transform himself, Olenin will confront again and again the stubborn fact that his human weakness is just as powerful a force as his human will.[15] The truth that the novel communicates lies neither in Olenin's idealism nor in the cynicism of his acquaintances, but somewhere in between, in a realm in which idealism and realism coexist in creative tension.

Tolstoy's subtle manipulation of the narrative voice thus reveals something of the author's own stance toward the hero. While he holds up Olenin for good-humored laughs, he also views Olenin's efforts at self-transformation as noble and courageous. In the end he does make value judgments, preferring the exuberant, proactive Olenin to his lifeless, world-weary acquaintances, who are on their way to nowhere. Their physical stasis is mirrored internally by their moral-spiritual stupor and lack of social conscience, which Olenin possesses in abundance. Tolstoy knows that Olenin's self-contented acquaintances may be wiser than the hero in the ways of the world, but he also shows that they lack the sensitive and soaring inner life that makes Olenin intriguing and perplexing to those who encounter him.

Tolstoy never permits the reader's sense of life to become ossified; rather, he creates a sense of openness through the dynamic relationship between the narrator's objective view and Olenin's subjective sense of things. An example of this can be seen in the second chapter, where the narrator is speaking about Olenin:

> On leaving Moscow he was in that happy state of mind in which a young man, conscious of past mistakes, suddenly says to himself, that was all not the real thing [*ne to*], that everything that went before was accidental and unimportant, that until then he had not really tried to live, but now with his departure from Moscow a new life was beginning—a life in which there would be no mistakes, no remorse, and certainly nothing but happiness. (91, 2)

A page later, as Olenin is recalling his entry into society, we learn that he had heard a voice that always whispered: "'*That's not it; that's not it.*'" [*Ne to, ne to*] (91, 2). Olenin's twofold repetition of the narrator's words sets up a tension between the two voices: the narrative consciousness is superior to Olenin and knows the hero is deluding himself, while at the same time it spars with Olenin's own consciousness. The closed world of inevitability, whose master is the all-knowing narrator, thus coexists with the open world of creative dialogue and possibility.

Another instance of the dialogue between narrator and hero centers on Olenin's inner contradictions. The narrator tells us: "He had come to the conclusion that *there is no such thing as love*, yet his heart always overflowed in the presence of any young and attractive woman. He had long been aware that *honors and position were nonsense,* yet involuntarily he felt pleased when at a ball Prince Sergius came up and spoke to him affably" (90, 29) [italics mine]. A few pages later, we hear Olenin's own voice, corroborating the narrator's. Just after Olenin muses about the submissive young woman he will meet and educate in the Caucasus, the hero thinks to himself: "'Oh, what nonsense!'" The text continues:

> But his fancy again began searching for the "nonsense" he had relinquished, and again fair Circassians, glory, and his return to Russia with an appointment as aide-de-camp and a lovely wife rose before his imagination. "But *there's no such thing as love,*" he said to himself. "*Fame is all rubbish.* But the six hundred and seventy-eight rubles? . . . And the conquered land that will bring me more wealth than I need for myself. I shall have to distribute it. But to whom? Well, six hundred and seventy-eight rubles to Cappele [his tailor] and then we'll see." (94, 2) [italics mine]

Why this corroboration? Why not simply have either Olenin or the narrator tell the reader? Instead of repeating the narrated speech exactly, Olenin's words are more like an echo than an exact repetition. They subsume the narrated text into Olenin's subjective consciousness, creating in the reader a sense of *déjà-vu,* the conviction that he has heard these words before, but not in quite the same way. This dialogue between narrator and hero, which mirrors Olenin's "interior monologue,"[16] continues to play an important role as Olenin discovers the mountains.

Most readers of the novel agree that Tolstoy demystifies Olenin's romantic illusions about the Caucasus by showing that the reality of the region does not square with his notions of what he will find there. But, if this is the case, how does the image of the Caucasus acquire such poetic force? Tolstoy demonstrates that there is indeed something grand and romantic about the Caucasus—but it does not lie in dreamy abstractions. The uniquely Tolstoyan poetry of the Caucasus arises from the concrete, ever-changing specificity of the natural surrounding. For Olenin, the poetic quality of the region is associated with abstract images that he has taken from the popular literature about the Caucasus that was widespread in his day: "All his dreams of the future were mingled with pictures of Amalat-Beks, Circassian women, mountains, precipices, terrible torrents, and perils. All these things were vague and dim, but the love of fame and the danger of death furnished the interest of that future" (93, 2). Olenin's "vague and dim" visions of the Caucasus not only contrast with the author's own more concrete rendition; they form a kind of psychological refuge for him, subsuming and neutralizing unpleasant, specific details from his past:

> As soon as he pictured anything definite, familiar Moscow figures always appeared on the scene. Sashka B fights with the Russians or the hillsmen against him. Even the tailor Cappele [to whom Olenin owes a debt of 678 rubles] in some strange way takes part in the conqueror's triumph. If amid these he remembered his former humiliations, weaknesses, and mistakes, then these recollections were not disagreeable. It was clear that there among the mountains, waterfalls, fair Circassians, and dangers, such mistakes could not recur. (93–94, 2)

Thus, the future is associated in Olenin's mind with the abstract, the general, and the ideal; the past with the concrete, the specific, and the real. His desire to escape his past is also a desire to replace what is real and specific in his life with the possibilities associated with an unknown future. Tolstoy makes this strikingly clear in the scene in which Olenin first encounters the Caucasian mountains. He expects them to correspond to a mental image of the Caucasus he has gleaned from the stories told by others, stories which are themselves influenced by previous literary sources. Thus, he fails to appreciate what he actually sees: "He could find nothing beautiful in the mountains of which he had so often read and heard. The mountains and the clouds appeared to him quite alike, and he thought the special beauty of the snow peaks, of which he had so often been told, was as much an invention as Bach's music and the love of women in which he did not believe. So he gave up looking forward to seeing the mountains" (96, 3).

But when Olenin gives up his mental expectations, suddenly the mountains present themselves to him in all of their surprising and beautiful specificity. He sees "pure white gigantic masses with delicate contours, the distinct fantastic outlines of their summits showing sharply against the far-off sky" (96, 3). Significantly, the narrator does not use the word "mountains" here to name what Olenin sees. Instead, the reader, like Olenin, is shown the highly specific features that make up the mountains: "delicate contours," "distinct fantastic outlines," "summits showing sharply." By referring to the mountains by means of synecdoche, Tolstoy thus makes a distinction between the mountains as they are experienced by an eye unclouded by preconceptions—that is, in the specific features that make them up—and the generalized concept of "mountains," which existed in

Olenin's mind as a prefabricated and abstract mental construct when he first encountered them on the previous day.

No sooner do the old myths begin to fade in Olenin's mind than they are replaced by a new one, a deeply personal response to the concrete facts before his eyes. He experiences a moment of genuine awe at the grandeur of the mountains: "When he had realized the distance between himself and the sky and the whole immensity of the mountains, and felt the infinitude of all that beauty, he became afraid that it was but a phantasm or a dream" (96, 3).

He then subsumes this newly discovered "dream" into a kind of grand new Truth against which the value of everything may be measured anew. The mountains diffuse their grandeur into his consciousness: "From that moment all he saw, all he thought, and all he felt, acquired for him a new character, sternly majestic like the mountains! All his Moscow reminiscences, shame, and repentance, and his trivial dreams about the Caucasus, vanished and did not return. 'Now it has begun,' a solemn voice seemed to say to him" (97, 3). The influence of this Romantic notion—the possibility of heightened awareness under the influence of natural beauty—is palpable in Tolstoy's description of the deeply affecting "immensity" and "infinitude of all that beauty" of the mountains.[17] They become a weighty new presence that begins to dominate Olenin's consciousness. The first half of each sentence contains the details of Olenin's surroundings, relayed to us by the objective narrator. Then there appears the phrase "but the mountains" ("*a gory*"), followed by an ellipsis.[18] The repeated phrase "but the mountains" bubbles forth as a kind of disembodied presence in the text, existing in opposition to that which comes before it in each sentence:

> Two Cossacks ride by, their guns in their white cases swinging rhythmically behind their backs, the white and bay legs of their horses mingling confusedly; but the mountains . . . Beyond the Terek can be seen the smoke from a Tartar village; but the mountains . . . The sun has risen and glitters on the Terek, now visible beyond the reeds; but the mountains . . . From the village comes a Tartar wagon, and women, beautiful young women, pass by; but the mountains . . . (97, 3)

The mountains, now associated in Olenin's mind with the mysterious grandeur of both the Caucasian landscape and the hero's inner world, begin to take over all the other details of his surroundings, subsuming everything external to them. This process is reinforced in the final sentence of the passage, in which Olenin's voice effectively merges with and, as it were, begins to predominate over that of the narrator: "'Abreks canter about the plain, and here *I* am driving along and do not fear them; *I* have a gun, and strength, and youth . . . but the mountains'" (97, 3) [italics mine].

Here the reader first glimpses the subtle emergence of a self that gropes for self-assertion, but which does not yet have anything specific to say. It is a self that is full of youthful vigor and a feeling of endless possibility, but which has not yet discovered an adequate form through which to channel its abundant energies. The mountains, a large and inchoate presence in Olenin's mind, both embody and nourish his expansive, inner life. The next stage in his development will occur during his first hunting expedition in the forest with Daddy Eroshka, the old Cossack, who serves as his primary guide through the luxuriant natural world of the Caucasus.

TWO HUNTERS AND A STAG: OLENIN AND EROSHKA

The worldview of Eroshka, that wise old pantheist, allows Olenin to fulfill his youthful quest to embrace the world in its entirety and live spontaneously, while maintaining a sense of ethical responsibility to his surroundings.[19] Eroshka tells his protégé: "God has made everything for the joy of man. There's no sin in any of it" (141, 14). Like Nimrod of the Bible, to whom he is compared at one point, Daddy Eroshka is a physically powerful and respected hunter-provider, and thus a father figure to Olenin, who is painfully aware of his incompetence in practical affairs, particularly in matters of personal survival in the rugged environment of the Caucasus.

Attracted as he is to Eroshka's earthy, all-embracing attitude toward life, Olenin remains his charmingly naïve, overly analytical self, and this becomes particularly evident in the scene when he is hunting with Daddy Eroshka. The scene begins with a beautiful, laconic description of the natural surroundings. By focusing on visual details, the omniscient narrator's description slowly transports the reader away from the bustle of village life, into a world apart, alive with a movement and excitement of its own:

> The mist had partly lifted, showing the wet reed thatches, and now was turning into dew that moistened the road and the grass beside the fence. Smoke rose everywhere in clouds from the chimneys. The people were going out of the village, some to their work, some to the river, and some to the cordon. The hunters walked together along the damp, grass-grown path. The dogs, wagging their tails and looking at their

masters, ran on both sides of them. Myriads of mosquitoes hovered in
the air and pursued the hunters, covering their backs, eyes, and hands.
The air was fragrant with the grass and with the dampness of the forest.
(159–60, 19)

Olenin and Eroshka appear fully immersed in the natural surroundings. Yet, in the very next sentence, we see that Olenin is easily distracted:
"Olenin continually looked round at the ox-cart in which Maryanka sat
urging the oxen with a long switch" (160, 19).

He interprets the meaning of his experience, and intellectualizes his
fearful responses: "Olenin knew that danger lurked in the forest, that
Abreks always hid in such places. But he knew too that in the forest, for
a man on foot, a gun is a great protection. Not that he was afraid, but he
felt that another in his place might be" (160, 19). As the hunters move
further into the pristine regions of the forest, Olenin's sense of surprise
and disorientation grows: "The vigor of the growth of this forest, untram-
pled by cattle, struck Olenin at every turn, for he had never seen anything
like it. This forest, the danger, the old man and his mysterious whisper-
ing, Maryanka with her virile upright bearing, and the mountains—all this
seemed to him like a dream" (160, 19).

But the narrator snaps Olenin out of that momentary dream with the
first words spoken aloud in this scene: "'A pheasant has settled,' whispered
the old man, looking round and pulling his cap over his face—'Cover your
mug! A pheasant!' he waved his arms angrily at Olenin and pushed forward almost on all fours. 'He don't like a man's mug'" (160–61, 19). The
union between man and nature, suggested at the beginning of the scene,
has now been wholly undermined. As if to emphasize this revised order of
things, the narrator has the inexperienced Olenin briefly supersede Daddy
Eroshka in hunting prowess, thus undercutting his heroic stature. Apparently Daddy Eroshka "could not hit a flying bird," while, surprisingly,
Olenin can.

The thrill of the hunt intensifies when Daddy Eroshka points out a
footprint. "'Yes, well?' said Olenin, trying to speak as calmly as he could.
'A man's footstep'" (161, 19). Olenin misunderstands that the footprint
belongs to Eroshka, who has pointed it out to Olenin in order to prepare
him to recognize another print, that of the stag. But before Olenin—or the
reader—learns of Eroshka's intention, Olenin's mind makes various associations and interpretations: "Involuntarily a thought of Cooper's *Pathfinder*
and of Abreks flashed through Olenin's mind, but noticing the mysterious
manner with which the old man moved on, he hesitated to question him

and remained in doubt whether this mysteriousness was caused by fear of danger or by the sport" (161, 19). Just as Olenin relied on romantic literary images in his earlier dreams about the Caucasus, so now, when confronted with another unfamiliar experience—the "mysteriousness" of this crucial moment in the hunt—he evokes a literary model to make sense of the moment. Cooper's 1841 novel *Pathfinder* was popular in Russia in the 1840s and 1850s, and its theme mirrors the general situation in *The Cossacks:* the confrontation of civilized man with the primitive peoples of the frontier. Like Olenin, the Pathfinder combines elements of the kind of person Olenin actually is—an outsider from another world—and who he would like to be: an Eroshka-like hunter, accepted by the natives and at home in the ways of the frontier.[20]

Despite Olenin's mental circumlocutions, the narrator keeps the reader grounded in the immediacy of the moment and the full force of the natural environment. A few seconds later the two hunters trace the footsteps of a stag to his lair. In Tolstoy's characteristically cinematic fashion, at the very moment of possible entrapment, the stag runs away, heard but not seen. The hunters' disappointment is suddenly transformed into an acute awareness of the instant, in which they become transfixed by the reverberations of the stag escaping through the trees. To this brief instant the narrator devotes an entire paragraph, and he reveals it to be an event that is both transitory and timeless:

> Suddenly they heard a terrible crash in the forest some ten paces from where they stood. They both started and seized their guns, but they could see nothing and only heard branches breaking. The rhythmical rapid thud of the galloping was heard for a moment and then changed into a hollow rumble which resounded farther and farther off, re-echoing in wider and wider circles through the forest. Olenin felt as though something had snapped in his heart. He peered carefully but vainly into the green thicket and then turned to the old man. Daddy Eroshka with his gun pressed to his breast stood motionless; his cap was thrust backwards, his eyes gleamed with an unaccustomed glow, and his open mouth, with its worn yellow teeth, seemed to have stiffened in that position. (162, 19)

Olenin's analytical mind turns off, his need for verbalizing is suspended, and that higher Tolstoyan truth—which is neither rational nor verbal but sublimely palpable nonetheless—seizes him. It also seizes Daddy Eroshka, who becomes in this moment a kind of human apotheosis of that truth.

His motionless, stiffened stance, open mouth, and eyes gleaming "with unaccustomed glow" suggest an iconic human presence, a man both frozen, deathlike, in the moment, and extraordinarily alive. The Russian word used to describe Eroshka's position, *zamer*, "stiffened," comes, in fact, from the same root as *umeret'*, to die. In the description of Daddy Eroshka, the concrete immediacy of the here-and-now (the gun pressed to his breast, the cap thrust backwards, the gleaming eyes, open mouth, and worn yellow teeth) acquires the quality of transcendence.

During the hunt scene, when Olenin *senses* without trying to make sense of things, he embraces, for a brief instant, what Eroshka knows intuitively and the narrator knows completely: that the beauty of nature in the Caucasus lies both in its concrete, sensual immediacy and in its capacity to transform human awareness. But that extraordinary moment of discovery is too short-lived for the hero. When Olenin and Eroshka return to the village in the evening, the extraordinary, heightened experience of the hunt dissolves, as the ordinary rhythms of everyday life reassert themselves. Like the stag who eluded him, it must be recaptured. Olenin attempts to do just that when he returns to the stag's lair the next day.

In his extraordinary solitary encounter with the stag, Olenin, while not fully "merging" with nature, feels a distinct affinity for the animals that surround him, and knows himself to be like them in an essential way. For a brief moment this animal essence defines him, making his social standing irrelevant and providing a temporary cessation of his inner torment. That moment is key to understanding Olenin's larger moral-philosophical quest. The name Olenin contains the word *olen'*, or "stag," in Russian, suggesting that the desire to connect with his animal nature is at the core of Olenin's existential search.

Initially resisting the pull of the animal world, Olenin finds himself surrendering to it, and as he does so his voice grows increasingly self-aware. This process begins from the moment Olenin finds himself in the same spot where he and Daddy Eroshka had discovered the stag on the previous day:

> Having been covered by the myriad of mosquitoes, Olenin was ready to run away from them and it seemed to him that it was impossible to live in this country in the summer. He was about to go home, but remembering that other people managed to endure such pain, he resolved to bear it and gave himself up to be devoured. And strange to say, by noontime the feeling became actually pleasant. . . . These myriads of insects were so well suited to that monstrously lavish wild vegetation, these multi-

tudes of birds and beasts which filled the forest, this dark foliage, this
hot scented air, these runlets filled with turbid water which everywhere
soaked through from the Terek and gurgled here and there under the
overhanging leaves, that the very thing which had at first seemed dreadful and intolerable now seemed pleasant. (163, 20)

As Olenin lies down in the stag's lair and enjoys a moment of physical
comfort and relief, in which "[h]e felt cool and comfortable and did not
think or wish for anything," he begins to reflect on his condition and is
struck by a heightened sense of both himself and his surrounding:

> Suddenly, with extraordinary clearness, he thought: "Here I am, Dmitry
> Olenin, a being quite distinct from every other being. . . . Here I sit, and
> around me stand old and young trees, one of them festooned with wild
> grape vines, and pheasants are fluttering, driving one another about and
> perhaps scenting their murdered brothers." He felt his pheasants, exam-
> ined them, and wiped the warm blood off his hand onto his coat. "Per-
> haps the jackals scent them and with dissatisfied faces go off in another
> direction: above me, flying in among the leaves which to them seem
> enormous islands, mosquitoes hang in the air and buzz: one, two, three,
> four, a hundred, a thousand, a million mosquitoes, and all of them buzz
> something or other and each one of them is separate from all else and is
> just such a separate Dmitry Olenin as I am myself." He vividly imagined
> what the mosquitoes buzzed: "This way, this way, lads! Here's some
> one we can eat!" They buzzed and blanketed him. And it was clear to
> him that he was not a Russian nobleman, a member of Moscow soci-
> ety, the friend and relation of so-and-so and so-and-so, but just such a
> mosquito, or pheasant, or deer, as those that were now living all around
> him. "Just as they, just as Daddy Eroshka, I shall live awhile and die,
> and as he says truly: 'grass will grow and nothing more.'" (164, 20)

In this extraordinary passage, we hear two distinct voices: the hero's
earnest tone as he simultaneously recognizes the individuality of all living
things and his own animal nature, and the narrator's ironic voice, mocking the absurdity of his hero's thinking insects. Yet, in spite of his irony,
we sense his empathy with the hero, who exhibits that characteristically
Tolstoyan aspiration to both embrace and transcend the limitations of
otherness.

Of course, Olenin's attempt at a simplistic identification of himself with
the mosquitoes immediately breaks down. He is a creature of desire after

all: "'But what though the grass does grow?' he continued thinking. 'Still I must live and be happy because happiness is all I desire'" (164–65, 20).

In his unself-conscious state when he feels "cool and comfortable" and does "not think of or wish for anything," the confusion and contradictions of Olenin's inner world seem to melt away. But the moment immediately gives way to one of moral and intellectual recognition of his responsibility toward other beings. He realizes that, whether he is an animal or a bit of God, "still I must live in the very best way I can" (165, 20) and concludes that personal happiness lies, ultimately, not in self-gratification but in "living for others." "Love and self-sacrifice" are the only desires that may be satisfied "despite external circumstances," whereas desires aimed purely at self-gratification are subject to the whims of uncontrollable outside forces and therefore cannot ensure individual happiness (165, 20).

Underlying this scene and imbuing it with universal significance is the archetype of the Garden of Eden.[21] When Olenin feels "cool and comfortable" and does "not think or wish for anything," and when he senses the "rightness" of the mosquitoes and his feelings of harmony with his environment, he is like Adam in the Garden of Eden. But he is swiftly expelled when he becomes aware of his own blissful state—his own innocent "nakedness," as it were. In this fallen world, Olenin evokes the theme of fratricide—Cain's slaying of Abel—when he surmises that the fluttering pheasants scent their "murdered brothers." The choice of words suggests that Olenin is experiencing a sense of guilt, which, moments ago, in the exhilaration of hunting, was alien to him.

For Olenin, as for Adam, self-consciousness and expulsion from the Garden are accompanied by considerable rewards, above all the ability to perceive his surroundings in a fresh and dynamic way. He becomes a kind of artist, capable of reorganizing the external world through acts of the imagination. Like his own creator, Leo Tolstoy, Olenin invites the reader to think differently about the relationship between man and nature: to perceive the organic synthesis of natural, cultural, and individual human experience.

But when Olenin transforms this creative perspective into an ethical program a few moments later, the integrated truth the hero has momentarily tapped into becomes replaced by a narrowly systematic one. Olenin goes from being a temporary creative subject of his world to the object, once again, of Tolstoy's ironic eye.

Olenin thus remains an actor in the narrator's archetypal story of man's expulsion from the Garden of Eden, which reaches its denouement when he leaves the stag's lair and becomes afraid of his "nakedness" amidst the natural surroundings, which now appear gloomy and menacing to him. In a subtle reference to the wilderness in which Adam and Eve were made to wander, "[Olenin] called to his dog who had run away to follow some animal, and his voice came back as in a desert" (165–66, 20). Shortly after this, Olenin's sense of moral guilt intensifies; he doubts his ability to fulfill his ethical program of living for others. Not until he hears the "sounds of Russian speech" does he experience a relief so intense it borders on a sense of spiritual salvation: "Suddenly it was as though the sun shone in his soul. He heard Russian being spoken, and also heard the rapid smooth flow of the Terek" (167, 21). The soothing sounds of the Terek River evoke the River Jordan, which the Israelites crossed in order to enter the Promised Land. But Olenin's promised land is his native, Russian-speaking one! The natural man who could translate the buzzing of mosquitoes has vanished inside the Russian aristocrat.

And it is this civilized being who now attempts to apply what he believes he has "learned" in the stag's lair—his systematic theory of the happiness to be found only in self-sacrifice—to the everyday world of the Cossacks. But when he gives Lukashka, the dashing young Cossack and Maryanka's sweetheart, his horse later that evening, his altruism is deformed by its contact with the reality of human relations and he ends up achieving the very opposite of what he intended. As soon as his theory, supposedly motivated by a genuine desire for self-sacrifice, is put into practice, other, less noble motivations—such as the desire to be recognized by others—rear their unlovely heads: "Olenin expected that Lukashka would go to share his joy with Maryanka, but though he did not do so Olenin still felt his soul more at ease than ever before in his life. He was delighted as a boy, and could not refrain from telling Vanyusha not only that he had given Lukashka the horse, but also why he had done it, as well as his new theory of happiness" (174, 22). What the narrator knows and his naïve hero fails to recognize is that, in the dust and heat of human affairs, purely selfless behavior is an impossibility. Moreover, Tolstoy points to a fatal contradiction between what Olenin wants to express—his expansiveness of spirit, love of the world, and desire for self-transcendence—and his attempt to express it through the limiting medium of a rationally planned ethical program.

IN SEARCH OF A HEROIC IDEAL

No such dichotomy plagues Lukashka, Olenin's ideal and would-be comrade, rival, and foil. Dwelling as he does in the world of the senses, and in a world that is "beyond good and evil," he comes much closer to achieving that ideal of inner harmony which continually eludes his young Russian counterpart. Later in the novel, Olenin will be troubled by Lukashka's murder of the Chechen brother: "'What are you so glad about?'" Olenin remonstrates with Lukashka. "'Supposing your brother had been killed; would you be glad?'" (170, 21). If Olenin experiences the moral consciousness of man expelled from the Garden, Lukashka is unconcerned with questions of good and evil. He retorts, "'Well, that happens too! Don't our fellows get killed sometimes?'" (171, 21).

Tolstoy develops the existential distance between his protagonists by contrasting their experiences of nature: Olenin's in the stag's lair, Lukashka's in the cordon. These scenes differ radically in both form and content, reflecting the stark differences between the two characters.

The opening sentences of each scene have nearly identical structures. In the cordon scene we read, "The night was dark, warm and still." In the stag's lair scene: "The day was perfectly clear, calm, and hot." Lukashka's moment alone in nature takes place in the darkness of night, Olenin's in the full light of day. Lukashka's association with the night heightens the reader's sense of his mysterious and ultimately hidden inner nature. If Olenin is portrayed as a young man with an emerging individual perception of the world, then Lukashka is described largely as an extension of his surroundings: a wild animal, incapable of moral or intellectual reflection, totally in tune with the rhythms of nature:[22] "The rhythmic sounds of night—the rustling of the reeds, the snoring of the Cossacks, the hum of mosquitoes, and the rushing water, were every now and then broken by a shot fired in the distance, or by the gurgling of water when a piece of bank slipped down, the splash of a big fish, or the crashing of an animal breaking through the thick undergrowth in the wood" (115, 8). While in the distance shots can be heard, in the camp there appears to be a complete harmony between the natural and human worlds, a harmony that is highlighted in the rhymed phrases: *khrapenie kazakov, zhuzhzhanie komarov* ("the snoring of the Cossacks, the hum of mosquitoes").

The recurrence of the mosquitoes is significant. In the stag's lair scene Olenin projects his thoughts onto them, using them as a vehicle for self-exploration. In contrast to this, the mosquitoes in the cordon scene have no relation to Lukashka's inner world, which is not developed in the novel. They are but one element in the tapestry of nature, which unfolds of its own accord, independent of human will.

Lukashka's inner life scarcely exists within the novel, and when it does appear in the form of a brief thought about his mistress or excited anticipation about his killing of an *abrek*, it is devoid of any of the moral and intellectual awareness that animates Olenin's inner world. He is a kind of noble savage, a man of primitive sentiment and raw, unreflective action—part Rousseauian, part Homeric. In his diaries of the period, Tolstoy wrote about the need to substitute a Christian ethic of universal love for the supramoral Homeric poetry of violence and nature. But there is no hint of rebuke in his treatment of Lukashka. Instead, the description of the young Cossack exalts the Homeric vision of nature as beautiful but essentially amoral—a vision that Tolstoy was powerfully drawn to but wished to suppress in himself.

If the struggle between Homeric and Christian values is central to Olenin's search for himself, they exist within *The Cossacks* as a whole, in the comparison of Lukashka's amoral, naïve experience of nature with Olenin's self-conscious one. Tolstoy is not mystifying one and demystifying the other, but creating within the novel an internal dialogue between these two poles of human experience. *The Cossacks* represents a tension between these two ways of being, and demonstrates that both are essential aspects of the totality of human experience.

We see this with even greater nuance and clarity in the battle scene, where the two men play apparently opposite roles. Lukashka is the fearless and brash warrior, leading the Cossack troops in their battle against the Chechens, while Olenin, the fumbling if genuinely curious outsider, attempts to make sense of an event in which he is clearly out of his element. While Tolstoy's emphasis in the scene is on the differing ways Lukashka and Olenin react to and participate in the battle, the author gives the reader a small but significant detail that briefly deflects and then refocuses his attention on the Lukashka–Olenin comparison. A cornet, who is described as no less confused and out of place in the scene than Olenin, sees the wounded Chechen who fired at Lukashka. "The cornet went up to him as if intending to pass by, and with a quick movement shot him in the ear" (238, 41). There is something ignoble and cowardly in the cornet's action. Lukashka's killing of the Chechens is driven by a natural inner force, an irrational, Achilles-like love of battle. His noble savagery is beyond moral categories, and the young Tolstoy describes it with undisguised admiration.

In contrast, the cornet's furtive act of shooting the Chechen in the ear after having pretended to walk by him is cowardly and sly. It reveals the presence of a moral universe so removed from the noble spirit of the fighting Cossacks that the Olenin–Lukashka contrast pales in comparison. The cornet is, in fact, the only character in the novel that Tolstoy consistently derides. He is beyond the pale of acceptability in Tolstoy's spiritual universe. His presence in the novel serves to remind readers that Lukashka and Olenin, despite their differences, are alike in possessing a mythic grandeur and vitality. The cornet has neither Lukashka's abundant physical vitality nor Olenin's rich inner life. In comparison to the two youths, he appears small and petty. The reader is reminded that alongside the novel's philosophically ambivalent portrait of life, there exists an authorial consciousness that does finally possess a sense of right and wrong. Characters who embody a fullness of life—either by means of an unconscious primitive spirit (Lukashka) or through conscious moral strivings (Olenin)—are "right." They ennoble human life. Characters who lack these qualities, such as the cornet and Olenin's Moscow tavern acquaintances, are "wrong." They impoverish and deaden life—both within themselves and in others.

If Lukashka represents to Olenin Homeric courage in a world "beyond good and evil," and if Daddy Eroshka is a father figure and a pantheist ideal, then what is Maryanka's significance to Olenin? She is, from the very first, the feminine ideal to be revered and conquered, the ultimate touchstone for all of Olenin's great expectations about the Caucasus and the perfect love he will experience there. All his romantic hopes and feelings of endless possibility are projected onto the figure of the mysterious "*she,*" who is firmly fixed in the hero's imagination, before he even arrives in the Caucasus.

Maryanka, with her "tall, shapely figure," "firm, maidenly form," and "beautiful black eyes," fills this role for Olenin from the moment he first sees her (126, 10). He imposes upon her the same sort of preconceived notion of beauty that he imposed on the mountains earlier, so that at first he fails to see Maryanka as she truly is. "This is she," he thinks, but then instantly feels a sense of disappointment: "'There will be many others like her' came at once into his head" (126, 10). And as in the mountain scene, here, too, Olenin will notice the full beauty of Maryanka only moments later, after he has time to adjust to the reality of who she is: "Her firm youthful step, the untamed look of the eyes glistening from under the white kerchief, and the firm stately build of the young beauty struck Olenin even more powerfully than before" (127, 10). He now sees her not as a romantic abstraction, but in the context of her specific, elusive, and unglamorous domestic reality. She wears a print smock, patters down the porch steps past Olenin, apparently going about her daily chores, "looking round hastily with laughing eyes at the young man" (127, 10). Still, he tries to hold on to the original, romantic image of "her": "'Yes, it must be she,' he thought, and troubling his head still less about the lodgings, he kept looking round at Maryanka as he approached Vanyusha" (127, 10).

Our sense of Maryanka is filtered through Olenin's consciousness, a focus that enables the narrator to highlight the hero's intense romanticizing of love. Maxim Gorky once quoted Tolstoy as saying that romanticism stems from an inability to look into the face of truth—a truth that Olenin's relationship with Maryanka amply illustrates. For all his sincere passion, Olenin is still incapable of mature love, precisely because he is incapable of a mature perception of the world. Maryanka is still for him largely the manifestation of an ideal and a compensation for his own internal deficiencies. In his unsent letter home in chapter 33, Olenin exhibits a flash of personal insight into these deeper psychological motives for his love for Maryanka, even as he continues to idealize her:

> "What is most terrible and yet sweetest in my condition is that I feel that I understand her but that she will never understand me; not because she is inferior: on the contrary she ought not to understand me. She is happy, she is like nature: consistent, calm, and self-contained; and I, a weak, distorted being, want her to understand my deformity and my torments. . . . Perhaps in her I love nature: the personification of all that is beautiful in nature . . . Loving her I feel myself to be an integral part of God's joyous world." (213, 33)

Given the high emotional stakes of Olenin's attraction to Maryanka, it is not surprising that he pursues her with a desperation bordering on obsession.

As for the real Maryanka, for all her shrewd insight, she is not as "above" Olenin as he often considers her to be. Despite her elusiveness and earthy "wisdom," Maryanka is herself part of a larger human drama, told by the narrator. A creature of contradictions, at the same time that she finds Olenin naïve, perplexing, and intrusive, she is undeniably attracted to him. In a scene that subtly encapsulates the broader contours of their relationship, Olenin and Maryanka meet briefly in the vineyard and reveal a mutual attraction that is as fleeting as it is real. The spontaneity of the moment is first evident in Olenin's recognition of Maryanka's blue smock from among the rows of vines, "by some instinct"; he does not consciously pursue her. Their initial moment of physical connection is also unexpected; Olenin's and Maryanka's hands touch suddenly as Olenin shows her the grapes he has harvested, and she looks at him, smiling. They are briefly transported into a metaphorical garden: not the Garden of Eden of the stag's lair scene, but the vineyard of the premodern Homeric epic. Here the Homeric ethos of battle and hunting (Olenin is carrying his gun with him) coexists with the life-affirming traditions of agriculture (grape harvesting, wine-making). The Homeric subtext is further reinforced by the time of year—August, the high season of haying and harvesting, which occurs on the heels of the other typically Homeric motifs of celebration (merrymaking and singing), and progeneration (Maryanka's betrothal to Lukashka), described in the chapters leading up to this one. These epic overtones, brought into a modern context, suggest the larger human drama that is being enacted by Olenin in this scene, and indeed, throughout the novel: that of modern man's striving to recover a lost organic union of man and nature, and to discover the kind of love that might exist between man and woman within that lost world.

But the Homeric motifs in this fallen world are inevitably skewed. Olenin introduces a jarring note into the environment. By intruding the normally acceptable values of the hunter into the world of the harvester, he evokes the threat of violence toward women: "'You'll be shooting women with your gun like that,'" Maryanka tells him (206, 31). In his attempt to play the heroic role of Maryanka's suitor, he betrays Lukashka:

"Do you love Lukashka?"
　"What's that to you?"
　"I envy him!"
　"Very likely!"
　"No really. You are so beautiful."
　And he suddenly felt terribly ashamed of having said it, so commonplace did the words seem to him. He flushed, lost control of himself, and seized both her hands.
　"'Whatever I am, I'm not for you. Why do you make fun of me?'" replied Maryanka, but her look showed how certainly she knew he was not making fun. (206, 31)

Here, in Maryanka's first moment of genuine empathy for Olenin, the tone of the scene shifts from a gentle comedic to a tragicomic register. Her pity for him belies her efforts to push him away. Olenin's frustration grows and Maryanka's half-hearted verbal attacks reach a crescendo when she cries, "Leave me alone, you pitch!" The word "*smola*" (pitch, resin, tar), suggesting something sticky and heavy, implies that Olenin is metaphorically beginning to stick to her, in both a negative and a positive sense (206, 31).[23] The positive implication is reinforced in the next line: "But her face, her shining eyes, her swelling bosom, her shapely legs, said something quite different" (206, 31).

Yet Olenin is unable to accept Maryanka's attraction to him. He continues to idealize her, unable to accept the possibility that Maryanka, so superior to him in his own estimation, might be no less human than he. His ordinarily fertile imagination fails him when it comes to considering perhaps the most human possibility of all: that Maryanka is not above love, and that she likely sees in Olenin the same sort of attractive, exotic "other" that he sees in her.

In typical Tolstoyan fashion, the brief moment of human connection is suddenly interrupted by Ustenka's high voice from behind the vineyard, calling for Olenin. Vestiges of what has just transpired briefly linger on: "Maryanka went on cutting and continually looked up at Olenin." And suddenly Olenin, who "was about to say something, . . . stopped, shrugged his shoulders and . . . walked out of the vineyard with rapid steps" (207, 31). The flicker of intimate possibility is extinguished, never to return.

The final and decisive break occurs when Lukashka is wounded at the cordon. Olenin naïvely asks Maryanka after the battle, "'What are you crying for? What is it?' She sternly answers: 'Cossacks have been killed, that's what for'" (238, 41). Now that the stakes have been raised, Maryanka's flirtation with Olenin is no longer acceptable to her. In a time of community crisis she rediscovers and reasserts her true allegiances to Lukashka, as well as to the Cossack community. The narrator intentionally leaves the reader uncertain as to whether Lukashka will survive, thereby highlighting the impact that the mere potential of his death has for Maryanka.

Had Tolstoy carried out his plans to develop *The Cossacks* into a larger saga, Olenin would have fared no better. In this unrealized version, Olenin returns to the Caucasus, courts and eventually cohabits with Maryanka, before experiencing his final disenchantment and being murdered, either by her, or by a jealous lover. Tolstoy could envision Olenin and Maryanka's physical union, but the notion of spiritual harmony between these beings from different worlds clearly violated his sense of the possible.

As Olenin leaves the Caucasus at the novel's end, multiple levels of irony reflect off one another to create a vision of reality that transcends the viewpoint of any one character. Daddy Eroshka filches a gun from Olenin, while "sobbing quite sincerely" about his friend's departure. Vanyusha, Olenin's lackey and a shrewder judge of character than his master, remarks: "'What a lot you've given the old fellow . . . he'll never have enough! A regular old beggar. They are all such insubstantial people'"

(242, 42). Vanyusha is, of course, partly correct. Eroshka is greedy, and Olenin fails to recognize that his erstwhile mentor has taken advantage of him. But Vanyusha misses the mark when he generalizes that all Cossacks are insubstantial. The text has created a far more complex view of these mountain people, as we have seen. Tolstoy thus winks ironically at Vanyusha, in the same way that Vanyusha ironizes Olenin in this final scene.[24]

The novel's final sentences leave the reader with a sense of the unsentimental truth about the objective nature of things: "Olenin turned round. Daddy Eroshka was talking to Maryanka, evidently about his own affairs, and neither the old man nor the girl looked at Olenin" (243, 42). In the end, Olenin is a passing curiosity for the Cossacks, never a permanent fixture in their world; the internally free Cossacks represent for Olenin a human ideal he will never fully realize. The Cossack village, which Olenin once believed to be his true spiritual home, becomes but a stopover on the hero's ongoing journey to self-discovery.[25]

As the novel opens, Olenin is an idealistic aristocratic youth, desperate to exchange the fetters of civilization for the natural freedom of a primitive people. By the novel's end he has grown spiritually closer to the narrator, becoming a writer-philosophizer who reflects at length on the contradictions of modern existence. Olenin breaks out of the two-dimensionality of a specific Russian literary type and comes to embody the human struggles and contradictions of modernity at large.

As such, he has something vital to say to those of us today who feel the world's falseness and injustice and who struggle with the issue of how to "make a difference" in an increasingly complex and threatening global environment. To whom are we to turn for inspiration in that struggle? Who are our heroes? Who are our moral pigmies? The younger generation continues to be bombarded with a smorgasbord of titillating heroic images—Hollywood celebrities, political dynamos, corporate executives, sports heroes, evangelist preachers—without knowing which of them is worthy of their emulation. What, they might well ask, makes an odd seeker such as Olenin, or a noble savage such as Lukashka, worthy of their attention, when the more recognizable type of the suave, cynical Muscovites or the showy cornet so readily charms and impresses them? In *The Cossacks* Tolstoy reawakens us to an ideal of greatness that transcends the seductions of the moment and instead illuminates timeless truths and reminds us of the epic possibilities of the human spirit.

While not exactly a social activist in the sense we think of today, Olenin is a spiritually *active* human being. His internal world, while conflicted and contradictory, is also marked by continual movement and growth. His sensitive nature registers injustice and falsehood, even as his own desire to do good often founders on the all-too-familiar rocks of human egotism and insensitivity. What distinguishes Olenin, though, is the sincerity of his intentions and the tenacity of his quest. For Tolstoy, as for his spiritual offspring, Mahatma Gandhi and Martin Luther King, Jr., this inner aliveness is the foundation of genuine social change. Productive worldly activity must arise—not from the compulsion to do the socially sanctioned thing or to ennoble one's resume—but from the stirrings of a genuine moral conscience: a nagging inner voice that insists that living out society's unexamined dictates and values is a betrayal of one's best self. For those willing to search for that self, which for Tolstoy was the "natural," authentic, Rousseauian self that precedes socialization, Dmitry Olenin makes an excellent guide and traveling companion.

four

$\mathcal{W}$AR AND PEACE

Life's "Labyrinth of Linkages"

One of the unfortunate byproducts of academic literary criticism over the past three decades is its failure to help readers appreciate the essence of *War and Peace*. The influence of postmodernist thought has led many well-meaning scholars to extract from the greatest novel ever written various ideological constructs about war, politics, and society. Other scholars, in the interest of "specialization," have plucked from Tolstoy's delightfully overflowing garden a single species of growth—a theme, a technique, a motif—and replanted it within their own conceptual frameworks. After reading analyses of Tolstoy's use of repetition, his preference of metonymy to metaphor, or his allusions to Greek philosophy, one scratches one's head, wondering: And where is *War and Peace*?

This "loose baggy monster" of a work, as Henry James famously called it, is a cornucopia of human experience. The novel embodies what Tolstoy called life's "labyrinth of linkages"—the deep interconnectedness of everyone and everything in the universe. As such, it is perhaps the grandest literary celebration ever conceived of "globalization"—not merely the unifying social, economic, and cultural forces that connect us today, but the transposition of these connections to a higher realm of spiritual unity.

Tolstoy worked on *War and Peace* during a creative period marked by great spiritual tranquility. Happily married to Sofya Behrs since 1862, settled comfortably on his family estate at Yasnaya Polyana, and intoxicated by his growing literary reputation, Tolstoy wrote *War and Peace* from 1863 to 1869 "under the best conditions of life."[1] The writer's calm inner state is reflected in the novel itself. In contrast to his angst-ridden first novel, *War and Peace* is a majestic meditation on life's holism. If in *The Cossacks* we hear an intense dialogue between the narrator and his hero, in *War and Peace* the narrator focuses our attention on the inner life of many heroes and on the deep interconnectedness of each individual with the cosmic forces of nature and history.

The result is a unified vision of the world that had not yet materialized in *The Cossacks*. The narrator of *War and Peace,* gazing with Olympian repose on his wondrous creation, is fundamentally different from the more ironic and divided narrator of *The Cossacks.* Despite his authoritarianism, like the God of the Old Testament, he has an almost paternalistic love for the humanity of all of his imperfect creatures.

A grand celebration of all that constitutes reality, whether "good" or "bad," *War and Peace* moves back and forth between private lives and public spectacles, ballrooms and battles, marriages and massacres. No character is too small and no subject too large for this epic masterpiece. Characters are born, they marry, grow old and die within a fictional world where the clock ticks on with slow, implacable calm. This has led some readers to sense in the novel a spirit of fatalism. But it is also an inspiring vision of the world's physical plenitude and of the meaningful moral choices it offers. These characters discover that their individual lives are both finite and full of possibility, both solitary and part of a unified tapestry of human history and nature. Only Prince Andrei is unable to reconcile his noble ideals with reality. He is the novel's one tragic hero.

As characters' personal destinies become increasingly intertwined with the encroaching forces of war and history, the "peace" and "war" sections of the novel become so intertwined that it appears virtually impossible to disentangle them. Power politics, schemes, and stratagems are as rampant in the Petersburg drawing rooms as on the battlefield, and characters are as apt to achieve spiritual illumination in the throes of war as in the joys of family life. The "peace" of the novel's title refers not only to peacetime but also to the spiritual tranquility characters seek amidst the confusion of modern life.[2]

If *The Cossacks* focuses on Olenin's view of life from outside the lost Garden and his desperate efforts to get back into it, then *War and Peace* presents a glimpse of what the Garden might actually look like from within. Unlike the first novel, *War and Peace* does not merely describe characters' quest for perfection in an imperfect world. Its underlying struc-

ture and vision *model* this coveted destination. The essential truth of life
the protagonists seek is already present in the work's epic wholeness, in its
portrait of a mythical totality of human existence, in which heaven and
earth, ideal and real, coexist in total equilibrium. If this sense of wholeness
was, as the critic Georg Lukacs has argued, organic to the ancient worldview, then Tolstoy has come as close as possible to resurrecting it in an
alienated, modern age.[3]

THE ART OF *WAR AND PEACE*
IN AN IDEOLOGICAL ERA

War and Peace meditates on the majestic order of the universe as a kind
of artistic compensation for an era that was anything but orderly and
harmonious. The growing ideological divisiveness and social dislocations
feared by the author of *The Cossacks* had in fact materialized. Alexander
II put the Great Reforms, which democratized the society, into effect in the
1860s. The greatest of those reforms, The Emancipation of the Serfs, was
enacted in 1861. To the ongoing debates about social reform were now
added discussions about Russian national identity, Russian history, and
historiography in general. Fierce journalistic and scholarly controversy
continued to sharpen the rift between the old guard and the radical revolutionaries. Divisions also widened between the Slavophiles, who argued
that Russia's destiny lay in a return to its unique national traditions, and
the Westernizers, who believed that Russia's development ought to follow
European models of political governance and social reform.

The opinionated author of *War and Peace* was not above the ideological fray. A proud landed aristocrat, Tolstoy was deeply concerned about
the personal loss of prestige and social chaos portended by the Great
Reforms. Furthermore, as a soldier during the Crimean War, and author of
the patriotic *Sevastopol Tales,* which immortalized the heroism of Russian
soldiers during that war, Tolstoy resented the liberal argument that Russia's "humiliating" defeat in the Crimea proved the necessity of sweeping
reform.[4]

But art and ideology are not, finally, interchangeable. *War and Peace*
assimilates Tolstoy's personal beliefs—many of them conflicting—into
an artistic and philosophical whole that transcends whatever polemical intentions the author may have initially had for the work. Kathryn
Feuer makes a similar point in her important *Tolstoy and the Genesis of
War and Peace.* She describes the strong social and political overtones of

Tolstoy's earliest work on *War and Peace,* a period defined by the author's "rejection of the Spirit of 1856," the time of reform-minded enthusiasm. Feuer then traces the slow and tortuous process by which *War and Peace* grew from a sociopolitical novel with overt ideological intentions into a masterpiece, in which the demands of artistic truth, which at first serve the author's ideological agenda, ultimately supersede it.[5]

While Feuer describes the transition from ideology to art, Boris Eikhenbaum argues in *Tolstoi in the Sixties* for a fundamentally opposite trajectory. He points out that what began as a family chronicle eventually was transformed into a historical epic. This is exemplified by Tolstoy's progressive inclusion of historico-philosophical essays, which Eikhenbaum likens to the authorial digressions in a Homeric epic. Furthermore, these essays prove to Eikhenbaum that Tolstoy's writing was becoming more rather than less polemical, as the author became increasingly engrossed in the controversies of the late 1860s. Still, as this astute critic argues, it is nearly impossible to fit Tolstoy neatly into any of the warring ideological camps of the 1860s, because the author's "archaistic" thought patterns combine so many conflicting traditional and progressive tendencies.

Taking Eikhenbaum's insights a step further, I propose that *War and Peace* unites the intellectual oppositions of the 1860s within an artistic world that transcends ideology altogether. Against the backdrop of the author's luxuriant, expansive canvas, questions about whether Tolstoy was a conservative or a liberal, a Slavophile or a Westernizer, become moot. Just as the vast Russian countryside in *War and Peace* engulfs the invading French army, so Tolstoy's massive literary landscape assimilates a web of conflicting ideas and influences into a synthetic creation whose deepest artistic sympathies are panhuman and pantheistic.[6]

There is no denying that Tolstoy's social conservatism seeps into *War and Peace* in his idealized depiction of the harmonious landlord–peasant relationship; he seems to suggest that such feudal relations are part of a timeless historical pattern that existed long before discussion of reform.[7] However, despite the obvious ideological underpinnings of the novel's rather poetic presentation of peasant–aristocrat relations, this vision of social harmony serves a non-ideological purpose, as well. It is integral to the work's overall sense of timeless historical cycles and the interconnectedness of man, nature, and history within a "great chain of being."[8]

Through his depiction of class harmony, Tolstoy creates for the divided Russian society of the 1860s a vision of a mythical, harmonious past, in which Russians are un-self-consciously secure in their collective national identity and spiritually united in their response to an invading army. In the novel Russia ends Napoleon's worldwide anarchy, and thus unleashes the forces that would lead to her own Decembrist Revolution of 1825.[9] In this way, Russia becomes a vital link in the vast chain of historical evolution, in which timeless patterns of revolution and retreat, social chaos and order, eternally recur.

To take another example of how the novel assimilates authorial ideology into an artistic whole, consider the novel's portrait of Mikhail Speransky, the influential government reformer under Alexander I, who, when Prince Andrei idolizes him in Volume Two, Part Three, is at the height of his career. While many historians in Tolstoy's time and after admired Speransky's accomplishments as an administrator, Tolstoy ridicules him in the novel, looking down on him as titled gentlemen often looked down on priests' sons who became opportunistic government bureaucrats. What's more, with his grating, high-pitched laugh and lowbrow narrow-mindedness, Tolstoy's Speransky has the qualities that Tolstoy disliked in many of the radical reformers of his own day: he is abrasive, contemptuous of others, and deaf to the larger historical and natural forces that move life forward. But even if the ideologue in Tolstoy has Speransky play the role of polemical whipping boy for his pro-aristocratic, antireformist stance, the artist in Tolstoy perceives Speransky from a much wider vantage point. Speransky is, in fact, *essential* to the larger life processes and trajectory of the novel as a whole.

When Prince Andrei becomes bitterly disenchanted with him, this is but a variation on the recurrent theme of ideal creation and disillusionment that is experienced by all of the novel's main characters. Prince Andrei's disenchantment with Speransky is the final blow to his grandiose delusions about human power. Having discovered earlier, on the battlefield of Austerlitz, that his idol Napoleon is but a buzzing fly in the fabric of history, Prince Andrei learns through his encounter with Speransky that social reformers are equally ineffectual—and irrelevant. Psychologically freed, at least for the moment, Prince Andrei can now open himself to new possibilities for achieving personal happiness and meaning. For one of the few times in the novel, he listens to the wisdom of his emotions and heeds the call of his love for the young and vibrant Natasha Rostova.

Yet this emotional flowering is temporary. Prince Andrei's capacity to live in concert with the forces of life and his own emotional needs is limited. Tragically unable to free himself from the shackles of duty and rationality, he postpones his happiness by giving in to his father's demands that the wedding to Natasha be postponed for a year. It is significant that, when he returns to Moscow nearly a year later, at the end of Volume Two,

Part Five, and learns of Natasha's infidelity during his absence, Prince Andrei's first words are a defense of his former idol, Speransky, "the news of whose sudden exile and alleged treason had just reached Moscow" (530; II, 5, 21).[10] He deals with his bitterness towards Natasha—and presumably towards himself—by attempting to resurrect an idol long dead to him, and now to Russia as well. Thus, Speransky's rise and fall from power roughly parallel Prince Andrei's own emotional trajectory in the novel. Despite Tolstoy's ideological opposition to Speransky's politics and personality, the artist in him sees Speransky as a necessary part of that timeless ebb and flow of life processes, which, in the context of the novel, is the highest, most enduring truth.

THE OBJECTIVE MIRROR AND THE TRANSFORMATIVE LENS: ARTISTIC "REALITY" IN *WAR AND PEACE*

To speak of the holism of *War and Peace* is not to imply that the work contains, literally, a comprehensive picture of reality. No work of art could possibly achieve this, even one as vast as *War and Peace*. In a response to criticism leveled against him in 1869, the author admitted that there was much he intentionally left out of his depiction of the era: "the horrors of serfdom, the immuring of wives, the flogging of grown-up sons . . . and so on."[11] John Bayley makes a telling point when he writes that "Tolstoy only created a world that seems to embrace all of reality by sealing off things that worried and disturbed him."[12] Indeed, Tolstoy's factual omissions stem from his desire to focus on the mythical social harmony of an earlier age, and to distill from that era the universal norms, rather than the extreme limits, of human behavior:

> If we have come to believe in the perversity and coarse violence of that period, that is only because the traditions, memoirs, stories, and novels that have been handed to us record for the most part exceptional cases of violence and brutality. To suppose that the predominant characteristic of that period was turbulence is as unjust as it would be for a man seeing nothing but the tops of trees beyond a hill, to conclude that there was nothing to be found in that locality but trees.[13]

Tolstoy himself repeatedly rejected the notion of the novel as an objective reflection of reality. Art's purpose, he insisted, is not to transfer historical experience exactly (an impossibility in his view) but to transmute it to the literary canvas, which contains its own internal set of laws and relationships. In response to readers who criticized him for having Napoleon speak both French and Russian, Tolstoy compared himself to the painter who is blamed for putting a black spot on his subject's face to create the impression of a shadow: "I would only ask those to whom it seems absurd that Napoleon should speak now Russian and now French, to realize that this seems so to them only because they, like the man looking at the portrait, notice a black spot under the nose instead of observing the face with its lights and shades."[14]

Tolstoy's defense of his artistic choices goes beyond questions of ideology or literary technique. It touches on his central ideas about the unique capacities and aims of art. As this quotation makes clear, what concerns the author above all is a distinction between artistic reality and empirical reality, between an artistic representation of the world and that world as it is seen by the naked eye, or experienced by the senses with empirical objectivity. This distinction, which appears obvious from our post-Formalist standpoint, was not widely accepted in the anti-aesthetic, materialist, and utilitarian intellectual climate of the 1860s in Russia.

To appreciate this, we need only consider Nikolai Dobroliubov's influential article "What is Oblomovitis?" published in 1860, about Ivan Goncharov's novel *Oblomov*, or the essay "Bazarov," about Ivan Turgenev's *Fathers and Sons*, published in 1862 by the radical social critic Dmitry Pisarev.[15] These critics blithely ignore the line between art and life and treat the novels as if they were objective mirrors of reality, thus turning them into sociological documents. Rather than discuss the emotional complexity of the works and the deep ambivalence of both authors towards their heroes, Dobroliubov and Pisarev treat each fictional hero as if he were an actual living being, and they diagnose contemporary social ills based on this "empirical" literary evidence. In other words, these critics treat art in precisely the way that Tolstoy said that art should not be approached: as an exact mirror of objective reality. For Tolstoy, art is not a mirror but a transformative lens. It distills from the objective facts of nature and society a higher poetic truth.

Tolstoy develops these ideas further in a notebook entry from April 1870, about a year after the completion of *War and Peace*. The author describes why he believes art is superior to "historical science" for understanding historical truth:

The first condition of history, like that of every art, must be lucidity, simplicity, and affirmativeness, not conjecture. But then *history-art* does not have the constraint and the unachievable goal of *history-science*. *History-art,* like every art, aims not for breadth but for depth, and its subject-matter can be the description of the life of all of Europe and the description of one month in the life of a 16th century peasant.[16]

Tolstoy considers "history-art" a superior form of knowledge because it peers into the inner reality and penetrates the deeper significance of historical facts, whereas "history-science" contents itself with an enumeration of the facts themselves. The limitation of "history-science" is that it focuses on the external reality of a historical era, and that it fails to incorporate into its narrative the innumerable forces—many of them metaphysical—that play a crucial role in the movement of history. To capture historical truth "[a] knowledge of *all* the details of life is necessary. Art—the gift of artistry—is necessary."[17]

In other words, the artist must capture the totality of the universe, the overarching order that encompasses all the details, not an enumeration of each and every detail. In a notebook entry written a month earlier, in March 1870, Tolstoy further explains why he believes that art, not science or rational thought, is uniquely capable of illuminating the "essence" of life:

> The work of thought leads to the vanity of thought. It is not necessary to return to thought. There is another tool: art. Thought requires figures, lines, symmetry, movement in space and time and thereby destroys itself. . . . What do chemistry, physics, astronomy, and especially the most fashionable zoology do? They bring everything under their requirements of symmetry and continuity (the circle), and arrive at a thought, but the essence of the object [of study] remains. . . . Only art knows the conditions neither of time, nor space, nor movement. Only art, always inimical to symmetry and the circle, gives the essence.[18]

Conspicuously absent from Tolstoy's reflections on the superiority of art to scientific thought is any reference to the human subject, to the artist himself, who creates the work. In speaking about art as though it existed outside of the participation of and manipulation by human beings, Tolstoy reveals the depth of his desire to believe in a pure, unconstructed truth of life. And yet, the writer was equally aware of how necessary, and even empowering, humanly imposed structures can be. Indeed, it is precisely through the author's brilliant manipulation of artistic *form* that *War and Peace* captures life's plenitude and holism.

Tolstoy understood that the capacity of art to reflect life's deepest truths depends not only on poetic inspiration and metaphysical insight but also on a finely honed artistic craft, a subject that preoccupied him throughout his life. One of his most illuminating ruminations is found in an unlikely place, his essay "Why Do Men Stupefy Themselves?" published in 1890 as a preface to a book, *Drunkenness,* about the Temperance Movement in Russia.[19] One of the essay's well-known passages about the use of details in art hearkens back to Tolstoy's earlier reflections, in his 1870 notebook entries, on art's unique capacity to reveal life's "essence." Here the writer provides a tantalizing clue about how exactly art does that:

> [The painter] Bryullov one day corrected a pupil's study. The pupil, having glanced at the altered drawing, exclaimed: "Why, you only touched it a tiny bit, but it is quite another thing." Bryullov replied: "Art begins where the tiny bit begins."
>
> That saying is strikingly true not only of art but of all of life. One may say that true life begins where the tiny bit begins—where what seems to us minute and infinitely small alterations take place. True life is not lived where great external changes take place—where people move about, clash, fight, and slay one another—it is lived only where these tiny, tiny, infinitesimally small changes occur.[20]

This passage reveals as much about Tolstoy's artistic technique as it does about Bryullov's: the attention to detail that allowed him to capture the subtle movement of human consciousness and the moment-to-moment flow of everyday reality. "True life" is lived in those "minute" and "almost imperceptible" moments when the mind is moving forward ever so slightly, making those successive tiny decisions that lead to major consequences. It is in that "almost imperceptible" space that the future drug or alcohol addict is born, according to Tolstoy. By giving in to a seemingly insignificant impulse to indulge, the future addict thus initiates a process that ramifies well beyond the initial, isolated act of smoking or drinking.

It is also in that "almost imperceptible" space that the holism of Tolstoy's artistic vision in *War and Peace* is born. Focusing on minute processes, he illuminates a vast web of associations. His poetics of the "tiny bit" permits him to go not only into the "breadth" but also into the "depth" of his subject. Yet not just any detail will do. In a little-known article, "How Count Tolstoy Writes," published in Boston in 1899 by

Charles Johnston (an Irish journalist and writer who knew him person-ally), Tolstoy explains what constitutes the necessary detail:

> "You should not neglect the slightest detail in art: because sometimes some half-torn button may light up a whole side of the character of a given person; and that button must be faithfully represented. But all efforts, including the half-torn-off button, must be directed exclusively to the inner reality, and must by no means draw away attention from what is of first importance to details and secondary facts. One of our contemporary novelists, in describing the history of Joseph and his wife, would certainly not miss the chance to exhibit his knowledge of life, and would write: 'Come to me!' murmured she, in a languishing voice, stretching out her arm, soft with aromatic unguents, on which shone a bracelet decorated, and so on, and so on, and these details not only would not light up the heart of the matter more clearly, but would cer-tainly obscure it."[21]

Let us observe how the Russian master, in contrast to those "con-temporary novelists," uses details to "light up" "the inner reality" of the moment in *War and Peace*. Here is Prince Andrei discovering that his wife, Lise, has died during childbirth:

> He went into his wife's room. She lay dead in the same position in which he had seen her five minutes before, and, despite her still eyes and pale cheeks, there was the same expression on that lovely, timid, child-ish face, with its lip covered with fine black hair.
>   "I loved you all and did nothing bad to anybody, and what have you done to me? Ah, what have you done to me?" said her lovely, pitiful dead face. In the corner, something small and red snorted and squealed in Marya Bogdanova's white, trembling hands. (327–28; II, 1, 9)

The details Tolstoy selects cause us to experience along with Prince Andrei the shock of discovery that the face he (and we) had seen only moments before is now dead. Prince Andrei's shock has a moral dimension as well; projecting onto his wife's dead face his own sense of guilt toward her, he perceives in it words of rebuke. By attributing them to the "lovely, timid, childish face," only after we hear them, the narrator creates for us a momentary sense that Lise is actually speaking. Thus, as we read the text, we experience Andrei's inner reality, as he realizes that Lise is dead and is overcome by the sense that he is somehow responsible.

Figure 1   L. N. Tolstoy in the study at his Yasnaya Polyana home, November 3, 1909. Photograph by his wife, S. A. Tolstaya. Tolstoy liked the portrait: "The portrait is wonderful, because it was not posed. The hands are wonderful, the expression is natural." Published in *Tolstoi v zhizni* (Tula, 1988), vol. 1, p. 145. Courtesy of L. N. Tolstoy State Museum, Moscow.

Wherein lies true, objective experience, and what is subjective perception? We are momentarily unsure. We know and feel what Prince Andrei knows and feels, but also more than he does. It is unclear whether he sees what is happening in the corner of the room, but we certainly do. The final details describing the birth of his son reinforce for us the sense of life's ultimate continuity and integrity. The scene's overall pathos, then, is one of tragedy combined with tenderness and optimism. We begin to understand

Lise's death both from Prince Andrei's limited perspective and also from the narrator's wide-seeing, life-affirming vantage point. The scene highlights the objective truth about life and death, while simultaneously evoking the fluid subjectivity of the individual who confronts that truth with a sense of confusion and vulnerability.

In this dual perspective lies the scene's "inner reality," made palpable to us not through abstract emotionalism or realistic embellishment but by means of concrete details that reveal both the surface of things and their hidden truths. The details in this passage thus "*light up the heart of the matter more clearly*" (italics added), by illuminating one of the cornerstones of the novel's overarching design: its sense of the world as a place defined by the immutable, ongoing cycles of life and death, and as a place in which human joy and tragedy are forever present in equal measure.

WAR AND PEACE IN THE EYES OF TOLSTOY'S CONTEMPORARIES

Despite Tolstoy's repeated emphasis on the holism of art and his lifelong search for a technique that would capture it, *War and Peace* seemed to its contemporary readers anything but whole. Far from discovering that "essence" Tolstoy described in his notebooks, or uncovering the novel's "labyrinth of linkages," contemporary critics repeatedly referred to the work's strangeness, incomprehensibility, and lack of a guiding principle.

The author of an unsigned review of the first parts of *War and Peace*, published in 1866 in *Book Herald* (*Knizhnyi Vestnik*), remarks that Tolstoy's novel "seems strange and indeterminate. Evidently the author himself does not know what he is writing."[22] In 1867 the critic and minor novelist N. D. Akhsharumov echoes this point by emphasizing the generic indeterminacy of the work: "We cannot place this work categorically in any of the usual literary genres."[23] In his 1868 review of the work, P. V. Annenkov writes: "The big wheel of the novel in our opinion can only be the plot and the central idea of the work which is inextricably connected with it. The plot is nowhere to be seen, not even in the scenes of political and social life, however remarkable they might be."[24] The author of an unsigned review in *Affair* (*Delo*) writes that "the pictures and characters are not united by any controlling idea or anything which would give an inner life or logic to the events: everything is mixed up into a general mass where one can see neither the reasons for nor the consequences of the events or the appearance of heroes or facts."[25]

For some of Tolstoy's contemporary critics, the size and formlessness of the work were a reflection of Tolstoy's own unformed, prodigious personality. In a letter to I. P. Borisov, for instance, Ivan Turgenev remarks that "Tolstoy is a real giant among the rest of our literary fraternity—and he produces on me the impression of an elephant at the zoo: clumsy, even preposterous, but enormous—and how intelligent!"[26] A reviewer for the *Westminster Review* in England speaks of the novel as "this prodigal outpouring of a careless genius."[27] And the American writer and critic Henry James famously called the novel "a splendid accident."[28]

There was one glaring exception to this general trend in the contemporary reception of *War and Peace*. Not surprisingly, it came from the critic and philosopher Nikolai Strakhov, who wrote three articles about the novel, published in 1866, 1869, and 1870. These articles not only established Strakhov's reputation as an important literary critic but also were responsible for sparking Tolstoy's interest in the critic, and initiating their lifelong friendship.[29] In their time Strakhov's articles were the most unequivocally admiring responses to the novel, counterbalancing the generally hostile reaction to it in the influential radical press.

To this day Strakhov's readings remain among the most sensitive—and underappreciated—attempts to grasp the novel's mysterious holism. By discussing the novel's artistic and philosophical vision, Strakhov became one of the first critics to appreciate that "labyrinth of linkages" that Tolstoy would later define as "the essence of art." He was also among the first to touch on an aspect of Tolstoy's art that has thrilled readers for generations: the "realism" feels so true to life, and yet at the same time captures the extraordinariness of everyday reality. The critic asserts that, while no "abstract paraphrase" will do justice to *War and Peace*, the novel *does* do justice to the complexity of life: "A complete picture of human life. A complete picture of Russia of those days. A complete picture of the things in which men set their happiness and greatness, their sorrow and their shame. That is what *War and Peace* is."[30]

If Strakhov, like other contemporary critics, found the novel incomprehensible, it was not because it lacked a guiding principle, but rather because of its artistic richness and philosophical profundity, which, he felt, were beyond the reach of the ordinary, rational intellect: "Count L. N. Tolstoy is a poet in the old and best sense of the word. He carries within him the deepest questions of which man is capable. He sees things clearly and opens up to us the most sacred secrets of life and death."[31] In a not so subtle swipe at the radical intelligentsia, who mocked the novel's refined "elegance" and its "philosophy of stagnation,"[32] Strakhov asks: "How do you want people to understand him, people for whom such questions completely fail to exist, and who are so obtuse or, if you wish, so intelligent that they don't find any secrets either within themselves or around them?"[33]

To appreciate the uniqueness in its time of Strakhov's approach to *War and Peace,* we may compare it to another important contemporary article, "Staroe Barstvo" ("The Old Gentry"), published in 1868, by Dmitry Pisarev, mentioned earlier. As was characteristic of the radical intelligentsia, Pisarev used Tolstoy's novel as a springboard for his discussion about the "pathology of Russian society" of the era of Alexander I and, by extension, of the current era as well.[34] In *War and Peace,* Pisarev argues, Tolstoy "poses and decides the question about what happens to human minds and characters in those conditions which create the possibility for people to get by without knowledge, without energy, and without labor."[35]

Pisarev is referring here, of course, to the gentry, one of the radical intelligentsia's favorite targets. Pisarev censures two characters in the novel, Boris Drubetskoi and Nikolai Rostov, but he sees Boris as the lesser of the two evils. Despite his aristocratic pretensions, he is a practical-minded careerist who possesses skills that could potentially make him a productive member of society. Nikolai, on the other hand, is a self-indulgent and weak-willed child of privilege. Boris "seeks solid and tangible benefits" for himself, whereas "Rostov wants more than anything, and come what may, bustle, glamour, strong sensations, effective scenes and bright pictures."[36]

The reason Boris "is more intelligent and has a deeper character than Rostov" is that he is grounded in empirical reality. He has "a far greater capacity to observe attentively and to make sensible generalizations about surrounding phenomena,"[37] by which Pisarev means specifically material facts. "With the proper development of his talents Boris would make a good investigator while Rostov with the same proper development of his would make in all probability an exceptional artist, poet, musician, or painter."[38] Without denigrating the value of art as a professional pursuit (Pisarev is himself a literary critic, after all), he makes it clear that a rational, scientific approach to the world is preferable. Still, Nikolai might at least leverage his penchant for "bustle" and "glamour" into a socially useful artistic career, in which he can share his "strong sensations" and interest in "effective scenes and bright pictures" with the rest of society.

Despite his deep-seated distrust of art created by an idle aristocrat of Tolstoy's ilk, Pisarev does not deny that *War and Peace* is an important work of art. On the contrary, he argues that "precisely because the author spent much time, labor, and love . . . that truth, throbbing with the life of the facts themselves, that truth, bursting forth apart from the personal sympathies and convictions of the story-teller, is especially valuable for its irresistible persuasiveness."[39] Tolstoy, it seems, is just the kind of socially useful artist Pisarev hopes Nikolai might one day become. His authorial eye becomes a photographic lens, accurately, if accidentally, reflecting the objective reality that gave rise to it. *War and Peace* is, in spite of itself, a valuable sociological document,[40] because it reveals the concrete, empirical reality of the world that produced it. While uninterested in Tolstoy's creative imagination, his personal attitudes, and subjective perception of objective reality, Pisarev seems to believe that an artist of Tolstoy's caliber must *necessarily* record reality with total accuracy.

It is no wonder, then, that Nikolai Rostov so incensed Pisarev. One of the novel's expansive personalities, Nikolai —with his impulsiveness, sense of life's poetry, and deep patriotism, often expressed with childlike abandon—offends Pisarev's sober faith in the supreme importance of objective reality. Any individual who strives—through reverie, art, or any other means—to overcome or otherwise transform that reality is, for Pisarev, delusional and a drag on social progress. Objective reality exists outside of our subjective consciousness; it is something "you can't conceal in a bag."[41]

Strakhov's article about *War and Peace* shares two assumptions with Pisarev's article: that the novel presents an indisputable truth about the world, and that its capacity to do so lies in the author's great artistry. But here is where the similarity ends. For Pisarev, the author is a passive vehicle through which objective reality is filtered. Strakhov, however, focuses on the productive act, not just the final result, of the author's engagement with his world. For Strakhov the human subject—and this includes both the author and his characters—do not merely exist in the world. They do not merely see or fail to see external reality for what it is. They participate in the world and proactively engage in it, seeking its hidden meanings, searching out its deeper truths. According to Strakhov, Tolstoy does not merely present life's phenomena; he penetrates them, transforming them artistically and illuminating their inner essence.

"There is realism and then there is realism [*Realizm realizmu rozn'*]," Strakhov writes. "Art essentially can never reject the ideal and always strives for it; and the more clearly and vividly one senses that striving in the creation of realism, the loftier that realism is, the nearer it is to being truly artistic."[42] Herein lies the difference, according to Strakhov, between Tolstoy's realism and that of his less gifted contemporaries who turn their souls into a simple photographic instrument and photograph with it whatever pictures happen to arise. Our literature produces many such pictures: but then simple-minded readers, imagining that before them appear genuine artists, will be not a little surprised upon seeing that absolutely nothing comes of these writers. The matter, however, is understandable; these writers were faithful to reality not because it was brightly illuminated by their ideal, but because they themselves did not see further than that which they depicted. They stood on the same level as the reality that they described.[43]

Although Strakhov does not name the specific practitioners of what he calls "photographic realism," we may assume that he is referring to those prose writers who became popular in Russia in the 1860s for their stark, journalistic reportage of the various social ills.[44] Strakhov had a strong distaste for their radical political positions. Interestingly, though, his critique of "photographic realism" focuses not on its misguided ideology but on its creative and philosophical shallowness.

What Strakhov disliked most about the politics of the radicals of his generation—their valuing the material over the spiritual; their mechanistic and atomistic sense of life; their inability to recognize an ideal of transcendent beauty in the world—is precisely what he disliked in the art of the "photographic realists," as well. Like their counterparts in the political sphere, these realist writers see only empirical facts, never the unifying truths and higher spiritual beauty contained within those facts.

Tolstoy, on the other hand, is able to rise above this "photographic" realism and to "penetrate that poetry which is hidden in reality."[45] Tolstoy's realism is infused with the ideal: "A realistic depiction of the human soul was essential [to Tolstoy] in order that a genuine realization of the ideal, however weak, might appear before us all the more powerfully and all the more truthfully."[46] The novel celebrates the "genuine inner beauty, genuine human dignity" of the individual, not by means of abstract generalization or by romantic distortion, but by capturing "each feature, each trace of genuine inner beauty, of genuine human dignity" of the individual, struggling nobly against the implacable forces of history.[47] "The broader subject of the author," Strakhov writes, "is, simply, *man*."[48]

Tolstoy's art does not pit the "wonderful life" against "ordinary everyday reality."[49] Far from a vision of Utopia, Tolstoy's ideal, for Strakhov, exists "in the pure light of day"[50]: right here, right now, within this imperfect world and its flawed, striving inhabitants. He "tries to find and define with complete precision, in what way and in what degree man's striving for the ideal is realized in actual life."[51] The author's ideal emerges, not only in heightened moments or striking scenes; it pervades the artistic fabric of the entire text, in that mysterious authorial voice that reveals the imperfect world to us with utter verisimilitude, while at the same time illuminating life's poetic grandeur. And yet, as readers of the novel have discovered, to their delight or dismay, one of its most original features is the existence of a second authorial voice—polemical, rational, severe—that regularly punctuates the text, rudely puncturing that shimmering narrative fabric.

TWO HEDGEHOGS:
ART AND ARGUMENT IN *WAR AND PEACE*

This second voice confronts us with a fundamental problem: how are we to make sense of the openly polemical historical-philosophical treatises—those cantankerous, rigidly rational intrusions into an otherwise expansive vision of life? These essays, scattered among the artistic portions of the novel, and increasing in length and number towards the end, are of two types: abstract philosophical treatises and specific polemical attacks: against Napoleon, who believes that he shapes events; at historians who accept the great-man theory of historical evolution; and at all manner of strategists, military and otherwise, who believe that rational planning affects the outcome of events. If there is a consistent thesis in these essays, it is that great men are history's slaves and that free will is an illusion, albeit a necessary one to help us get through life.

For many contemporary readers the digressions were only one of many examples of the work's structural confusion and indeterminacy. In his article about *War and Peace,* published in 1870, Strakhov pinpointed the problem of these essays: while their ideas are excellent, he wrote, they detract from the work's overall philosophical spirit. The essays reduce the celebration of life's fullness, evoked in the artistic portions, to a one-sided system of ratiocination, which dissects rather than integrates, and thus gives an "incomplete" picture of life:

> [The] formulas about knowledge are in and of themselves cold, passionless, indifferent; they capture neither beauty, nor goodness, nor truth, that is to say, that which is higher than all else on earth, in which consists the most essential interest of our life. . . . For science the world becomes a dead, one-sided play of reasons and consequences; but for a living person the world has beauty, life, it constitutes an object of

despair or delight, blessing or repulsion. . . . The mind finds nothing in the world besides some sort of endless and senseless mechanism; but the heart shows us another meaning, which at bottom is singularly important.

And so, the primary meaning of *War and Peace* is not to be found in the philosophical formulas of Count L. N. Tolstoy, but in the chronicle itself, where the life of history is illustrated with such amazing fullness, where there are so many profound discoveries for our heart.[52]

Strakhov's ideas guided Tolstoy as he himself grappled with this issue of the difference between an artistic representation of the world and rational argumentation, throughout the late 1860s and 1870s.[53] In fact, even as he worked on the novel in the 1860s, the author vacillated, entertaining serious reservations about whether the polemical digressions should remain at all. Eventually, he came to believe that art, with its ability to speak in images, can reveal things that rational thought cannot, and decided to remove the essays from the main section and place them in a separate appendix, called "Articles about the Campaign of 1812," in the 1873 edition of *War and Peace*. Under the wrong-headed assumption that Tolstoy considered the original version of the novel definitive, future editors adopted the practice of reinstating the essays in the main body of the text.[54]

If we examine what, specifically, is problematic about the essays in the context of the novel as a whole, and why Tolstoy had ongoing reservations about them, we uncover the essence of his narrative art. The author of the theoretical essays destroys his intellectual competition by mounting a point-by-point assault against the "false" theories of historical evolution and then carefully leading the reader through his own "correct" reasoning processes. The voice is that of a severe and humorless social critic, an intellectual crank, whose spirit reminds one more of the later author of "What Is Art?" and the moralistic fiction than the broad-minded, life-affirming narrator of *War and Peace*. These captious authorial musings reinstate, in fact, the very intellectual divisiveness of the era (the 1860s) that the artistic narrator seeks to transcend.

The artistic narrator does not argue rationally for or against abstract intellectual positions. In and of themselves, ideas are sterile and irrelevant to his conception of the world. What counts are the infinitely complex natural and historical processes, in which rational ideas play, at best, a trifling role. The artistic narrator is concerned above all with the human capacity to live successfully within these organic processes—a capacity that depends not on ideas, but on the person behind the ideas, on the person's emotional, intuitive responsiveness to the world.

We see this in Tolstoy's treatment of Speransky, whose shortcoming is not only his faulty conclusions but his faulty approach to living. As Prince Andrei discovers, Speransky's ideas can have no bearing on his or anybody else's happiness, and his clever words, which lacked that "something which constitutes the salt of merriment" (465; II, 3, 18) embody the ultimate sterility of the man himself. By contrast, Pierre, whose ideas are frequently confused or half-baked amalgams of other peoples' thought, leaves a lasting effect on other people through the warmth of his personality and the sincere quality of his words. "'[Y]our friend's a fine fellow, I've come to love him!'" Old Prince Bolkonsky says to his son, Andrei, after Pierre's departure. "'He fires me up. Another man talks cleverly, and you don't want to listen to him, but he talks nonsense, yet he fires me up, old as I am'" (394; II, 2, 14).

While the narrator's irony can be harsh indeed in the artistic sections, as we see in the Speransky passages, it stops short of outright contempt and is always counterbalanced by a paternal, godlike benevolence. In contrast, the narrator of the theoretical essays openly scoffs at the narrow-mindedness of the historians and philosophers he discredits. The artistic narrator bestows a full-blooded, complex humanity on even the most reprehensible of characters.

What reader is not gripped by sudden compassion for the cruel, maleficent Dolokhov, when Nikolai Rostov unexpectedly discovers that "Dolokhov, this rowdy duelist, lived in Moscow with his old mother and hunchbacked sister, and was a most affectionate son and brother"? (317; II, 1, 5). The narrator of the theoretical treatises cannot surprise us with such a revelation, because his perspective is defined and circumscribed by the nature of the genre in which he is writing: a mixture of philosophical disquisition, historiography, and polemical journalism. His purpose is to conquer his audience with the power of rational, linear argument, not to invite us to share emotionally in the fate of his characters and in the complexities of their lived experience.

In the theoretical essays, we, the readers, are passive recipients of the world. In the artistic portions of the novel, however, we are invited to be active participants in, indeed co-creators of, the universe alongside the narrator. Carried along by the overwhelming lifelikeness of the narrator's invented world, we achieve the sort of clear, comprehensive vision of the universe that Prince Andrei, Nikolai, and Pierre, Napoleon, Speransky, and the military strategists covet but cannot attain. We fully empathize with the characters' struggles and vicariously participate in them while calmly recognizing, along with the narrator, the concealed patterns and unifying truths hidden from the characters' gaze. This awareness only intensifies our empathy for the characters, widening our understanding of their individual experiences and, by extension, our own.

"'Can it be they're running to me? Can it be?'" Nikolai Rostov thinks while standing in an open battlefield after having fallen from his horse and sprained his arm during battle. "'And why? To kill me? *Me*, whom everybody loves so?'" (189; I, 2, 19). The brilliance of the narrative perspective resides in the narrator's ability to embrace both the poignancy of the moment and also the comic naïveté of Nikolai's thought. The gung-ho young hussar knows that he is at war, and "though a moment before he had been galloping only in order to meet these Frenchmen and cut them to pieces," now in his heart of hearts he cannot conceive of anybody trying to hurt him, the beloved son and brother and "young master"! Beyond this, Tolstoy is gently mocking the self-dramatization and obviously unheroic conduct of this youthful warrior, who "seized his pistol and, instead of firing it, threw it at the Frenchman, and ran for the bushes as fast as he could" (189; I, 2, 19).

We both feel *with* Nikolai and shake our heads at his childish amazement and jejune behavior. The narrator's omniscient perspective is benevolent and responsive to multiple emotional levels in a way that the more severe voice of the polemical narrator, constrained by the limits of the genre in which he is writing, cannot be.

Not all critics are willing to grant this extraordinary success to the narrator. In a recent study, Jeff Love argues that "While *War and Peace* strives towards absolute vision, it also certainly fails to achieve such vision, what amounts to a hyperborean view belonging to the gods or God alone. In this very failure is the secret of its remarkable realism, or rather, the illusion of realism which has struck so many readers of the novel."[55] I would argue, on the contrary, that readers are struck by how Tolstoy's realism *does* achieve a comprehensive, transcendent vision while never eschewing the rough edges, the gaps, the imperfect ebb and flow of the ordinary. Finitude may be a condition of the characters, but not of the narrator—and, by extension, of us, the readers. Therein lies the peculiar power of what Boris Eikhenbaum has described as the narrator's "otherworldly voice" (*potustoronnii golos,* or, literally: "a voice from the other side"), by which I take him to mean not only a voice that speaks from the perspective of eternity but also one that is forbearing and humane in a way that only God can be.[56]

As distinct from the narrator of the theoretical treatises, the artistic narrator's synoptic vision is never abstractly philosophical. His transforming presence can be felt in the concrete, sensual details of the here-and-now. As Ivan Turgenev said, "Whenever [Tolstoy] touches the ground, he, like Antaeus, regains his powers."[57] And those powers are felt most palpably in the way the narrator illuminates both what is and what lies beyond what is, the extraordinary in the ordinary. One of Nikolai Rostov's most intensely religious experiences in the novel—his desperate prayer to God to send the wolf his way during the hunt—is also one of the novel's most earthbound. A seemingly unremarkable moment, such as Prince Andrei's surveying of the battlefield the night before the Battle of Schöngrabern, grows into a vast chain of metaphysical and artistic ramifications when viewed in the context of his life's—and the novel's—larger trajectory.

The question of the novel's unity has been at the center of the critical debate right up to our own time. One particularly influential twentieth-century critique is Isaiah Berlin's famous essay *The Hedgehog and the Fox: An Essay on Tolstoy's View of History*, first published in 1951. Berlin argues that Tolstoy the artist celebrates the diversity of life in *War and Peace*, while Tolstoy the thinker strives for a unifying philosophical vision. "The fox knows many things, but the hedgehog knows one big thing," Berlin cites the Greek poet Archilocus at the outset of his essay. He explains: "[T]here exists a great chasm between those, on one side, who relate everything to . . . a single, universal organizing principle in terms of which alone all that they are and say has significance—and, on the other side, those who pursue many ends, often unrelated and even contradictory, . . . related by no moral or aesthetic principle."[58]

Because Berlin associates Tolstoy's integrative wisdom with the thinker and foxlike skepticism with the artist, he looks for Tolstoy's unified vision in his theories, not his art. Berlin cannot take seriously the possibility that Tolstoy, the artist, also strives for a holistic vision of the world. Is it possible that there are two hedgehogs in *War and Peace*? In fact, there are. Both the artist and the thinker try to articulate a unifying conception of life—the artist through imagery, and the thinker by means of rational polemics. In this competition of the hedgehogs, I propose that the artist wins, because his vision of life is the fuller and ultimately more humane of the two.

Whereas Berlin separates the thinker and the artist, Gary Saul Morson in his *Hidden in Plain View: Narrative and Creative Potentials in "War and Peace"* tries to put these two sides of the writer's personality back together. Morson is astute in many of his observations—particularly in one of his central conclusions, that Tolstoy cherished ordinary moments in human life. But I believe that he is wrong to link this and other aspects of the novel to a systematic Tolstoyan thesis about the absence of any unifying patterns at all in the world. In doing so, it seems to me, Morson fails to appreciate how the novel transforms a mountain of "ordinary" facts into an extraordinary vision of human life as something inexhaustible and yet organically unified.

Among contemporary scholars, Sergei Bocharov, George Clay, and Jeff Love have offered compelling alternatives to the Berlin–Morson reading of *War and Peace*. Rather than trying to extract from the novel a systematic idea or thesis, these scholars present nuanced, sensitive readings from which they discover unifying patterns in the complex poetics of the work itself. George Clay describes a "phoenix design," a pattern of literal and symbolic deaths followed by metaphorical resurrections, which recurs throughout the artistic portions of the work.[59] Proceeding from Tolstoy's injunction to critics not to look for "ideas" in art, Bocharov creatively guides the reader through several compartments in the work's "labyrinth of linkages."[60] Love sees the genius of the work stemming from the artist's struggle to represent the fluidity of experience in the fixed form of language. In Love's reading, the unresolved tension between infinite desire and finite capacity in Tolstoy's artistic representation of life is the source of the novel's singular creativity and philosophical dynamism.[61]

Yet, as we have seen, the artist and the thinker are at odds with one another in the novel, as Berlin first pointed out, and the artistic narrator does succeed in capturing life's holism in a way that the polemical narrator does not. In my reading of the novel, the author and his characters engage in a continual, simultaneous effort to create order out of chaos, and higher forms of meaning out of the prosaic facts of reality. In the end, the omniscient narrator discovers that order even when the characters cannot see it, and the artist touches the transcendent where the thinker falls short.

When in the second part of the epilogue the narrator presents his calculus of history thesis—that historians must stop trying to seek causes and discover instead the laws that unite the "unknown infinitely small elements" of the universe—he is merely offering an analytical clarification of the truths the novel's artistic canvas has created for us from the beginning: that every human being, individual moment, or decision is both irreducibly distinct and also an integral part of an inexhaustible, unified tapestry of human experience. The narrator's calculus thesis is at best a gloss on the multilayered experience of life already realized in the "labyrinth of linkages" contained in the artistic sections of the work. The theorist writes

WAR AND PEACE   **73**

about unity, he writes *about* the need to integrate. But the artist unites, he integrates. He gives us a glimpse of that "essence" which Tolstoy described in his 1870 notebook as the fundamental aim of artistic expression.

We may agree or disagree with the narrator's theories but never with his created universe. We may choose to accept the terms of that universe, strive to appreciate its mysteries, understand how it came to be and what its constituent elements are. But in that universe there is no "idea" being put forth or thesis being argued, no hidden ideology to be exposed and explicated. There is only that "endless labyrinth of linkages that makes up the stuff of art."

five

$\mathcal{A}$NDREI AND NIKOLAI
Intersecting Spiritual Orbits

Nowhere in *War and Peace* is the "labyrinth of linkages" more important and compelling than in the interconnected tales of its main characters. The novel creates spiritual echoes among its protagonists by revealing
deep similarities in their philosophical quests and life trajectories. In this
chapter we will discover such resonances in an unexpected quarter: the
stories of Andrei Bolkonsky and Nikolai Rostov. On the surface the novel
calls for no obvious juxtaposition of Nikolai and Andrei, in the same way
that it invites comparisons, for instance, between Pierre and Andrei, who
are friends from the beginning and who engage in frequent philosophical
dialogue. *War and Peace* offers readers a unified view of mankind that is
concrete and rooted in the complexities of actual experience. Nikolai with
his earthy impetuousness and Andrei with his icy, philosophical grace are
radically different men—and they almost never interact in the novel. Yet
they exist within one another's spiritual orbit from the beginning. Proud,
patriotic, and intensely idealistic, both Andrei and Nikolai pursue their
ideals by joining the war effort; both eventually confront the imperfect
realities of a world in which history does not happen as they wish and in
which the definition of the good is not absolute.

The spiritual echoes between Andrei and Nikolai are not merely a
strategy for helping readers to orient themselves in the novel's sprawling
landscape. These echoes also prod us to discover life's inner truths and

harmonies beneath its ostensibly messy veneer.[1] In this chapter we will trace these harmonies through two kinds of analysis. The first is a close reading of the passages in Volume One, Part Two, in which Andrei and Nikolai participate in the Battle of Schöngrabern. We will then stand back and trace the life trajectories of Prince Andrei and Nikolai in the context of the novel as a whole. As we move from microcosm to macrocosm, we will reproduce the poetics of *War and Peace,* in which each moment of experience is distinctly textured and intrinsically meaningful, while also an essential link in life's vast chain of interconnectedness.

In this reading of *War and Peace,* the novel becomes a giant oak tree with proliferating branches extending in all directions.[2] Each scene is a single branch of that tree. It possesses a unique contour and combination of texture, color, and smell, and may therefore be regarded as a complete creation in itself. But it is also connected to the large trunk from which it extends. The unifying truth of the work lies neither in the combination of finely wrought details that make up the branches nor in the massive breadth of the trunk, but at the point where trunk and branch—unifying order and its unique manifestations—intersect.

It is, of course, neither possible nor necessary to examine *all* the novel's details as they relate to one another and to the work's unified vision. In fact, attempting such an analysis would violate Tolstoy's definition of "history-art" as an approach that captures life's essential holism, not by enumerating every detail, but by selecting just the "right" ones and organizing them with the "right" artistic focus.

MICROCOSM:
PRINCE ANDREI SEEKING THE BIG PICTURE

Let us begin with the scene in Volume One, Part Two, Chapter Sixteen, in which Prince Andrei surveys the battlefield on the night before the Battle of Schöngrabern. This scene is an important one, both for what it tells us about Prince Andrei's psychology, and for the way in which it encapsulates the novel's larger philosophical concerns. The chapter opens with this paragraph:

> Having ridden all along the line of troops from the right flank to the left, Prince Andrei went up to the battery, from which, according to the staff officer's words, one could see the whole field. Here he got off his horse and stopped by the last of the four unlimbered cannon. In front

of the cannon paced an artillery sentry, who snapped to attention before the officer, but at a sign from him renewed his measured, tedious pacing. Behind the cannon stood their limbers, further behind a hitching rail and the campfires of the artillerists. To the left, not far from the last cannon, there was a newly plaited lean-to from which came the animated voices of the officers. (177; I, 2, 16)[3]

Andrei wants to grasp the whole picture of the upcoming battle by viewing the battle site panoramically, from a single perspective. But Tolstoy sets up a counterpoint to his hero's intent. By showing the reader details of camp life—the pacing of the sentry, the bonfires of the artillery men, and the wattle shed from which the officers' voices emerge—he creates a sense of the interaction of diverse human experiences which no single human perspective could fully embrace. Only the narrator can see the totality of the situation. In the next paragraph the narrator subsumes Andrei's act of surveying the field as an "event" into his own "story" of the night before the Battle of Schöngrabern:

Indeed from the battery a view opened out of almost the entire disposition of the Russian troops and the greater part of the enemy's. Directly facing the battery, on the crest of the knoll opposite, one could see the village of Schöngraben; to the left and right it was possible to make out in three places amidst the smoke of their campfires the masses of the French troops, of whom the greater part were evidently in the village itself and behind the hill. To the left of the village, in the smoke, appeared something resembling a battery, but it was impossible to see it well with the naked eye. Our right flank was disposed on a rather steep elevation, which dominated the positions of the French. On it our infantry was disposed, and at the very end one could see the dragoons. In the center, where Tushin's battery stood, from where Prince Andrei was surveying the position, there was a gently sloping and direct descent and ascent to the stream that separated us from Schöngrabern. To the left our troops adjoined a woods, where smoked the campfires of our infantry, who were cutting firewood. The French line was wider than ours, and it was obvious that the French could easily encircle us from both sides. Behind our position was a steep and deep ravine, through which it would be hard for artillery and cavalry to retreat. Prince Andrei, leaning his elbow on the cannon and taking out his notebook, drew a plan of the disposition of the troops for himself. In two places he penciled some notes, intending to tell Bagration about them. He proposed, first, to concentrate all the artillery in the center; second, to transfer the cavalry back to the other side of the ravine. Prince Andrei had been constantly at the commander in chief's side, had followed the movements of masses and the general orders, had constantly been taken up with historical descriptions of battles, and in this forthcoming action involuntarily considered the future course of the military operations only in general terms. (177–78; I, 2, 16)

Note that the narrator does not merely relay facts in an objective, impersonal manner, but actually becomes an involved, humanized *raconteur.* For instance, he uses the colloquial expression *khoroshenko* in the phrase *nel'zia bylo rassmotret' khoroshen'ko* ["was impossible to see it well"]. And he makes frequent reference to "our" flank, infantry, and position.

And yet at the same time that the narrator comes down to earth and momentarily becomes one of "us," he also rises above "us" and reveals things that "we," in our limited awareness, fail to perceive. The narrator tells us, for instance, that from the position Andrei occupies "there was a gently sloping and direct descent and ascent to the stream that separated us from Schöngrabern." This becomes an important detail several lines later when we see Prince Andrei drawing up plans for the upcoming battle. His position affords him a naïve enthusiasm about the prospects of success in the battle that the more far-seeing narrator, and we, the readers, do not have. The reader understands the irony here: Andrei will not be able to prepare a fully adequate plan because he fails to see *all* of the details that such a plan would need to include.

The fact of Prince Andrei's limited perspective is underscored in another detail, as well: "All the while he was in the battery by the cannon, as often happens, he had never stopped hearing the sounds of the officers' voices, talking in the lean-to, but had not understood a single word of what they were saying" (178; I, 2, 16). In the previous paragraph the narrator showed us the larger physical context of which Prince Andrei was not fully aware. Now we are told that Andrei's failure to understand the officers' voices is one instance of a larger pattern of human nature, to which, once again, only the narrator is privy. It seems that Andrei's failure to pay full attention to his surroundings is both a unique event, occurring in a specific time and place, and also an expression of a universal human shortcoming: the tendency of human beings, "as often happens," to overlook the details of their immediate surroundings.

Such neglected details nevertheless force themselves upon us: "Suddenly the sound of voices from the lean-to struck him with such soul-felt tones that he involuntarily began to listen" (9, 217; 178; I, 2, 16). Significantly, Andrei has been "struck" by the sound of the voices, and when he does begin to listen, he does so "involuntarily," as if motivated by some internal force. The narrator enlists his considerable resources, from sound play to psychological insight, to suggest a larger, encompassing reality. The verbal association of the vowel *u* in the rhymed pair of words *vdrug-zvuk* (suddenly, sound) creates an inherent linkage between these two notions. On the psychological level, Tolstoy links the soldiers' reflections about death and Andrei's own meditations on the upcoming battle. Just as the soldiers find solace in talking about their fear of death, so Prince Andrei finds comfort in attempting to organize the impending battle in his head.

At the very moment, then, that Prince Andrei's perception begins to focus on the minute details of his surroundings, the text creates the impression of a commonality of human experience, which is organically linked to those details. The narrator's—and by extension, the reader's—vision, drawn to suprapersonal, universal concerns, coexists with Andrei's perception, which is becoming narrower and more focused on specific details of his surroundings. Minute details and universal experience become so organically linked in this moment that an increase in our perception of these dimensions occurs simultaneously.

What Prince Andrei seeks in this moment of the novel is an embodiment of what he seeks philosophically throughout the work: a sense of mastery over his environment, that is, the assurance that he is a creative subject, and not merely a created object, of his world. It is this need to mentally "conquer" the world that motivates his aspiration to become, like Napoleon, a literal conqueror. Andrei's imaginative narrative of the upcoming battle may thus be read as an act of authorship in the deepest sense of the word: authorship as an act of sense-making, of creating meaning out of chaos, and of self-mastery. Indeed, there is a similarity between Andrei's surveying of the field of battle and Tolstoy's own "surveying" of the grand landscape of life in this novel. It seems that Andrei's instinct for mastery over his world has been implanted in him by a creator who himself possesses an instinct to harness and give form—artistic form—to the staggering vastness of human life.

And yet the omniscient narrator, who sees the "whole" picture, speaks with a touch of irony about the hero's attempts to embrace a similarly full vision. The reader senses that Andrei *is* deluding himself here, and this we know even before we are given an account of the actual battle in the following chapters, in which almost nothing happens according to Andrei's or Prince Bagration's or anybody else's plans. Andrei lacks the narrator's capacity to perceive in the limited number of facts available to his finite awareness a unifying vision. He lacks the narrator's ability to think and speak in multiple registers at once, as both one of us and as somebody superior to us, as somebody attuned both to each individual human experience and to the universal truths of which it is part.

The integrative wisdom of the narrator has its human counterpart in the figure of the Russian commander-in-chief, Field Marshal Mikhail Illarionovich Kutuzov, a military man and survivor, whose approach to battle—and life—is the diametric opposite of Andrei's. Unlike Andrei, and despite his blindness in one eye, Kutuzov understands the essence of a situation with a single glance. The text subtly contrasts this Kutuzov-like wisdom with Andrei's more reductivist approach by juxtaposing the latter's surveying of the battlefield of Schöngrabern with Kutuzov's review of the troops several pages earlier, at the beginning of Volume One, Part Two.

Whereas Andrei remains largely oblivious to the complex human realities as he gazes across the battlefield, Kutuzov is attuned to the minutest gesture or look indicating a character's state of mind and personal story. In a glance Kutuzov instinctively senses the decency of Timokhin, who, unbeknownst to the commander-in-chief, had been chided unfairly moments before by the regimental commander. Timokhin's missing teeth, pockmarked face, and feeble deference point to his life of patriotic devotion and quiet suffering. With his innate wisdom and humanity, "Kutuzov, evidently understanding his situation, and wishing the captain, on the contrary, nothing but good, hastened to turn away" (117; I, 2, 2). When the demoted Dolokhov insolently and cloyingly beseeches the commander-in-chief for an opportunity to prove his devotion to the Tsar, Kutuzov "turned away and winced, as if wishing to express thereby that all that Dolokhov had said to him and all that he could say had long, long been known to him, that it all bored him, and that it was all by no means what was needed" (118; I, 2, 2).

Prince Andrei also lacks Kutuzov's ability to submit instinctively to the impersonal forces over which he has no control, and in that act of submission, to become empowered, rather than defeated, by those very forces. With his scarred face and blind eye, Kutuzov's very being testifies to his brushes with death in battle. History's immutable truths etched into his war-hardened body are a testament to his improvisational virtuosity in the theater of life. Kutuzov's reaction to Napoleon's offer of battle at Borodino is further evidence of his wisdom. "In offering and accepting battle at Borodino," the narrator writes in Volume Three, Part Two, "Kutuzov . . . acted involuntarily and senselessly" (754; III, 2, 19). And yet, as the novel bears out, his instinctive reactions proved fruitful, for the Battle of Borodino wounded the French army irrevocably, leading to a Pyrrhic victory and the taking of Moscow, which paved the way for the army's ultimate destruction during their retreat out of Russia.

If Kutuzov survives by embracing historical flux on its own unknowable terms, at Schöngrabern Andrei believes that he can control the outcome of historical events through the power of his rational intellect. An internal transformation begins to take place, however, after the battle, at the end of Volume One, Part Two. Andrei's realization that unforeseen contingencies and social intrigue play a crucial role in events is further deepened at the Battle of Austerlitz. He participates in the council of war, at which Kutuzov sleeps while his military advisors play psychological games of one-upmanship under the guise of strategic planning.[4] "'Can it really be that, for court and personal considerations, tens of thousands of lives must be risked—and my own, *my* life?' [Prince Andrei] thought" (264; I, 3, 12).

On one level, Andrei is still looking at his world from afar, separating himself from the collective of soldiers, as he did when surveying the battlefield at Schöngrabern. On another level, though, Andrei most fully grasps an abstract philosophical truth—the limits of his individual freedom—by making that truth concrete and personal, by appreciating how it applies to "*my* life." Personal and universal understanding go hand in hand for Andrei. This trait, which prevents him from connecting with others, is also the quality that allows him to feel the pain and aspirations of humanity most deeply. That is why Andrei, one of Tolstoy's most flawed characters, is also one of his most heroic.

Unlike the careerists Boris Drubetskoi, Nikolai's childhood friend, and the officer Alphonse Berg, who seek worldly success for the sake of personal security and comfort, Prince Andrei seeks the love and esteem of men. Berg and Boris embody narrow-minded mediocrity. Prince Andrei, on the other hand, wants to transcend the limits of the world he inhabits and to achieve heroic greatness and permanence. Before the Battle of Austerlitz he reflects:

> "[W]hat am I to do if I love nothing except glory, except people's love? Death, wounds, loss of family, nothing frightens me. And however near and dear many people are to me—my father, my sister, my wife—the dearest people to me—but, however terrible and unnatural it seems, I'd give them all now for a moment of glory, of triumph over people, for love from people I don't know and will never know, for the love of these

people here," he thought, listening to the talk in Kutuzov's yard. From Kutuzov's yard came the voices of orderlies preparing to sleep; one voice, probably of a coachman who was teasing Kutuzov's old cook, whom Prince Andrei knew and whose name was Titus, said: "Titus, hey, Titus?"

"Well?" replied the old man.

"Titus, don't bite us," said the joker.

"Pah, go to the devil!" a voice cried, drowned out by the guffawing of the orderlies and servants.

"And still, the only thing I love and cherish is triumph over all of them, I cherish that mysterious power and glory hovering over me here in this mist!" (265; I, 3, 12)

Like the voices that Prince Andrei involuntarily overhears while surveying the battlefield at Schöngrabern, the voices he overhears now bring his attention back to earth, back to the quotidian—and in this instance, comic—realities of everyday life. But here as elsewhere in the novel, Prince Andrei refuses to allow his lofty musings to be punctured by such an unwelcome intrusion. Andrei notices the joking voices and the laughing orderlies, but "still" he seeks his Toulon: he wants to rise above the ordinariness of everyday life. When the battle begins several pages later, it appears to Andrei that he will get his wish: "'Here it is, the decisive moment has come! Now it's my turn,' thought Prince Andrei, and spurring his horse, he rode up to Kutuzov" (278; I, 3, 16). A page later, after realizing that Kutuzov has been wounded, Andrei, "feeling sobs of shame and anger rising in his throat," spontaneously jumps from his horse, repeats the phrase "here it is," seizes the standard, and charges with the troops into battle (280; I, 3, 16).

Each time Andrei says "here it is" it appears to him that he is breaking decisively from his ordinary past and lurching into an extraordinary, heroic future.[5] But what appears to Andrei to be a decisive break is, from the perspective of the omniscient narrator, a repeated pattern of behavior, an ongoing quest with no final resolution. Still, the reader never judges or laughs at Andrei for his false conclusions, for each of these moments does contain heightened emotional intensity and a poetic grandeur felt by both character and reader. In such "moment[s] of self-creation," as Natasha Sankovitch calls them, "characters have a sense of their lives taking shape, and it is this sense that sets these moments apart from others."[6]

The moment in which Prince Andrei leads the charge against the French is indeed unique, for it is one of the few times in the novel when Andrei's emotional impulse overpowers his rational intellect. An internal transformation, however fleeting, has taken place in Andrei, and it is critical to his overall trajectory. His impulsive act of charging into the thick of battle is what will soon get Andrei wounded and lead him, in turn, to one of the most important discoveries of his life: the sight of the lofty, infinite sky, as he lies prostrate on the battlefield. Having set out to win his Toulon, Prince Andrei instead secures a radically different but, for him, no less significant victory. Through the haze of his blurred vision, resulting from a wound to his head, Andrei sees for the first time and with profound clarity the immensity of the universe, indifferent to his worldly plans and ambitions:

> There was nothing over him now except the sky—the lofty sky, not clear, but still immeasurably lofty, with gray clouds slowly creeping across it. "How quiet, calm, and solemn, not at all like when I was running," thought Prince Andrei, "not like when we were running, shouting, and fighting; not at all like when the Frenchman and the artillerist, with angry and frightened faces, were pulling at the swab—it's quite different the way the clouds creep across this lofty, infinite sky. How is it I haven't seen this lofty sky before? And how happy I am that I've finally come to know it. Yes! Everything is empty, everything is deception, except this infinite sky. There is nothing, nothing except that. But there is not even that, there is nothing except silence, tranquility. And thank God!" (281; I, 3, 17)

This glorious epiphany, fundamental to Andrei's spiritual trajectory, is one of the most breathtaking and famous moments in *War and Peace*. It is also one of the most beguiling. Prince Andrei's vision, glorious and compelling as it may be, is, in the metaphysics of the novel, only a partial truth. The whole the hero glimpses is not quite the holism of the narrator; something is missing. Lying prostrate with his gaze turned upward away from the earth, Andrei sees the totality that lies entirely out there, in the misty infinitude of the sky, excluding all that is down here, in the clearly visible pettiness of the world. Andrei's earlier aspiration to worldly glory has been replaced by his striving to embrace the heavenly grandeur of the universe. But are the two impulses really so different? Are not his earlier pursuit of his Toulon and his submission to the power of the lofty, infinite sky but variations on the same theme of Andrei's quest for permanence, for transcendence?

Yet Prince Andrei's great revelation becomes, paradoxically, a source of anguish. The vision of the sky at Austerlitz temporarily lifts Andrei up, only to remind him from that moment on of the vast distance separating the transcendent he has briefly glimpsed from the everyday reality he regularly sees. The heightened vision at Austerlitz thus becomes the philosophical noose around Prince Andrei's neck, his tragic "leitmotif," as Sergei Bocharov has called it.[7] Not coincidentally, later in the novel, after Andrei learns of Natasha's infidelity, the narrator emphasizes that the hero's growing mental agony is not softened, but rather intensified, by his recollections of the lofty sky at Austerlitz:

> He not only did not think those former thoughts that had first come to him as he gazed at the sky on the field of Austerlitz, which he had liked to enlarge upon with Pierre, and which had filled his solitude in Bogucharovo and then in Switzerland and Rome; but he was even afraid to remember those thoughts that had opened boundless and bright horizons. He was now concerned only with the most immediate and practical interests, unconnected with his former ones, which he grasped at the more eagerly the more closed to him the former ones were. As if that boundless, ever-receding vault of the sky that used to stand over him had suddenly turned into a low, definite, oppressive vault, in which everything was clear and nothing was eternal or mysterious. (628; III, 1, 8)

As this passage reveals, Prince Andrei's heightened awareness of life's "boundless and bright horizons" becomes a wistful memory and an unfulfilled yearning. Far from embracing what Tolstoy once called life's "innumerable, inexhaustible manifestations," Prince Andrei after Austerlitz becomes overwhelmed by life's mundane truths, which he continues to see all too clearly—and incorrectly. Andrei sees the ineffectiveness of the political and military leadership. He sees the shortcomings of married life. He sees Pierre's naïveté. He sees his father's cruelty towards his sister, Princess Marya. And after Austerlitz he sees the falseness of his own aspirations to greatness. But his insights are all negative, unveiling the falsity and inadequacy of life. He does not possess an integrative vision in which human foibles and quotidian reality might be subsumed within something greater and more hopeful.

Prince Andrei never discovers the higher truth he seeks, because it doesn't exist in the form in which he expects to find it. The unifying truth in *War and Peace* lies not only in what the world actually is but also in the hidden beauty and spiritual possibilities contained in what is. In Andrei's meditation on the sky at Austerlitz, he envisions the transcendent in isolation from the earthly. Throughout much of the rest of the novel he sees the earthly dimension but not the transcendent. Andrei never grasps Tolstoyan truth, because he tries to understand the world through an "either-or" binary construct. But for the narrator a complete vision of the world must include "both-and." Truth in *War and Peace* exists in a realm where the ordinary and transcendent realms of life coincide, where prosaic and poetic perception intersect, where each moment, meaningful in itself, also contains a microcosm of the beauty and grandeur of the larger universe.

FROM MICROCOSM TO MACROCOSM

Prince Andrei is not the only character for whom the confrontation of the real and the ideal is a central philosophical and psychological dynamic. All of the novel's main characters experience this. *War and Peace* is, on one level, a Bildungsroman about young people who grow up, grow old, and grow wise. Pierre's spiritual journey, for instance, revolves around his learning to love life despite its imperfections. Natasha, who, as a vivacious, self-involved young woman, sees the world as a glittering ballroom, eventually appreciates life's darker sides and embraces a more integrated conception of life, in which pain and self-sacrifice are necessary elements. Princess Marya is attached to a narrow ideal of pious self-abnegation, but comes to appreciate that earthly happiness and spiritual goodness are not mutually exclusive. And, as we will now examine in depth, Nikolai Rostov, who starts out as a fiery young patriot exclaiming that "the Russians must either die or conquer" (64; I, 1, 17), ultimately adopts a more nuanced understanding of the world when he becomes a seasoned military man, father, and husband.[8]

For all the differences between them, Nikolai and Andrei are both idealists who join the war against Napoleon in search of higher meaning in their lives. The black-and-white view of the world that the young Nikolai still holds is precisely what Andrei is trying to retrieve and recreate in his own life. What Nikolai believes when the novel begins—that the world may be divided between us and them, courageous and cowardly, honorable and dastardly—is precisely the sort of naïve worldview that Andrei has long ago lost and is trying to recover. Thus they share a single-mindedness in their pursuit of their goals, both personal and public, a desire for glory, and a tendency to project their ideals onto the world around them. Prince Andrei, who is in his early thirties and feeling trapped in an unfulfilling marriage when the novel begins, wants to prove his significance by winning his Toulon and gaining power over others. Nikolai, over a decade younger and feeling at once nurtured and stifled by his doting family, wants to prove his manhood as a soldier on the battlefield. Prince Andrei wants to rise above the crowds; Nikolai wants to lose himself in them. In Volume One, Part Two, both characters go through a similarly painful process of disillusionment as a result of their first major military experience.

The narrator creates a sense of this commonality in the way he structures the plot of Volume One, Part Two. Early in the book he describes Andrei's impatience with two soldiers who joke after the news of a lost campaign. "'What's with me?' said Prince Andrei, stopping in agitation. 'Understand that we're either officers serving our tsar and fatherland, and rejoice in our common successes and grieve over our common failures, or we're lackeys, who have nothing to do with our masters' doings'" (127; I, 2, 4). The soldiers relieve tension by laughing, but Andrei, intense and serious, cannot allow himself this sort of reflexive venting. For him, the military defeat is a personal affront. His patriotism stems from his need for clarity and purpose in his world—a world in which irreverent soldiers, like the vagaries of history, continually challenge his idealistic aspirations.

Later in the same book, the young Nikolai, like Andrei, learns that those around him don't always admire or share his noble intentions. After Nikolai publicly exposes a certain Telyanin, an old soldier who has stolen Denisov's money, he is chided by the staff captain for confronting Telyanin in front of other officers. Nikolai responds: "'It's not my fault that the conversation started in front of other officers. Maybe I shouldn't have spoken in front of them, but I'm no diplomat. I joined the hussars because I thought there was no need for subtleties here'" (135; I, 2, 5). For Nikolai, placing honesty above tact is an indisputable virtue. He believes in an absolute code of honor and considers it his responsibility to uphold it. The scene reveals, however, that there are many competing codes of honor in the military world, and that Nikolai's is merely one among them.

Both Nikolai and Andrei, then, share a pride, an intensity of spirit, and a single-mindedness in their worldviews. And both confront the imperfect realities of a world in which events unfold in mysterious ways, and in which there are no absolute definitions of virtue. The unique experiences of these two very different characters unfold separately and without direct relation to one another in Volume Two. The two characters are not even aware of each other's existence at this point in the novel. And yet, even as their stories unfold separately in this book, they also echo one another, like two parallel subjects of a single musical fugue.

The narrator reinforces the unity of their two storylines in the double ending of Part Two of Volume One. Andrei's story ends with these lines: "Prince Andrei looked at Tushin and, saying nothing, walked away. Prince Andrei felt sad and downhearted. All this was so strange, so unlike what he had hoped for" (199; I, 2, 21). Then with his characteristically cinematic intuition, the narrator shifts the lens immediately to Nikolai, who has sprained his arm and reflects on his unsuccessful first military venture: "'Nobody needs me!'" he exclaims several paragraphs later. "'There's nobody to help me or pity me. And once I was at home, strong, cheerful, loved'" (200; I, 2, 21).

Both of these moments occur simultaneously, although in distinct, if nearby, locales. And both moments poignantly express the disintegration of each character's earlier ideals and the accompanying feeling of isolation. By juxtaposing these parallel situations, the narrator admits us to each man's private suffering, while simultaneously inviting us to transcend it through recognition of a common human experience. From the point of view of the characters themselves, this is perhaps shallow consolation. But the early Tolstoy was too honest a writer to offer artificial solutions to the challenge of life. Instead, in *War and Peace* he distills life's disappointments and imperfections into an art form that combines the rhythmic principle of poetry with an unflinching attention to the particular details of lived experience, characteristic of realist prose.[9] The rhythmic principle in the novel, as we have seen, is not merely verbal, as one critic has argued.[10] It is also thematic. That is, there are situations and experiences that play off one another in a manner similar to the way that parallel sounds and rhythms interact with one another in poetry.[11]

R. F. Christian was among the first critics to recognize "situation rhymes" as important to the work's aesthetic organization.[12] What I am arguing here is that these rhymes are organically linked to the novel's metaphysics, as well. By means of internal resonances within the text itself, the narrator artistically links the truth of a single moment in an individual's life to the larger truth of our shared human experience. Thus, despite the novel's attention to life's tragic truths, *War and Peace* is an essentially optimistic work. The novel's fundamental sense of life's goodness is not a kind of psychological "band-aid" that the author has pasted onto an otherwise tragic conception of life, in the same way that some of Tolstoy's later moralistic writings are sometimes felt by readers to be. Rather, optimism is organic to the artistic and philosophical holism of the novel itself.[13]

INTERSECTING PATHS

The intersecting trajectories of Andrei and Nikolai in Volume One, Part Two are echoed and deepened in Volume One, Part Three. For the first and only time in the novel the two heroes meet. Significantly, their meeting comes only two weeks after the Battle of Schöngrabern and a few days before the Battle of Austerlitz, two formative events in both characters' lives. The presence of Berg and Boris serves as a foil to their meeting. Berg, who has been promoted to the rank of captain, recounts stories of his calm under fire—a calm matched by the coolness of his speech and the sterility of his personality. Boris, ever the opportunist who has dedicated his energies to making important professional connections, has brought a letter of recommendation to Andrei from Pierre in the hopes of attaining a position on Kutuzov's staff. By having the meeting between Andrei and Nikolai take place in their presence, the narrator highlights the spiritual affinities between these two heroes when viewed against the backdrop of the more circumscribed worldview and spiritual mediocrity of Berg and Boris.

In contrast to Boris, whose nobility comes from his father's service to the state, not his birth, and Berg, who is of the bourgeois class, Andrei and Nikolai are aristocrats by birth and in spirit. An intense, fraternal chemistry—full of respect and rivalry—at once develops between them. Nikolai is immediately repulsed by Andrei, whom he scorns as a mere staff officer; but at the same time, like an admiring younger brother, he grows quiet and confused in Andrei's presence: "In spite of Prince Andrei's unpleasant, mocking tone, in spite of the general disdain which Rostov, from his fighting army point of view, had for all these staff adjutants, to whom the newcomer obviously belonged, Rostov felt embarrassed, turned red, and fell silent" (243; I, 3, 7). After a heated exchange, in which Nikolai openly insults Andrei for his being on the staff rather than among the fighting soldiers, Andrei, in a tone of patronizing benevolence, tries to end the conversation and let their disagreements stand. Disturbing feelings linger on in Nikolai's soul, as he mulls over how he should have responded. In a wonderfully pithy final sentence, the narrator captures the powerful emotional sway Andrei continues to have over him: "Now he thought spitefully of what a pleasure it would be to see this small, weak, and proud man's fear in the face of his pistol, then he was surprised to feel that, of all the people he knew, there was no one he so wished to have for a friend as this hateful little adjutant" (244; I, 3, 7).

This beautifully succinct description of the meeting between these two characters captures the nature of their connection in the novel. Despite their differences in personality and the fact that they meet only once in the novel, Andrei and Nikolai orbit the same spiritual axis. The intensity of their reaction to one another creates the sense that they have known each other since long before they met. And in a sense, they have. Like two comets colliding in space, they are made of the same stuff and are guided by the same laws of attraction.

In the very next chapter, we see Nikolai happily losing himself in the cheering crowd during the Emperor's review. On one level his behavior contrasts directly with that of Andrei, whose impulse is often to stay close to the commanders at the top. But upon closer inspection, we recognize a surprising similarity between their actions. For Nikolai's immersion in the crowd and Andrei's lofty stance above it are two sides of the same coin. Both heroes seek to transcend the here-and-now. Both strive for the extraordinary, the wonderful, the heightened experience. Both crave spiritual intoxication, a rousing sense of human possibility and permanence in an imperfect, finite world. Only their strategies differ: Nikolai immerses himself in the communal moment, surrendering his individual self. Andrei lifts himself above that moment, asserting his individuality and the primacy of personal conquest.

After their meeting at Olmütz, Andrei and Nikolai go their separate ways, never to interact directly again. But their spiritual energies continue to resonate and harmonize, now fading into the background, now coming forth like prominent melodies in the symphony of historical events. Just as they have similar experiences in the Battle of Schöngrabern, so they grow in similar ways during the Battle of Austerlitz. While Andrei's old perceptions are radically altered as he gazes at the lofty, infinite sky, Nikolai's ideas about courage and heroism and patriotic devotion are dismantled at Austerlitz. Like a lover in pursuit of the object of his affection, Nikolai passionately fulfills his assigned duty to look for Kutuzov and the Emperor near the village of Pratzen. When Nikolai finally comes upon the Tsar in an open field, he is at last confronted with the possibility he has longed for: to show his ardent devotion to his leader. And he falters:

> But as a young man in love trembles and thrills, not daring to utter what he dreams of by night, and looks about fearfully, seeking help or the possibility of delay and flight, when the desired moment comes and he stands alone with her, so now Rostov, having attained what he desired more than anything in the world, did not know how to approach the

sovereign and presented thousands of considerations to himself for why it was unsuitable, improper, and impossible. (287; I, 3, 18)

When Captain von Toll rides up to the Emperor moments later, Nikolai chastises himself for his weakness. He makes a second attempt, but when he turns around, the Emperor and the captain are gone. To Nikolai, his failure to act is devastating, a sure sign of his weakness. But to the narrator—and consequently to the reader—Nikolai's weakness is actually a sign of strength. His failure to act is an expression of his budding maturity. During his internal debates moments before about whether he should approach Alexander, Nikolai instinctively, if inconclusively, senses that there would be something inappropriate, something self-serving and artificial, in approaching the Emperor. The speeches Nikolai had prepared in his mind for such an occasion don't quite fit the current scenario. "Those speeches were for the most part held under quite different conditions" (288; I, 3, 18): for moments of fairy-tale glory, in which the dying soldier is praised by the grateful Tsar for his heroic, patriotic deeds.

But here the battle has not yet started, and it is Alexander, not Nikolai, in need of assistance; precisely what kind of assistance is far from clear. Moral support? A helping hand? These far-fetched possibilities, which come to Nikolai's mind, cause us to smile. We sense, along with Nikolai, the awkward ambiguity and uniqueness of the situation, and we know, like the hero, that his fairy-tale script must now end. The hero's hesitation is a sign of his growing wisdom, of his understanding that heroism and patriotism are fluid, situation-specific notions, and that his boyish fantasies are and must always remain just that.

Nikolai discovers this truth at the same time that Andrei discovers the sky in Volume One, Part Three. Both characters grow and replace their old paradigms with new, more nuanced understanding. Both Andrei, while looking at the sky, and Nikolai, while looking at the empty field where the Tsar stood a few moments earlier, are forced to dismantle their respective fantasies about what it means to be a hero. At Austerlitz they lose their old ideals but gain insight into their own natures and into the true nature of the world.

So when Moscow society celebrates the Russian "victory" at Austerlitz in Volume Two, Part One, the reader cannot help smiling at this irony. In Tolstoy's universe wartime battles, like any event, have no clear winners or losers. The "official" interpretation of the Battle of Austerlitz is, like all human attempts at after-the-fact historical interpretation, artificial and reductive. The narrator captures a much more complex, fluid truth: all that exists are the continual cycles of life, the eternal march of time, and the ongoing processes of human consciousness, moving between disillusionment and discovery, in its search for truth.[14]

Just as the narrator connects the experiences of Andrei and Nikolai through the double ending of Volume One, Part Two, here, too, he further links them through the repetition of a minor detail. In the moment just following Nikolai's disappointment at not having approached the Emperor, he hears the same joking voices saying the almost identical words—"Titus, don't bite us!"—that Andrei overhears during his grandiose reflections before the Battle of Austerlitz. As in the earlier scene with Andrei, so the joking orderlies now draw Nikolai's attention earthward, towards messy everyday reality, and away from the mirage of heroism. Nikolai is not to be Alexander's savior, just as Andrei is not to be the conqueror he dreams he will be.

But here, as elsewhere in *War and Peace,* and indeed throughout Tolstoy's *oeuvre,* ironic deflation is not the final note. Demystification and remystification occur together. Even as Nikolai's and Andrei's lofty ideals are dismantled by an ironic narrative detail, the mysterious beauty and grand unity of the universe reassert themselves. This repeated bit of buffoonery, "Titus, don't bite us!" creates the impression of life's coherence and continuity, the sense of a "perpetual present."[15] Suddenly the trivial becomes significant, and the repeated details breathe concrete life into the philosophical truism that "the more things change, the more they stay the same."[16] Indeed, Andrei and Nikolai will continue to search for their place in God's grand design, just as the orderlies will continue to live out their everyday lives, making silly jokes to pass the time while their caravan traverses the Russian countryside.

Military convoys still crisscross the countryside, in Iraq, Afghanistan, and elsewhere in the world, as the wheels of war grind on in our time. As if Austerlitz and Borodino were not sufficiently horrific, warfare in the age of terror and nuclear weapons, where the "face" of the enemy is the blast of an improvised explosive device, has become even more dehumanizing. Yet soldiers' stories remain strikingly the same. From Studs Terkel's Pulitzer Prize–winning *The Good War,* detailing the experiences of ordinary Americans during World War II, to the more recent PBS series *Operation Homecoming,* documenting the experiences of soldiers in the Iraq War, soldiers' journeys through the vast physical and spiritual landscape of warfare still stir us. The poems in Iraq War veteran Brian Turner's prize-winning collection *Here, Bullet* bring the horrors of that war painfully alive, while never failing to show us "the shine of light on the broken."[17]

They remind us yet again that war, which brings out the best and worst in man, pitting personal wills against impersonal forces, is still one of the clearest windows we have into the universal truths of human life. As maimed and traumatized veterans returning from Iraq today seek new avenues for hope and self-respect, they discover, as do Nikolai and Andrei, that life must be built and rebuilt day by day, one small victory at a time. Whether our veterans find renewed meaning in the joys of family life, as Nikolai eventually does, or in the spiritual illumination only death can provide, like Prince Andrei, one thing is clear: the quest to make meaning out of the messiness of their lives remains their most important battle, as it does for all of us—in war and in peace.

six

$\mathcal{P}$ATTERNS OF
DISILLUSIONMENT AND DISCOVERY

Throughout *War and Peace* the intersection of Andrei's and Nikolai's spiritual paths remains a key structural element in the novel, an implicit framework for its exploration of alternative fates and temperaments. Significantly, as the novel progresses the two characters are linked more by their differences than by the similarities of their trajectories. Volume One, Part Three ends with the wounded Andrei left, "among other hopelessly wounded," to the care of the inhabitants of the local village, his fate uncertain (294; I, 3, 9). Volume Two, Part One begins with Nikolai's jubilant homecoming. The contrast between the joyous atmosphere of the Rostov home and the dark melancholy of the Bolkonsky home at Bald Hills is made explicit by the narrator. Andrei, presumed dead and all but forgotten by society, is the source of anguish intermingled with flickers of desperate hope at Bald Hills. This shroud of anxious gloom—lifted ever so slightly by the calming presence of Lise, Andrei's wife, in her delicate state of pregnancy—is counterbalanced by the spirit of family happiness that fills the Rostov home. Andrei, whose physical separation from his family mirrors the spiritual isolation that defines much of his life, struggles for survival alone, while Nikolai is ensconced in the warm embrace of his family. Such will be the diverging paths of the two heroes for the remainder of the novel, until the epilogue, in which their paths cross once again.

In a scene cloaked in Romantic gloom, Andrei mysteriously returns to Bald Hills on a wintry night amidst "snows and storms" of "desperate malice," to witness the birth of his son, and then also witnesses the death of his wife, Lise, during delivery (325; II, 1, 8). The gothic, almost funereal atmosphere surrounding Andrei's return from the dead, as it were, reinforces our sense of him as a figure standing on the threshold between life and death. The image of Andrei sitting quietly alone in a separate room during the baptism of his child captures his deep loneliness, even amidst family, and his literal absence from the world.

Burdened by guilt over his wife's death and devoid of faith in the possibility of military glory, Andrei will withdraw to a life of quiet desperation on his father's estate. His encroaching spiritual death is slowed only infrequently by his half-hearted participation in local civic affairs and by his fulfillment of his fatherly responsibilities. It will not be until Pierre visits him nearly a year later at Bogucharovo, in Volume Two, Part Two, that Andrei's cold spirit begins to thaw under the influence of his friend's infectious vision of life's endless possibility.

Andrei's progressive estrangement from life and Nikolai's increasing harmony with it are thus played off one another like point and counterpoint in Volume Two, Part One. And yet, even as the narrator reveals the unmistakable divide between these two characters, he also makes us aware of hidden commonalities. Their evolving story lines embody similar patterns of disillusionment and discovery, as the pendulum of their lives swings gently back and forth between sorrow and joy.

Just as Andrei's dark homecoming and growing despair are lightened by the birth of his child, so Nikolai's boundless *joie de vivre* is tempered by his growing confusion about his feelings for Sonya and, even more significantly, by the shame and depression he experiences after losing 43,000 rubles to Dolokhov. Volume Two, Part One thus ends with both characters, Andrei and Nikolai, trying to put their cracked worlds back together, each in his characteristic way: Andrei by withdrawing from military life and Nikolai by reentering it.

EMBRACING LIFE AND ITS DISCONTENTS

After his severe gambling losses to Dolokhov, Nikolai seeks solace by returning to his regiment, where there

was not all that disorder of the free world, in which he found no place for himself and made wrong choices; there was no Sonya, with whom he had or did not have to talk things over. There was no possibility of going or not going here or there; there were not those twenty-four hours in a day which could be spent in so many different ways; there was no numberless multitude of people, of whom no one was close, no one was distant; there were none of those unclear and undefined money relations with his father; there was no recollection of that terrible loss to Dolokhov! Here in the regiment everything was clear and simple. (395; II, 2, 15)

As he painfully discovers, all is not so clear and simple, even in the army, where his friend Major Denisov is facing possible court marshal for seizing a transport of food to feed his hungry regiment, which has been denied provisions for two weeks. During his journey to Tilsit, where he plans to deliver his petition directly to the Tsar on Denisov's behalf, Nikolai visits his friend in the hospital. There he witnesses the smells and sights of human suffering in all of their concreteness, and his faith in the military world, already unstable because of the injustice done to his friend, begins to crumble further. When he arrives at Tilsit, Nikolai desperately assures himself that "'[the Emperor] would understand whose side justice is on . . . No, I'm not going to let the chance slip now as I did after Austerlitz . . . I'll fall at his feet and plead with him. He'll raise me up, listen to me, and even thank me'" (411; II, 2, 20).

But just as at Austerlitz, so at Tilsit reality will rear its ugly head. Boris, embarrassed to be seen with his childhood friend, a mere hussar in civilian clothes, receives Nikolai coldly. The next day an unnamed member of the Emperor's suite rebuffs Nikolai for his audacity in delivering the petition without the approval of his commander. In a momentary reversal of fortune, a general finally offers to take the petition, as Nikolai happily joins the crowd, which cheers the arriving Tsar who is about to consummate an official truce with Napoleon. However, unlike the Emperor's review at Olmütz, something is seriously amiss here for Nikolai. Not only does he fail to understand why it has been so difficult to get his petition on behalf of Denisov accepted, but he also is beginning to question the very justification of the war itself. So many people killed and wounded, and now, after Tilsit, Russians have become friends with the French!

While Nikolai desperately tries to make sense of what he sees, the narrator calmly stands above the fray and deconstructs Napoleon's sham performance, in which he pompously presents the Legion of Honor to a Russian soldier. The narrator sprinkles the scene with ironic details such as Napoleon's "small, plump hands" reaching out to take an order from a page who runs to him with pathetic alacrity. Even more cuttingly, Tolstoy shows Napoleon presenting the order to a Russian soldier named Lazarev (from the Russian *Lazar,* or "Lazarus"), whom, he arrogantly believes, he is metaphorically raising from the dead: "It was as if Napoleon knew that, for this soldier to be happy, rewarded, and distinguished from everyone else in the world, it was only necessary that his, Napoleon's, hand deign to touch the soldier's breast" (415; II, 2, 21). Napoleon's obsequious underlings accord meaning and power to his performance, but Nikolai and the narrator do not. Whereas the narrator can look upon that performance with ironic amusement, Nikolai only descends further into despair:

> Painful work was going on in his mind, which he could not bring to an end. Terrible doubts arose in his soul. Now he remembered Denisov with his changed expression, his submission, and the whole hospital with those torn-off arms and legs, that filth and disease. He imagined so vividly now that hospital stench of dead flesh that he looked around to see where the stench could be coming from. Then he remembered that self-satisfied Bonaparte with his white little hand, who was now an emperor, whom the emperor Alexander liked and respected. Why, then, those torn-off arms and legs, those dead people? Then he remembered the rewarded Lazarev and Denisov punished and unforgiven. He caught himself in such strange thoughts that it made him frightened. (416; II, 2, 21)

The truce between his beloved Tsar and the enemy is the final insult. Nikolai's world seems to be crumbling—again. Now everything he has lived for—honor, justice, and courage in the name of the Emperor—appears to have been for naught. There is a fissure in his universe, which he will try to repair with a little help from the bottle. At a celebration later that evening, Nikolai, who is in a stupor, bursts out at a Russian officer: "If it pleases the sovereign emperor to recognize Bonaparte as emperor and conclude an alliance with him—it means it has to be so. And if we start judging and reasoning about everything, then there'll be nothing sacred left. Next we'll be saying there's no God, no anything . . . Our business is to do our duty, to cut and slash, not to think, that's all" (416–17; II, 2, 21).

The officer, of course, never said a word about the Emperor, as he himself points out, but that is irrelevant to Nikolai. Here again we see the young man, who, as at Schöngrabern, refuses to play the "diplomatist" and make compromises, and instead sees the world as divided between patriots and imposters, dutiful soldiers and doubting Thomases. In other words, Nikolai attempts to smooth over the world's moral ambiguity through hortatory simplification. But Tolstoy's world does not submit to such reductivism. In order to achieve happiness, Nikolai will have to find another way of healing his wounds. In the midst of his rhetorical outburst, he finally immerses himself in the confusing thick of things, embraces his pain, and finds solace in community:

> "Our business is to do our duty, to cut and slash, not to think, that's all . . ." [Nikolai] concluded.
> "And to drink," said one of the officers, unwilling to quarrel.
> "Yes, and to drink," Nikolai picked up. "Hey, you! Another bottle!" he shouted. (417; II, 2, 21)

"Another bottle!" now becomes Nikolai's verbal leitmotif, in the same way that "And still" was Andrei's before Austerlitz. Concrete and earthy, Nikolai's "another bottle!" is the diametric opposite of Andrei's abstract and intellectual "And still." And yet Nikolai, like Andrei, finds solace by numbing his pain. Along with the other soldiers who relieve their tension by drinking and merrymaking, Nikolai now finds solace, not by pursuing perfection, but by submerging himself in the moment. Here he rediscovers the lesson of Schöngrabern: that even in his regiment, a supposed refuge from the complications of the world, life is complex and the definitions of virtue and patriotism are ambiguous. But whereas the earlier revelation led him to despair, now, by giving in to the world (*mir*) and accepting it on its own imperfect terms, he finds temporary peace (*mir*). (In Russian the words for "world" and "peace" are the same: *mir*.)[1]

A TALE OF TWO LOVES

Nikolai's growth during this part of the novel is echoed in Andrei's trajectory, as well. Just as Nikolai's disillusionment in Volume Two, Part Two concludes with a kind of temporary emotional uplift, so Prince Andrei's depression is partially lifted by his encounter with Pierre at Bogucharovo in the same part of the novel. Significantly, Nikolai finds emotional relief amid the community of soldiers and under the influence of alcohol, while Prince Andrei's is revived by his closest friend, whose expansive presence gives Andrei a renewed sense of possibility and reconnects him with the world. At the conclusion of their philosophical discussions, Prince Andrei, glancing

> with a luminous childlike, tender gaze looked into the flushed, rapturous face of Pierre . . . looked at the sky Pierre had pointed to; and for the first time since Austerlitz saw that high, eternal sky he had seen as he lay on the battlefield, and something long asleep, something that was best in him, suddenly awakened joyful and young in his soul. This feeling disappeared as soon as Prince Andrei re-entered the habitual conditions of life, but he knew that this feeling, which he did not know how to develop, lived in him. The meeting with Pierre marked an epoch for Prince Andrei, from which began what, while outwardly the same, was in his inner world a new life. (389; II, 2, 12)

The feeling "which [Andrei] did not know how to develop" is an ability to embrace the world's beautiful imperfection, when his rational intellect can see only the tragic reality of life's injustices and contradictions. On the battlefield at Austerlitz Andrei has glimpsed a vision of the gloriousness of the universe, but it was somehow abstract and otherworldly. During his conversations with Pierre, he glimpses yet another grand vision, through which he senses a deep connection to his immediate surroundings. Andrei is moved not by the intellectual content of his conversations with Pierre, but by the soothing, inspiring presence of the natural surroundings and of Pierre himself.

Andrei's encounter with Pierre thus helps to prepare the soil for the slow flowering of his withered spirit and his eventual return to life in Volume Two, Part Three. But before that happens, Andrei will need to have one more crucial, life-transforming encounter, with a young, vibrant girl, whose infectious life force and ability to live fully moment to moment is diametrically opposed to Andrei's own aloof and conflicted nature. That girl is Natasha Rostova, whom Andrei first meets while visiting Natasha's father, Count Ilya Rostov, the Marshal of the Nobility, during an overnight business trip to their estate at Otradnoe, which means "comforting" in Russian.

Natasha, whose vitality infuses Andrei with feelings he cannot name, is a mystery to him, and this, in part, is the source of her power over him. "'What is she so glad of? What is she thinking about?'" Andrei asks himself when, upon arriving at Otradnoe, he first sees Natasha, indifferent to his presence, running and laughing with the other girls (421; II, 3, 2).

Natasha's indefinable charm, like the enigmatic allure of his own awakening emotions, begins to exhilarate Andrei.

Later that evening, when he opens the window and suddenly hears Natasha's voice, quietly singing and speaking rapturously to Sonya about the beauty of the evening, Andrei is overwhelmed by inexplicable emotional pangs: "In his soul there suddenly arose such an unexpected tangle of youthful thoughts and hopes, contradictory to his whole life, that, feeling himself unable to comprehend his own state, he fell asleep at once" (422; II, 3, 2). At Otradnoe he begins to recognize the plenitude that lies within. His encounter with Natasha thus continues the process, begun in his meetings with Pierre, of unloosening Andrei's internal shackles and opening him up to new perceptions and possibilities. Even the external world seems to expand and renew itself, thus echoing the process of renewal that takes place within him.

On the previous day, as he drove to Otradnoe, the oak tree, "old, angry, scornful, and ugly," with "huge, gnarly, ungainly, unsymmetrically spread arms and fingers," seemed to Andrei to echo his own sentiments about life's hopelessness (419; II, 3, 1). Now, when he sees the oak again, the ungainly monster with sprawling limbs appears to be "quite transformed" and "spreading out a canopy of juicy, dark greenery." The oak becomes for Andrei—and the reader—a beautiful, sturdy monument to nature's permanence and resilience:

> "Yes, it's the same oak," thought Prince Andrei, and suddenly a causeless springtime feeling of joy and renewal came over him. All the best moments of his life suddenly recalled themselves to him at the same time. Austerlitz with the lofty sky, and the dead, reproachful face of his wife, and Pierre on the ferry, and a girl excited by the beauty of the night, and that night itself, and the moon—all of it suddenly recalled itself to him.[2] (423; II, 3, 3)

Like the oak, which at first Andrei does not recognize after a light rain, Andrei, too, has been washed by the soothing, regenerating spirit of Otradnoe. Is it Andrei's subjective perception that has changed—or objective reality? The narrator suggests that both processes are at work. Andrei's consciousness both moves in tandem with and also reflects the processes of nature.[3]

This is different from Andrei's experience both at Schöngrabern, when he tried to impose his internal vision onto the external world, and at Austerlitz, when he envisioned a vast universe that overshadows the human individual. What he feels in this scene comes closest to what he felt during his meeting with Pierre at Bogucharovo. Now, as then, Andrei's spirit expands, precisely because he tries neither to control nor to transcend the world, but remains present in the moment and fully connected to his changing surroundings. Under the influence of this changed inner state, Andrei reconnects to his inner truth:

> "No, life isn't over at the age of thirty-one," Prince Andrei suddenly decided definitively, immutably. "It's not enough that I know all that's in me, everyone else must know it, too: Pierre, and that girl who wanted to fly into the sky, everyone must know me, so that my life is not only for myself; so that they don't live like that girl, independently of my life, but so that it is reflected in everyone, and they all live together with me!" (423; II, 3, 3)

Significantly, Andrei's renewed sense of individual possibility is expressed in his revitalized desire to be known and loved by others. But unlike his earlier desire for greatness, which was motivated by a Napoleonic love of conquest, his grandiosity here is rooted in a deep humanitarianism and in a sense of noblesse oblige. Paradoxically, he wants to rise above the crowds in order to inspire them.

When he returns to public life later in this section, it is to work with Mikhail Speransky, whose promise as a social reformer especially attracts Andrei in his renewed state of idealism. Yet he soon discovers the stark contrast between Speransky's socially conscious reforms and his cold, calculating intellect, and so learns the truth faced by many of Tolstoy's searching characters: that social activism is often a mask for personal egoism. This is true not only of Speransky but, to some degree, of Andrei as well, in whom the impulse to do good is never far removed from the desire to be known.

Prince Andrei's brief foray into the vortex of public life ends in both disillusionment and discovery. Realizing that public power cannot possibly lead to his personal happiness, he withdraws into private life. But instead of falling into despair, as he did after Austerlitz, Andrei remains under the rejuvenating force of Natasha and her home, which he begins to visit more frequently. He confides his feelings for Natasha to Pierre, but as soon as he shares them with Natasha herself, in the form of a marriage proposal, they begin to evaporate. Even Natasha's family senses that there is something not quite right in their daughter's impending union with Prince Andrei, who "seemed a man from an alien world, and Natasha spent a long time getting the household accustomed to Prince Andrei and proudly assured them all that he only seemed so peculiar, but that he was the same as everybody else" (480; II, 3, 24).

The reader knows that Andrei is not like the Rostovs at all, and that this is, in fact, an important source of his attraction to their vivacious, emotion-driven world, which is so different from the tone and atmosphere of his own family life. The tragic reality is that Natasha is, and could only be, an unachievable ideal to Andrei. The powerful, irrational force that had gripped him ever since his visit to Otradnoe is not strong enough to withstand Andrei's analytical nature and need for order. His attachment to his irascible old father proves stronger than his burgeoning love for Natasha. Andrei would rather preserve his familiar life of quiet desperation than plunge further into the exhilarating but foreign world of romantic feelings. That is why Andrei quickly bows down to his father's insistence that the wedding to Natasha, whose wealth and social rank is beneath that of the Bolkonskys, be postponed for a year.

Prince Andrei's subservience to his father's wishes belies his passionate vow to Pierre one day before that "he could not sacrifice his happiness to his father's whim," and that "he would make his father agree to this marriage and love her, or else he would do without his consent" (475; II, 3, 22). For Andrei does sacrifice his personal happiness to his father's wishes. His love for Natasha suddenly becomes a "duty," as he helplessly allows the shackles of reason and responsibility to be placed on him once again:

> Prince Andrei held her hand, looked into her eyes, and did not find the former love for her in his soul. Something suddenly turned over in his soul: the former poetic and mysterious delight of desire was not there, but there was pity for her woman's and child's weakness, there was fear before her devotion and trust, a heavy but at the same time joyful consciousness of duty that bound him to her forever. The actual feeling, though not as bright and poetic as the former one, was more serious and strong. (479; II, 3, 23)

This moment marks the end of Prince Andrei's brief foray into the world of the emotions and his return to the cold, if comfortable, world of duty and routine. When we last see him at the end of Volume Two, Part Three, Andrei leaves neither for his estate nor for the battlefield, as he had done in previous moments of disillusionment, but to Europe, the favorite gathering place of so many disenfranchised nineteenth-century Russian aristocrats and intellectuals. The narrator thus links Prince Andrei's personal tragedy with the larger drama of nineteenth-century Russian history.

His turning to Europe at this critical point in his life suggests that his psychological inability to integrate into the Rostovian world is indicative of a deeper incapacity—shared by many of the so-called superfluous men in nineteenth-century Russia—to find a spiritual home within the world of purely Russian values. The spontaneous, life-affirming spirit of tradition and family togetherness, embodied by the Rostovs, appears permanently beyond Andrei's reach.

When he returns to Moscow from Europe a year later, at the end of Volume Two, Part Five, and learns that, in his absence, Natasha has been tempted by Anatole Kuragin, Andrei's tragic fate is sealed. The possibilities of love and personal happiness that had once opened up before him become only tormenting reminders of a path now closed to him forever. Though the text does not state so explicitly, the reader senses through Andrei's combination of agitation, iciness, and stoic avoidance of the topic of Natasha's infidelity that he realizes that he is complicit in his own unhappiness. He has asked Natasha to do something that she, with her passionate, vibrant nature, could not possibly do—wait for the gratification of love.

This moment is a turning point both in Andrei's life and in the historical trajectory of the novel. Andrei's honor has been violated, his spiritual world invaded, his sense of order shattered. So, too, will Russia be invaded in the very next section, when Napoleon crosses the Nieman River in June of 1812 in an act of willful aggression and open violation of the Russian–French truce signed at Tilsit. In a state of profound despair, Andrei will go into battle again, this time not in search of his Toulon, but in pursuit of his betrayer, Anatole, and his lost honor.

In Volume Two, Part Three, the world is reborn for Andrei with his visit to Otradnoe, only to be lost again through his fatal weakness. Similarly, Nikolai's return to his regiment ends in his bitter disappointment at Tilsit and his subsequent return home, in Book Two, Part Four, to his family, whose financial affairs are in shambles. The narrator puts it succinctly: "Things were not cheerful in the Rostovs' house" (517; II, 4, 8). In the same way that Prince Andrei's spirit was temporarily uplifted after his visit to Otradnoe, the heaviness weighing on Nikolai is momentarily lightened by the exhilarating wolf hunt and the following evening of merrymaking, at which "Uncle" plays the balalaika and Natasha sings. But the overriding spirit in the Rostov home in this section is one of dreariness. Nikolai feels this particularly strongly, as his attraction to Sonya appears to be in conflict with his duty to his family and his mother, who wants him to marry the wealthier Julie Karagina in order to help put the family financial affairs in order. In addition to this more obvious conflict, another, more subtle internal struggle is taking place within Nikolai—he must now clarify the depth of his feelings for Sonya.

At Christmas, under the influence of their holiday role-playing during the mummer celebration, Nikolai sees Sonya "with totally new eyes. It seemed to him that it was only today, for the first time, owing to that cork mustache, that he had known her fully. Indeed, that evening Sonya was merrier, livelier, and prettier than Nikolai had ever seen her before" (528; II, 4, 4). This moment of discovery faintly echoes the earlier scene in which Andrei first hears Natasha's voice at Otradnoe and begins to see the world anew. For both characters, the intense moment of emotional connection takes place in an atmosphere of nocturnal enchantment. In both cases the feelings seem real and powerful, yet ultimately unsustainable.

In the case of Andrei, his self-denying nature intervenes. He simply cannot break free of his internal shackles and give himself over to the power of Natasha's essential nature. For Nikolai, Sonya seems able to rise to the level of enchantress only in costume. He looks at Sonya during the Christmas sleigh ride and thinks: "'The same happy, smiling Circassian with a little mustache and shining eyes, looking from under a sable hood . . . was Sonya, and this Sonya was certainly his future happy and loving wife'" (530; II, 4, 12). The costume is what allows Nikolai to perceive this girl he has known all his life in a fresh, exciting light.

However, as the novel bears out, Nikolai's belief that Sonya is destined to become his wife is an illusion. He manufactures this sense of destiny in the same way that the whole Rostov family actively looks for signs that the union between Andrei and Natasha was meant to be, in order to stifle their well-founded doubts. The narrator's sobering exposure of his characters' false sense of destiny is counterbalanced by his inspiring vision of the truer, higher destiny that actually does guide their lives.

The reader feels these fatidic forces most palpably in the climactic Volume Three, Part Two, which creates the mythical, patriotic aura of 1812. In this section, the novel's longest, the forces of violence, personal survival, and social upheaval dominate. Yet underlying these elemental energies is the guiding vision of the narrator, who reveals that there is a higher ordering principle at work. Social distinctions are temporarily transcended, as the peasants and the nobility unite against the French. Even the distinction between the categories of war and peace disappear, as war has penetrated all of Russia.

At the same time, various plotlines merge, loose strands are temporarily resolved, and important new unions are formed. Andrei's father dies, thus freeing Andrei from his earthly duties and foreshadowing his fatal wound at Borodino, which brings his ultimate liberation from the world he could not learn to love. Pierre's incarceration by the French begins the process of spiritual resurrection that will eventually lead him back to Natasha, whom he can marry only after Andrei's death.

It is in this heightened historical moment of 1812 that Nikolai's "chance" encounter with Princess Marya appears to be not so accidental. It smacks of destiny. Nikolai, now a squadron commander, rides into the Bolkonsky estate, Bogucharovo, in order to protect its inhabitants from the invading French army.[4] While there, he suppresses the peasant rebellion on the estate and reestablishes order; in this atmosphere of chivalry, he and Marya fall in love. "Rostov immediately imagined something romantic in this encounter" (733; III, 2, 13). And in contrast to his earlier infatuation with the costumed Sonya, it has lasting consequences.

He and Princess Marya see each other in their most exposed state, amid the tumult of 1812, in which they, like Russia, are stripped down to their most essential qualities. "'And what meekness, what nobility in her features and expression!' he thought, listening to her timid account" (733; III, 2, 13). Gentleness and nobility are Princess Marya's defining features, which her father and her male suitors, put off by her physical plainness, could never fully appreciate. Only her brother, Prince Andrei, and now Nikolai, recognize her inner beauty. By having Nikolai see Princess Marya in this way, the narrator reveals Nikolai's fundamental nobility of spirit, as well as his deeper spiritual connection to Marya's brother, the high-minded Prince Andrei.

The heightened romantic circumstances of their meeting in 1812 allow Nikolai and Marya to see the noble qualities in each other, in the same way that all of Russia manifests its essential honor, courage, and collective spirit in a time of national crisis. In the union of Nikolai and Marya the narrator asserts the fundamental unity of the Russian national character by bringing together its opposite poles: the earthy, family-focused principle, embodied in the Rostovs and their Otradnoe estate, and the spiritual-religious principle, embodied in the Bolkonskys and Bald Hills. Nikolai and Marya thus complement one another on multiple levels, and their ultimate union seems perfectly consistent with the general spirit of holism in the novel.

These characters could not have known their destinies before the crucial events of 1812, that watershed historical moment that exposes characters' authentic emotional truths, reveals the world's larger design, and gives the lie to all human falsehood. Just as Napoleon's reputation for greatness and military prowess, formerly admired and feared, is shown in 1812 to be a fleeting mirage in history, so now Nikolai's formerly childish notions of virtue and patriotism, as well as his youthful infatuation with Sonya, are shown to be passing vagaries. Similarly, Princess Marya's once rigid attachment to a life of pious spinsterhood is replaced by a more balanced, holistic notion of happiness that embraces both spiritual and earthly pleasures.

Their more mature worldview eventually will bear fruit in the epilogue. Nikolai's and Marya's inspired, fairy-tale-like meeting at Bogucharovo in 1812 will be transformed into the calmer union of husband and wife, who will raise a family in the soothing, pastoral atmosphere of Bald Hills after the war. The formerly impetuous young hussar now will prove his manhood not on the battlefield but in the home, by ensuring the financial security of his family and protecting the honor of his deceased father, whose debts Nikolai insists on repaying. Nikolai will become a successful estate manager and rebuild the family fortune, thanks to the same single-mindedness, sense of duty, and hot temper he has always exhibited: "'He was a real master . . . The muzhiks' affairs first, and then his own. But he never went easy on us. In short—a master!'" his peasants will say of him (1146; Epilogue, 1, 7).

Princess Marya, with her gentle spirituality, will be the ideal complement to Nikolai. She will help him to control his "old hussar habit of making free with his fists" (1146; Epilogue, 1, 8), and she will quietly accept the mysteries of her husband's personality with her characteristic spiritual devotion and acumen. She cannot understand why "her kind Nikolai" refuses the request of the peasants who turn to her asking to be released from work, yet she instinctively accepts that "he had his special world, which he passionately loved, with some sort of laws that she did not understand" (1146; Epilogue, 1, 7). Those laws, the narrator tells us, derive not from any abstract notion of Christian charity but from an authentic, healthy egoism: "And—it must have been because Nikolai did not allow himself the thought he was doing anything for others out of virtuousness—all that he did was fruitful" (1146; Epilogue, 1, 7). Princess Marya unobtrusively supports her husband, because she instinctively knows that, in doing so, she is helping to realize one of Tolstoy's most cherished values: the preservation of the family. That is something that her brother, Andrei, with his inflexibly high ideals, was unable to do.

DEATH AND ILLUMINATION

After he hears the news of Natasha's infidelity and returns to the battle-field in Volume Three, Part One, Prince Andrei falls into a despair from which he will recover only in his dying hours. He will become the tragic hero, whereas Nikolai will become the survivor. Even in his most despairing moments, Nikolai is grounded by a life-affirming acceptance of the world and by the strong communal instinct that is a uniquely Rostovian principle.

It is just this instinct that Prince Andrei lacks. His Bolkonskian nature is too strong in him. The nobility of spirit that makes all of the Bolkonskys—Andrei, his father, and his sister, Marya—attractive to others is also their Achilles' heel. Their conception of life is grand, but not in the way Tolstoy most valued. It stems not from an appreciation of life's fluid totality, but from unbending, binary constructs.

If the Rostovian sense of life is generative and malleable, then the Bolkonskian worldview is rigid and even life-denying. The Old Prince, an embittered scion of an old, aristocratic order, will hold onto his outmoded social ideals at all costs, including that of his daughter's happiness. Under no circumstances will he allow the snow to be swept from his steps for the arrival of a French doctor, whom he suspects, quite ludicrously, of espionage. Old Prince Bolkonsky dies a relic of the past. Princess Marya eventually survives, however, because, unlike her father, she overcomes her rigidity. Like his sister, Prince Andrei discovers a fuller, more fluid way of being, but, tragically, only in death.

Caught between an awareness of his finitude and his aspiration towards the lofty, infinite sky he glimpses at Austerlitz, Prince Andrei is led to an acute awareness of the very self he seeks to transcend. What begins as a heroic fire eventually fades to a faint glow. But this recognition of the idealist's movement from grand conception to deflated resignation is but one dimension of the narrator's wisdom, which lies in his embracing of both the heavenly and the earthly, the hopeful and the tragic, as two equally important and organically linked dimensions of the human experience. The narrator shows us that ordinary, earthly moments in fact contain a touch of the heavenly within them, when perceived with a full, open spirit. That fullness of spirit is precisely what Andrei has when he meets Natasha earlier in the novel, and it is what he has lost by the time of the Battle of Borodino.

The disappointment of great expectations is a common theme in other works of nineteenth-century Russian literature, beginning with Mikhail Lermontov's Romantic novel *A Hero of Our Time,* and culminating in the dark, spiritually tormented Dostoevskian heroes. Lermontov's Pechorin famously laments: "'How many people, in starting out in life, dream of ending it as Alexander the Great, or Lord Byron, but meanwhile all their life remain titular councilors?'"[5]

Prince Andrei echoes Pechorin's words when he speaks to Pierre before the Battle of Borodino in a tone of morbid resignation and foreboding: "'Ah, dear heart, lately it's become hard for me to live. I see that I've begun to understand too much. And it's not good for man to taste of the tree of the knowledge of good and evil . . . Well, it won't be for long!'" (776; III, 2, 25). During the next day's battle Prince Andrei will make good on his promise when he watches with an almost eerie passivity as his world, his physical world, is destroyed by the bursting shell. That moment—more of a whimper than a bang—is the beginning of the end of Andrei's struggle against that "low, definite, oppressive vault" of reality that has haunted him since Austerlitz (628; III, 1, 8).

We are prepared for this moment of resignation by the scene in which Andrei surveys the battlefield before the Battle of Borodino—a mirror image of Andrei's surveying of the battlefield at Schöngrabern, but with important differences. Now it is Andrei, not the soldiers, who reflect on the life-and-death implications of the upcoming battle. And whereas at Schöngrabern Andrei stood at the highest position, from which he tried to see the whole field and to plan the upcoming battle, here we see him "propped on his elbow in a broken-up shed" (769; III, 2, 24), viewing his surroundings "[t]hrough an opening in the broken wall." What Andrei sees through that gap are just the kinds of quotidian details he overlooked at Schöngrabern. But these quotidian details are not a source of inspiration for him; their ordinariness haunts him: "And the birches with their light and shade, and the fleecy clouds, and the smoke of the campfires— everything around was transfigured for him and appeared as something dreadful and menacing. A chill ran down his spine" (770; III, 2, 24).

Andrei's descent from his privileged vantage point at Schöngrabern to his more grounded perspective here is, for him, a descent into tragic awareness, not a source of inspiration or a stepping stone to a higher wisdom. Yet even at the fatal moment, he gropes towards some kind of understanding of the world and his place in it. A mysterious vitality flickers within him: "'Can this be death?' thought Prince Andrei, gazing with completely new, envious eyes at the grass, at the wormwood, and at the little stream of smoke curling up from the spinning black ball. 'I can't, I don't want

to die, I love life, I love this grass, the earth, the air . . .' He was thinking all that and at the same time remembered that he was being looked
at" (810–11; III, 2, 36).[6] The grass, the wormwood, and the streamlet of
smoke are intensely real to him. How different this scene is from Andrei's
experience at Austerlitz, where, close to death, he concludes that "everything is empty, everything is deception, except this infinite sky" (281; I, 3,
16). What for Andrei appears to be a descent from his perception of something great and important to a frustrated awareness of life's pettiness is, in
the context of the larger novel, not a descent at all but rather an ascent.
The movement of Andrei's vision from the lofty sky of Austerlitz to these
simple, earthly sights implies sharpened powers of perception, a renewed
capacity to appreciate life's details.

Andrei's vision at Austerlitz is directed upward towards the heavens;
his vision at Borodino is downward, toward the earth. In the artistic universe of *War and Peace,* these two poles—earth and heaven, microcosm
and macrocosm, the real and the ideal—always exist in equilibrium. As
we have seen in examining Prince Andrei's surveying of the battlefield at
Schöngrabern, the more the reader's focus is drawn to concrete, specific
details and circumstances in the novel the greater his awareness of the universal order of things becomes. But for Andrei these two poles exist in
opposition. Concrete, ordinary reality is for him something to be suffered
through and overcome, while the transcendent is an ideal that cannot be
attained on earth. The possibility that imperfect earthly reality might contain the very transcendent qualities he seeks is beyond Andrei's sustained
imagination. He glimpses this Tolstoyan truth briefly at various points
in the novel—at Austerlitz, when he philosophizes with Pierre on the
ferry raft, when he first hears Natasha's voice in a moment of nocturnal
enchantment—but he cannot hold onto it.[7]

So, too, when the shell lands in front of him at Borodino, at the very
moment that Andrei grasps beauty around him, he "remembered that
he was being looked at" (811; III, 2, 36). Even in this critical instance,
Prince Andrei's intense rationality and overpowering sense of propriety
cloud his vision and stifle in him his life-embracing impulse. He is instinctively more concerned with appearances than with survival. The moment
before, a spinning shell landed between Prince Andrei and the adjutant.
"'Get down!' (*Lozhis'*) cried the voice of the adjutant, throwing himself to
the ground. Prince Andrei stood undecided" (810; III, 2, 36). To Andrei it
must seem craven to exhibit fear in front of a mere adjutant, and especially
an adjutant who has just addressed him, quite audaciously, in the singular,
informal thou-form.

"'It's a shame, officer!' he said to the adjutant. 'What an . . .' He did not finish"[8] (811; III, 2, 36). What is shameful? To lie down? To want to live? To be concerned with what others are thinking about him in such a critical moment? Or is Andrei perhaps reflecting more generally on the slaughter on the battlefield and his participation in it? The text intentionally doesn't tell us. What we hear instead is the internal dialogue of a bruised and divided consciousness with deep feelings of shame lying beneath the calm, noble exterior.

That dialogue, presented in the text as conversation with the adjutant, is, on a deeper level, Andrei's dialogue with himself. And just as his words are cut short by the shell's explosion, so Andrei's internal debate ends without resolution. The war between heart and head, instinct and reason, rages on within him. His failure to connect with the adjutant stems from his failure to connect with himself, to bridge the gap between his competing impulses.

The narrator reinforces this inner battle by contrasting Andrei's intellectual reaction to the bursting shell with the panic of a horse, who, "not asking whether it was good or bad to show fear, snorted, reared up, nearly throwing the major, and leaped aside. The horse's terror communicated itself to the men [liudiam]" (810; III, 2, 36). Prince Andrei is not infected by the horse's terror, because he is not truly among "the men," [liudiam], or literally "the people," suggestive of the collective. He is at a remove from the collective, because he is at a remove from the immediacy of the moment itself. Even in this moment of temporarily heightened perception, when, confronted with the possibility of death, Prince Andrei glances enviously at his surroundings, he still seems to be looking at his world from a slight distance, just as he gazed from afar upon the battlefield at Schöngrabern.

And he maintains that distance even at the end of the chapter, when he joins the wounded soldiers crowded together as they await their turn to be admitted into the nursing tent. The soldiers "wheezed, moaned, wept, shouted, cursed, begged for vodka" (812; III, 2, 36), and they listen to the talk of an officer. Andrei, who is physically among them and who also listens to the officer, doesn't groan or sigh or weep or scream. Instead, he philosophizes quietly to himself: "'But does it make any difference now? . . . Why was I so sorry to part with life? There was something in this life that I didn't and still don't understand'" (812; III, 2, 36).

In these words we hear the sincere pathos of a man who feels that his lifetime of searching and suffering have been for naught; they hover over us like a soft, melancholy veil, dwelling, like Andrei himself, in a realm just removed from the concrete, immediate details of his surroundings. While the men react viscerally to their circumstances, Prince Andrei responds intellectually. Not until the end of the chapter, when he sees a suffering Anatole in the operating tent, does he briefly exhibit uncontrolled, spontaneous emotion:

> Prince Andrei could no longer restrain himself, and he wept tender, loving tears over people, over himself, and over their and his own errors.
>
> "Compassion, love for our brothers, for those who love us, love for those who hate us, love for our enemies—yes, that love which God preached on earth, which Princess Marya taught me, and which I didn't understand; that's why I was sorry about life, that's what was still left for me, if I was to live. But now it's too late. I know it!" (814; III, 2, 37)

There is an almost beatific quality, a compelling vulnerability and sincerity, to Andrei's thoughts and words. But at the same time they are rarified, abstract. A tendency towards analytical distance overtakes the rawness of Andrei's feelings. His behavior emerges organically out of the circumstance of the moment and the truth of his nature. The intellectual aloofness that has characterized him from the beginning now becomes, appropriately, his downfall.[9]

The special purpose for which Tolstoy had intended Prince Andrei from the earliest drafts has been realized. Tolstoy knew early on that he "needed a brilliant young man to die at Austerlitz," as he wrote in a letter in 1865.[10] Tolstoy later revised this to have that young man—the future Andrei Bolkonsky—only wounded, because "he would be needed later on." It seems that the purpose Tolstoy settled on—probably unconsciously—was to have his hero's death pave the way to Pierre's marriage to Natasha and Princess Marya's marriage to Nikolai.[11]

Moreover, had Prince Andrei died at Austerlitz, as the author initially intended, he would have experienced none of the extended inner drama that is essential for his ultimate illumination. Instead, he would have left the world believing in the beauty of the infinite, unattainable by human beings. But in the metaphysics of *War and Peace*, this is only a half-truth, for it excludes the beauty of all that is concrete and craggy about the here-and-now.

So, too, Andrei's meditation about compassion in the operating room, at the sight of a wounded Anatole, is only a partial truth. If *War and Peace* can be said to teach anything, it is the universality of human suffering, and the spirit of forbearance that this recognition inspires. But the power of the novel lies in its ability to communicate this truth without stating it abstractly. The lesson of compassion and acceptance, of loving an imperfect world and flawed human beings, is evoked by the all-embracing poetics of the novel itself.

Andrei wants to distill that discovery into a moral maxim. But in doing so he overlooks a larger truth: intermingled with his sublime feelings are also hints of satisfaction in seeing his personal desire for revenge carried out by fate. Andrei "remembered Natasha with her slender neck and arms, with her frightened, happy face ready for rapture. . . . He now remembered the connection between him and this man" (814; III, 2, 37). The connection, of course, is that this man, Anatole, caused Natasha's rapturous young face to be disfigured with tears of shame, and at the same time shattered Andrei's own hopes for happiness. It is significant, then, that Andrei's attention is particularly focused on Anatole's bloody, amputated leg. Deep down, we suspect, Andrei would still like to see this virile young rake castrated.

The brilliance of this scene is that it captures these contrasting emotional registers at once. When Andrei meditates on compassion, he is missing the larger human reality of the moment. The grand, life-affirming wisdom of *War and Peace* cannot be distilled into abstract philosophical nuggets. It lies everywhere, all around Prince Andrei, in the rich multiplicity of human experience. And it also lies inside him, in his bruised yet striving spirit, which, right up until the very end, continues to glimmer with life and yearn for permanent meaning in a world whose beauty both beckons and eludes him.

Andrei's last days and hours are characterized by the same aloofness that defines his life. Yet the note of tragic solemnity on which his life concludes is mingled with sublimity. Not coincidentally, Natasha tells Princess Marya when they meet before Andrei's death that "'he's too good, he can't, can't live, because . . .'" (978; IV, 1, 14). Natasha cannot finish her thought, because what she wants to say is beyond the capacity of ordinary language to communicate. She senses that Andrei's death has a higher purpose in the mysterious order of things, yet she is unable to reduce that purpose to a "because" clause. She knows that Andrei must die, not in spite of, but precisely because of, his goodness, that Andrei is perhaps too good for this world. Yet where is the logic in that? How can rational language capture such a realization? With Natasha we, too, begin to apprehend a more integrative truth about Prince Andrei's life: that his tragic flaw—his inability to reconcile himself with reality—is also his supreme gift. Prince

Andrei's fatal weakness—obdurate idealism—is also, as Natasha now understands, the mark of his greatness.[12]

For Natasha—vibrant, life-embracing, earthbound—to admit this is to challenge the foundation of her worldview. But Tolstoy's world remains intact, for in the universe of *War and Peace,* real and ideal, tragedy and optimism, are integrated into a harmonious whole. Natasha's personal metaphysics must expand to include this broader wisdom.

Prince Andrei never wins his Toulon, but, in his dying hours, he has another sort of victory: illumination. The unattainable, beautifully mysterious realm that has attracted and tormented him since Austerlitz now no longer burdens him. It envelops him in its soothing embrace and gives him clarity: "The dread, the eternal, the unknown and far off, of which he had never ceased to feel the presence throughout his life, was now close to him and—by that strange lightness of being he experienced—almost comprehensible and palpable" (982; IV, 1, 16).

The quiet clarity of Andrei's consciousness communicates itself to those around him, as well. Natasha and Princess Marya "both saw how he sank deeper and deeper, slowly and peacefully, somewhere away from them, and they both knew that it had to be so and that it was good" (985–86; IV, 1, 16). The final sentence of Volume Four, Part One communicates, with sublime simplicity and elegance, the power and meaning of Prince Andrei's death for the two closest women in his life. The prolonged reaction of Natasha and Princess Marya provides the final note of quiet acceptance combined with profound illumination that Andrei's death produces: "Natasha and Princess Marya also wept now, but they did not weep from their own personal grief; they wept from a reverent emotion that came over their souls before the awareness of the simple and solemn mystery of death that had been accomplished before them" (986; IV, 1, 16).

If, as Tolstoy believed, a person's death is a measure of the goodness of his life and the quality of his soul, then the angelic peacefulness and noble beauty of Prince Andrei's last hours would suggest that his life was one of virtue and an almost divine grace. Fatally flawed Andrei Bolkonsky becomes, paradoxically, an inspiring beacon of hope. There is in his death a touch of that sublime, peaceful beauty that accompanies the death of the tree in Tolstoy's 1858 story "Three Deaths."[13] As the shackles of duty and reason are finally removed, and the trappings of ego and ambition fall away, Andrei's fundamental goodness and nobility of spirit are revealed to be his dominant, lasting qualities.

After Prince Andrei's death, his spiritual orb continues to intersect with Nikolai's, for it is his death that makes the eventual marriage between

Nikolai and Princess Marya, Andrei's sister, possible. Andrei's spirit lives on in his son, who, significantly, is named Nikolai. He is raised by Princess Marya and Nikolai Rostov, who "in his heart did not like Nikolenka, but whom he was always ready to acknowledge as nice" (1173; Epilogue, 1, 15).

At issue is not merely that Nikolai Rostov has difficulty in forming an attachment to somebody else's biological son. We also have here a subtle variation on a theme, on the psychological subtext, that runs throughout the Nikolai–Andrei storyline. Nikolai's feelings of repulsion and pity for Andrei's son are an echo of the young Nikolai Rostov's conflicted feelings towards Prince Andrei, when he first met him years earlier at Olmütz. Nikolai's intense, fraught reaction to Andrei at Olmütz, with its tinge of fraternal conflict, reproduces itself in his future paternal relationship with Andrei's son, thus reinforcing the eternal, transgenerational linkages between the two characters.

In the novel's epilogue, the ongoing spiritual connection between Nikolai Rostov and Andrei Bolkonsky reaches its culmination. But in order fully to appreciate Tolstoy's vision, we must first turn our attention to the third—and most central—searcher in the novel: Pierre Bezukhov.

$\mathcal{T}$HE DOG AND THE GLOBE

Pierre's Journey to the Truth

A doll-sized bronze dog and a small porcelain globe, two of Tolstoy's favorite boyhood toys, are on display in an enclosed plexiglas case in the Tolstoy Museum in Moscow. When I first saw these objects, I glanced at them briefly, trying to picture them in Tolstoy's young hands and wondering where and under what circumstances he played with them. What childish fantasies did they feature in? What role did they play in his imagined adventures? Musing, I moved on. Years later, those two apparently random images, almost forgotten, came to mind again, demanding renewed attention. They reemerged, surprisingly, in connection with one of the central protagonists of *War and Peace*, Count Pierre Bezukhov.

In Volume Two, Part Three, Pierre dreams that he is surrounded by dogs, and that one of them seizes his leg and won't let him go. "Lord, Great Architect of nature!" Pierre writes in his diary after the dream, "help me to tear off the dogs—my passions" (443; II, 3, 10). This connection intrigued me. The dog was a fixture of nineteenth-century aristocratic life, in the home and on hunts. Tolstoy's own beloved spaniel-poodle, present at family events at Yasnaya Polyana, makes a brief appearance in the film footage of Tolstoy's eightieth-birthday celebration. But in the Russian cultural imagination dogs are also associated with impure, anti-Christian forces—the dangers of egoism and the spiritual chaos unleashed by the physical passions.[1]

Rooted in a seemingly minor image, then, is a larger motif that runs throughout *War and Peace,* and most profoundly in connection with Pierre himself—the battle between his ego and his moral-spiritual aspirations, between his animal-like receptiveness to the world and his intense inner life. This struggle takes place to some degree, of course, in all of Tolstoy's searching characters. But few have Pierre's insatiable appetite for the pleasures of this world combined with an equally acute hunger for higher spiritual truth. Few characters are as consistently seduced and enraptured by the earth's beauty or as incessantly tormented by its suffering, injustice, and cruelty.

Of all the male characters in *War and Peace,* Pierre best embodies both the dramatic tensions and the inexhaustible fullness of the world, which permeate the entire work. Even in a novel in which each of the leading male characters is a projection of Tolstoy's personality, Pierre, the novel's "central image" and the "main hero," as one critic called him, most fully dramatizes Tolstoy's core as man and artist.[2] Ego and soul, the sensual and the spiritual, the real and the ideal, clash and unite inside him as in few other characters. He possesses a Tolstoyan largeness of being.

And so it is fitting that his creator gives Pierre a second motif, a globe—the symbol both of life's holism and of the mind capable of grasping it. The globe also suggests the Russian Orthodox belief in an underlying unity in the diversity of life—a belief, in other words, in the divine perfection of the universe. And it evokes the soothing feminine roundness and nurturing orderliness associated with the image of "Mother Russia." The onion-domed Orthodox churches throughout Russia call forth both these religious and national associations. In Volume Four, Part Three, Pierre dreams of a liquid, vibrating globe shown to him years earlier by his boyhood geography teacher. On the globe drops continually move, change places, expand outward and compress into one another, divide and merge. "'This is life,' said the old teacher. 'How simple and clear it is,' thought Pierre" (1065; IV, 3, 15). The answers to his most vexing questions, Pierre realizes, are to be found within everyday life—always in motion and in tension, yet perfect and whole, like the globe.

A bronze dog and a small porcelain globe—two seemingly unremarkable museum objects I had once found mildly intriguing—suddenly illuminated for me Pierre's essence and pointed to a core Tolstoyan truth: that the extraordinary is available to us right here, right now, in the ordinary details of everyday life. Pierre's own journey repeatedly enacts this truth. Forever mistaking deception for truth, moving from one disillusionment to another, he never stops asking his accursed question: *Zachem?*

What for? The meaning he seeks emerges incrementally, as half-forgotten details unexpectedly reappear in a new light and reveal to him—and to the reader—that he has been connected to life's hidden "labyrinth of linkages" all along.

LIFE AND "THE MIND'S GAME OF CHESS"

One of the few male characters present in Tolstoy's earliest conception of the work and surviving its numerous revisions, Pierre through his struggles embodies for Tolstoy the "great era" that captured the writer's imagination. His tortuous path from innocence to wisdom parallels the path taken by Russia herself during the years of her confrontation with Napoleon. Tolstoy could not "write about our triumph in the struggle against Bonaparte's France without having described our failures and our shame. . . . If the cause of our victory was not accidental, but lay in the essence of the character of the Russian people and army, then that character must be expressed still more clearly in the period of failures and defeats [1805–11]."[3] Similarly, the author cannot speak of the wisdom attained by Pierre at the end of the novel without writing about the many mistakes and delusions on his path to illumination. For the author of *War and Peace* triumph is not the absence of failure but the integration of inevitable human failure into views of oneself and the world.

To understand the meaning of Pierre's trajectory, then, we must follow him through the peaks and valleys of his tumultuous journey. The unifying pattern of his odyssey is expressed best by Tolstoy himself, writing in his diary while working on *War and Peace:* "The mind's game of chess goes on independently of life, and life of it."[4] So it is with Pierre's every intellectual conviction and rational intention. Whether in the ballroom or on the battlefield, his ideas and plans disintegrate like meteor dust as soon as they come into contact with real life.

General Kutuzov defeats Napoleon not because he has a superior strategy but because he instinctively senses the inevitable course of events. Pierre, whom we might consider a civilian version of Kutuzov, lives in a correct Tolstoyan way, because he is above all a believer and a feeler, not a rational thinker or a shrewd operator.[5] This symbolically nearsighted young man who wears glasses might be naïve about how society functions, but he is in sync with life's vital rhythms. Like Don Quixote, who mistook windmills for giants and a prostitute for his Dulcinea, Pierre misreads much of what he sees. Yet, like Quixote, he continually marches on, feel-

Figure 2   L. N. Tolstoy, A. L. Tolstaya, D. P. Dolgorukov, and P. I. Biriukov going to Yasnaya Polyana village to attend the inauguration of a rural library. Yasnaya Polyana, 1910.
Photo by V. G. Chertkov. Source: *Lev Tolstoy in Photographs by Contemporaries* (Moscow: Publishing House of the USSR, 1960). Courtesy of *Tolstoy Studies Journal*, online
Tolstoy Image Gallery.

ing the world's pain, imbibing its pleasures, and embracing its possibilities
as few other characters do.[6]

A bastard and an orphan after his mother's death, Pierre is twenty
years old and unsettled professionally and personally when the novel
opens. He has just returned from an extended stay in Europe, a favorite
nineteenth-century gathering place for uprooted Russian noblemen and
intellectuals. Everything about him—his stout figure, his illegitimate birth,
and his over-the-top defense of Napoleon—contributes to salon hostess
Anna Pavlovna's anxiety: "At the sight of the entering Pierre uneasiness
and fear showed in Anna Pavlovna's face, like that expressed at the sight
of something all too enormous and unsuited to the place" (9; I, 1, 2).

Pierre is unsuited for another reason, as well—he threatens to intro-
duce a spirit of authenticity into a social world that thrives on intrigue
and stratagem. His smile, which is "not like that of other people, blending
into a non-smile" (21; I, 1, 4), seemed to say, "'Opinions are opinions, but

you see what a good and nice fellow I am.' And everyone, including Anna Pavlovna, involuntarily felt it" (22; I, 1, 5). Readers sense from the beginning what even the salon-goers cannot deny—that Pierre is somehow more authentic and alive than the polished pragmatists in the room.

Still, Prince Andrei will gently admonish his closest friend later: "*Mon cher,* you can't go saying what you think everywhere" (24; I, 1, 6). This well-meaning advice falls on deaf ears, for impulsive Pierre does not understand life in society as does the more cerebral Andrei. Pierre says what he thinks when and where he thinks it. It is a mark of his broad responsiveness to life, and to the contradictions of his era, that he can daydream at the beginning of the novel that he is Napoleon slaughtering the British and then later believe, in all seriousness, that he will be Napoleon's assassin.

Like the young Tolstoy, the young Pierre leads a dissolute life at the beginning of the novel. He is still under the influence of his acquaintances, Anatole Kuragin and Dolokhov, both morally stunted egoists in pursuit of personal gratification. Pierre will eventually break free of their influence, but only after he is tempted down the twin paths of sensual pleasure and social acceptance and discovers that neither satisfies his deepest needs.

Living in the world of society but not truly a part of it, Pierre all too easily falls victim to its natural predators. On the eve of his father's death, which will make him the beneficiary of one of the largest fortunes in Russia, he acquires a host of new friends and benefactors. Prince Vasily Kuragin, father of Anatole and Hélène, and Anna Mikhailovna Drubetskaia accompany him to his father's deathbed, ostensibly to watch over his interests but in actuality to watch over their own and those of their children. As his self-designated benefactors shuffle hurriedly back and forth along the corridors of his father's house, exchanging significant looks and carrying on secret conversations, Pierre looks on in confusion. He tries to convince himself "that this had necessarily to be so" (76; I, 1, 19), but the reader knows that he is merely seeking a rationalization of processes he cannot stop. Life washes over him, and his mind plays its futile game of chess. Just how futile his mind's game of chess is in this moment can be seen further in the fact that his intellectual conclusions are self-contradictory: "Pierre did not understand what it was all about . . . but he understood that it all had to be so" (77; I, 1, 19).

Over the coming months, Prince Vasily will take Pierre under his wing, kindly managing Pierre's estate by keeping it for himself. Prince Vasily secures a minor governmental appointment for him and chaperones him to high-society events, where the young heir is now treated with utmost respect. The prince also carefully orchestrates Pierre's courtship of his beautiful, empty daughter, Hélène, seducing him into an unhappy marriage. Eager not to disappoint his benefactor and new admirers, Pierre "had no time to ask himself about the sincerity or insincerity of these people. He was constantly busy, he constantly felt himself in a state of mild and merry intoxication" (202; I, 3, 1).

Tolstoy has chosen the word "intoxication" (op'ianenie) carefully.[7] The future author of the pro-temperance essay "Why Do Men Stupefy Themselves?" is attuned to the ways in which human beings fill their inner emptiness with subtle diversions and addictions of all sorts. Pierre is literally drunk on the adoration he thinks he is receiving. But if the later Tolstoy will criticize self-stupefaction as a way of avoiding life's serious moral questions, then the younger author of War and Peace has a different task—to reveal just how powerful the feelings and forces guiding Pierre are.

In a moment of sobriety Pierre begins to think about recent events. Dimly realizing that he doesn't love Hélène, he senses that there is something wrong about his impending union with her. Still, that awareness is no match for the sheer power that Hélène's sensual beauty has over him: "[T]error came over him at the thought that he might already have bound himself in some way to go through with something which was obviously not good and which he ought not to do. But while he expressed this realization to himself, on the other side of his soul her image floated up in all its feminine beauty" (208; I, 3, 1). Pierre's mental chess game goes on, while the pleasures of the body and the joys of worldly success hold sway.

It will be months before Pierre's intuitive realization that he does not love Hélène becomes conscious. Try as he may, he cannot recreate the sequence of events that led him to say to her those fateful words that indicated only the presence of lust: "Je vous aime." As he attempts to do so, "he suddenly pictured her" (318–19; II, 1, 6) just as he had done earlier. Only now her image is repugnant to Pierre. In a rare act of self-assertion, he brandishes a slab of marble tabletop during an argument with Hélène and threatens to kill her. The "enthusiasm and enchantment of rage" (320; II, 1, 6) he feels in that moment foreshadows the liberating turmoil he will experience years later, in 1812, as the catastrophe of war descends upon Moscow, destroying old patterns and ways of being. Just as new possibilities emerge from that destruction, Pierre's angry break with Hélène opens the way for new growth and discovery.

After his separation from Hélène and his duel with Dolokhov, whom he suspects of a secret liaison with his wife, Pierre leaves for Petersburg in a state of depression. At the Torzhok post station his troubled mind transforms the ordinary post station into a crucible of existential reflection: "'For me it's good, for some traveler it would be bad, and for the postmaster it's inevitable, because he has nothing to eat,'" Pierre thinks as he suspects the postmaster is trying to fleece him for more money (347; II, 2, 1). "'And what does she need the money for?'" he thinks about a peddler woman selling her wares. "'As if this money can add one hair's breadth to her happiness, her peace of mind? Can anything in the world make her or me less subject to evil and death?'" (348; II, 2, 1).

Of course, Pierre is also thinking about himself, the inheritor of a vast fortune still tormented by unhappiness. Yet even in his despair he is ready to believe. At Torzhok Pierre is drawn to the wise old man, the Freemason Osip Alexeevich Bazdeev, whose "intonations, convictions, and heartfelt emotion," "glittering old man's eyes, grown old in conviction," and "calmness, firmness, and knowledge of purpose which shone in the Mason's whole being" offer Pierre solace (351; II, 2, 2). The reader senses in Bazdeev something of a smooth spirituality peddler, but Pierre is moved by his warm paternal presence and inspiring vision of universal brotherhood, which speak to his deepest yearnings: "[H]e wanted to believe with his whole soul, and did believe, and experienced a joyful feeling of peace, renewal, and return to life" (352; II, 2, 2).

In his spiritual hunger and uncritical surrender to belief, Pierre is surely our contemporary, an easy mark for televangelists and spiritual gurus of every persuasion. One can almost imagine him as a "how-to" junkie, prowling the aisles of megabookstores for the latest roadmap to salvation. But what lifts him above this stereotype is his essential spiritual honesty, which prevents him from deceiving himself for long. Moreover, Pierre is no empty vessel waiting to be filled; he has only to recognize his own fullness.

Tolstoy, who believed in the truth of lived experience rather than the utopian promises of organized religious and spiritual movements, describes Pierre's sudden conversion to Freemasonry with undisguised irony. During the initiation ritual in the next chapter, Pierre is blindfolded and led on an allegorical "journey." He "noticed that they referred to him now as *the seeker,* now as *the sufferer,* now as *the postulant,* and made various noises with hammers and swords" (359; II, 2, 4). This symbolic pilgrimage is only a pale reflection of Pierre's actual journey in the novel, during which he is knocked, not by symbolic hammers and swords, but by the slings and arrows of real life. Pierre genuinely searches and suffers and demands of life answers to his urgent question *Zachem?* What for? Freemasonry, on the other hand, offers illusory promises expressed through empty rituals.

Pierre does not yet see this. He mistakenly believes that Freemasonry can give him the answer he seeks.

"'I'm still so weak that I love my life,'" Pierre thinks during the initiation ritual, when he learns that "love of death" is one of the Masons' seven virtues (357; II, 2, 3). Yet Pierre's inability to accept that preaching is a sign not of his weakness, as he believes, but of his life-affirming spirit. The Masonic doctrine is yet another example of the "mind's game of chess" being played independently of life. Still, the narrator carefully distinguishes between how that game is played in the minds of the Masons and how Pierre plays it. While he is animated by a spirit of genuine seeking, the Masons are motivated, like so many modern spirituality movements, by the interests of their own organization. The narrator does not fail to point out that the Masons include the most highly placed people in society: the young Polish count, Willarski; an Italian abbé whom Pierre had met two years before at Anna Pavlovna's soirée; and "a rather important dignitary" (360; II, 2, 4). The narrator also notes that before departing for his estates Pierre leaves the Masons "large sums for alms" (363; II, 2, 5).

"ONLY UNCONSCIOUS ACTIVITY BEARS FRUIT . . ."

Feeling himself spiritually reborn, Pierre attempts to implement social reforms on his estates, just as the young Tolstoy tried to do in his twenties. Tolstoy's attempt was a comedy of errors and disappointments, as he confessed in his diary at that time.[8] Over a decade later, a wiser Tolstoy observes his hero's efforts with empathic objectivity.

Too many forces conspire against the realization of Pierre's noble intentions. There is the wily chief steward, "who considered all the young count's ventures near madness, unprofitable for himself, for Pierre, and for the peasants" (379; II, 2, 10). Nevertheless, he appeases his master by staging receptions that "would impress and deceive" Pierre, all the while extracting from the peasants more labor than before. Then there is the cross-bearing priest, who thanks Pierre for providing funds needed to educate the peasant children while forcing the children to work on his private plot of land and exacting money from their parents.

Pierre is blind to all this, seeing only the new schools and hospitals being built, mostly for show and by increased peasant labor. He is touched by the expressions of gratitude and ceremonies in his honor. Traveling blissfully through his estates, filled with warm thoughts about all the good he has achieved, he exults: "'How easy it is, how little effort it takes, to do so much good'" (380; II, 2, 10). Tolstoy knows better. He understands just how difficult it is and how much effort it takes to do good in the world. He also reveals that Pierre's utopianism is motivated partially by his own need to be admired and to feel that he is making a positive contribution to the world. Pierre's experience was part of a larger utopian trend in the nineteenth century, not only in Russia but in the United States as well. Social experimentation, inspired by the ideas of Thoreau, Emerson, and the Transcendentalists, was in full swing, yet experimental programs often were dropped as quickly as they were adopted.

Pierre is attached to an *idea* of the good, and he holds on to it in defiance of reality—and his own deep-seated doubts: "In his heart of hearts Pierre agreed with the steward that it was hard to imagine happier people and that God knows what awaited them in freedom; yet Pierre insisted, albeit reluctantly, on what he considered right [*chto on schital spravedlivym*]" (381; II, 2, 10).

"Right." The Russian word "*spravedlivym*" has powerful connotations; its root, "*pravda*," means "truth." "Justice" implies an absolute morality, immune from compromise and above political or intellectual debate. It is precisely this maximalist notion that would animate the future Russian revolutionaries, who sincerely believed that they were creating an earthly paradise.[9] They proved sadly mistaken, building instead the Soviet hell on earth.[10] Tolstoy, who vehemently opposed their violent means, was nonetheless sympathetic to the utopian impulse underlying the revolutionary agenda. Lenin famously called him the "mirror of the Russian Revolution" in an essay by that title. It is no wonder, then, that while the narrator gently ironizes Pierre's ill-fated attempts at social reform, he warmly admires his hero's uncompromising insistence on doing "what he considered right."

What's more, Pierre's idealistic aspirations presage the actual reformist course that Russian society would take during the nineteenth century. In the novel's earliest conception, Tolstoy intended Pierre to be a participant in the future Decembrist Revolt of 1825, when a small band of Russian officers would lead 30,000 men in a protest against the assumption of power by Tsar Nicholas I. The final version of the novel ends in 1820, and there is no mention of the revolt or of Tolstoy's attitude towards it. Still, Tolstoy clearly marks Pierre with the traits of a socially conscious reformer ahead of his time, thus giving him a larger historical significance that Tolstoy's contemporary readers living in the 1860s certainly would have recognized.

Despite his failure in carrying out the reforms, Pierre acts, nevertheless, in harmony with larger historical processes, of which he is unaware.[11] His failed efforts illustrate the truth of the narrator's words later in the novel: "Only unconscious activity bears fruit, and a man who plays a role in a historical event never understands its significance" (944; IV, 1, 4). Indeed, Pierre's social aspirations would find resonance almost two generations later during the Great Reforms of Alexander II, implemented in the 1860s, when all of Russia would be consumed by the spirit of social reform that had inspired Pierre in 1806 and 1807.

The story of Pierre's failed reforms is thus also the tale of how the "mind's game of chess goes on independently of life, and life of it." Pierre plans and God laughs, and all that remains is the truth of history's overarching design, which is beyond the grasp of rational understanding. Pierre's life will continue to evolve in accordance with that design, even though it remains hidden from his awareness. The reader sees it, however. Through all its twists and turns, Pierre's journey unfolds with the force of destiny and as if by the grace of God.

Over the next two years Pierre's relationship with Freemasonry deepens. Finding himself "involuntarily . . . the head of the Petersburg Masons" (433; II, 3, 7), he grows increasingly dissatisfied with the external rituals and institutional realities of Freemasonry and wishes to penetrate its deeper essence. He travels abroad, where he is initiated into the higher secrets of the order. Inspired by these new, yet unspecified revelations, he returns to Petersburg and delivers a rousing speech, in which he calls upon his fellow Masons to disseminate "pure truth and to bring about the triumph of virtue" (435; II, 3, 7)—an idealistic point he passionately makes over and again throughout his speech. To Pierre's surprise, the speech not only does not achieve its intended effect but is "received . . . with a coldness that surprised Pierre" (436; II, 3, 7). He painfully discovers that even Freemasonry, which once appeared to him to be the coveted destination on his spiritual quest, cannot give him what he had hoped it would:

> Pierre was struck for the first time at this meeting by the infinite diversity of human minds, which makes it so that no truth presents itself to two people in the same way. Even those members who seemed to be on his side understood him in their own fashion, with limitations and alterations which Pierre could not agree to, since his main need consisted precisely in conveying his thought to others exactly as he understood it himself. (436; II, 3, 7)

Alas, reality—with its inevitable miscommunications, compromises, and clashes of wills—exists even among the Masons. Pierre realizes that his trying journey must continue, and again he is overtaken by depression. In search of consolation, he visits his benefactor, Bazdeev, who encourages him to continue to live in accordance with the Masonic virtues. Softened and inspired, Pierre returns to Petersburg and attempts to reconcile with his wife, Hélène, from whom he has been separated for nearly two years.

The pages describing Pierre's internal processes at this point are intimate and poignant. The narrator reproduces long passages from Pierre's personal diaries, which, in their searching tone and confessional honesty, echo many of Tolstoy's own diaries from an earlier period in his life. "Grant me, O Lord, that I may live without sin and suffering and die without fear and despair," the twenty-four-year-old Tolstoy wrote in his diary.[12] "My God," Pierre writes in his, "help me and strengthen me so that I may walk in Thy paths" (441; II, 3, 10). The large-souled narrator invites readers to empathize with the character's pain, even as he makes them aware that Pierre's reconciliation with Hélène, undertaken out of desperation, is doomed to failure.

As society continues to live in its one-dimensional world, with its superficial labels and judgments, the narrator shows the reader the full-blooded, complex humanity of Pierre's situation. Society sees only "the somewhat blind and ridiculous husband of a famous wife, an intelligent eccentric, a do-nothing, but one who harmed nobody, a nice and kind fellow" (440–41; II, 3, 9). One recent scholar fell prey to just this sort of oversimplification when he tried to fit Pierre into his own narrow paradigm, by calling him a "special type of narcissistic personality."[13] This unhelpful epithet only serves to reinforce the simplistic notion—as prevalent in today's intellectual climate as in the world of Tolstoy's novel—that people can be understood through a single conceptual lens, psychoanalytic or otherwise. But the narrator reminds readers that "a complex and difficult work of inner development was taking place, which revealed much to him and led him to many spiritual doubts and joys" (441; II, 3, 9).

Over the coming year Pierre will descend further into despair. Because of Hélène's intimacy with a royal prince, Pierre "unexpectedly" is made gentleman of the bedchamber, and finds himself more deeply immersed in the court society he finds so oppressive. To make matters worse, he observes the growing intimacy between Prince Andrei and Natasha, and contrasting "his own position with that of his friend . . . intensified [his] gloomy mood still more" (474; II, 3, 22). The counterpoint rhythm between the diverging fates of the two friends intensifies and reaches a climax at the beginning of Volume Two, Part Five. Prince Andrei, already engaged to Natasha, is traveling in Europe, and Pierre, the unhappy "rich husband of an unfaithful wife, a retired gentleman-in-waiting" (536; II, 5, 1), remains buried in Moscow.

It is in this section of the novel that the reader begins to feel that Pierre's envy of Andrei's happiness runs deeper than first meets the eye. When Princess Marya presses Pierre for information about her future sister-in-law, Natasha, Pierre blushes "without himself knowing why," and responds: "'I simply cannot analyze her. She's enchanting. But why, I don't know: that's all one can say about her'" (548; II, 5, 4). These words, stemming as they do from instinct rather than analysis, and delivered with an involuntary blush, speak volumes. What they say becomes clearer later in Part V, when we learn that "Pierre had been avoiding Natasha. It seemed to him that he had a stronger feeling for her than a married man ought to have for his friend's fiancée. Yet some sort of fate constantly brought them together" (589; II, 5, 19).

The "fate" that now throws them together is the note Pierre receives from the Rostov family friend and Moscow society matron Marya Dmitrievna, requesting him "to come to her on a very important matter concerning Andrei Bolkonsky and his fiancee" (589; II, 5, 19). The matter is Anatole Kuragin's recent attempted abduction of Natasha, and her sudden decision to break off her engagement with Andrei. On his way to the Rostovs, Pierre runs into Anatole, his brother-in-law, dressed, appropriately, in the dashing accouterments of a lady-killer. Pierre, who does not yet know that Anatole has just attempted to abduct Natasha, thinks "with envy" to himself: "'Yes, indeed, there's a true wise man! He doesn't see anything beyond the present moment of pleasure, nothing troubles him—and therefore he's always cheerful, content, and calm. I'd give anything to be like him!'" (590; II, 5, 19).

The narrator ingeniously has Pierre think these words just as he is on his way to protect Natasha's honor from the "wise man" he so admires. The implication is clear: Pierre, not Kuragin, is the true "wise man" in this moment—and in the novel. By acting out of his instinctive concern for another human being rather than out of calculating self-regard, as does Anatole, Pierre lives in harmony with life's larger design and the higher Tolstoyan truth in the novel. This will be borne out shortly, when Pierre consoles Natasha in her sadness and shame, and glimpses the truth that the reader has sensed all along—that he is in love.

The revelation disorients Pierre at first. When he leaves the Rostovs and his coachman asks him where he would like to go, the bewildered

Pierre can only respond: "'Where to? Where can I go now? Not to the club or to pay visits.' All people seemed so pitiful, so poor in comparison with the feeling of tenderness and love he experienced, in comparison with that softened, grateful glance she had given him at the last moment through her tears" (600; II, 5, 22).

Suddenly, the darkness and confusion that have been weighing on Pierre for months are replaced by illumination, which is embodied, significantly, in the same lofty sky that Prince Andrei glimpsed while lying on the battlefield at Austerlitz. Just as Andrei experienced an epiphany then, so Pierre is reborn now, but with important differences. The lofty sky "with gray clouds slowly creeping across it" showed Andrei that "everything is empty, everything is deception" on earth (281; I, 3, 16). What the sky reveals to Pierre is the presence of the sublime in the mundane. A moment earlier, when "[a]ll people seemed so pitiful" in comparison with his heightened feelings, he mentally separated the heavenly from the human, the ideal from the real, but now, when he looks at the sky, he unites these opposite realms in his consciousness: "Only looking at the sky did Pierre *not* feel the insulting baseness of everything earthly compared with the height his soul had risen to" [emphasis mine] (600; II, 5, 22).

Whereas Andrei perceives in the sky portents of the grey quiet of eternity, Pierre sees the bright beauty of life, embodied in the scintillating stars and the brilliant comet of 1812, which "answered fully to what was in his softened and encouraged soul, now blossoming into new life" (600; II, 5, 22). Out of the ruins of old perceptions, new energies begin to stir inside Pierre. At the same time, Andrei begins his final fatal trajectory in the novel, culminating in his passivity before the bursting shell at Borodino and his eventual death. The indifferent sky of Austerlitz hovers over Andrei like a grey cloud of fate, while Pierre's starry firmament illumines his path towards new discoveries and transformations.

1812 AND THE "HITCHING UP" OF THE WORLD

Significantly, this watershed moment in Pierre's life occurs in 1812, the year in which Napoleon crosses the Niemen and enters Russia. This coincidence reinforces the impression, created throughout the novel, that Pierre's personal trajectory parallels larger historical processes. Indeed, at the very moment that Pierre experiences the soul-expanding frisson of love, all of Russia is absorbing the shock of Napoleon's invasion. And, in the same way that Russia unifies in a time of national crisis, Pierre's own consciousness begins to gain new clarity and coherence: "That terrible question—'Why? What for?'—which used to present itself to him amidst every occupation, was now replaced for him not by another question and not by the answer to an old question, but by *her* image" (664; III, 1, 19).

"Her" image refers literally to Natasha, but it suggests Russia, as well. Pierre's love for Natasha is integrally, if subconsciously, linked with his love for Russia. That dual love now becomes the muse that will carry him forward and inspire him to acts of personal heroism, which he exhibited only in rare instances earlier in the novel. At the end of Volume Three, Part One, the Moscow noblemen, including Pierre, "astonished at what they had done" at the Sloboda Palace assembly, in the presence of the Emperor promised both their property and their lives to the war effort. "Pierre had no other feelings at that moment except the desire to show that it was all nothing to him, and he was ready to sacrifice everything" (681; III, 1, 23). He promises a thousand of his serfs to the war effort. In the pulsating atmosphere of 1812, formerly muted emotions rise to the surface, and once distant possibilities become real presences.

In his roused state Pierre soon will abandon his life in Moscow altogether. He is consumed by the instinctive feeling that something profound and transformative is taking place: "The worse the state of any affairs, and especially his own, the more pleasant it was for Pierre, the more obvious it was that the catastrophe he expected was approaching" (750; III, 2, 18). War, that destructive-creative force which moves history in the novel, moves Pierre to new emotional heights:

> He now experienced a pleasant sense of awareness that everything that constitutes people's happiness, the comforts of life, wealth, even life itself, is nonsense, which it is pleasant to throw away, in comparison with something . . . With what, Pierre could not account for to himself, nor did he try to clarify to himself for whom and for what he found it so particularly delightful to sacrifice everything. He was not concerned with what he wanted to sacrifice it for, but the sacrificing itself constituted a new, joyful feeling for him. (753; III, 2, 18)

As Pierre's life becomes increasingly intertwined with forces of war, a radical reordering of values takes place inside him. What once appeared significant now seems trivial, and the uncertainty that once caused him angst now delights and intoxicates him. In the feverish atmosphere of 1812, Pierre's capacity for intoxication—formerly a liability in the calculating world of society—is one of his greatest assets. In his roused state

Pierre later will make a spontaneous, "irrational" decision to protect an Armenian woman from a French soldier. That event will lead to his arrest and captivity, where, at last, he will discover the answer to his nagging existential question: *Zachem?* What for?

But first he will go to the front in his white summer hat, wide-eyed, like a boy ready to play at war. When seen through Pierre's innocent eyes, the Battle of Borodino and its aftermath embody the transcendent energies coursing through the universe of the novel. Just as Prince Andrei earlier surveyed the battlefield at Schöngrabern, Pierre ascends the barrow at Gorky in the hopes of seeing the whole battlefield. However: "Everywhere there were fields, clearings, troops, woods, smoking campfires, villages, barrows, streams, but not the battlefield he had expected to see; and much as he tried to make it out, on this living terrain he could not find a position and could not even distinguish our troops from the enemy's" (761; III, 2, 21). How different this is from Prince Andrei's earlier surveying of the field at Schöngrabern, where he falsely believed that he could foresee the various positions and contingencies of the upcoming battle. Just as Pierre strives in vain to grasp life's ultimate purpose throughout much of the novel, so here he has difficulty seeing the battlefield as a unified whole.[14]

When the battle begins, however, the disconnected details are suddenly transformed into a glorious panorama of bright colors and mass movements:

> Going up the steps to the barrow, Pierre looked ahead of him and froze in delight at the beauty of the spectacle. It was the same panorama he had admired from the barrow the day before; but now the whole terrain was covered with troops and the smoke of gunfire, and the slanting rays of the bright sun, rising behind and to the left of Pierre, cast over it, in the clear morning air, a piercing light of a pink and golden hue, and long, dark shadows . . . It was lively, majestic, and unexpected . . . (789; III, 2, 30)

When Pierre ascended the Gorky barrow for the first time, he expected to see the battlefield as he imagined it should appear. Now the dynamic beauty of that battlefield strikes him in all of its "unexpected" vividness and majesty. Recalling the most intoxicating moments in Pierre's life—his seduction by Hélène and his sudden social popularity, his encounter with the Freemason Bazdeev at Torzhok, his inspired promise of a thousand serfs to the war effort during the Sloboda Palace assembly, and his realization that he is in love with Natasha—we recognize that they were all "unexpected."

Pierre sees the majestic beauty of the battlefield and the grandeur of war when he is not looking for it. His presence at the front thus becomes a microcosm of his entire journey. He searches consciously for life's ultimate design, without realizing that his life is unfolding within it.

Like a child instinctively drawn to the flames of his first fire, "Pierre wanted to be there where those puffs of smoke, those gleaming bayonets and cannons, those movements, those sounds were" (790; III, 2, 30). Though "[h]e did not hear the sounds of the bullets whining on all sides, and of the shells that flew over his head, did not see the enemy on the other side of the river, and for a long time did not see the dead and wounded, though many fell not far from him," Pierre is, in his own way, wholly absorbed in his surroundings (791; III, 2, 31). He misses much, yet "with a smile that never left his face" (791; III, 2, 31), he internalizes the expansive energy of the moment. In the same way that his realization of his love for Natasha lifted him to new emotional heights, so now the invigorating shock of war plunges him into an acute awareness of the sheer joy of being.

But his exhilaration will soon be mixed with horror, as the whole reality of war—its poetry and its ugliness—dawns on him. "'No, now they'll stop it, now they'll be horrified at what they've done,'" Pierre thinks after seeing the wounded and the dead, some of whom he recognized (793; III, 2, 31). But they do not stop, and they are not horrified. The forces of violence continue, and Pierre is inescapably caught in the flow of events. But there, in the midst of the fray, he will have more revelations.

He ascends the so-called Raevski's Redoubt, but "precisely because he was there" he thinks it "one of the most insignificant places of the battle" (793; III, 2, 31). On the contrary, the narrator tells the reader, that location "was the most important place in the battle" (793; III, 2, 31). It is the place where tens of thousands fell, and which the French regarded as key to their position. More importantly for Pierre, Raevski's Redoubt is where he encounters death, not abstractly, but concretely, in the image of the young soldier doubled over "on the ground like a bird shot down in flight" (796; III, 2, 31). It is there, too, that Pierre has a skirmish with a French soldier, during which he realizes that, in the thick of battle, distinctions between victor and vanquished, "I" and "other," are artificial constructs. "'Am I taken prisoner or have I taken him prisoner?' each of them thought" (797; III, 2, 32). Pierre comprehends viscerally the creative chaos of war—the great, irrational force that both kills and unites human beings.

After the Battle of Borodino, Pierre leaves the front and returns to

Mozhaysk, where he had stayed before the battle. His overwhelming desire is "to get away as quickly as possible from those dreadful impressions in which he had lived that day," and to "return to the ordinary conditions of life. . . . But there were no ordinary conditions of life anywhere" (840; III, 3, 8). Napoleon is on the outskirts of Moscow and chaos is everywhere. As he falls asleep in a lodge at Mozhaysk, Pierre continues to hear the sounds of battle outside and dreams about the Russian soldiers he saw in battle: "*They*—these strange people, hitherto unknown to him—*they* were clearly and sharply separated in his mind from all other people. 'To be a soldier, just a soldier!' thought Pierre as he fell asleep, 'to enter the common life with my whole being, to be pervaded by what makes them that way'" (842; III, 3, 9).

What Pierre fails to grasp is that he already *has* entered communal life. He is integrally connected to the transformative events sweeping through Russia. In his dream he wonders at the soldiers' calmness and bravery, but at Raevski's Redoubt the soldiers wondered at his. "'How is it you're not afraid, master, really!'" a soldier asked Pierre, who "looked around with a smile" as he brushed off the dirt thrown up by a shell bursting near him. When Pierre answered, "it was as if they did not expect him to talk like everybody else and were glad of this discovery" (794; III, 2, 31). Pierre is as much an intriguing presence in their eyes as they are in his. Pierre and the soldiers share a curiosity, as well as similar projections and assumptions, about the other.

Another dimension of their commonality is the breakdown of class biases. Pierre, the future Decembrist, senses the unified social fabric and national spirit, which Tolstoy believed ultimately responsible for Russia's conquest of Napoleon in 1812. Pierre understands viscerally what Prince Andrei has explained to him the evening before the Battle of Borodino— that success in the battle, as in any battle, depends not on position, equipment, numbers, or on those in command, but rather on the collective, patriotic spirit of the people.

Americans experienced something similar in the aftermath of September 11. In the tense, heightened atmosphere of those days political grievances and social tensions gave way to a renewed sense of community and purpose. This shift in attitude was palpable and could be seen on people's softened faces, in the look of resolve in their eyes, in their gentler interaction with one another. Older Americans who had lived during World War II compared the patriotic atmosphere to the national spirit they felt during the war. This healthy collective resolve soon was replaced by an arrogant triumphalism, which was closer in spirit to the French patriotism depicted in *War and Peace,* and which counteracted the sense of possibility that temporarily had opened before us.

After he leaves Mozhaysk the first time, Pierre recalls the wounded soldiers he saw there and feels the connection between them and the working peasants he now sees. He grasps the collective Russian spirit and knows that he, too, is a part of it: "The sight of these bearded muzhiks working on the battlefield, with their strange, clumsy boots, with their sweaty necks, and some with their side-buttoned shirts open, revealing their sun-burned collarbones, impressed Pierre more strongly than anything he had seen or heard so far about the solemnity and significance of the present moment" (760; III, 2, 20). These thoughts are echoed in Pierre's dream about the soldiers when he is in Mozhaysk the second time, after the Battle of Borodino. In that dream his mind wanders among seemingly unrelated thoughts, and he tries to find their connection:

> "The most difficult thing" (Pierre went on thinking or hearing in his sleep) "consists in being able to unite the meaning of all things in his soul. To unite all things?" Pierre said to himself. "No, not to unite. It's impossible to unite thought, but to *hitch together* all these thoughts— that's what's needed! *Yes, we must hitch together, hitch together!*" Pierre repeated to himself with inner rapture, feeling that precisely these and only these words expressed what he wanted to express and resolved the whole question that tormented him.
>
> "Yes, we must hitch together, it's time to hitch together."
>
> "We must hitch up, it's time to hitch up, Your Excellency! Your Excellency!" some voice repeated, "we must hitch up, it's time to hitch up . . ."
>
> It was the voice of his groom, waking Pierre up. (843–44; III, 3, 9)

This moment goes to the heart of the transformation taking place inside Pierre. He intuitively grasps the Tolstoyan wisdom of "hitching up" the world, of bringing together people, facts, and phenomena without diminishing the individuality of any one of them. This is a very different concept from the one Pierre first evokes in his dream, when he hears the word "*soedinyat'*" (to unify), whose root, "*edin*" ("one"), suggests a homogenized oneness, a bringing together of things in which the individuality of each entity or phenomenon is made secondary to the "whole" and thereby diminished. This was the intellectual route taken by the philosophical searcher before 1812. But now, his yearning for an abstract unifying principle is displaced by a growing sense of the immense power inherent in bringing together the talents and energies of a diverse people at a crucial point in their history.

Pierre awakes and helps to prepare the horses, but the reader's attention lingers on the echo between the words he hears in his dream (*"we must hitch together"*) and those he hears from his valet in the waking world ("Time to hitch together"). We all have had this experience. We wake up from dreams of water, dams bursting, and so forth, only to realize we have to go the bathroom! This does not invalidate Pierre's inner vision. It merely shows that inner vision giving way to a waking reality. When he awakes, he sees "the dirty inn yard" with soldiers watering their horses. Pierre turns away from this reality "with revulsion" and tries to recreate the vision of his dream (844; III, 3, 9). But the vision is gone. Life has flowed on.

So, too, has Moscow changed upon Pierre's return. It has become what the narrator calls a "queenless beehive" (844; III, 3, 9). Tolstoy, who was intimately familiar with beekeeping, chooses the metaphor aptly. Just as the empty hive with dead and enfeebled bees scattered about is only a stage in the ongoing evolutionary process, so the evacuated city, in which "a few people still stirred meaninglessly," is only a temporary reality (875; III, 3, 20). The queen reproduces eggs elsewhere, and Russia, preparing for its regeneration, is in a state of quiet gestation. Ordinary consciousness sees deadness in the streets, but the more far-seeing narrator knows that new life is blossoming beneath the surface.

The same processes are taking place inside Pierre. While in Moscow he goes for the last time to the home of his benefactor, Osip Bazdeev, who has died. In Bazdeev's study Pierre finds temporary refuge from the whirlwind of the past two days. But the "gloomy" study, which Pierre "used to enter with such awe," is now "gloomier still" (869; III, 3, 18). The dark room gives him some moments of peace, but the inspiration he once received from Bazdeev's actual and symbolic presence has dissipated. The reader recalls Pierre's earlier visit to the large, gloomy house of his dying father. That house, too, had rooms that he entered with fear, or not at all. Yet as the novel reveals over and over again, the truth Pierre seeks will be found, not in the dark, mysterious rooms of a father's home, but on the brightly lit path that is uniquely his own.

Near the Sukharev water tower he is stopped by the Rostovs, who are departing Moscow. During their brief, awkward meeting, Natasha, who has not seen Pierre for months, asks, "But what's the matter with you, Count? You don't look yourself . . ." He responds, "Ah, don't ask me, don't ask me, I know nothing myself" (867; III, 3, 17). This seemingly perfunctory response suggests a deeper reality about Pierre's current situation. Like the spectacular metamorphosis in which a larva molts into a butterfly, he is growing a new identity. The processes of shedding are still underway, and the rebirth has not yet taken place. He feels only the exciting pull of new possibilities.

In his roused state Pierre is overtaken by the notion that he is destined to assassinate Napoleon and thereby put an end to the misery of Europe. On his way to save Russia, he instead saves the French soldier, Ramballe, who has been fired upon by Bazdeev's drunken, half-crazy brother. Pierre's heroic intention "had fallen into dust at the first contact with a human being" (909; III, 3, 29). He quickly befriends the cloyingly grateful Ramballe; they drink wine together, and chat, among other things, about love. The apparently random conversation sparks memories in Pierre of his last meeting with Natasha at the Sukharev water tower, and "now it seemed to him that that meeting had had something very significant and poetic about it" (912; III, 3, 29).

Suddenly, the poetry of love and simple connection with another human being overshadows thoughts of heroic triumph. At this moment Pierre sees the same starlit sky that he saw after his fateful meeting with Natasha nearly six months prior. And now its illumination is intermixed with that of the campfire. The poetry of life glows for Pierre once again, not through the haze of heroic conquest, as he had expected, but in the beauty of the here-and-now:

> Looking at the high, starry sky, at the crescent moon, at the comet, and at the glow, Pierre experienced a joyful tenderness. "See how good it is! What more does one need?!" he thought. And suddenly, remembering his intention, his head whirled, he felt sick, and had to lean on the fence so as not to fall. (913; III, 3, 29)

Under the animating influence of the Moscow fires and the general unrest, Pierre will make a final attempt to stoke once again his original intention to kill Napoleon. As he is on his way to do so, he is stopped again, this time by a woman who begs him to save her child from a burning building, and then by a shrieking Armenian woman being harassed by a French soldier. Once again, life takes over, and Pierre's final heroic intention dissolves when he is arrested on suspicion of arson and becomes a prisoner of war. But out of the ruins of his dream of heroism the greatest revelations of his life will arise. For in captivity he will discover true spiritual freedom, and in deprivation he will enjoy a new kind of plenitude.

"THERE IS NOTHING FRIGHTENING IN THE WORLD . . ."

In captivity Pierre finds his former strivings replaced by a focus on the cold in his body, the pain in his swollen feet, and the hunger in his stomach. Once spiritually homeless, Pierre is now literally homeless and nameless. "'I will not tell you who I am. I am your prisoner. Take me away,'" Pierre says in French to the soldier who arrests him in Moscow (931; III, 3, 24). From that moment on he will be referred to by the French as "he who does not divulge his name," a designation that also encapsulates the larger truth of his existence at this point in the novel (962, 963; IV, 1, 10).

Like Job stripped of his every possession, Pierre finds that his existence becomes, as it were, a dog's life. The metaphor is reinforced by the appearance of a little blue-grey dog who, like Pierre, is homeless and nameless. Also like Pierre, who eats horseflesh to stay alive, the dog feeds on the flesh of different animals—"from men to horses"—for sustenance (1061; IV, 3, 13). Formerly, in the artificial world of society, Pierre's carnal desires led him into the grip of Hélène and her entourage of social predators. Now that same animal instinct is what keeps him alive.

Yet Pierre is not an animal, but a human being with a need for existential meaning. Nowhere is that meaning more challenged than when he believes he has been sentenced to execution. The powerful life force that once lifted Pierre to great emotional heights now threatens to crush him. He wonders who has sentenced him to death: "It was the order of things, the turn of circumstances. Some order of things was killing him—Pierre—depriving him of life, of everything, annihilating him" (963; IV, 1, 10).

Pierre learns that he has been brought to the execution only as a witness. Still, the brief confrontation with the possibility of extinction is enough to destroy his every intellectual conceit about life, his every illusion about human power, and his faith in "the world's good order, in humanity's and his own soul, and in God" (968; IV, 1, 12). His world has crumbled, and he "felt that to return to faith in life was not in his power" (969; IV, 1, 12). In a sense, he is right—it is not in his power. All he can do is give himself over to that implacable life force that he now feels in all its raw immediacy. He stops fighting, planning, and searching, and submits to the will of the universe. And in that act of submission, the universe awakens inside him as never before.

After witnessing the execution, Pierre is placed in a "small, devastated, and befouled church" (968; IV, 1, 12). He sits silently in a dark corner on a heap of straw, opening and closing his eyes with almost catatonic regularity. He notices "the strong smell of sweat" emanating from a small man sitting beside him. He watches the "rounded, deft movements" of the man's arms removing leg bands, and the smooth, even movements of his hands cutting something (969; IV, 1, 12). The man sitting next to him is Platon Karataev, the wise old peasant who, the narrator later writes, would always remain for Pierre "the unfathomable, rounded, eternal embodiment of the spirit of simplicity and truth" (974; IV, 1, 13). But whatever symbolic meaning Karataev later will have, his soothing power for Pierre lies initially in the concrete, sensual details of his immediate presence.[15]

Karataev gives Pierre a potato—a symbol of the nurturing roundness of both Platon himself and the Russian earth—and it is the best food Pierre ever has eaten.[16] A simple act of physical nourishment becomes profound emotional nourishment. Thus, Pierre's final spiritual rebirth in the novel begins not with the hope of realizing a utopian ideal, nor in the rapture of love, nor under the intoxicating influence of battle or heroic fantasy, but rather in the simple fulfillment of his immediate bodily needs. Never before have the ordinary rhythms of moment-to-moment experience so enraptured Pierre. Never has he immersed himself so freely and unselfconsciously in the greatest pleasure of all—the joy of simply being alive.

How, then, are we to understand his seeming indifference to the death of his friend and mentor, Karataev, weeks later? This is one of the moments in the novel that perplexes and bothers readers. Exhausted and delirious, Pierre does not make the connection between the howl of the dog and the killing of Karataev only meters away. Instead, he falls into reverie, just as he did at Mozhaysk after the Battle of Borodino. Karataev briefly flits across his mind, but then Pierre sees in his dream another "meek old teacher," his boyhood geography teacher, who shows him a vibrating liquid globe. "'This is life,' said the old teacher. 'How simple and clear it is,' thought Pierre. 'How could I not have known before?'" (1065; IV, 3, 15).

The geography teacher in Pierre's dream further develops the lesson of the vibrating globe:

> "In the center is God, and each drop strives to expand in order to reflect Him in the greatest measure. It grows, merges, and shrinks, and is obliterated on the surface, goes into the depths, and again floats up. Here he is, Karataev, see, he spread and vanished. Have you understood, my child?" said the teacher.
>
> "Have you understood, damn it?" shouted the voice, and Pierre woke up. (1065; IV, 3, 15)

The dream of the globe appears at first to be an irrelevant diversion from what should be most important to Pierre in this moment—Karataev's death. But upon further consideration we realize that there could hardly be a better tribute to Karataev's memory than Pierre's nonreaction to his execution. For what does Karataev represent, if not the futility of worldly striving and the necessity of total submission to the will of the world? Pierre's nonreaction reveals that he indeed has internalized Karataev's wisdom.

Moreover, Pierre has not forgotten about Karataev. The peasant has become etched indelibly in his subconscious. He is one of the globe's drops, which spread out and disappear and eventually reemerge. And so Karataev will reemerge, for months and years afterwards, as the leitmotif of Pierre's calmer, wiser life. Though Pierre does not react to Karataev's actual execution, he half-consciously knows that his mentor has died. In his dreamlike state Pierre therefore knows more than ordinary consciousness can provide him. He knows the *whole* truth about Karataev's death. He intuitively knows that Karataev, although physically gone, will continue to be a presence in his world.

This holistic sort of knowledge is mirrored artistically by the text, when the shouting voice that wakes Pierre up with "'Have you understood . . . ?'" echoes the teacher's voice in the dream. Just as when he dreams about "hitching up" at Mozhaysk, here, too, his inner world and external realities merge. In his state of delirium, Pierre is able to tap into a higher truth inherent in his subconscious associations. Ordinary perception is transformed into extraordinary awareness, and for a moment Pierre's insight into the world becomes as transcendent and all-encompassing as that of the narrator.

Pierre awakes from his dream, and "[s]uddenly, simultaneously" images come to him. He is on the verge of putting them together and realizing consciously that Karataev has been killed, when he falls to dreaming once again, "still not connecting the memories of that day and not drawing any conclusions about them" (1065; IV, 3, 15). Now he sees a summer evening he had spent with a beautiful Polish lady on the veranda of his house in Kiev.

The globe reappears in connection with that vision and the memories of bathing, and he imagines that he sinks into the water, which closes over his head. Pierre having metaphorically given himself up to the world, the world, in turn, embraces, soothes, and cleanses him. When Natasha meets Pierre again after he has returned to Moscow, she remarks to Princess Marya: "'He's become somehow clean, smooth, fresh—as if from the bathhouse, you understand? Morally from the bathhouse. Hasn't he?'" (1118; IV, 4, 17).

The bath in which Pierre has been cleansed is the bath of suffering, life at its rawest, most immediate, and real. Paradoxically, when he is most fully immersed in reality, Pierre finally transcends it. Only when he stops searching for truth does he discover it. In captivity Pierre realizes "not with his mind but with his whole being, his life," that there is a purposeful order to the universe, and that, as he himself now understands, "there is nothing frightening in the world" (1060; IV, 3, 12). Tolstoy believed that there is a benevolent order to the universe, and that every human being has the capacity to feel it and is instinctively attracted to it.

Readers will look in vain for manifestations of evil in *War and Peace*, in the same way they find evil in the literary worlds of Lermontov and Dostoevsky, in Dante and Milton. The moment in which the Governor of Moscow, Count Rostopchin, orders the execution of the prisoner Vereshchagin, in order to placate the seething mob, is sometimes cited as proof that Tolstoy did, in fact, see evil in the world. But this scene shows something quite different. Rostopchin acts not out of an "evil" impulse but out of desperate attempt to guide the ship of state in the "historical sea," to reclaim control over the uncontrollable: "'See what they've done to Russia! See what they've done to me!' Rostopchin thought, feeling an irrepressible wrath rising in his soul against someone to whom he could ascribe the cause of all that was happening" (887; III, 3, 25). That "someone" will be Vereshchagin. Violence begets violence and the mob nature takes over: "The crime had begun, it was necessary to go through with it" (890; III, 3, 25). Rostopchin's after-the-fact rationalization to himself that he ordered Vereshchagin's death in the name of "*le bien public*" ["the public good"] is an example of the "mind's game of chess" being played. In actuality, Tolstoy shows that Rostopchin is a coward and a show-off, who plays to the mob, and that he was driven ultimately by a survival instinct and by circumstances beyond his control—he has drowned in the sea of history. But Pierre has learned to thrive in it. The world of *War and Peace* is filled with cruelty and suffering, but these are counterbalanced by human grace and goodness. And they are always subsumed into the holistic, life-affirming worldview held by the narrator that has now become part of Pierre himself.

How appropriate, then, that, upon his return to Moscow, Pierre rediscovers his love for Natasha. Like every other revelation, this one, too, comes unexpectedly. At first Pierre does not recognize Natasha when he meets her at Princess Marya's house. Not the spirited girl he once knew, she is to him nothing more than Marya's companion in a black dress "who would not hinder his heart-to-heart talk with Princess Marya" (1112; IV, 4, 15). When he realizes who is before him, he is suddenly transformed. That moment, one of the most beautiful in the novel, is worth quoting in full:

> "But no, it can't be," he thought. "This stern, thin, pale, aged face? It can't be her. It's only a reminiscence of that one." But just then Princess Marya said: "Natasha." And the face, with its attentive eyes, with difficulty, with effort, like a rusty door opening—smiled, and from that open door there suddenly breathed and poured out upon Pierre that long-forgotten happiness of which, especially now, he was not even thinking. It breathed out, enveloped, and swallowed him whole. When she smiled, there could no longer be any doubt—it was Natasha, and he loved her.
>
> In that first moment, Pierre involuntarily told her, and Princess Marya, and above all himself, a secret he himself was unaware of. He blushed joyfully and painfully. He wanted to conceal his excitement. But the more he wanted to conceal it, the more clearly—more clearly than the most definite words—he said to himself, and to her, and to Princess Marya, that he loved her. (1112; IV, 4, 15)

That all-powerful life force, which Tolstoy felt so acutely in all of its destructive and creative beauty, has whirled through Pierre's life, carrying him inexorably through the crucible of error and discovery, and now has led him back to Natasha. Ever since their encounter at the beginning of 1812, Pierre's love for Natasha has remained constant through all the twists and turns of his journey. Similar to the drops on the vibrating, liquid globe, his love for her has grown, subsided, at times lain dormant, and again reemerged, like everything else that is authentic and alive in Tolstoy's world. Pierre's marriage to Natasha in the novel's epilogue will mark his return to the quotidian realities and ordinary rhythms of everyday life. It also will bring full circle the "labyrinth of linkages" that unites his destiny with those of the other searching characters in the novel, and with the fate of Russia herself.

eight

*F*ROM GENERATION TO GENERATION

"What is *War and Peace*? It is not a novel, even less is it a poem, and still less an historical chronicle. *War and Peace* is what the author wished and was able to express in the form in which it is expressed."[1] So claimed Tolstoy in a separate article about the novel, published in 1868, in response to critics who were baffled by the work's formal oddities. The addition of a two-part epilogue to the already expansive literary landscape did little to lessen readers' bewilderment. Well might they ask why Tolstoy needed the epilogue and what it could possibly add to the book. What more could the author wish to convey? As we shall see, the epilogue, in which three generations of Rostovs and two generations of Bolkonskys live together in the self-contained country world at Bald Hills, rounds out Tolstoy's vision of harmony and continuity, both ending his novel and leaving it open-ended.

The epilogue is divided into two parts. The first is a continuation of the stories of the characters' lives, while the second is a complex treatise about free will and determinism. The treatise has the gravitas of a philosophical tome, yet it unintentionally raises more questions than it answers. The first part of the epilogue, on the other hand, intentionally refuses to tie up loose ends. Its openness stems from the passion of the literary visionary who wrote that an artist's goal "is not to solve a question irrefutably, but to force people to love life in all its innumerable, inexhaustible manifestations."[2] In the first part of the epilogue, the grand "labyrinth of linkages" that is *War and Peace* remains visible and continues to grow before our eyes. Only by examining it can we see the "roundness" of the novel's conception.

The narrator shows us life's inexhaustible fullness by inviting us to reflect calmly on the long journey we have taken. In roughly sixty pages, Tolstoy covers seven years (from 1813 to 1820), which is the same time span depicted in the novel's first thousand pages (from 1805 to 1812). Time accelerates. The narrator's brushstrokes become broad and generalizing. The moment-by-moment unfolding of experience stands out in bold relief against the relentless passage of time from year to year, generation to generation.

The peace with which the novel began has returned. Yet something seems to be missing in this post-Napoleonic world. Gone is the narrator's loving, sensual description of how Count Rostov's plump, nimble body twisted and twirled on the dance floor while Natasha pulled at the spectators' sleeves, urging them to "look at papa!" The narrator gives us only a brief sentence describing how Nikolai, in the absence of his wife, "allowed himself to give his daughter a gallop around the room" (1153; Epilogue, 1, 19). He quickly becomes out of breath, removes little Natasha from his shoulders, presses her to his heart, and thinks about how one day he will dance the "Daniel Cooper" with her just as his father used to do with *his* daughter Natasha. What strikes the reader is not the exhilaration of the dancing itself, but Nikolai's poignant reflections about it, not the beauty of the timeless moment, but the bittersweet recognition of the movement of time.

What the narrator says of Moscow after the war is true of the whole world of the novel: "everything has been destroyed, except for something indestructible, immaterial" (1108; IV, 4, 13). That "something" is the life force, which continually renews itself. The seething forces of history have risen up, uprooted characters' peaceful existences, and then subsided, as if in accordance with the harmonic ebb and flow of nature. So, too, there is in the characters' respective fates a poetic justice, a "harmony" of life, which, Tolstoy wrote in his diary, "only art feels": "So-called self-sacrifice and virtue are only the satisfaction of one morbidly developed propensity. The ideal is harmony. Only art feels this. And only that is real which takes as its motto: there are no guilty people in the world. He who is happy is right! The self-sacrificing person is more blind and cruel than the others."[3] These words reaffirm the holistic vision of life at the heart of the novel, and they also reveal Tolstoy's admiration of the value of healthy egotism: healthy because it is vital, spontaneous, and life-producing, not calculating and smug, as in the case of such characters as Boris Drubetskoi, Dolokhov, and the Kuragins.[4] (The latter family's name, significantly, echoes the Russian word "*kuraga*," or "dried apricots.")

"'I'm not to blame that I'm alive and want to live; and you do, too,'" Pierre says to Natasha when they meet after the war (1118; IV, 4, 17). That kind of life-affirming selfishness bears fruit in the novel. Pierre and Natasha, Nikolai and Marya, survive the traumatic events of 1812 and create families.[5] Boris Drubetskoi does not appear again. There is no further mention of Anatole in the novel after his leg is amputated, and his sister, Hélène, dies during childbirth. Their father, Vasily, now old and pathetic, fills his emptiness with a new post and fresh decorations. While there are "no guilty people in the world," there are, for Tolstoy, people who live "correctly" and those who don't. The surviving couples are endowed with the gift of living well, because they are intuitively in harmony with life's vital forces and higher truth, with what Arthur Schopenhauer, one of Tolstoy's favorite philosophers, called the "will" of the world.[6]

However, as the characters discover time and again, the world wills both joy and suffering. In *War and Peace* the two are inseparably linked. One flows continuously into the other. Natasha has to learn what it is to fall from innocence and to suffer before she can discover a new kind of happiness in the duty-bound roles of mother and wife. Each of her various romances before Pierre are the temptations she must pass through (Boris, the future careerist; Andrei, the disillusioned idealist; Anatole, the debauched), until she finds her destiny as the wife of a new, enlightened Pierre, who also has passed through the crucible of experience. On one level, the whole novel is the labyrinth through which they find each other, and Prince Andrei's death becomes a central event leading to the possibility of their union.

Andrei's death is also a shared loss for Natasha and Marya, who grow closer because of it. Their increasing intimacy permits each to recognize the other's unique gifts—something they were unable to do when they first met and disliked each other in Moscow years earlier. Ironically, Marya will be the one who brings her former antagonist together with her brother's best friend. Though Marya can't fully forgive Natasha's joy so soon after the death of Andrei, she instinctively wants Natasha to be happy in marriage, just as she wants happiness for herself. Once she and Nikolai Rostov confess their love, the family happiness that had eluded Princess Marya for most of her life becomes hers, and her gift to others. "'Never, never would I have believed that one could be so happy,'" she whispers to herself in the presence of her husband and daughter, significantly named Natasha (1153; Epilogue, 1, 9). But even as a smile lights up her face, she sighs with the realization "that there was another happiness, unattainable in this life" (1153; Epilogue, 1, 9). Her devout religious nature endures, even though it is overwhelmed by the stronger pull of family happiness.

In the same way that Prince Andrei's death leads to the creation of new relationships and family unions, so Petya Rostov's death is part of a larger, life-affirming design, as well. The young man's tragic death is counterbalanced by the survival and spiritual rebirth of his namesake, Pierre. Their two fates play off one another like point and counterpoint, when Pierre is rescued by the very same Russian soldiers with whom Petya is fighting when he is fatally shot. There are other counterpoint rhythms in this moment of the novel, as well. The caravan of Russian prisoners in French captivity suddenly is transformed into a procession of French soldiers now under Russian control. The mass eastward movement of troops now becomes a mass movement westward. And the formerly demoted Dolokhov, now renowned for his bravery, is in charge of directing the cavalcade of French prisoners. This triumphant Dolokhov, with his "cold glassy gaze, which promised nothing good" (1066; IV, 3, 15), marching behind the Cossacks carrying Petya's body, is the same man whose "light, cold gaze" (336; II, 1, 13) fell upon Petya's brother, Nikolai, during the poker game in which he attempted to destroy Nikolai financially, as revenge for having been refused by Nikolai's cousin, Sonya. Dolokhov's essential ruthlessness has found its proper arena in battle, transforming him from scoundrel to war hero.

The Rostovs are devastated by Petya's loss, but their innate resilience allows them to transform their pain into something positive and productive. "[T]he same wound that half killed the countess, this new wound called Natasha to life" (1080; IV, 4, 3). The emotional and financial blows that strike the old Count Rostov are absorbed by his son, Nikolai, who successfully dedicates his efforts to restoring the family name and ensuring the future security of his children. The expansive Pierre, spiritually reborn in captivity, will rediscover Natasha and unite his life with hers. Dolokhov, who is never mentioned again in the novel, presumably will continue to be a force for destruction and cruelty in the world, as he always has been. Life and death, goodness and cruelty, creation and destruction: these are the undercurrents of Tolstoy's world, forever intermingling in his changing landscape.

If Borodino was the embodiment of the forces of war, at once destructive and creative, then the Bald Hills of the epilogue is the peacetime expression of life's ultimate wholeness. Modeled on Tolstoy's own family estate at Yasnaya Polyana, it is described as a kind of ideal Russian community:

> As in every real family, several totally different worlds lived together in the house at Bald Hills, each maintaining its own particularity and yielding to the others, but merging into one harmonious whole. Every event that occurred in the house was equally—joyfully or sadly—important for all these worlds; but each world had its own reasons, independent of the others, for rejoicing or lamenting over whatever the event might be. (1160; Epilogue, 1, 12)

This description recalls the image of the vibrating liquid globe, which Pierre sees in his dream while in French captivity. Each drop is distinct, and at the same time continually interacting with and merging with every other drop, while the overarching wholeness of the globe remains. The world at Bald Hills is a microcosm of the world of the novel, in which the teeming diversity of life coexists with a higher unifying principle. For beyond the ongoing biological processes of life (the birth of new children, the creation of new families, the death of the older generation),[7] there is also a coming together of distinct essences. Rostovian earthiness and Bolkonskian spirituality unite in the marriage of Nikolai and Marya. Prince Andrei's intense drive and Pierre's spiritual expansiveness merge in fourteen-year-old Nikolenka Andreevich, Andrei's son, who is being raised by Nikolai and Marya. The merging of these heritages in the figure of this engaging adolescent endows him with a pivotal significance in the novel's overall design.

For the young Nikolenka Andreevich, this joining of essences is far from a perfect union. Whose progeny is he? Given the epilogue's overt exploration of the theme of family creation and generational cycles—issues that will be central to Tolstoy's next novel, *Anna Karenina*—this is a crucial question. While stopping short of a definitive answer, the epilogue offers clues. Biologically, Nikolenka Andreevich is the offspring of Prince Andrei and the little Princess Lise, who died delivering him. Psychologically and spiritually, though, his parents are Prince Andrei and Pierre. They will be his dominant shaping influences, not Princess Marya and Nikolai, who are already emotionally absent. "'I'm afraid I forget about him because of my own,'" Marya laments to her husband. "'We all have children, we all have relations; but he has nobody. He's eternally alone with his thoughts'" (1173; Epilogue, 1, 15). Nikolenka's fragile family connections, as well as the size of the emotional void he must fill, suggest that his journey will be as tumultuous as Pierre's and Andrei's.

And he will begin to fill it with the stories Uncle Pierre tells him about his own and his father's involvement in the Napoleonic wars. Pierre, whom Nikolenka calls "a hero and a sacred figure" (1161; Epilogue, 1, 12), and Prince Andrei, who "appeared to him as a deity, whom it was impossible to imagine and of whom he did not think otherwise than with a thrill in his heart and tears of sadness and rapture" (1161; Epilogue, 1, 12), merge in his imagination. They become central characters in the heroic mythology that will live and grow inside of Nikolenka. That mythology will awaken in him spiritual rather than military aspirations. He "did not want to be a hussar or a chevalier of St. George like Uncle Nikolai; he wanted to be learned and intelligent and kind, like Pierre" (1161; Epilogue, 1, 12).

The epilogue concludes with Nikolenka Andreevich awakening from a dream—a moment that is both deeply private and also a microcosm of the entire world of the novel. Here external and internal reality, ordinary experience and extraordinary youthful conceit, merge into a prophetic whole. Nikolenka dreams that he and Uncle Pierre are leading a large army of soldiers, helmeted like those in the writings of Plutarch, whom Nikolenka has been reading. The army in the dream is made up of the "slanting white lines that filled the air like the spiderwebs that fly about in the fall and that Dessalles [the boy's tutor] called *les fils de la Vierge* [the thread of the Virgin]. Ahead was glory, just the same as these threads, only slightly denser" (1177–78; Epilogue, 1, 16). The army is stopped by Nikolai Rostov, who says that he has orders from Arakcheev (a ruthless general and conservative statesman serving under Alexander I) to execute them if they continue to march. When young Nikolenka turns to look at Pierre, he sees his father, Prince Andrei, comforting and pitying him. But when Nikolai Rostov moves closer, young Nikolenka awakens in terror.

The dream is an allegory of Nikolenka's future as the orphan with uncertain family connections and unclear purpose, who is spiritually close to the forces of rebellion (Pierre), threatened by the forces of reaction (Nikolai Rostov and Arakcheev), and both inspired and calmed by the hazy heroic image of his father (Prince Andrei).[8] Yet through his troubled journey he will remain protected by the privileged cocoon of his aristocratic upbringing (Dessalles) and enveloped by nature's beauty (the autumnal light that spreads like spiderwebs). But how solid will that cocoon actually be? An army consisting only of metaphorical spiderwebs cannot protect him forever. Moreover, the dream implies that the future glory towards which he is marching will also be flimsy—only slightly denser than the spiderwebs. The "thread of the Virgin," while beautiful in its delicate innocence, will never be as solid as the vibrant, secure aristocratic world in which Nikolenka's elders grew up.

The forces of reaction and rebellion, represented by Nikolai Rostov and Pierre, do battle in the dream, just as they did in Russian society in those days. Young Nikolenka's large, receptive consciousness internalizes that conflict and becomes the crucible through which it will be played out. He will be nineteen in 1825, when the future Decembrists will take to Senate Square in Petersburg, demanding a constitutional government. Will Nikolenka join them? While this is beyond the scope of the novel, Tolstoy's original conception of the work as the story of a Decembrist returning from exile leads us to wonder about this. The fire of rebellion, fueled by the same ambition to win the love and admiration of men that motivated his father, already burns inside the fourteen-year-old: "'I know they want me to study. And I will study. But some day I'll stop. And then I'll do it. I ask God for only one thing: that it's the same with me as with the men in Plutarch, and I'll do the same. I'll do better. Everybody will know me, love me, admire me'" (1178; Epilogue, 1, 16).[9]

"'And then I'll do it.'" The narrator leaves "it" intentionally unclear, just as the "glory" towards which Nikolenka and Pierre march in the dream is dense and murky. The author doesn't define "it," because "it" is bigger than any specific career or conquest. "It" is that elusive end pursued by all of Tolstoy's searching characters: the ultimate answer that is never ultimate, the final destination that is never final, the coveted blissful peace that is continually being disturbed by the forces of strife and war. "The historical sea did not, as formerly, direct its surges from one shore to another: it seethed in its depths," the narrator tells us near the beginning of the epilogue (1129; Epilogue, 1, 1). Indeed, still present is the sense of impending cataclysm, which could be felt in the novel's bristling opening monologue by the angry salon hostess Anna Pavlovna Scherer, as she railed against the ruthless Napoleon, who was then encroaching on all of Europe. The forces of rebellion still lurk beneath the surface, and now it appears that something unprecedented is brewing.

The intensity of public debate, though more muted in the epilogue's calm pastoral world of Bald Hills, is still palpable in the heated discussions between Nikolai Rostov and Pierre, who frequently travels to Petersburg, where he is active in antigovernment circles. The reader also senses the movement of those depths in the inner turmoil of young Nikolenka

Andreevich. The rumbling of the impending cataclysm that will take place in 1825 can be heard in his words, with which the novel ends. After awaking from his troubled dream, Nikolenka is asked, in French, by his tutor, Dessalles, "Are you unwell?"

> "*Non,*" replied Nikolenka, and he lay back on the pillow. "He's kind and good, I love him," he thought of Dessalles. "But Uncle Pierre! Oh, what a wonderful man! And father? Father! Father! Yes, I'll do something that even *he* would be pleased with. . . ." (1178; Epilogue, 1, 16)

"*He*" participated in the great Battle of Borodino in 1812. "*His*" son might well be present during the Decembrist uprising of 1825. The next generation will witness the Alexandrine Reforms of the 1860s, the era in which Tolstoy wrote *War and Peace.* Another generation will experience the Russian Revolution of 1905, which led to the establishment of a constitutional regime. Yet another generation will bear witness to the Revolution of February 1917, which deposed the Tsar and established a democratic republic, only to be forcefully dismantled eight months later by the Bolsheviks, who arrogated all power to themselves and attempted to create a utopian state called the Soviet Union. Still another generation will watch as the Soviet regime is itself dismantled by the Gorbachev counterrevolution in the 1980s, while another will live through the resurgence of Tsarist-style authoritarianism under Putin. From revolution to revolution, rupture to rupture, the giant wheel of life spins on and on, always changing, always the same. The human spirit strives ceaselessly for something better.

While today's readers may resonate with Tolstoy's grand vision of the human historical trajectory, we also wonder whether it is too naïve for our postmodern sensibilities. Have we become too sophisticated or jaded to embrace this kind of idealism? Emerging from a tragic century of failed "isms," haven't we seen only too clearly how ideologies, once "implemented," not only fall short of salvation but often deliver the opposite of what they promised?

To many, utopian strivings are not merely the quaint relics of an innocent past worldview but a present danger. The critics of the failed Communist dream in Russia are justified in pointing out that its script was drafted by progressive thinkers in nineteenth-century Russia, who sincerely believed they were creating a kind of heaven on earth. As history revealed, they created a hell of earthly corruption and social inequality even worse than the tsarist autocracy they sought to replace. In his *Soviet*

Civilization: A Cultural History, Soviet writer Andrei Sinyavsky explains this paradox. For him the Soviet experience is a case study in the way in which ideals of universal goodness and perfect social justice, when applied to reality, necessarily end up leading to their exact opposite.[10] The reason, he argues, is that such idealism is often accompanied by ideological absolutism, enforced by a tyrannical ruling minority.

Following Sinyavsky's line of thinking, the best alternative would seem to be the kind of value-free secular pluralism that flourishes today among "enlightened" political thinkers, in many segments of the public at large, and in academic circles, where the very notion of literature as a reflection of man's deepest spiritual longings is all but dismissed as a relic of a bygone era in literary criticism. Yet the quest for ultimate meaning, which is at the very core of Tolstoy's art and thought, remains a burning human need. Modern man wants more than progress, prosperity, and pluralism. Man is also hungry for a higher purpose.

The upsurge of fundamentalism in many parts of the world is testimony to this. The recent explosion of religion in Russia and the former Soviet republics since the fall of the Soviet Union reveals the extent to which religious impulses, stifled by state-imposed atheism, had lain dormant all along. The strengthening of religious extremism in the Muslim world attests that secular solutions to modern-day problems do not satisfy large populations of people. In our own country, we need only look to the upsurge of Evangelicalism as a manifestation of the desire for an absolute faith that dictates the solution not only to spiritual needs but also to political ones.

For those of us who look to our great writers for the elucidation of life's meaning, Tolstoy offers a rare and necessary commodity: idealism without absolutism. The messianism of a Pat Robertson, an Ahmedinejad—or of Tolstoy's contemporary, Dostoevsky, who sincerely dreamed of a pan-Slavic Orthodox empire led by Russia—was alien to him. Yet he understood and sympathized with the basic human longing that inflames such utopian dreams. In *War and Peace* the author describes the spiritual quest of the major protagonists with relish and empathy, while never overlooking the potential dangers and limitations inherent in their idealistic strivings. *War and Peace* does not force readers to choose between ideals and reality, between their spiritual longings and their earthly existence. It offers an idealism that is neither dangerous nor simplistic, because it does not attempt to transform the world's complexity into a homogenous uniformity. The vision of the novel therefore provides an alternative to the political and religious ideological absolutism of our era without at the same time asking readers to accept a value-free secular pluralism. The novel stimulates readers to grapple actively alongside Tolstoy and his characters with their most fundamental questions. It encourages them to lay down their mental telescopes, as Pierre eventually does, and to apprehend the concrete beauty and infinite possibility all around them.

nine

$\mathcal{L}$EVIN

"To Err and to Dream"

If *War and Peace* is a grand, free-flowing celebration of the wholeness of the universe, *Anna Karenina* is more like a taut string ready to snap. It is a novel less about the world's infinite possibilities than about the difficult choices people must make in a society that has lost its moorings. Written and set in the decade following the Great Reforms of Alexander II, *Anna* portrays the cultural and spiritual splintering that was taking place at all levels of society. The novel's second sentence, "All was confusion in the Oblonsky's house" (1; I, 1), is a metaphor for the entire age.[1]

The traditional landed aristocracy to which Tolstoy belonged was losing its influence to an increasingly powerful radical intelligentsia that raised rational thought to the level of religion, made a mockery of moral absolutes, and preached the gospel of "progress at any cost." At the same time, Russia was making a transition to a capitalist economy, which resulted in the emergence of a new professional class—one that introduced Western materialism and individualism into a society formerly nourished, Tolstoy believed, on the ideals of community and compassion. Many would (and in Tolstoy's time did) object to such a characterization of a society based on autocracy and serfdom. Tolstoy himself was deeply bothered by the many injustices of these institutions. Yet he believed that there was a "natural," centuries-long bond between aristocrats and peasants that transcended politics altogether, one based on shared spiritual and cultural ideals.

Tolstoy watched in despair as the new system of values—or rather, lack of values—affected all aspects of contemporary life, including the one most sacred to him: family. In *Anna Karenina* he writes with urgency about the breakdown of the family ideal as both a catastrophe in its own right and as the embodiment of the larger processes of disintegration he saw all around him.[2] While the fashionable women's liberation movement was heating up and his close relatives and friends were getting divorced, Tolstoy became ever more vehement in his opposition to the modernizing, "progressive" trends of his time.[3] Tolstoy's glorified view of the past might remind some of the nostalgia felt today by Russians who long for the idyllic order of the Soviet Union. That is all the more reason to try to understand this very real human feeling explored throughout the novel.

Anna Karenina is Tolstoy's most confessional novel and the one that Russians discuss most heatedly today, because the issues it raises are precisely the ones confronting their society at the beginning of the twenty-first century. As they make yet another transition, this time from a deformed socialism to capitalism, Russians are asking themselves the same difficult questions Tolstoy poses in the novel: Is it possible for men and women to form truly loving bonds and for happy families to flourish in a world dominated by the values of Western-style individualism and economic competition? What is the place of faith and spirituality in a hyperrationalized, technological society? Can people of diverse backgrounds and perspectives in an increasingly fragmented world share a belief in any unifying ideal? Russians have returned to Tolstoy's masterpiece, and Americans are beginning to do the same, because the novel offers a gripping exploration of that perennial Russian—and human—question: *Kak zhit'?* How to live in the modern world?

Tolstoy began *Anna Karenina* as a novel about a fallen high-society woman. As he progressed, he added the Levin–Kitty plotline, which not only acted as a counterpoint to Anna's fateful affair with Vronsky but gradually came to overpower it as the philosophical center of the novel. By the time Tolstoy finished the work in 1877, Levin had replaced Anna as its central hero. Not only does he embody the writer's faith in the redemptive potential of marriage and family. He expresses Tolstoy's belief that constant striving towards an ideal, no matter how elusive, is the most fruitful response to the challenges of modern life.

The German poet Friedrich Schiller's phrase "Zu erren and zu traumen"—"To err and to dream"—was one of Tolstoy's favorites, and he quoted it often. It is the leitmotif of each of his searching characters, including the most autobiographical of all: Konstantin Levin. Readers wanting to learn about Tolstoy's spiritual journey in the 1870s need only follow Levin's trajectory through the pages of *Anna Karenina*. Tolstoy wrote few diary entries in those years. Instead, he poured his most private passions and silent sufferings into his hero.

Why, then, didn't he call the novel *Konstantin Levin*? Because Anna and her tragic story reflect the truth that broken families, ungrounded passions, and human isolation are central to the modern experience. It is against these realities that Levin, with his questing spirit and commitment to firm ideals, must fight. He belongs to a minority in his time—as he would in ours, which is why his story is vitally important today. Levin strives for meaning that neither the scientific worldview, nor the moral relativism, nor the pseudoreligiosity of his era can provide. Through Levin Tolstoy reveals an alternative truth that lies beyond the numbing habits and spiritual poverty of modern life. That truth never comes in the form of neatly packaged life lessons, of the sort we have come to expect today in self-help books and how-to guides to happiness. Levin's truth is more of an attitude than an answer, a way of living rather than a concrete set of solutions. Here is a complex portrait of one of Russian literature's great conscientious objectors. Like the Amish and other small communities in America today, both traditional and experimental, Levin resists an entire way of life that, in his view, fails to nourish man's highest moral and spiritual potential.

"Whatever Levin's shortcomings, there was no hint of sham in him," the narrator tells us (267; III, 9). In a society drenched in falsehood and self-deception, Levin still believes in Tolstoy's celebrated hero: Truth. Striving towards it comes at a cost, however, as Tolstoy's friend the philosopher and critic Nikolai Strakhov pointed out: "[Levin] is terribly solitary, and solitary in proportion to his sensitivity, genuineness, and sincerity, which do not allow any compromises and turn away from all falsehood. Thus the best of the people introduced in the novel is least of all capable of merging with the surrounding life."[4]

Strakhov's admiring response to Levin was exceptional at the time. Many of Tolstoy's more progressive contemporaries regarded him as a naïve, though amiable, country bumpkin.[5] Some saw in him only a stale recapitulation of the clumsy, questing Pierre of Tolstoy's earlier masterpiece, *War and Peace,* published nearly a decade earlier. "We have read it all before . . ." wrote one contemporary reviewer. "Here and there pages of *War and Peace* come to the surface; the figure of Levin becomes confused with that of Pierre Bezukhov."[6] But *had* they read it all before? The problem for Tolstoy was precisely that the world *had* changed, and that idealistic young noblemen with searching minds and hearts were growing extinct.

In contrast to *War and Peace,* in which there are multiple searching heroes, *Anna Karenina* has only one. Levin combines the moral intensity of Pierre Bezukhov with the traditional landowner's ethos of Nikolai Rostov. Nikolai is in his teens and Pierre is twenty when *War and Peace* begins. Levin is thirty-two at the beginning of *Anna.* Unlike the characters from the earlier novel, who are in a formative stage of self-discovery, Levin knows what he values—family, tradition, authenticity—and he fights to preserve them in a hostile environment.

LEVIN AND THE "HIGHER THING"

Through Levin, Tolstoy injects the expansive spirit of *War and Peace* into an age that had become cold and constrained. The thrill of youthful possibility in *War and Peace,* fueled in part by impending war, is no longer in the air. The main characters in *Anna Karenina* are older and married, the majority of them unhappily so. Their lives have become routinized, and in many cases comfortably numb. Dolly, the paragon of womanly virtue, lives a life of quiet desperation with her philandering husband, Stiva Oblonsky. In her selflessness and devotion to duty, Dolly resembles the long-suffering Princess Marya from the earlier novel. Yet Marya finds happiness in her union with Nikolai, which is consummated in fairy-tale-like circumstances amid the heightened energies of 1812. Dolly's life almost never reaches such poetic heights. She stays mired in the realm of the prosaic.

For critic Gary Saul Morson, in his recent book *"Anna Karenina" in Our Time: Seeing More Wisely,* this very immersion in the mundane makes Dolly the novel's real hero. "If by the hero of the work we mean not the character who occupies the dramatic foreground but the one who most closely embodies the author's values, then the hero of *Anna Karenina* is Dolly." This view trivializes and distorts Tolstoy's values. True, Dolly is "a good mother," and she "lives a life focused on the everyday and on that most ordinary of institutions, the family."[7] But the author encourages us to do more than pay "constant attention to the prosaic details of daily life," as Morson put it elsewhere.[8] Tolstoy also invites us to see the extraordinary in the ordinary, to open ourselves to life's wonder and godliness.

One of Dolly's most vital moments—the bathing of her children in Part Three—is moving, not because of how ordinary it is but precisely because of how remarkable it becomes. For a brief instant in her otherwise melancholy existence, the prosaic is suddenly transformed into the poetic: "To touch all those plump little legs, pulling stockings on them, to take in her arms and dip those naked little bodies and hear joyful or frightened shrieks; to see the breathless faces of those splashing little cherubs, with their wide, frightened and merry eyes, was a great pleasure for her" (265; III, 8).

In this instance Dolly feels a measure of what Levin does when he sees Kitty at the skating rink, mows with his peasants in the fields, and witnesses the death of his brother, Nikolai, and the birth of his son. These moments lift him out of the realm of the ordinary and into the sublime. Other characters have similar moments, but Levin experiences them more profoundly and more frequently than the others. They are his leitmotif, the essential subtext of his life. He has a gift, possessed by few others, of catching glimpses of eternity. Nowhere is this quality more beautifully evident than when he witnesses the birth of his child, a scene that made Tolstoy's close friend, the poet Afanasy Fet (1823–92), "jump up" and claim: "Nobody since the creation of the world had done that nor will anybody."[9] Here is a brief passage from that scene:

> [Levin] knew and felt only that what was being accomplished was similar to what had been accomplished a year ago in a hotel in a provincial capital, on the deathbed of his brother Nikolai. But that had been grief and this was joy. But that grief and this joy were equally outside all ordinary circumstances of life, were like holes in this ordinary life, through which something higher showed. And just as painful, as tormenting in its coming, was what was now being accomplished; and just as inconceivably, in contemplating this higher thing, the soul rose to such heights as it had never known before, where reason was no longer able to overtake it. (713; VII, 14)

Levin sees that "higher thing." He is one of "those few *real* people," about whom Tolstoy spoke in an 1876 letter to Fet, "who in this life look beyond its bounds . . . [and] always stand on its very verge and see life clearly just because they look now at Nirvana, the illimitable, the unknown, and now at Samsara [life on earth with its cares and contingencies], and that view of Nirvana strengthens their vision."[10] Tolstoy endows Levin with this gift of dual vision. While most other characters hide from life through stultifying habits and subtle forms of self-deception, Levin is both completely of the world, and standing "on its very verge," descrying its higher meaning. For all her admirable qualities as a wife and a mother, Dolly lacks this deeper Tolstoyan vision.

THE PURSUIT OF HAPPINESS: LEVIN AND OBLONSKY

Levin's singular nature stands out even more vividly when we compare him with the novel's other major male characters. Anna's husband, Karenin, and Levin's half-brother, Koznyshev, shrink from life by donning their straitjackets of rules and rationality. Vronsky, too, lives in a carefully constructed house of habits and regulations, only to have it come crashing down under the weight of his passion for Anna. At the other end of the spectrum, there is Stepan Oblonsky, affectionately called "Stiva" by his intimates, who prefers not to live for too long in any abode at all, even with his wife and children. Like his sister, Anna, Oblonsky is responsive to the emotional and the sensual—momentarily. Stiva is like a balloon, floating away from the earth amid dreams of dinner parties and dancing girls. In Tolstoy's wry formulation, Stiva is well-meaning, yet constitutionally incapable of commitment: "Hard as Stepan Arkadych tried to be a solicitous father and husband, he never could remember that he had a wife and children" (260; III, 7). His answer to the complexities of life is "to live for the needs of the day, in other words, become oblivious" (4; I, 2). This is different from the "oblivion" Levin feels during his transcendent moments, which have about them a quality of heightened awareness and intense spiritual connection with the surrounding world. Oblonsky's "oblivion" is less about self-transcendence than self-stupefaction.

Tolstoy uses the friendship between Oblonsky and Levin to compare their differing worldviews throughout the novel, much in the same way that he juxtaposes those of Prince Andrei and Pierre in *War and Peace*. Only now the author's emphasis is less on underlying philosophical harmony than on ineradicable difference. "To each of them [Levin and Oblonsky] it seemed that the life he led was the only real life, and the one his friend led was a mere illusion"[11] (17; I, 5). Both lives, of course, are real, but in the fictional universe of *Anna Karenina* Levin's is driven by a moral and spiritual quest and is therefore the fuller and wiser of the two.

For Oblonsky, to be fully alive means to satisfy personal desires, and often the most superficial, bodily ones at that. Levin, by contrast, is only too ready to give up his freedom as a bachelor, because he understands the Tolstoyan truth that happiness comes not from the fleeting pleasures of immediate personal gratification but from the lasting spiritual fulfillment that only deep human relationships, with all of their sorrows and joys, can provide. No choice is perfect, and no commitment is without its challenges, as the many unhappy marriages in the novel attest. But to conclude from this, as Oblonsky does, that every value or decision is as valid as every other, is to fall prey to the moral relativism that Tolstoy saw as one of the illnesses of his time—a form of inner laziness masquerading as a positive belief system.

"You have a wholesome (*tsel'nyj*) character, and you want all of life to be made up of wholesome phenomena, but that doesn't happen," Oblonsky chides Levin. "All the variety, all the charm, all the beauty of life are made up of light and shade" (42; I, 11). Of course, Oblonsky's observations are perceptive and realistic. The problem is that he uses them to justify his own self-indulgence. For him, enjoying life's "charm" and "beauty" frequently amounts to a refusal to believe in any absolute values. In our postmodernist era, such a philosophy might strike many as highly attractive. What could be more "enlightened" than accepting all value systems, and refusing to impose any absolute standards of right and wrong? Such moral relativism—or, as Oblonsky might prefer to call it, "openness" to the world—certainly serves *his* interests well. In the name of enjoying life's charming diversity, he can have his family and his French actresses, too. He can eat his oysters and enjoy the smell of sweet rolls after a filling meal, which he will pay for later, if he has the money. It is hardly surprising that "Oblonsky felt relieved and rested after talking with Levin, who always caused him too much mental and spiritual strain" (42; I, 11). Levin forces Oblonsky to do something he has little practice at—grappling with life's serious existential and moral challenges.

Yet most readers like Oblonsky. In fact, the novel's opening pages lure the reader into empathizing with the disgraced husband, who has just been caught cheating with the family governess. We are seduced by his innocent sincerity as well as the sensuality of his "full well-tended body," which doesn't want to awake from a pleasant, dreamlike sleep on the sofa. Even a clear-eyed social thinker of the caliber of Allan Bloom is enchanted by Oblonsky: "Oblonsky is one of the sweetest characters in all of Tolstoy. . . . He brings life and goodwill wherever he goes."[12]

But Oblonsky's charm is deceptive, and our attraction to his "sweetness" says more about our needs than about Tolstoy's values. This man who spreads goodwill everywhere sows seeds of pain and destruction in the lives of those closest to him. By the end of the novel, Stiva has become rather pathetic. Having brought financial ruin on his family, he now desperately manipulates his way into a job, any job. His lack of self-discipline and inability to commit himself deeply to anybody or anything has come back to haunt him. The floating balloon has been punctured and is rapidly descending.

While Oblonsky is superficially responsive to everything and everyone, Levin is both more passionate and more selective. And in contrast to the other idealists depicted in the novel—the materialists, pietists, positivists, proto-Communists, Slavophiles, nationalists, and spiritualists—Levin is driven not by a fashionable "-ism" or an abstract theory, but by a visceral need to live a life of meaning in the here-and-now. "I don't accept a life without love," Oblonsky tells Levin at one point (162; II, 14). But love as Oblonsky defines it—the gratification of personal desire—is meaningless to Levin. Only a higher form of love satisfies him: love as genuine spiritual connection, love as devotion to a community, a tradition, a set of ideals. For Levin, such love is the only real solution to the emptiness of modern life. And its fullest expression is to be found in what for him and for Tolstoy was the most ordinary *and* extraordinary institution of all: family.

DESPAIR AND DREAMS:
LEVIN IN LOVE

Tolstoy imparts his love of family to his hero and makes it the linchpin around which his life revolves. Levin's "notion of marriage was . . . not like the notion of the majority of his acquaintances, for whom it was one of the many general concerns of life; for Levin it was the chief concern of life, on which all happiness depended" (95; I, 27). More than an ideological position or a conservative's rejection of liberal values, Levin's attachment to the ideal of family reflects his hunger for a meaning to his existence that death cannot destroy.

The embodiment of that ideal is the house Levin has inherited from his parents. That house "was a whole world [*mir*] for Levin. It was the world [*mir*] in which father and mother had lived and died. They had lived a life which for Levin seemed the ideal of all perfection and which he dreamed of renewing with his wife, with his family" (95; I, 27). The twice-repeated word "mir," or "world," carries important philosophical and psychological associations. "Mir" also means "peace" in Russian—not only as the opposite of war, but also as a state of an internal, existential calm.[13] "Mir" also means "community" or "commune" and specifically refers to the peasant-village communes of old Russia that were disintegrating in

Figure 3   L. N. Tolstoy with his granddaughter, T. M. Sukhotina. Yasnaya Poly-
ana, 1909. Photo by V. G. Chertkov. Source: *Lev Tolstoy in Photographs by
Contemporaries* (Moscow: Publishing House of the USSR, 1960). Courtesy of
Tolstoy Studies Journal, online Tolstoy Image Gallery.

Tolstoy's postemancipation era. Levin's dream of preserving the bygone
way of life of his deceased parents is, at its core, a longing for connection,
for inner calm and clarity amid the confusion of modern life.

When we first meet him in Part One, Levin has come to Moscow from
his country estate at Pokrovskoe to propose to Kitty Shcherbatskaya.[14]
For years he has loved the Shcherbatsky family, "especially the female
side," which "seemed to him covered by some mysterious poetic veil,"
beneath which he suspected only "the loftiest feelings and every possible
perfection" (21; I, 6). As we watch him observing Kitty at the skating

rink with "the joy and fear that overwhelmed his heart," we almost blush right along with him, so infectiously sincere are his feelings. In a single sentence Tolstoy communicates all the pathos of his innocent love: "The place where she stood seemed to him unapproachably holy, and there was a moment when he almost went away—he was so filled with awe" (28; I, 9).

This and similar details give us a clue as to why Levin abruptly left Moscow in the past, without proposing: not because he was too proud, as Kitty's slightly cynical mother wrongly presumes, but because he was too much in love. No wonder Kitty's mother misreads Levin. In the "sophisticated" atmosphere of high society, Levin's almost childlike love for a woman is so unusual that it must appear strange, like his bashful blushing, which discomfits even Oblonsky. And that is just the point: Levin *is* strange. He is a man from a different universe, not only geographically, but emotionally and spiritually, as well.

When Kitty refuses him, mistakenly thinking that the more dashing Vronsky is about to propose to her, she shakes his entire foundation. From the perspective of contemporary American culture, where divorce rates are at 50 percent and three and four marriages not uncommon, Levin's reaction seems extreme. So it didn't work out; it's time to regroup and move on. Surely he'll be able to find another suitable match. In the world of this novel, such pragmatic thinking about romantic relationships is also the norm. High society is replete with marriages of convenience, empty marriages, and other varieties of unhappy marriage. The stultifying pleasures of soirées, malicious gossip, and casual adultery fill the emptiness. Had divorce been easier to obtain at the time, it would likely have become as popular a solution to marital dissatisfaction as it is in our day.

But Levin isn't blasé about love or practical about male–female relationships. He approaches them with a seriousness that betrays both his idealism and his inner depth. Significantly, Kitty's father, the wise old Prince Shcherbatsky, always a judge of sincerity and sometimes a mouthpiece for Tolstoy's own ideas, considers Levin "a thousand times better" than "this little fop from Petersburg," Vronsky, who attempts to seduce Kitty for sport[15] (55; I, 15).

After Kitty's refusal of him, Levin goes back to Pokrovskoe and settles into bachelor life in the country. Winter passes, spring arrives, and thoughts of Kitty continue to grow slowly inside him, like the spring, which "was a long time unfolding" (152; II, 12). Ironically, as thoughts of Kitty prick at Levin, Oblonsky arrives for an unplanned visit and sees only his friend's good fortune:

"No you're a lucky man. You have everything you love. You love horses—you have them; dogs—you have them; hunting—you have it; farming—you have it."

"Maybe it's because I rejoice over what I have and don't grieve over what I don't have," said Levin, remembering Kitty. (162; II, 14)

Levin's is a noble sentiment, but the next pages reveal just how much he does grieve over what he doesn't have. His disappointment about Kitty becomes the cause of his rapidly souring mood, which culminates in a verbal diatribe, first against the merchant Ryabinin, and then against Vronsky.

When Oblonsky sells off a piece of his wife's forest to Ryabinin, for far below its actual value, Levin is furious: ". . . [I]t's vexing and upsetting for me to see on all sides this impoverishment of the nobility, to which I belong and, despite the merging of the classes, am glad to belong. . . . Ryabinin's children will have the means to live and be educated, and yours may not!" (170–71; II, 17).

When the conversation turns to Vronsky, Levin launches into one of his most extended diatribes, against fake aristocrats such as Vronsky, "whose father crept out of nothing by wiliness, whose mother, God knows who she didn't have liaisons with . . . ," and who cannot point, as Levin can, "to three or four honest generations in their families past, who had a high degree of education, . . . and who never lowered themselves before anyone, never depended on anyone . . ." (172; II, 17).

Eikhenbaum has pointed to Levin's arguments in these pages as illustrations of Tolstoy's conservative social ideology.[16] Yet, while it is true that Tolstoy's conservatism seeps into the fabric here, as it does throughout the novel, we must distinguish art from argument. In placing his own views in Levin's heart and on his lips, Tolstoy is not advancing an ideology but enriching a highly nuanced character whose yearnings transcend ideology altogether.[17] Within Levin, personal hurt over Kitty and Russia's social confusion are interrelated branches of the same psychological tree—the disintegration of meaning in his crumbling universe. His passion for Kitty and his social polemics, while breathed into him by his socially conservative creator, stem from a longing for existential meaning that is the unifying force of his life.

"I LOVE *HER*"

In Part Three Levin visits Dolly at her family estate in Yergushovo, after receiving a request to do so from Oblonsky, who is busy spending the family money in Petersburg, where he has gone to search for a job by day and bachelor pleasures by night. Levin feels Dolly's embarrassment at her husband's absence. At the same time he sees her "in all her glory," doing what she does best—bringing order to a house that has been left in shambles by her negligent husband. When Levin watches the "mother hen" in her domestic grandeur, he finds himself "before one of the pictures of his imaginary future family life" (266; III, 9). Like Dolly, Levin can look beyond her unhappiness to find what is beautiful in her married life. Still, we muse, how different Dolly's life might have turned out had she married a Levin rather than an Oblonsky. Luck might not have been on her side, but maybe, just maybe, it will be for her sister, Kitty. This is a possibility that the jaded Dolly still clings to. She explains to Levin why her younger sister, confused about her feelings, could not accept his proposal months earlier but now might be able to.

"'If you realize what pain you're causing me!'" Levin responds, his wound reopened. "'It's the same as if your child were dead, and you were told he would have been like this and that, and he might have lived, and you would have rejoiced over him. And he's dead, dead, dead . . .'" (271; III, 10). But such children do not die in Tolstoy's world. Levin's exalted love for Kitty is a seed that has continued to grow inside him, just as the seeds sown on his estate in the spring are now sprouting into thick wheat and rye.

Two months after his visit to Yergushovo, after an intoxicating day of mowing with his peasants, Levin sits on a haystack, depressed. He watches his peasants at work and listens to their singing. As much as he wants to join in "expressing this joy of life," he realizes that all he can do is "lie there and look and listen," painfully aware of the distance between his own "burdensome, idle, artificial and individual life" and "this laborious, pure and common, lovely life" (275; III, 12). For hours Levin reflects under the pacifying influence of the nighttime calm. When morning arrives, he has made the decision to transform his life. "[T]his night has decided my fate. All my former dreams about family life are nonsense, not the right thing [ne to]. . . . All this is much simpler and better . . ." (276; III, 12).

"Ne to": These are the same words Olenin in *The Cossacks* uses to refer to his inglorious past, which he plans to cast off by going to live among the wild Cossacks. But just as he discovers that his past will always be with him, so Levin realizes that his dreams about family life were and still are "the right thing." As suddenly and imperceptibly as his decision to join the peasant way of life came over him, so destiny mysteriously unfolds before his eyes. Walking down the road towards the village, he makes out a young woman in a traveling carriage:

Bright and thoughtful, all filled with a graceful and complex inner life to which Levin was a stranger, she looked through him at the glowing sunrise.

At the very instant when this vision was about to vanish, the truthful eyes looked at him. She recognized him, and astonished joy lit up her face.

He could not have been mistaken. There were no other eyes in the world like those. There was no other being in the world capable of concentrating for him all the light and meaning of life. It was she. It was Kitty. He realized that she was driving to Yergushovo from the railway station. And all that had troubled Levin during that sleepless night, all the decisions he had taken, all of it suddenly vanished. He recalled with disgust his dreams of marrying a peasant woman. There, in that carriage quickly moving away and bearing to the other side of the road, was the only possibility of resolving the riddle of his life that had been weighing on him so painfully of late. (277; III, 12)

It will be several weeks before Levin and Kitty actually meet again, but here their fate is sealed. A man and a woman—each with a rich inner world beyond the comprehension of the other, each traveling along a different life path—find themselves, literally and metaphorically, on the same road, their destinies joined. At this moment, both fleeting and sublime, Levin's shattered world begins to repair itself. The "strange mother-of-pearl shell of white, fleecy clouds," crawling across the "inaccessible heights" (276; III, 12), which Levin saw overhead minutes earlier, before sunrise, have disappeared, along with his fantasy of marrying a peasant woman. In their place a new radiance shines forth:

The sky had turned blue and radiant, and with the same tenderness, yet also with the same inaccessibility, it returned his questioning look.

"No," he said to himself, "however good that life of simplicity and labour may be, I cannot go back to it. I love *her*." (278; III, 12)

OUT IN THE FIELD OF LIFE: LEVIN'S AGRICULTURAL REFORMS

When next we encounter Levin, in Part Three, the narrator tells us: "The night Levin spent on the haystack was not wasted on him" (320; III, 24). That night, as well as his mowing in the fields, has planted in him an important kernel of insight, which now forms the basis of a book about agricultural reform he is writing. Though he rejects the fantasy of going over to the peasant life, Levin nevertheless continues to feel inspired by the peasants' "laborious, pure and common, lovely life," and he wants to incorporate their holistic wisdom into his ideas about improvements in farming.

He now sees that his former approach to agricultural reform, in which he, like many progressive landowners at the time, tried to force upon his peasants European-influenced technological fads, has led to "a cruel and persistent struggle between him and his workers" (320; III, 24). He searches for another way, one that is sensitive to the humanity of each worker and true to the communal wisdom already embodied in the peasants.

While seemingly "reactionary" in his approach, Levin is actually ahead of his times. He instinctively understands what today's most forward-thinking entrepreneurs—whether business leaders or international development planners—know: borrowed theories, imposed from above by an impersonal corporate bureaucracy or a foreign culture, can often hurt productivity while impoverishing the souls of both the workers and their bosses. Success depends upon recognizing the uniqueness of the human individual and his culture—what Levin calls the "natural order of things."[18]

Levin's livelihood will depend on his success in not merely retaining his peasants, who, after the Emancipation Reform of 1861, had the right to leave their masters, but in creating an environment in which they can work in the manner best suited to them. Levin's book is the urgent working out of ideas that are vital to his financial survival as an estate manager, and to his spiritual survival as a human being. Given the book's importance to Levin, it is no wonder that its ideas, while specific to his immediate circumstances as a farmer, transcend time and place. Tolstoy implicitly contrasts Levin's book with that of Koznyshev, mentioned later in the novel, over which this highly respected intellectual labors for years with the highest of hopes. Alas, that book, with its apparently meticulous formulations and rather pompous title, *An Essay in Survey of the Principles and Forms of Statehood in Europe and Russia,* is passed over in silence in his time, and has little to offer ours either.

How could it be otherwise? While Levin's ideas are born from his deeply felt experiences—getting to know his peasants as they truly are, suffering in love, struggling with life's meaning in the face of death—Koznyshev's notions are manufactured in the dusty cobwebs of his cool, rational mind. Koznyshev "did not like contradictions, especially the sort that kept jumping from one thing to another and introduced new arguments without any connection" (244; III, 3). The irony, of course, is that Levin, not Koznyshev, follows ideas to their logical limits and senses the larger connection among things.

Levin asks questions that he *must* answer for himself. His is a responsive soul that feels as well as thinks, intuits as well as analyzes, embraces the complex totality of life rather than mentally slicing life up into nice, neat categories, as Koznyshev does. The very title of his book suggests Koznyshev's tendency to divide the world into "forms" and "principles." By contrast, the overarching purpose of Levin's book—to define the elements of a productive, healthy relationship of the individual to the land and to the "natural order of things"—is the essential impulse underlying his larger quest for meaning. And that impulse, in turn, gives rise to his utopian socialist tendencies. He muses:

> Agriculture as a whole, above all the position of the entire peasantry, must change completely. Instead of poverty—universal wealth, prosperity; instead of hostility—concord and the joining of interests. In short, a revolution, a bloodless, but great revolution, first in the small circle of our own region, then the province, Russia, the whole world. (344; III, 30)

In these exuberant words we hear the utopian longings that would inflame future generations of Russians, leading ultimately to the socialist Revolution of 1917 and the formation of the Soviet Union. But in the context of *Anna Karenina,* the yearning for "concord and the joining of interests" transcends the social and political to become an expression of a universal human striving for community.

Since these are the very things that Levin once hoped marriage to Kitty would provide him, it is not surprising that, at the very moment he dreams of utopia, Levin remembers his unrequited love for her: "I, Kostya Levin, the same one who came to the ball in a black tie and was rejected by Miss Shcherbatskaya and is so pathetic and worthless in his own eyes," will be the very person to spark a revolution and bring about social harmony (344; III, 30). Subconsciously he hopes that the realization of his social ideal will supply his life with the meaning that his former dream of family life, shattered by Kitty's refusal, could not.

Yet these hopes are only a temporary psychological band-aid. For Levin instinctively knows that no social vision can fill the void left by his lost ideal of family happiness. How could a society composed of individuals with bruised souls and broken or nonexistent families, or a society drenched in moral hypocrisy, hope to create ultimate harmony on earth? We need only think of those political and religious figures in our time who preach moral goodness and family values while cheating on their spouses and deceiving their constituents, to appreciate the contemporary relevance of this question.

For Levin, as for Tolstoy, social harmony without domestic harmony is an unrealizable goal. Both the character and his creator believed that family happiness alone can heal the wounds inflicted by modern life and console man in the face of death. Part Three ends, appropriately, with the poignant meeting between Levin and his other brother, Nikolai, who is dying of consumption. Levin's encounters with his two brothers—Koznyshev at the beginning of Part Three and now Nikolai—thus frame this section of the novel, creating a sense of roundness and casting new light on Levin's mysteriously touching encounter with Kitty at dawn. The fate of his love for Kitty has now become a matter of Levin's spiritual survival in the face of "a new, insoluble problem—death" (349; III, 31).

"SOMETHING HE HAD NOT UNDERSTOOD BEFORE . . ."

After Nikolai's visit, as Levin is increasingly tormented by thoughts of death, the possibility of salvation through marriage comes ever nearer. Levin and Kitty meet again at Oblonsky's dinner party. The general atmosphere is one of lively repartée, helped along by the irrepressible Oblonsky; but the energy surrounding Levin and Kitty is different. Just as Levin knew weeks earlier at dawn, instinctively and not rationally, that he loved "*her*," so now he knows "[i]n the depths of his soul" that Kitty would be there. And though he tries rationally to "assure himself that he had not known it," "when he heard that she was there, he suddenly felt such joy, and at the same time such fear, that his breath was taken away and he could not bring out what he wanted to say" (382; IV, 9). Sensing the powerful connection between Kitty and Levin, Oblonsky deftly places them next to each other at the table. There they carry on a private conversation, "or not a conversation but some mysterious communication that bound them more closely together with every minute and produced in both of them a feeling of joyful fear before the unknown into which they were entering" (390; IV, 11).

Much of the interaction between them is seen from Levin's point of view, and his thoughts and feelings begin to merge with the omniscient narrator's perspective and even dominate it. The reader is invited not only to notice Levin's ecstasy but also to feel what he feels and even to join him as he ascends to a higher level of experience: "Not just in that room, but in all the world, there existed for him only he, who had acquired enormous significance, and she. He felt himself on a height that made his head spin, and somewhere below, far away, were all these kind, nice Karenins, Oblonskys, and the rest of the world" (385; IV, 9). Even Koznyshev, not normally attuned to others' feelings, can sense something unusual in his brother: "'What's got into him tonight? Such a triumphant look'" (385; IV, 9). The communion between Levin and Kitty, consummated during their wordless conversation, was taken directly from Tolstoy's life. Just as Tolstoy did with his future wife, Sofya Behrs, Levin proposes to Kitty and she accepts by writing the first letter of each word in chalk. Levin cannot make out the most important sentence of all, Kitty's acceptance, "but in her lovely [*prelestnykh*] eyes shining with happiness he understood everything he needed to know!"[19] (398; IV, 13).

And that love, in turn, continues to be inseparable from Levin's ongoing thoughts about death. Tolstoy compares Levin's anxiety during the hours between the dinner party and the next morning, when he would formally propose, with his fear of death. Such are the stakes of the impending meeting. Kitty's acceptance is his key to recapturing a lost unity, asserting his permanence, staving off death:

> When Kitty had gone and Levin was left alone, he felt such anxiety without her and such an impatient desire to live quickly, the more quickly, till tomorrow morning, when he would see her again and be united with her forever, that he became afraid, as of death, of those fourteen hours that he had to spend without her. He absolutely had to be with and talk to someone, so as not to remain alone, so as to cheat time. (398; IV, 14)

His anxiety is matched only by the dizzying happiness of his impending engagement. When seen through Levin's rose-colored glasses, the whole world suddenly becomes a place of boundless joy and universal brotherhood. The local zemstvo meeting, formerly a venue full of strife and petty politics, now is made up of kind, sincere, and loving men. Levin sees the goodness of his lackey, Yegor, whom he "had never noticed before," and uses the occasion to instruct Yegor, who is married with four children, on the joys of family life. Levin conveys "his thought that the main thing in marriage was love, and that with love one was always happy, because happiness exists only in oneself" (401; IV, 14). Yegor becomes "infected by Levin's rapture," and tells his young master about his own "remarkable" life. Such is the power of Levin's contagious enthusiasm. Though Tolstoy's gentle irony can be heard in the background, these pages depicting Levin's ecstasy, in which he "had felt himself completely removed from the conditions of material life" (402; IV, 15), communicate an experience that is real and powerful. Once again we catch a glimpse, along with Levin, of that "higher thing."

Yet as Levin will discover, happiness in marriage also requires work, compromise, and the ability to see the world from another's point of view. His soaring wings are momentarily clipped when he learns, to his surprise, that Kitty also "had certain requirements of her own regarding their future life" (438; V, 1). And he realizes that absolute authenticity is an unattainable—and inadvisable—goal. In his innocent exuberance Levin does exactly what Tolstoy had done with his future wife, Sofya Behrs: he gives Kitty all his private diaries, which describe in detail the moral struggles and concupiscence of his bachelorhood, because "[h]e knew that there could not and should not be any secrets between them" (408; IV, 16). The wall of secrecy is indeed shattered, but, unfortunately, so is Kitty. In handing over his diaries Levin has thought about his needs, but "he did not realize how it might affect her, he did not put himself in her place" (408; IV, 16). Marriage, he learns, is not only a profound expression of togetherness. It is also the coming together of two beings with distinct perspectives, feelings, and needs.

Tolstoy beautifully captures this dual aspect of marriage—unity and separateness—in the scenes portraying the wedding ceremony in Part Five. The difference in perspectives between Levin and Kitty is unmistakable. Levin responds powerfully to the priest's mention of "unity" and the "indissoluble bond of love," but he mistakenly concludes, "by the look in [Kitty's] eyes, that she understood it as he did. But that was not so; she had almost no understanding of the words of the service and did not even listen during the betrothal" (452–53; V, 4). Yet these differences in perception pale in comparison to the intensity of their shared experience. Kitty may not be moved by the ceremony in the same way that Levin is, but her connection to him is profound nonetheless: "All her life, all her desires and hopes were concentrated on this one man, still incomprehensible to her, with whom she was united by some feeling still more incomprehensible than the man himself . . ." (453; V, 4). For his part,

> Levin felt more and more that all his thoughts about marriage, all his dreams of how he would arrange his life, were mere childishness, and

that it was something he had not understood before, and now understood still less, though it was being accomplished over him; spasms were rising higher and higher in his breast, and disobedient tears were coming to his eyes. (454; V, 4)

The "incomprehensible" feeling that overwhelms Kitty, and the "something he had not understood before" that dominates Levin, is a force that Tolstoy does not name in the way that the priest attempts to do by means of the obscure Orthodox liturgy. Nor does Tolstoy offer symbolic representations of that power, as the ceremony tries to do with its official prayers, hymns, and candle-lightings. Instead, the author permits that force to remain as incomprehensible yet palpable to the reader as it is to the characters themselves. The candles are lit, the rings eventually make their way onto the fumbling fingers of the bridal pair, and the guests gossip and interpret what they see. But Levin and Kitty are half-oblivious to all of this. They are overwhelmed and united by their shared experience of something great and ineffable, something beyond the power of words and symbols to capture.

In the months following the ceremony, Levin will come face to face with the other, less glorious, realities of married life. Kitty's "trifling preoccupation" with housekeeping and building her nest, and the couple's frequent quarrelling are an affront to his exalted ideal of marital bliss. Their honeymoon, from which "Levin had expected so much—not only had no honey in it, but remained in both their memories as the most difficult and humiliating time of their life" (483; V, 14).[20] However, these very disenchantments become for him "new enchantments." The reality of married life, with its struggles and imperfections, offers fresh illumination. The suffering caused by conflicts with his wife gives Levin renewed faith in the connection between them. When Kitty unjustly accuses him of returning late from the farmstead,

[h]e was offended at first, but in that same instant he felt that he could not be offended by her, that she was him. In the first moment he felt like a man who, having suddenly received a violent blow from behind, turns with vexation and a desire for revenge to find out who did it, and realizes that he has accidentally struck himself, that there is no one to be angry with and he must endure and ease the pain. (482; V, 14)

Levin's realization may set off alarm bells for some contemporary readers, signaling what is known in popular psychology as an unhealthy "codependency." But for Tolstoy, Levin's discovery is a measure of both his growing realism about marriage and his increased level of inner development. Anybody who has checked himself from expressing indignation at a spouse's unwelcome and unfair reproach knows what Levin knows here—that self-restraint, while difficult, is an effective way to defuse a tense moment and also an expression of one's ability to choose among possible responses. In choosing restraint, Levin shows that he is committed to a union that transcends the immediate needs of his ego. This decision is accompanied by a feeling of wounded pride, but it also deepens the bond between him and his wife. Far from diminishing Levin, the constraints of married life, in fact, expand his very sense of self.

"DEATH"

The close connection between Levin's love for Kitty and his ongoing confrontation with questions of mortality, suggested earlier in the novel, is explored further in the exquisite pages describing the death of his brother, Nikolai, in Part Five. "DEATH," the only titled chapter in *Anna Karenina*, appears at the structural center of the work, when the opposite trajectories of the two couples are firmly established. Kitty and Levin, having just returned from a less than perfect honeymoon, nevertheless settle into married life, whereas Anna and Vronsky gallivant about Europe on their own sort of honeyless "honeymoon," which symbolizes their ever-deepening estrangement from Russian society—and from one another.

Death serves not only as the structural center but also as the philosophical fulcrum of the novel. No sooner does Levin find some degree of contentment in the joys of family life than the stark face of death stares him down, threatening the foundation of his happiness. Just as his former ideas about marriage are dismantled by the actual experience of married life, so Levin's former concepts about dying prove inadequate when he is confronted with the real thing. He "had expected" to feel a particular kind of pity for his dying brother, Nikolai, and to see only a slight deterioration in his physical condition. "But he found something else entirely":

> In a small, dirty room with bespattered paint on the walls, divided by a thin partition behind which voices could be heard, in an atmosphere pervaded with a stifling smell of excrement, on a bed moved away from the wall, lay a blanket-covered body. One arm of this body lay on top of the blanket, and an enormous, rake-like hand was in some incom-

prehensible way attached to the long arm-bone, thin and straight from wrist to elbow. The head lay sideways on the pillow. Levin could see the sweaty, thin hair on the temples and the taut, if transparent, forehead.

"It cannot be that this terrible body is my brother Nikolai," Levin thought. (491; V, 17)

Death is no longer abstract to Levin; it is something he can see, smell, and touch, yet it remains utterly bewildering. Levin gropes for rational answers, but none appear. Instead, he is absorbed by terror before the unknown, much like what he felt in the hours before consummating his engagement to Kitty. Then, Levin was both "afraid, as of death," of his separation from Kitty, and overwhelmed by his connection to her. Now, too, his fear of death and his love for his wife are intertwined, and they intensify in proportion to one another:

[H]e felt even less capable than before of understanding the meaning of death, and its inevitability appeared still more horrible to him; but now, thanks to his wife's nearness, the feeling did not drive him to despair: in spite of death, he felt the necessity to live and to love. He felt that love saved him from despair and that under the threat of despair this love was becoming still stronger and purer. (504–5; V, 20)

Like two other critical moments in his life—his earlier engagement to Kitty and his later witnessing of the birth of his son—this one catapults Levin into a new kind of awareness. And it does so, significantly, by directing his attention to the details of the here-and-now.

Despite his long meditations on death, Levin is rendered helpless in its actual presence. He is so concerned about exposing his innocent young aristocratic wife to the horrors of death and the dirtiness of the provincial hotel that his first impulse is to go alone. The wiser Kitty insists on joining him, and Levin is grateful she does. While he is paralyzed by fear and confusion at the sight of his emaciated brother, Kitty acts decisively and effectively. Her pity for Nikolai "produced none of the horror and squeamishness it did in her husband, but a need to act, to find out all the details of his condition and help with them" (493; V, 18).

While Kitty does not ponder questions of meaning, Levin concludes that she "unquestionably knew what life was and what death was" far better than those "many great masculine minds" and more ordinary masculine minds such as his own (496; V, 19). For Kitty to live in the face of death is to act, to create the comforts and structures of domesticity right up to the very end. In Kitty's hands Nikolai's small, dirty room becomes a modest domicile, and her own room is transformed by her homely touch. She lays out her things, "cleanly and neatly, somehow specially, so that the room began to resemble her home, her rooms: beds made, brushes, combs, mirrors laid out, doilies spread" (497; V, 19). With the assistance of Agafya Mikhailovna, Levin's former nurse and current housekeeper, who joins them, Kitty insists that Nikolai take communion. The two women create out of that provincial hotel a makeshift home that provides both Nikolai *and* Levin with the physical and spiritual comfort they seek.

How different this is from the attention of Marya Nikolaevna, Nikolai's former mistress, who now tends to him. "'Yes, that woman, Marya Nikolaevna couldn't have arranged it all,'" Levin admits to Kitty (498; V, 19). Marya Nikolaevna is a sympathetically drawn character, and her love for Nikolai is real. But theirs is an example of what Dostoevsky called "an accidental family" in a novel by that title, the coming together of two uprooted souls (Marya Nikolaevna is a former prostitute), and not the sort of ideal family Levin or Tolstoy imagined. Absent is the rich, productive union Kitty and Levin enjoy—a connection founded not only on mutual caring but also on the structures of domesticity, community, and religious traditions. "'She's the same as my wife, the same,'" Nikolai insists earlier in the novel (87; I, 24). In this scene Levin knows otherwise.

Yet he does not judge his brother. Levin understands that the young man who formerly "always wanted to do good" and who "had sought help from religion as a bridle for his passionate nature," but was mocked, has fallen into the only life available to him (85; I, 24). In a modern Russian society that preaches scientific materialism and trivializes the sanctity of marriage and tradition, Nikolai's tragedy is that he has internalized the dominant mores of his age.

When Kitty leaves the room Nikolai characteristically tells Levin after taking communion, "'I performed that comedy for her. She's so sweet, but it's impossible for you and me to deceive ourselves. This is what I believe in,' he said, and, clutching the vial over his bony hand, he began breathing over it" (500; V, 20). In one sense Nikolai is perceptive. He and his brother do share a passionate insistence on truth, and a refusal to accept intellectual fads. "'I know his soul, and I know that we resemble each other,'" Levin thinks to himself earlier in the novel (84; I, 24). Still, for all their spiritual similarities he and Nikolai have trodden fundamentally different paths. The materialist worldview inherited by Nikolai is precisely what Levin has rejected as an inadequate solution to the existential challenges of life. Whether because of bad genes or unfortunate circumstances,

Nikolai has only a vial of iodine to grasp onto in his dying hours, whereas Levin has something more substantial: a family, a community, a connection to the traditions and values of his noble upbringing. The final note in this chapter is one of optimism, of life's continuity. In the presence of his brother's dead body Levin reaffirms the grand mysteries of life and death as the ultimate touchstones of truth. He glimpses once again that "higher thing," precisely because he is deeply connected to both the pain and the possibilities of this imperfect world:

> No sooner had the one mystery of death been accomplished before his eyes, and gone unfathomed, than another arose, equally unfathomed, which called to love and life.
>   The doctor confirmed his own surmise about Kitty. Her illness was pregnancy. (505; V, 20)

THE FALLACY OF FULFILLED DESIRE, OR ANNA AND VRONSKY'S PATH

Levin and Kitty come face to face with life's ultimate contingency, and yet their connection to one another and their sense of rootedness in the world grow more solid as a result. By contrast, Anna and Vronsky, ensconced in European luxury, are insecure itinerants without a clear place or purpose in the world. Theirs is a truly haphazard existence. As Levin finds contentment in married life, Vronsky casts about like a "hungry animal" in search of new forms of stimulation, bringing to mind Proust's famous dictum "The real voyage of discovery consists not in seeking new landscapes, but in having new eyes." Levin is growing new eyes, whereas Vronsky is desperately trying to fill his void with new places and occupations, such as painting, which he abandons as quickly as he takes it up. No change of place or profession can assuage Vronsky for long, because the nagging emptiness he wants to fill is within his very nature, and in the nature of his love for Anna: "Vronsky meanwhile, despite the full realization of what he had desired for so long, was not fully happy. He soon felt that the realization of his desire had given him only a grain of the mountain of happiness he had expected. It showed him the eternal error people make in imagining that happiness is the realization of desires" (465; V, 8).

   Tolstoy's notion will inevitably draw objections from some of us, glutted as we are by a consumer culture of instant gratification. Certainly, readers of Rhonda Byrne's wildly popular "spiritual" book *The Secret* (New York, London, Toronto, and Sydney: Atria Books, 2006) will balk at these lines. Underlying Byrnes's book is the assumption that a major aim of life is getting what you want (the examples are most often of material things), and this you achieve by focusing positive thoughts on getting them: I *will* get a check in the mail today. What is happiness, Byrnes and her ecstatic readers might well wonder, if not a realization of one's desires? Tolstoy's answer—the sort of love Levin has for Kitty, rooted in a sense of place and purpose, nurtured by the spirit of forbearance, and deepened by its confrontation with life's inexorable truths.

When Anna accuses Vronsky of being in love with another woman, she is not entirely mistaken. He is in love with the earlier, more beautiful, confident, and alluring Anna. Once the thrill of romantic conquest has worn off, once Anna's destructiveness and their tragic situation become visible, Vronsky no longer knows what to do or how to love her.

The man who once reveled in his adulterous triumph now feels only vexation over Anna's "refusal to understand her position," when she flaunts her illicit affair in society's face by daring to go to the theater alone. Yet, in throwing down the gauntlet to society, Anna is merely exhibiting the same spirit of conquest and defiance that has defined her relationship with Vronsky *and* society from the beginning. From the very first, their courtship had none of the quiet tenderness that existed between Levin and Kitty. Rather, it was driven by raw animal attraction, the high drama of seduction and psychological battle. Their relationship illustrates the fleeting ecstasy of romantic struggle, and the tragic disappointment that comes from equating happiness with "the realization of desires."

Instead of strengthening their bond, much of Vronsky's energy later in the novel is dedicated to pacifying Anna, on the one hand, and extricating himself from her controlling grip, on the other. Newly obsessed with politics, Vronsky goes to the provincial landowners' elections in Kashin, "because he was bored in the country and had to assert his right to freedom before Anna . . ." (662; VI, 31). Levin, too, wants a degree of manly independence, but he doesn't have to fight as hard as Vronsky to get it. Kitty, now in confinement in Moscow, sees that her husband is bored, and encourages him to go to the elections. In fact, Levin's primary reason for going is to help his sister, who lives in Kashin, with an important financial matter.

The elections will be the first meeting since the beginning of the novel between Kitty's former suitors. Much has transpired, and the divergent life paths of the two men are now established. By having them meet again,

Tolstoy gives an incisive comparison, a sort of re-weighing of the scales. Not surprisingly, Vronsky is found wanting. He passionately engages in the political proceedings, which are shown to be fickle and superficial, whereas Levin has the more sober perspective, as he wanders about aimlessly, like Pierre on the battlefield of Borodino, trying to make sense of it all: "'I must confess that I have a very poor understanding of the significance of these elections among the nobility,'" Levin tells a landowner at one point. Tolstoy, in the guise of that landowner, responds: "'What's there to understand? There is no significance. An obsolete institution that goes on moving only by the force of inertia'" (656; VI, 29). For his part, Vronsky just can't understand how Levin, a permanent country-dweller, has not yet become a justice of the peace. "'Because I think the local court is an idiotic institution,'" he responds rather tactlessly, yet with the full approval of his creator (659; VI, 30). Anybody who has had to sit through the drudgery of a town hall meeting, or who has been forced to appear before a judge to explain why the tail light on his car was broken, can undoubtedly relate to Levin's frustration with political bureaucracy. But Vronsky seems to thrive on it.

We need not share Tolstoy's wholesale rejection of politics—an increasingly prominent aspect of his general Christian anarchism in the later years—in order to appreciate the psychological insight: Vronsky's involvement in politics is a way of escaping the problems in his relationship with Anna. When Anna sends him a desperate note begging him to return, his wall of denial comes tumbling down: "The innocent merriment of the elections and that gloomy, oppressive love he had to go back to struck Vronsky by their contrast. But he had to go . . ." (665; VI, 31).

Like Vronsky's painting in Italy, charitable hospital-building on his estate, and volunteering to defend his Slavic brethren in the Balkans in Part Eight, Vronsky's political passion feels brittle and false. Far from responding to an authentic inner impulse, it serves as a salve to ease his bruised spirit, a substitute for the essential meaning in his life that his relationship with Anna can no longer give him. And so he flits from passion to passion, without connecting finally to any authentic ideal or inner truth. Is this so different from Karenin's workaholism and love of power, from Oblonsky's inveterate womanizing, or from Koznyshev's academic philosophizing? For these spiritually lost characters, external activity becomes a substitute for genuine inner activity, and they cling to that substitute, as Karenin clings to the mumbo-jumbo spiritualism of Countess Lydia, "as if it were salvation indeed" (511; V, 22).

Levin is different. In a social world built on sham, he refuses to be swayed by the false gods of others. That is why, when he submits to society's values in Part Seven under the befuddling influence of "just talking, eating, and drinking" (703; VII, 11) in Moscow, we take notice. At the Moscow club he gets drunk with the other guys, joking and talking about subjects that don't really interest him. This scene is seductive, because the characters' interaction *seems* authentic. Who could find fault with a little light-hearted male bonding? Has Levin overcome his brooding and become part of the gang? Yes, and for that very reason his pleasure is cheap. It has none of the power of that infectious exhilaration, mingled with pain, that he felt watching Kitty at the skating rink, or when he saw her traveling at dawn in the carriage, or when he desperately counted down the hours before his engagement, or when he witnessed the birth of his son. Each of these bittersweet moments is authentic and moving, each is earned with the pain of emotional struggle. By contrast, the shallow pleasure of the club is inspired by men (Vronsky, Oblonsky, and the carousers Turovtsyn, Yashvin, and Gagin) whose romantic relationships are either in shambles or nonexistent. None of them save Vronsky has Levin's capacity to love deeply, and none of them is on any kind of spiritual quest. They have not risen to Levin's level; Levin has descended to theirs.

That descent is temporary. When he returns to the country, Levin is restored to himself. But the ease with which he begins to internalize society's mores during his short stay in Moscow is revealing. Like a concealed poison, the dominant values of the time seep insidiously into the soul. Family happiness will be Levin's surest antidote, constant moral questioning his best immunization against continued exposure.

Dostoevsky called Levin one of those "Russian people who *must have the truth*, the truth alone, without the lies we unthinkingly accept; these are people who, in order to find this truth, are prepared to give away absolutely everything they have."[21] And, we might add, they gain much in return. That gift, that abundance, is given to Levin but not to Anna, his spiritual twin, who also throbs with inner vitality. Why does Levin's journey end with his affirming the goodness of life, while Anna's ends in suicide? What wisdom has Levin found that Anna has not? These are the questions with which *Anna Karenina* concludes and to which we now turn.[22]

$\mathcal{T}$WO LIGHTS

Anna and Levin

In Part Seven of *Anna Karenina* Levin meets Anna, something he does only once in the novel. Sergei Rachinsky, Tolstoy's friend and a former botany professor, in a letter to the author called this meeting "one of the best episodes of the novel. Here the opportunity presented itself to tie together all the threads of the story and to provide a unified conclusion. But you did not want this." Tolstoy, he argued, lost the opportunity to correct "a basic deficiency in the construction of the whole novel. The novel lacks architectonics."[1] Tolstoy disagreed:

> Your opinion about *Anna Karenina* seems to me wrong. On the contrary, I'm proud of the architecture—the arches have been constructed in such a way that it is impossible to see where the keystone is. And that is what I was striving for most of all. The structural link is not the plot or the relationships (friendships) between the characters, but an inner link.[2]

Nowhere is this "inner link" more mysteriously palpable than in the meeting between Anna and Levin—but not for the reasons Rachinsky thought. The link consists in the intersection not of two plotlines but of two parallel energies. The "truthfulness" Levin senses in this "amazing, dear, and pitiful woman" is that of a kindred spirit (701; VII, 11).[3]

Tolstoy's close friend the poet Afanasy Fet was one of the first to see the connection between them, but few others in his time detected it: "[T]he inner, artistic link of Levin with [Anna] Karenina," Fet wrote, "stares you in the face throughout the whole novel."[4] The poet sardonically recommended that, in order to make the connection more clear, Tolstoy should rename the novel *Karenina, or the Adventures of a Lost Lamb, and the Stubborn Landowner Levin, or the Moral Triumph of a Seeker after Truth.* Yet to this day critics persist in seeing *Anna Karenina* as "two novels: Anna's and Levin's."[5] Gary Jahn explains that this is because readers often have "the perception that Anna's and Levin's situations are not morally comparable."[6] Our current intellectual climate makes it especially difficult to see parallels between them. The postmodernist insistence that values are relative, meaning is constructed, and truth is a matter of perspective has blunted our ability to perceive precisely the kind of "inner, artistic link" that Fet is referring to and that Tolstoy had in mind in his letter to Rachinsky.

Social constructionists argue that Anna's and Levin's divergent fates are explained by the difference in their genders and social positions. One contemporary critic, who echoes a main line of feminist interpretation of the novel, finds the work chauvinistic and oppressive. *Anna Karenina*, she argues, manipulates readers into accepting the "discrepancy between the gendered spheres: the circumscribed domain of the household for woman and the incomparably broader arena of estate management for men. . . . In questions of gender, *Anna Karenina* combines structural rigor with conceptual rigor mortis."[7]

Such a reading does a disservice to both Tolstoy and feminists, for not only does it blithely conflate art and ideology but it also underestimates Tolstoy's profound personal struggle with the very issue confronting Anna. Significantly, one of the original impulses for the novel was the suicide of Anna Pirogova, the mistress of Tolstoy's neighbor, A. N. Bibikov. Pirogova threw herself under a train after she found out that Bibikov was going to marry another woman. Tolstoy was so bothered by the story that he visited the woman's mangled corpse. Anna Karenina's death was written into the plot from Tolstoy's earliest conception of the novel, but in the final version her death represents much more than a social commentary. The issues she grapples with are too close to the ones that haunted Tolstoy for him to be able to treat her simply as an ideological whipping girl: How to reconcile insatiable passion with social commitments, and how to be authentic in a world that substitutes social dictates and feel-good spiritualism for genuine spiritual quest?

In this respect Anna is more similar than any other character to the autobiographical Levin. In an early draft of Part Eight, after hearing of Anna's death Levin goes to the train station to see her mangled body:

> "The organism is destroyed, and nothing remains," he thought. "But why is it destroyed? All of the parts are there, the energy has not gone anywhere. Where did it go?" he started to think. And suddenly, glancing at Anna's face, lovely in death, he began to sob over his own regret with his thoughts before that mystery, without whose resolution he could not live. And from that moment the thoughts occupying him became even more demanding and absorbed him completely.[8]

Tolstoy removed this scene from the final version of the novel, but the intense spiritual connection Levin feels for Anna in this scene remains a powerful subtext throughout the work. Ironically, it is Levin, not Anna, who finds the meaning both of them seek. The questions "'What am I? And where am I? And why am I here?'" (792; VIII, 11), which Levin asks explicitly in Part Eight, and which haunt him implicitly throughout the work, are the very questions to which Anna never finds satisfactory answers. She asks them, explicitly in fact, while on the rails: "'Where am I? What am I doing? Why?'" (768; VII, 31). If Levin's questions are forward-looking and still demand answers, Anna's have become desperate cries for help.

Socially, Levin has more options than Anna, but spiritually they both have only two choices: to be true to themselves, or not. Compromise, an instinctive reflex for most other high-society characters—what Eikhenbaum calls the "professional sinners" and Gary Jahn the "middle-grounders"— is not in their natures.[9] They wrestle with moral dilemmas in a way that is beyond the grasp of others.

Tolstoy's well-documented conservative views about the sacredness of marriage and family, and his valorization of motherhood, are clearly expressed in the Levin–Kitty storyline.[10] Yet if his original intention was to write a novel about a fallen woman who would serve as a proxy for everything he disliked about modern feminism, the final version of the novel transcends this polemical design.[11] It subsumes the hero and heroine in an artistic universe that brings into focus the discrepancy between their situations while illuminating their deep existential similarity. Had Tolstoy fulfilled his original plan for a novel about a fallen woman, *Anna Karenina* might well have become a social novel in the vein of Benjamin Constant's *Adolphe,* George Eliot's *Middlemarch,* or Flaubert's *Madame Bovary,* to which the novel is often compared. But it moves beyond the genre of the nineteenth-century European social novel to become nothing less than what Dostoevsky called a "monumental psychological elaboration of the human soul."[12]

We might try to imagine Anna in modern-day Petersburg or New York or Paris, where she could remarry more easily and where her defiance of conventional morality likely would meet with open approval. With the blessings of psychopharmacology, surely she could find a chemical solution to her depression and anxiety. Yet this exercise, which sees Anna's angst as conditioned by both her society and her biology, ignores the essence of Tolstoy's heroine. Her agitation and isolation have deeper roots. Discontentment is a part of her spiritual DNA, a condition of her soul. A Cassandra fated to doom, and aware of it, Anna knows and sees something others do not. Like Levin, she is different, an extraordinary case. Had she carried on a casual adulterous affair like Princess Betsy Tverskaya and the other "professional sinners," perhaps her society would have approved. Disloyalty to one's spouse, false virtue, and hypocrisy are condoned and encouraged in her world. But spiritual daring is not.

Beyond these apostasies, there is something innately tragic, mysterious, and contrarian about Anna. Dolly's observation that she "[looks] at things too darkly" (639; VI, 24), and Betsy Tverskaya's passing comment about Anna's inclination "to look at things too tragically" (298; III, 17), contain more than a grain of truth.[13] Before Anna is a social pariah, she is a spiritual outsider. Even in Part One she seems to have no close family other than her brother, Oblonsky, and no real women friends. True, Dolly loves her and her children cling to Anna, either because they "had seen that their mother loved this aunt, or because they themselves felt a special charm in her" (72; I, 20). That charm, which Kitty will later describe as "alien, demonic" (83; I, 23), contributes to the overall impression that Anna is in the world but not quite of it, that she is, in John Bayley's phrase, a "vivid insubstantiality."[14]

Her later rejection by society only pushes to the extreme the isolation that we sense in her from the beginning. Is there something about her insatiable passion that keeps her from forming close attachments? And why, when she does form one, does she choose Vronsky? Certainly, he is young, juicy, and handsome, and offers her both romantic devotion and animal passion—the very things lacking in her husband. But this "blunt fellow, with a mediocre mind," as Nabokov describes him, is too small a person to quench her voracious emotional appetite.[15] Perhaps no human being could fill her emotional void. Yet, by choosing Vronsky she substitutes one circumscribed, rule-obsessed Aleksei for another. Is this a coincidence, or is Anna's repeated attachment to a spiritually blunted Aleksei also somehow written in her stars, either because she is psychologically incapable of sustained intimacy, or because of a metaphysical destiny beyond her human will, or both?[16] Tolstoy leaves this question unanswered, and invites readers to grapple with it.

"A SURPLUS OF SOMETHING"

The novel's two largest characters have an uncanny insight into the universe and their own souls. Levin knows from a glance at Kitty riding in the carriage at dawn that his destiny lies with her. "'A bad omen,'" Anna says after the death of a watchman whose body had just been dismembered by an oncoming train. She is right. Her own life will end in just the same way: in physical and psychological dismemberment.[17]

That "higher thing" [*vysshee chto-to*, literally, "higher something"], which Levin glimpses during the death of his brother and the birth of his son, radiates from Anna the moment we first meet her at the Moscow train station in Part One. We notice along with Vronsky that Anna carries with her "a surplus of *something* that so overflowed her being that it expressed it beyond her will" in her "barely noticeable smile" and in the "light in her eyes," which she "deliberately extinguished" (61; I, 18) [emphasis mine]. This overabundance of life energy is still harnessed. When Vronsky calls on the Oblonskys, with whom she is staying, "a strange feeling of pleasure suddenly stirred in her heart, together with a fear of *something*" [emphasis mine] (75; I, 21). Kitty, initially mesmerized by this *grande dame* from Petersburg, later observes that "there's *something* alien, demonic, and enchanting about her" and "*something* terrible and cruel in her enchantment" (83; I, 23) [emphasis mine].

There is indeed "something" about Anna—a terrible vibrancy beneath the surface composure. When she returns to Petersburg her tense inner equilibrium breaks. "'Well, it's all over, and thank God!'" Anna tries to convince herself as she prepares to board the train in a raging blizzard (99; I, 29). But shameful thoughts of Vronsky continue to haunt her, just as Levin, a few chapters earlier, is filled with shame after being rebuffed by Kitty in Moscow. Just as he tries to forget her and move on, but cannot, so Anna's passion for Vronsky cannot be extinguished. The two characters who feel the most also deny their feelings most vehemently. Denial eventually becomes Anna's modus operandi. Openness to new spiritual possibilities becomes Levin's.[18]

If Anna becomes increasingly alienated from the traditional feminine roles of mother and wife, Levin connects more deeply to the feminine—to the emotions, the ideal of family, the natural birth cycles. Other major male characters—Karenin, Vronsky, Koznyshev—are associated with the linear, the rational, and the imperial bureaucratic order. Levin is rooted in the land, in tradition, the cycles of nature, life and death. Kitty's and Levin's love gestates over a long period of time, as if in harmony with the changing seasons. Their love is associated with the slow-moving natural and agricultural cycles of the Russian countryside, where the couple eventually will live and raise a family. Anna and Vronsky's love erupts and then fizzles, like a blizzard that has run its course.

Tolstoy deepens the connection between the two characters by juxtaposing Anna's and Levin's two most famous transcendent moments in nature. Anna's experience of "oblivion" during the blizzard at the train station is beautiful, yet terrifyingly solitary, whereas Levin's "moment of oblivion" while mowing with his peasants is a profoundly communal one. The blizzard—an extreme manifestation of winter's magical fury—is deeply ingrained in the Russian cultural imagination. To the Russian mind it is a symbol of life's poetry and chaos, of possibility and danger, of man's beautiful vitality and his tragic vulnerability. In Pushkin's 1831 story "The Blizzard," for example, the blizzard brings a pair of young lovers together, and it tears another pair apart. In Alexander Blok's poem "The Twelve" (1918), the blizzard is a metaphor for both the destructive and the creative forces of revolution. In Tolstoy's own story "The Blizzard" (1856), the storm reminds the youthful narrator both of his vulnerability and of his reliance on other human beings for his survival.

It is appropriate, then, that this symbol is directly associated with Anna Karenina herself—a vital force of nature who is ultimately consumed by her passion. She is a lone reed flailing in the storm. Levin is in harmony with nature and connected to a community of laborers working towards a common goal. Peasant and aristocrat work together. Body and spirit, mind and feelings, exist in harmony, each one intensifying and grounding the experience of the other.[19] In fact, almost every moment of individual epiphany for Levin takes place when he is connected to other human beings. Anna's frantic train ride in Part One, like her delirious flight from the world in Part Seven, is marked by her nearly complete isolation from both her surroundings and herself.[20]

On the train ride back to Petersburg, the cold blizzard rages bitterly on the outside, while Anna's nascent passion burns her from within:

[T]he feeling of shame became more intense, as if precisely then, when she remembered Vronsky, some inner voice were telling her: "Warm, very warm, hot!" "Well, what then?" she said resolutely to herself . . . "What does it mean? Am I afraid to look at it directly? Well, what of it? Can it be that there exist or ever could exist any other relations between me and this boy-officer than those that exist with any acquaintance?" (100; I, 29)

The answer, the reader understands, is a resounding "yes." That elemental "something" has been unleashed in Anna, and she both fears and welcomes it. She is beginning to feel with renewed intensity, and to see with excruciating clarity:

> She felt that her nerves tightened more and more, like strings on winding pegs.[21] She felt that her eyes opened wider and wider, that her fingers and toes moved nervously; that something inside her stopped her breath, and that all the images and sounds in that wavering semi-darkness impressed themselves on her with extraordinary vividness. (101; I, 29)

Anna has a heightened awareness, yet she is still only partially conscious, for she cannot feel her body as a whole organism or herself as an integral part of her surroundings. Does she actually feel her nerves tightening, her eyes opening, her fingers and toes moving, and something inside her stopping her breath, or does she feel "that" these things are happening? Tolstoy keeps open this subtle but crucial question. Anna's feelings, though intense, are also somehow abstract and alienated. Her perspective, though focused and precise, remains incomplete and fragmented:

> She kept having moments of doubt whether the carriage was moving forwards or backwards, or standing still. Was that Annushka beside her, or some stranger? "What is that on the armrest—a fur coat or some animal? And what am I? Myself or someone else?" It was frightening to surrender herself to this oblivion. But something was drawing her in, and she was able, at will, to surrender to it or hold back from it. (101; I, 29)

Anna focuses briefly on concrete reality when she sees a skinny peasant in a nankeen coat with a missing button entering to check the heat and thermometer, "but then everything was confused again" (101; I, 29). Anna's inner world here is a microcosm of the "confusion" depicted from the beginning in the novel's opening page, a world in disarray following Alexander II's Great Reforms in the 1860s. Just as little holds Russia together in this post-Emancipation era, so almost nothing holds Anna together psychologically in this scene. Not coincidentally, it takes place, like the other most important moments of Anna's life, in connection with the railroad, a symbol for Tolstoy of the fatal disarray underlying the seemingly rational organization and rigid power structures of modern life.[22]

Ironically, a skinny peasant—underfed and apparently too poor to afford a decent coat—looks after Anna's well-being when she cannot look after herself. Tolstoy's belief that the solution to Russia's moral-spiritual splintering lay in a return to the traditional wisdom of peasant culture is well documented in his letters of this era and in his essay "About the Education of the People" (1874). In the context of *Anna Karenina* and this scene in particular, the belief takes on specific implications. The peasant Anna sees is a "stoker," calling forth images of domestic pragmatism and the gift for survival exhibited by generations of peasants, who knew how to prepare for the harsh, subpolar Russian winters by harvesting oats, making preserves, curing meats, gathering firewood in the fall, and stoking fires through the freezing months. But when reflected through Anna's disoriented mind, the stoker becomes something dangerous and inhuman. He is there, not to protect, but to stoke the fire of passion and guilt burning inside her.

Readers who are sympathetic to Anna's plight sometimes regard the blizzard scene as the moment when she courageously chooses the path of inner freedom over the life of quiet desperation she has been living. But the more prescient narrator views her situation differently. What appears to Anna to be a leap into freedom is, in fact, for Tolstoy an escape *from* freedom, to borrow a phrase from the sociologist Erich Fromm.[23] Despite her connection with that mysterious "something," she is unable to give her most vital impulses a sustainable form in which to express themselves. She hopes that her union with Vronsky will give a purpose to her passion, but that union is too ungrounded to be able to do this. What she desires on the train is an ideal of absolute happiness, of complete liberation, not just from an oppressive marriage, but from reality itself.

Anybody who has been lost in a trance during meditation or a powerful musical performance knows well this allure of self-transcendence. Yet by giving herself over to the fantasy of complete liberation, Anna becomes a slave to her passions. Like her brother, Oblonsky, she becomes "oblivious in the dream of life," but with more serious consequences. The solution she believes she has discovered—to surrender to the "beautiful," "frightening," and "exciting" "oblivion"—turns out to be fatally inadequate. Anna fails to bring her subjective idealism into alignment with another, more limited—and limiting—objective reality, thus condemning herself to remain broken in a broken world.

For Tolstoy there is another kind of human fullness, one that is life-sustaining rather than life-destroying. This is Levin's path. In 1902 the author wrote that "[t]he spiritual is always created through material life, in space and time. The spiritual is created by doing."[24] If Anna moves between an intense fatalism and a sense of absolute agency, between a belief in complete freedom and total enslavement to circumstances, Levin discovers the ideal he seeks within the limits of imperfect reality, "through material life, in space and time."

On the train ride from Moscow to Pokrovskoe, three chapters before Anna's night journey to Petersburg, Levin experiences something similar to what Anna feels on the train. His trip to Moscow in the beginning of the novel was deeply unsettling, as it was for Anna. A new consciousness is born in both of them. Anna is consumed by the beautiful yet disturbing possibility of newly awakened love, Levin by the painful realization of his unrequited love for Kitty. While traveling on the train, he, like Anna,

> was overcome by the confusion of his notions, by dissatisfaction with himself and shame at something; but when he got off at his station, recognized the one-eyed coachman, Ignat, with his caftan collar turned up, when he saw his rug sleigh in the dim light coming from the station windows, his horses with their bound tails, their harness with its rings and tassels, when the coachman Ignat, while they were still getting in, told him the village news, about the contractor's visit, and about Pava having calved—he felt the confusion gradually clearing up and the shame and dissatisfaction with himself going away. (92; I, 26)

The world Levin returns to is as orderly, grounding, and nurturing as Petersburg is disordered and alienating to Anna. At Pokrovskoe he regains his lost sense of self: "He felt he was himself and did not want to be otherwise. He only wanted to be better than he had been before" (92; I, 26). In contrast, at the Petersburg train station, Anna "was especially struck by the dissatisfaction with herself on meeting Karenin" (104; I, 30).

The quiet, slow-growing union between Levin and Kitty becomes the alternative to the explosive relations between Anna and Vronsky, which are ignited by a single glance at the train station, flare up like a brush fire, or a blizzard, and eventually die with tragic abruptness.²⁵ Some readers consider the sudden intensity of their love to be insufficiently motivated and therefore an artistic weakness in the novel. For Tolstoy this is rather a sign of the fatal flaw in the relationship itself. Their love is all passion, pure *egoism à deux*. It is as natural and powerful as the pastoral love between Levin and Kitty, but it is deeply destructive and unsustainable. It exists in the realm of pure feeling, ecstatic fantasy. It lies outside all social and moral limits, beyond the bounds of ordinary, everyday reality—which is where, as Levin discovers, life must be lived.

If sheer vitality were the ultimate good in the novel, as some modern readers believe it to be, then the author would have had his heroine survive alongside Levin.²⁶ He would not have made her into such a neurotic, destructive, and self-destructive force by the end. Anna's vitality is too ungrounded, too individualistic, to satisfy Tolstoy, who repeatedly tried to reconcile his own leonine wildness (the "lev" in Lev Tolstoy and Levin means "lion" in Russian) with his desire for personal stability.²⁷ The novel's evolution from a polemical society tale into a meditation on the human search for stable, enduring meaning suggests something more than artistic evolution. It also reflects painful, internal processes within Tolstoy himself. Anna had to die so that Levin and his creator might live.

TWO FORMS OF ILLUMINATION

Following his heroine's tragic death, the writer's extensive portrayal, in Part Eight, of the discussions about the Serbian war, which broke out in 1876, and the upsurge of Russian patriotism towards persecuted fellow Slavs, at first seems like a non sequitur. But this conclusion to the novel has deep resonances with Anna's story—and Levin's.

The fashionable pan-Slavic movement (advocating the union of all Slavic peoples under the banner of the Russian Church) has had its supporters since the novel's beginning, and now it is more popular than ever. In Part One, the socialite Lydia Ivanovna, one of the movement's most passionate defenders, laments to Anna about the "'woe and wickedness in the world,'" surely brought on by "troubles and schemes against the cause of Church unity" (108; I, 32). Lydia Ivanovna then hurries off to a meeting of the Slavic committee, and Anna can only think: "'[I]t's ridiculous: her goal is virtue: she's a Christian, yet she's angry all the time, and they're all her enemies, and they're all enemies on account of Christian virtue'" (108; I, 32). In retrospect, Anna's comment is prophetic, for Lydia Ivanovna later will join the chorus of judgment against Anna, and become Karenin's confidante and protector against that "terrible woman" (513; V, 23).

With the exception of a brief conversation, in which Vronsky's mother condemns Anna for her selfishness, and a moment of regretful reflection by Vronsky himself, she is all but forgotten in Part Eight. Even her brother, the ever resilient Oblonsky, upon meeting Vronsky, who is off to Serbia as a volunteer, "had already quite forgotten his desperate sobs over his sister's body and saw Vronsky only as a hero and an old friend" (774; VIII, 2). The members of high society, awash in Christian compassion towards their Slavic brothers and sisters, cannot find similarly Christian feelings for Anna. The questions Anna quietly raised in Part One about Lydia Ivanovna have become part of a scathing interrogation of all of Russian society on the part of Tolstoy.

While Anna vanishes from the novel in Part Seven, Levin's story continues in Part Eight. Unlike Koznyshev and Katavasov, who have worked out solutions to social problems with methodical precision, Levin is unsure what his position is. All he knows is that the answers high society has found are abstract and impersonal. Something essential is missing from his brother's eloquent defense of Pan-Slavism, just as Anna sensed the falsehood of Lydia Ivanovna's Pan-Slavic Christian "virtue." Why, Levin wonders, is truth "limited to the Christian Church alone?" and how can warfare be waged in the name of Christian principles? (814; VIII, 18).

For him, as for Anna, self-congratulatory social epithets and ideologies are false. For the Pan-Slavists and populists, a narrow intellectual paradigm becomes irrefutable doctrine. But Levin rejects shibboleths about "the common good" and what Koznyshev calls "the spirit of the people." These catchphrases have the allure of universality, but Levin sees them as exclusionary and divisive. Moreover, they are espoused by individuals who have lost their grounding in life and who, unlike Anna, are unable to acknowledge it. Vronsky, who is leaving for the Balkans as a volunteer, and Koznyshev, who valorizes him, are running from reality. They have gaping inner holes to fill. Vronsky has lost Anna, and Koznyshev has spent six years on a book that was ignored. For them the bandwagon of the Balkan war has pulled into town at just the right time. They are seeking a stimulating new fiction, a fresh oblivion, a band-aid for their broken spirits. Levin is driven by a deeper spiritual hunger.

He has trouble believing, and fears that he might be a bad Christian, yet he lives with an instinctive understanding of what's right. He rejects social shibboleths about self-sacrifice, yet dedicates himself to his family. He acknowledges the selfish desires of his ego, yet joyfully lives within a community, a cultural tradition, a set of binding, transgenerational val-ues.[28] Levin's answers are therefore both more individual *and* more univer-sal than those offered by the fashions and ideologies of the times. Just as Pierre near the end of *War and Peace* recognizes that "God is here, right here, everywhere," so Levin comes to see that eternity is right now, in the ebb and flow of the ordinary, in the rhythms of family and communal life and work.

Levin goes on living with Kitty, raising his son, entertaining guests, managing his estate, beekeeping, and hunting, knowing that he has not found an ultimate justification for these activities. So agonizing does his lack of existential meaning become, in fact, and so unsatisfactory to him are the answers provided by science, philosophy, religion, and popular social movements, that he hides the guns and ropes so he will not hang himself—a detail taken directly from Tolstoy's own life.[29] "But Levin did not shoot himself or hang himself and went on living" (789; VIII, 9).

He knows that there will always be a wall between his inward experi-ence and that of other human beings, including his wife. He will continue to pray without knowing why, and he will suffer and sin and repent. Yet none of these realizations diminishes the strength of his widened world-view. His "whole life" makes sense to him, because he has found the right attitude towards living. He comes to embrace what Donna Orwin calls "Tolstoy's antiphilosophical philosophy."[30] Levin instinctively senses that there is a higher directive power in the universe and within him, even if that power cannot be seen, measured, or named. He knows that life is intrinsically good and purposeful, and that he has the power through moral choice to contribute to that purpose. Meaningful evolution, not revolution or modernist despair, becomes the novel's final note. He recog-nizes his own imperfections and inner contradictions, without conferring on them the power to negate the goodness and meaning of his life. Levin thinks:

> "I'll get angry in the same way with the coachman Ivan, argue in the same way, speak my mind inappropriately, there will be the same wall between my soul's holy of holies and other people, even my wife, I'll accuse her in the same way of my own fear and then regret it, I'll fail in the same way to understand with my reason why I pray, and yet I will pray—but my life now—my whole life, regardless of all that may happen to me, every minute of it, is not only not meaningless, as it was before, but has the unquestionable meaning of the good which is in my power to put into it!" (817; VIII, 19)

If Levin eventually learns to view life as a meaningful whole, Anna comes to see it as empty discord.[31] In her final hours Anna can acknowledge only life's evil and senselessness, and she does so with godlike certainty: "'I understand everything . . . the struggle for existence and hatred—the only thing that connects people'" (762; VII, 30).[32]

> And now for the first time Anna *turned the bright light* [*obratila . . . iarkij svet*] in which she saw everything upon her relations with [Vronsky]. What was he looking for in me? Not love so much as the satisfaction of his vanity. . . . Yes, there was the triumph of successful vanity in him. Of course, there was love, too, but for the most part it was the pride of success. . . . Yes, I no longer have the same savour for him. If I leave him, at the bottom of his heart he'll be glad."
>
> This was not a supposition. She saw it clearly *in that piercing light* [*v tom pronizitel'nom svete*] which now revealed to her the meaning of life and of people's relations. [my emphasis] (762–63; VII, 30)

A page later she formulates her worldview even more sharply, and with the same unwavering certainty. The narrowing of her perception can be seen in the fact that she becomes both speaker and respondent in a dialogue taking place within the confines of her imploding consciousness: "'Is anything—not even happiness but just not torment—possible? No, nothing!' she answered herself now with the least hesitation. . . . 'Aren't we all thrown into the world only in order to hate each other and so to torment ourselves and others. . . . ' And she was glad of the clarity with which she now saw her own and everyone else's life" (764; VII, 30).

Later Anna sees a married couple, and she is certain they are living in mutual resentment and deceit: "Anna could see their story and all the hidden corners of their souls, *turning her light* [*perenesia svet*] on them. But there was nothing interesting there, and she went on with her thinking" (766; VII, 31) [my emphasis].

Tolstoy was surely attuned to the triple entendre in his use of the word "*svet*," "light," which also means "high society," and even "world" in Russian. The illumination Anna directs onto her surroundings is not pure fantasy. It reflects an objective truth about social reality. Like Dostoevskian characters whose borderline insanity allows them to glimpse something others do not, the delirious Anna sees a tragic truth about her world that the novel corroborates. Despite her neurosis, or maybe because of it, Anna's words "'It's all untrue, all a lie, all deceit, all evil!'" (767; VII, 31) echo like a thunderbolt across the landscape of the entire novel.

They are, in one sense, truthful. Anna sees what Tolstoy sees: false gods being worshipped everywhere. In this respect, the light she shines repeatedly onto her world in her final hours *is* illuminating. Moreover, Anna has herself become the most perfect embodiment of the dominant worldview of her time: hyperrational to the point of irrationality, competitive, and individualistic. Tolstoy chillingly communicates this connection between her personal tragedy and her times when Anna overhears a woman speaking French:

> "Man has been given reason in order to rid himself of that which troubles him," the lady said in French, obviously pleased with her phrase and grimacing with her tongue between her teeth.
> The words were like a response to Anna's thought. (766; VII, 31)

As Barbara Lönnqvist has astutely observed, the woman's statement echoes Anna's own words earlier in the novel, when she justifies to Dolly her decision not to have any more children: "'Why have I been given reason, if I don't use it so as not to bring unfortunate children into the world?'" (638; VI, 23).[33] Of course, this rationalization is also a form of self-deception. Anna doesn't want any more children, either by Karenin or by Vronsky, and she appeals to reason, in part, to make her position appear more defensible. Reason has indeed provided Anna with compelling arguments, first against motherhood, and now against the value of existence itself.

We can only imagine what Tolstoy would have thought of the recent "rational" decision of Ms. Toni Vernelli, an Englishwoman, who had herself sterilized at the age of twenty-seven so as to reduce her "carbon footprint" and help "protect the planet."[34] Her story belongs to a growing contemporary movement of women who have chosen not to have children in the service of environmental causes. More extreme still is the work of the contemporary philosopher David Benatar, who lends academic cachet to a philosophy of rational nihilism in his recent book *Better Never to Have Been: The Harm of Coming into Existence*. He makes an argument Anna in her final hours would endorse: that "coming into existence is always a serious harm."[35] Here is a prime example in our time of a phenomenon that Tolstoy detected in his: the way in which reason is used as a self-protective screen, or to deny the value of living itself.

Yet the "enlightened" intellectual movements, fads, and fashions of her times are the only responses Anna is able to hear. She is tone-deaf to a deeper understanding of life, such as Levin attains. The apologists for materialism, liberalism, conservatism, positivism, pietism, communism, capitalism, spiritualism, and pan-Slavism all proffer their rational solutions to the problems of life, and all of them are found wanting by Tolstoy. The lady's panegyric amounts to rationalism's sneering coup de grace, its cold, cruel mockery of Anna's tragic denouement. Her nihilism turns out to be one more "-ism" among many: another inadequate solution to the challenges of life.

If Anna embodies the fragmentation of her age, Levin transcends it. In Part Eight he, too, sees a "light." As clearly as Anna glimpses the glaring truth of the tragic, just as powerfully Levin sees the beautiful glow of human possibility. Levin has just heard from a peasant, Fyodor, about another local peasant, "Uncle" Platon Fokanych, who "lives for the soul," whereas the innkeeper Mityushka "just lives for his own needs," and he is struck by the wisdom of these words: "A new joyful, feeling came over him. At the muzhik's words about Fokanych living for the soul, by the truth, by God's way, it was if a host of vague but important thoughts burst from some locked-up place and, all rushing towards the same goal, whirled through his head, *blinding him with their light*" [my emphasis] (794; VIII, 11).

Whether Fokanych provides Levin with the answer or points him towards it, what is important is that Levin's epiphany comes from a source other than his own mind. Whereas Anna repeatedly shines *her* light onto the world, Levin is awash in an illumination from another source.[36] Anna's light appears to illumine the whole of reality, yet it reflects her own increasingly dismal, subjective view of things. Her light makes everything seem clear to her, yet she is still blind to other possible meanings. Her absolute convictions only lead her further into a tragic dead end. Levin's "vague but important thoughts" are ill-defined, yet unifying; "rushing towards the same goal." Anna's epiphany rends her further apart. Levin's guides him towards a renewed sense of wholeness.

He glimpses what Rousseau, one of Tolstoy's favorite philosophers, called the "*lumiere interieure*," or "inner light," that innate perception of man's capacity for moral goodness. Significantly, this knowledge, which Tolstoy, following Rousseau, believed to be inborn, has been rekindled in Levin by the wisdom of a peasant. Anna, fundamentally a creature of the modern city, has been uprooted from the values of traditional Russian peasant culture. For her the Russian peasant is something incomprehensible and even dangerous, as suggested in her recurrent nightmare about a muzhik who hammers terribly on a piece of iron, just as life will hammer away mercilessly at her own soul.

In a passage in Part Eight that can be seen as a mirror opposite of the one in which Anna overhears the woman's praise of reason, Tolstoy offers through Levin a different kind of "solution":

> "Was it through reason that I arrived at the necessity of loving my neighbor and not throttling him? I was told it as a child, and I joyfully believed it, because they told me what was in my soul. And who discovered it? Not reason. Reason discovered the struggle for existence and the law which demands that everyone who hinders the satisfaction of my desires should be throttled. That is the conclusion of reason. Reason could not discover love for the other, because it's unreasonable." (797; VIII, 12)

Significantly, Levin is lying in the field on his estate, assisting a bug over a blade, and playing with stalks of grass when he has these thoughts. Anna was looking at the train tracks when she had hers. Reason, Levin discovers, is sly and seductive precisely because it offers the illusion of simplicity and clarity. Yet it is incapable of addressing life's most fundamental existential questions. The resolution of such questions, Tolstoy insists, depends on insight into dimensions of experience that lie outside the laws of science, empirical analysis, and logic. That dimension is precisely what Tolstoy gives us artistically in *Anna Karenina*. The novel captures it perhaps most beautifully, not only in its depiction of a vital life force coursing through the universe but also in the deep, mysterious parallelism between Anna's and Levin's spiritual journeys.

There is a moment in Part Three that expresses in miniature this larger "labyrinth of linkages." Anna has just broken off relations with Karenin, and Levin has rediscovered his love for Kitty, upon seeing her in the carriage at sunrise. This marks a turning point in both characters' lives. Their divergent trajectories are firmly established here, and mirrored in their different responses to nature. The same sky that for Levin is "blue and radiant," and that "returned his questioning look" with "tenderness," reveals to Anna four chapters later the inevitability of her tragic fate: "[Anna] stopped and looked at the tops of the aspens swaying in the wind, their washed leaves glistening brightly in the cold sun, and she understood that they would not forgive, that everything and everyone would be merciless to her now, like this sky, like this greenery" (290; III, 15).

Significantly, later Tolstoy will describe Anna's torment as a "painful state of expectation, between heaven and earth" (740; VII, 23). (*Nebo* means both "heaven" and "sky" in Russian.) What pains Anna, on the surface, is the separation from her son, her growing estrangement from Vronsky, and her social isolation—leading to her increased fits of desperate paranoia. On a deeper level Anna's agonizing position "between heaven and earth" is a metaphor for the state of her soul—a soul, like Levin's, hovering between the terrible weight of reality and the allure of limitless possibility.

In Anna's case, that dilemma eventually results in a concatenation of circumstances, external and internal, social and spiritual, so severe that neither she *nor* Tolstoy can offer clear, logical explanations for how she got there, or solutions for how to escape. Linear, rational language cannot capture the truth of her situation. For this Tolstoy needs a different form of expression—the language of art—which resolves contradictions and transmutes them to a higher plane of understanding. The sky points readers towards that other realm. At once terrible and tender, angry and inaccessible, the sky reflects each character's unique circumstances and personal projections, and at the same time it becomes a symbol of an all-encompassing truth, of a mysterious order of things, independent of subjective perception.

And yet, as Tolstoy reveals with excruciating clarity in this novel, subjectivity is the only tool we have for glimpsing that "higher something." Levin sees the sky only through the frame of his limited perception. He experiences the spiritual "through material life, in space and time," by reaffirming in the present the customs and traditions of the past. Far from negating his awareness of the spiritual realm, however, this narrowing of perspective deepens Levin's connection to it. In Part Eight he again sees the "high, cloudless sky," and thinks: "'Don't I know that it is infinite space and not a round vault? But no matter how I squint and strain my sight, I cannot help seeing it as round and limited, and despite my knowledge of infinite space, I am undoubtedly right when I see a firm blue vault, more right than when I strain to see beyond it'" (800; VIII, 13).

He is not merely right when he sees a vault instead of infinity; he is *more* right. By recognizing the limits of his subjective perception, by embracing his finitude, he is able to peer more deeply into the infinite. When he immerses himself fully in what is down here, in this imperfect world, Levin is able to do what Anna never could: touch the transcendent and survive.

$\int$TUMBLING THROUGH LIFE

The Death of Ivan Ilyich

"There was light and now there's darkness. I was here and now I'm going there! Where?"

—Ivan Ilyich to himself

In September of 1869, the same year he finished *War and Peace,* Tolstoy traveled with his coachman to a nearby province in order to purchase a plot of land. During the night he stayed at an inn in the town of Arzamas and had a severe panic attack. He described it two days later in a letter to his wife:

The day before yesterday I spent the night at Arzamas and something extraordinary happened to me. It was 2 o'clock in the morning. I was terribly tired, I wanted to go to sleep and I felt perfectly well. But suddenly I was overcome by despair, fear and terror, the like of which I have never experienced before. I'll tell you the details of this feeling later: but I've never experienced such an agonizing feeling before and may God preserve anyone else from experiencing it.[1]

The "Arzamas terror" was a defining moment for Tolstoy's later creative and philosophical outlook, much in the way that Dostoevsky's near-death experience in front of the firing squad before being sent to Siberian prison camp was central to his. Tolstoy had always been driven by existential questions, of course, but something shifted after the "Arzamas terror." The existential fear he experienced in 1869 would form a powerful subtext to nearly everything he wrote over the next twenty-five years.[2]

We already sense the writer's darkened perception at the end of *Anna Karenina,* written in the 1870s. Levin's doubts about the meaning of his life lead him to the verge of suicide, but his family, community, and work provide a foundation for survival in a socially and spiritually unstable Russia. If he is still able to live with an awareness of both reality and the transcendent, both Samsara and Nirvana, as Tolstoy described the two realms in his letter to the poet Fet, then Tolstoy was finding Samsara unsatisfactory and Nirvana unattainable. Financial difficulties and growing estrangement from his wife and family compounded the grief he was already experiencing from the recent loss of two children. In an unsent letter, written in December 1885, to his friend and disciple Vladimir Chertkov, Tolstoy wrote: "I'm living what may be the last hours of my life and living them badly, in despair and in anger with those around me. There are some things I do which are not what God wants, but I seek and do not find, and all the time I feel the same melancholy, despair, and worst of all, anger and the wish to die."[3]

"SOMETHING TERRIBLE, NEW, AND MORE IMPORTANT THAN ANYTHING BEFORE . . ."

The Death of Ivan Ilyich was the first work of fiction Tolstoy produced after finishing *Anna Karenina* in 1877. This cold, intense work encapsulates his growing preoccupation with death, and it captures the moral extremism and radical self-denial that pervaded Tolstoy's writing in his later years. Its pared-down, parablelike simplicity reveals the author's terror-stricken response to the question he faced personally while on the land-buying trip in 1869, and posed directly in his *Confession:* "Is there any meaning in my life that will not be destroyed by my inevitably approaching death?"[4]

Gone are the Caucasian vineyards and vitality of *The Cossacks,* the ballrooms and battlefields of *War and Peace,* the slow-growing love unions and sexual passions of *Anna Karenina.* Gone, too, are the beautiful natural tableaus, the intersecting plotlines, the multiple aristocratic heroes. From Olenin's verdant stag's lair, Andrei's infinite sky at Austerlitz, and Levin's and Anna's glimpse into that "higher something," our gaze has been directed inward and downward, towards the sofa, on which an ordinary judge, Ivan Ilyich, lies dying alone in a small, separate room, "facing the wall nearly all the time" (123, 10).[5] This "simple death of a simple man," as Tolstoy initially described the work to a friend, grew into a complex, harrowing portrait of one man's confrontation with the ultimate existential truth.[6]

We have met Ivan Ilyich Golovin before. This heady (*"golova"* means "head" in Russian) government lawyer-functionary is a descendent of the dry, calculating officer, Berg, and the rigid government reformer, Speransky, in *War and Peace*. We recognize Ivan in the pompous merchant, Ryabinin, and in the fly-swatting lawyer whom Karenin consults in *Anna Karenina*. We will see him again in *Resurrection* in the prison wardens, court officials, and civil servants populating various governmental institutions. But in no other work by Tolstoy does this character occupy such a prominent place, let alone the title role.

The "little man" with an overinflated ego was a popular figure in Russian literature of the 1880s and 1890s. Saltykov-Shchedrin, Garshin, Potapenko, as well as numerous minor artists wrote about small-minded bureaucrats, petty merchants, and other circumscribed characters from various social milieus. Anton Chekhov's Belov, the infamous "man in a case" in the short story by that name, memorialized the type. Belov is a direct descendant of Ivan Ilyich, but if Chekhov's diminutive hero is a model of poignant understatement, Tolstoy's Ivan offers a more sweeping moral-philosophical vision of modern man. But we must resist the temptation to think of Ivan as a social type, as a category of person, or as "man" as an abstraction. He is you and me. Tolstoy's original title was "The Death of a Judge," but he needed someone both more specific and more universal.[7] He found him in Ivan Ilyich: John, son of Ely, or Elias.[8]

After *Anna Karenina*, *The Death of Ivan Ilyich* is the most widely read of Tolstoy's works in American colleges. The National Endowment for the Arts recently added it to their list of required works for their national Big Read initiative. The novella continues to inspire new interpretations and studies from a variety of critical approaches, and it made no less powerful an impression on Tolstoy's contemporaries.[9] After reading the novella in French the writer Guy de Maupassant famously exclaimed, "I see that all of my work amounts to nothing, that my ten volumes aren't worth anything!"[10] The Russian critic Vladimir Stasov wrote in a private letter to Tolstoy: "I have never read anything like it in my life. Nobody anywhere on earth has produced such a work of genius. Everything is small, everything is trivial, everything weak and pale in comparison with these seventy pages."[11]

What make these seventy pages so powerful? To begin with, there is hardly a better literary depiction of what dying feels like in all its physical and psychological torment. A special 1929 edition of the Russian medical journal *Russian Clinic* recommended that every doctor read it with utmost attention, in order to discover "those abysses of terror and doubt, which the fatally ill experience."[12] The novella is still read in medical schools today; it asks the future doctor to see the world from the point of view of the terminal patient. It encourages her to recognize the limits of scientific training in the face of the eternal mysteries of life and death. The novella persuades her that no revolutionary medical invention—not even modern-day cryonics—can ease the suffering that is an inevitable part of our mortality. Even today's advanced methods for dampening physical pain cannot dull the psychological agony of life's ultimate encounter. Yet, as Tolstoy understood so well, "those abysses of terror and doubt" seldom register in our ordinary consciousness. Bringing that terror to our awareness is one of the work's most urgent goals.

Before telling us what death is, Tolstoy must first show us what we think it is. In doing so, he reveals how deeply rooted is the human impulse to block out all awareness of our own mortality, to put up protective walls against our authentic selves, against each other, against life itself. This is apparent from the novella's opening paragraph, which begins, like Tolstoy's earlier novels, *in medias res.* But in contrast to the earlier works, no vital life processes are underway. There are no brewing revolutionary forces, as in the opening of *War and Peace,* no nagging feelings of disorientation and guilt, as Oblonsky experiences at the beginning of *Anna Karenina.* Instead, Tolstoy plunges us into a world of talking dead men:

> During an interval in the Melvinsky trial in the large building of the Law Court the members and public prosecutor met in Ivan Egorovich Shebek's private room, where the conversation turned to the celebrated Krasovsky case. Fyodor Vasilievich fervently declared that it was not subject to their jurisdiction, Ivan Egorovich maintained the contrary, while Pyotr Ivanovich, not having entered into the discussion at the start, took no part in it, but looked through the Gazette which he had just been handed.
>
> "Gentlemen," he said, "Ivan Ilyich has died!"
>
> "You don't say so!" (83, 1)

We know that this conversation about the celebrated Krasovsky case, or a celebrated case just like it, has taken place many times before. So, too, minutes later, Pyotr Ivanovich and Shebek, upon realizing that they will now have to pay a visit to Ivan's widow, who lives "so terribly far away," will lightheartedly spar yet again on their favorite topic: "distances between different parts of the city" (84, 1). The death of a colleague becomes a mildly interesting piece of news, a dull thud in a dead world. And like the Krasovsky case, it, too, has been relegated to its proper jurisdiction, appearing in the form of a newspaper announcement, "surrounded by a black border" (83, 1), and written in colorless officialese. Being skillful lawyers, Ivan's colleagues quickly interpret and categorize the new information:

> Besides considerations as to possible transfers and promotions likely to result from Ivan Ilyich's death, the mere fact of the death of a near acquaintance aroused, as usual, in all who heard of it the complacent feeling that, "it's he who is dead and not I."
> Each one thought or felt, "Well, he's dead but I'm alive!" (84, 1)

Throughout Chapter One Tolstoy focuses our attention on Ivan's colleague and friend Pyotr Ivanovich, who, in an earlier draft, is given Ivan's private diary by the widow of the deceased. "'We must not, must not, and must not live like I lived and how we all live,'" Pyotr Ivanovich exclaims in that draft. "'Ivan Ilyich's death revealed this to me.'"[13] But Tolstoy removed these words from the final version and, in fact, emphasizes how Ivan's death has revealed nothing to Pyotr Ivanovich. Except for a few passing references, we never hear from him again after Chapter One. Even at the funeral, he,

> like everyone else on such occasions, entered [the room containing Ivan's body], feeling uncertain what he would have to do. All he knew was that at such times it is always safe to cross oneself. But he was not quite sure whether one should bow while doing so. He therefore adopted a middle course. (85, 1)

In other words, he treats this moment with the same propriety and safe, middling response with which Ivan approached everybody and everything in his own life. Pyotr Ivanovich, whose patronymic, Ivanovich, means "son of Ivan," is indeed Ivan's spiritual progeny—an unevolved, spiritual replica of his friend, just as Ivan is a replica of his own father. The "warning" he sees on Ivan's dead face "seemed out of place to Pyotr Ivanovich, or at least not applicable to him" (86, 1). When he later leaves the room to avoid the nauseating smell of incense, carbolic acid, and the sight of Ivan's dead reproachful face, he is still missing the point: Ivan's death *is* applicable to him. But he tries to assign it, in lawyerly fashion, to its correct category, which has nothing to do with his own fate.

If Pyotr Ivanovich shows us death through the eyes of the living, then Ivan Ilyich guides us through death as it is experienced by the dying.[14] The contrast between the two could not be starker. Pyotr Ivanovich hears from Ivan's widow at the funeral about how his friend suffered. But *we* actually hear Ivan's scream: that incessant, haunting "O"-sound, which reminds us simultaneously of the sob of a child and the chanting of a Buddhist monk. We feel that continual sharp, nagging pain in Ivan's side; we smell the foul taste in his mouth and the odor of his excrement. We are there with him every step of the way, as he goes from denial to anger to depression to reconciliation.[15] We lie with him for weeks, facing the back of the sofa, and we overhear Ivan's conversations with God, berating him for his cruelty and beseeching him for answers.

Tolstoy takes readers where few writers had taken them before: to the edge of the abyss we all must face. But Ivan does not want to look down. Like everybody around him, he clings to familiar paradigms. When he first becomes ill, his wife regards his irritability as yet another example of her husband's "dreadful temper" (102, 4). The doctor reduces the pain in Ivan's side to a matter somewhere "between a floating kidney and appendicitis" (103, 4). Ivan initially treats it like another intellectual challenge, a court case to be solved: "Reviewing the anatomical and physical details of what in the doctor's opinion was going on inside of him, he understood it all" (108, 5).

Of course, neither he nor the doctor has understood it all, a fact that becomes clear as Ivan tries in vain to find solace in the doctor's diagnosis, and in the diagnoses of "all the doctors" (107, 5) he had spoken to before that. Tolstoy's famous antipathy toward the medical profession is evident in these passages, but his commentary runs deeper than that.[16] Just as Fyodor Vasilievich and Ivan Egorovich fervently debate the Krasovsky case in the opening chapter, each one holding firmly to his point of view, so the doctors present their respective analyses of Ivan's condition, each drawing on the authority of science. But these brilliant analyses fail to address the real issue for Ivan: "'It's not a question of my appendix or my kidney, but of life and . . . death . . . Why deceive myself? Isn't it obvious to everyone but me that I'm dying . . .'" (109, 5).

The point is precisely that it is *not* obvious to everyone—at least not in the way he understands it, and how he experiences death is the only point of view that matters to him now. "One would have thought that it should have been clear to him that this exasperation with circumstances and people aggravated his illness, and that therefore he ought to ignore unpleasant occurrences" (104, 4). But "one" is not in pain; Ivan is, and he "drew the very opposite conclusion: he said that he needed peace, and he watched for everything that might disturb it and became irritable at the slightest infringement" (104, 4). Just as cool, rational responses to death no longer apply, so the schoolboy syllogism he learned from Kiesewetter's Logic cannot capture the irreducibly individual, strange, and messy thing happening to him: "'Caius is a man, men are mortal, therefore Caius is mortal,' had always seemed to him correct. That Caius—man in the abstract—was mortal, was perfectly correct, but he was not Caius, not an abstract man, but a creature quite, quite separate from all the others" (110, 6).

Ivan heeds the doctor's orders, takes his medicine, seeks clues to his condition in the ailments of others, secretly takes medicine prescribed by a homeopath, and considers a cure by a wonder-working icon—yet none of these eases his suffering. They are all just so many placebos. What formerly never registered in his consciousness suddenly becomes the most "important, intimate matter" (*vazhnoe, zadushevnoe delo*) (108, 5) and undeniable fact of Ivan's life:

> There was no deceiving himself: something terrible, new, and more important than anything before in his life, was taking place within him of which he alone was aware. Those about him did not understand or would not understand it, but thought everything in the world was going on as usual. That tormented Ivan Ilyich more than anything. (105, 4)

We might compare this with the passage in *War and Peace* in which Prince Andrei realizes that he is dying:

> Prince Andrei not only knew that he would die, but felt that he was dying, that he was already half dead. He experienced an awareness of estrangement from everything earthly and a joyful and strange lightness of being. Without haste or worry, he waited for what lay ahead of him. The dread, the eternal, the unknown and far off, of which he had never ceased to feel the presence throughout his life, was now close to him and—by that strange lightness of being he experienced—almost comprehensible and palpable.[17]

What a marked difference in the way these two characters confront death! Ivan writhes with terror, whereas Andrei revels quietly in the sublimity of his transformation. Ivan will call his family "fools" and "beasts" for singing while he is sinking. Andrei feels an even deeper spiritual connection to those around him. Why should Ivan's impending death evoke angry reactions from him but not from Andrei? For one thing, Ivan is dying of an unidentifiable illness brought about by unexplained causes, which only intensifies his sense of confusion and terror. Andrei is dying a soldier's death.

A second explanation gets at the heart of what it means for Ivan to die, and makes clear the change in Tolstoy's worldview from the 1860s to the 1880s. As Andrei nears death, he becomes ever more aware of the "eternal, the unknown and far off," which he has always coveted yet never attained. Ivan has not known this sort of Bolkonskian spirituality, has never glimpsed anything like the lofty, infinite sky Andrei sees at Austerlitz. Andrei's life is surrounded by gloom from the novel's beginning, yet his tragic aura evinces a fundamentally noble, striving nature. By contrast, the superficially cheery Ivan is, in essence, a walking dead man whose existence has become buried beneath a mountain of meaningless things, objects, and tasks.

Only in his final days does Ivan recall his former joys: "'There, in childhood, there had been something really pleasant with which it would be possible to live, if it could return'" (122, 9). But could we imagine Ivan, even in childhood, experiencing anything like Nikolai's happiness while hearing Natasha sing, or his ecstasy during the wolf hunt? Nikolai is a full-blooded epic hero from a mythical Russian past. For him the consciousness of death is a young man's innocent epiphany that his happy life might actually come to an end. But Ivan is an uprooted modern man, a bureaucrat and functionary to the marrow of his bones. For him dying threatens to destroy the tiny house of rules and conventions in which he has lived his life, and that is the only house he knows.

"[H]ow bitterly ridiculous it seemed" to Ivan that his death was caused by something as trivial as bumping his side on a window frame when he falls from the ladder while decorating his house, "for he knew that this illness originated with that knock" (112, 6). But do we? This tidy explanation comforts Ivan, and has been the assumption of many readers and critics. But nowhere does Tolstoy actually tell us what Ivan's illness is, or why he is dying. Medical doctors have praised Tolstoy for his clinical accuracy, and confirm that Ivan probably died of cancer. But Tolstoy shows us that all such diagnoses are irrelevant smokescreens, preventing direct confrontation with the sheer terrifying fact that Ivan *is* dying. Reason, logic, and laws of causality cannot help us in the face of this "challenge to all normal, human consciousness."[18] What makes death so frightening is that it is not only the elusive bogeyman under the bed. It is also the scary doll Ivan can see and touch. It is abstract and concrete, radically strange and terrifyingly ordinary:

It would come and stand before him and look at him. . . . And what
was worst of all was that *It* drew his attention to itself not in order to
make him take some action, but only so that he should look at *It*, look
it straight in the face: look at it and without doing anything, suffering
inexpressibly.

To save himself from this condition Ivan Ilyich looked for conso-
lations—new screens—and they were found and for a while seemed
to save him, but then they immediately fell to pieces or rather became
transparent, as if *It* penetrated them and nothing could veil *It*. (111, 6)[19]

To a Russian ear the impersonal pronoun "It" (*ona*, the feminine pronoun that means both "it" and "she" in Russian) has about it a quality of
both abstraction and intimacy. Death (*smert'*, a feminine noun in Russian)
is a concept Ivan cannot grasp, and at the same time it incessantly nags
at him, like his wife. It will not stay at home and mope, while he plays
bridge, or submit to his displays of power, as do his subordinates and liti-
gants. It will not be stuffed into a box, as Ivan does with all of his other
relationships. Ivan cannot *do* anything with death. He must simply stare at
it and be present with it.[20]

The Death of Ivan Ilyich comes closer than any other of Tolstoy's
works to offering a tragic conception of life, but unlike his contemporary,
Dostoevsky, or twentieth-century modernists, Tolstoy believed ultimately
in a stable order to the universe. For him the tragedy of Ivan Ilyich is not
that he lives in an absurd world, but that his approach to living is absurd.
In fact, in Tolstoy's formulation Ivan Ilyich never really lived, until he
started to die.[21]

A "LIFE . . . MOST SIMPLE AND
MOST ORDINARY AND MOST TERRIBLE"

"Ivan Ilyich's life had been most simple and most ordinary and most terrible," Tolstoy famously begins Chapter Two (89, 2). What is so terrible
about his life? Or, as critic Anthony Daniels puts it, "What should Ivan
Ilyich have been doing in his spare time other than playing bridge? Or are
we all to devote ourselves exclusively, not to taking in each other's wash-
ing, but to taking in each other's suffering, and therefore never to enjoy
ourselves?"[22]

Daniels is not the only one to raise this reasonable objection. Edward
Wasiolek thinks that Ivan's "life is not that bad, and the pain and terror are too much."[23] My former Russian literature professor at Moscow

State University refused to read the work with her students, because, having recently lost a brother, she believed that Tolstoy's artistic bludgeoning of Ivan was merciless and unfair. One of Tolstoy's contemporaries, the brother of the deceased judge on whom Ivan is based, felt similarly: "How much richer was his psychic register than that which Tolstoy gave to his hero!"[24]

In my classes and workshops on the novella I try an exercise: I ask students to imagine that they are going to die in six months. How would they live? The conclusion I have drawn from doing this exercise is that human beings have enormous difficulty making death real to themselves, and perhaps with good reason.[25] Our ability to put up psychological screens against the ultimate existential terror might well serve a practical purpose, as is evident in the case of soldiers I have heard about who have died in battle, not from enemy fire but from the fear of dying. Still, the inmates at the Virginia Beach Correctional Facility, where I led a workshop on *Ivan,* insisted that such screens have been unproductive in their own lives. Pushing death out of their minds, they told me, was an understandable form of self-protection amid the violence that was a regular part of their world. Yet these internal walls also made it easy for them to avoid asking the hard moral questions about their behavior that needed to be asked. Many of these inmates identified with Ivan's habit of avoidance and self-denial, and didn't like what they saw.

For example, one inmate, now in his thirties, had been in and out of prison for eighteen years. He had gotten several girls pregnant, recently married one of them, and was back in jail for selling illegal drugs to support his newborn son. He told the group that for years he had justified his life of crime with any number of excuses: He needed to survive; everybody broke the rules; American society was unfair; he had grown up without a father, and was raised by a physically and emotionally abusive mother. After reading Tolstoy's novella, this inmate was disturbed to discover that he had been rationalizing his behavior much like Ivan, who seems to excuse his moral failings with the comforting knowledge that he lives just like everybody else around him. "I had to come to this jail, this situation, to see what I was doing," the inmate remarked. "I learned something from this story I can use when I get out."

Whether we agree with Anthony Daniels, or share Tolstoy's censure of Ivan, one thing is clear: the persuasiveness of his descent into personal hell compels us, if not to accept, then at least to consider, the ideas Tolstoy intended to illustrate in the novella.[26] Even if we are bothered by the ideologue's equation of a "simple" and "ordinary" life with a "terrible" one, few readers deny the uncanny verisimilitude of the artist's created universe. There is indeed a convincing inner logic to the way in which Ivan's pleasant and satisfying life devolves into such extraordinary suffering.[27] That his agony is even greater because his family members "degrade this awful, solemn act [of dying] to the level of their visits, their curtains, their sturgeon for dinner" (114, 7) strikes us as consistent with the laws governing their world and his. That Ivan is treated by the doctors in the same dismissive way he himself handles prisoners in court also rings true and is consistent with the mores of the world he has internalized. The man who lived by the sword of egoism must die by the dull knife of abandonment.

One of the most heartbreaking moments in the novella is when Ivan Ilyich writhes with suffering, wants only to be petted and pitied, yet instead, "by force of habit" (115, 7), assumes a serious, professional air as soon as his colleague Shebek comes, and debates him passionately about a recent court case. This detail is all the more poignant because it is so true to character. Ivan's whole life has been defined by habits—copied from his father, adopted from his superiors, reinforced by his environment. So it is entirely consistent with the rationale of his existence that, when he most wants to express his authentic needs, he has only his habitual responses to fall back on. No wonder "this falsity around him and within him did more than anything else to poison his last days" (115, 7). The thing he needs most in his agony—genuine human connection—is the very thing that has always eluded him.

Before his conversion in the final chapter, Ivan is an accident of fate, a plaything of his biological and social environment. Like his father, who had been a "superfluous member of various superfluous institutions" (90, 2), Ivan is also an unnecessary institutional appendage. He is the mathematical average of the personalities of his older and younger brother: ". . . neither as cold and formal as his elder brother nor as wild as the young; he was a happy mean between them" (90, 2).

The first forty-four years of his "agreeable, easy, and correct life" (101, 4) pass like a shadow before his eyes. There is no mention of a single specific date except for the "new Code of 1864," and that in connection with Ivan's official duties. We get only large chunks of time: Ivan's boyhood followed by school, then his first post, where he served for five years, then two years as examining magistrate before meeting his wife, then seven years of married life, followed by another seventeen years. Ivan's biography reads like an unengaging encyclopedia entry, in which a life is reduced to a laundry list of periods of evolution and accomplishments. The tragedy is that he, in fact, experiences his own life in just this way. Tolstoy brilliantly captures this generalized quality of Ivan's cardboard existence, while creating Ivan himself as an artistically distinct individual. This Everyman is both a Nobody and somebody we recognize.

The word "new" appears nearly fifty times in this novella of under a hundred pages, yet the reader is continually struck by how stale and monotonous Ivan's life is. "On taking up the post of examining magistrate in a new town, he made new acquaintances and connections, placed himself on a new footing and assumed a somewhat different tone" (92, 2). After getting married, Ivan enjoys "new furniture, new crockery, and new linen" (93, 2). "The new and reformed judicial institutions were introduced, and new men were needed. Ivan Ilyich became that new man" (91, 2). But there is nothing new about this "new man." From examining magistrate, to Assistant Public Prosecutor, to the Department of Justice, his jobs and titles change, his salaries increase, and his circle of friends grows more refined, but the essence is always the same:

> He got up at nine, drank his coffee, read the paper, and then put on his uniform and went to the law courts. There the harness in which he worked had already been stretched to fit him and he donned it without a hitch: petitioners, inquiries at the chancery, the chancery itself, and the sittings, both public and administrative. In all this the thing was to exclude everything fresh and vital, which always disturbs the regular course of official business, and to admit only official relations with people, and then only on official grounds. (99, 3)

In Chapter Three we get another specific date, 1880, "the hardest year of Ivan Ilyich's life," in which he is passed over for a promotion, "the greatest and most cruel injustice" from his point of view, but "quite an ordinary occurrence" to everyone else, including his father, who refuses to help him financially (96, 3). In a world of egoists, one man's pain is completely ignored by others—a foreshadowing of the lonely death that awaits the hero among family and friends. After happening upon an even better career opportunity, Ivan recovers nicely from this "stumble" of 1880—a bitingly ironic choice of words, when we consider the actual stumble from the ladder pages later. In fact, Ivan's "*zapnuvshaiasia zhizn'*"—literally, his "stumbled" or "faltering" life—is already well underway (97, 3).

Alongside the omniscient narrator, speaking now with cold objectivity, now with overt censure, we also hear Ivan's childish voice, and feel the spirit of his atrophied life. Tolstoy conveys this not by means of any interior monologue—Ivan has no inner life to speak of until his confrontation with death—but by recreating in his very manner of writing Ivan's superficial and perfunctory attitude towards the world. In Part Three, for example, Tolstoy uses repetition to suggest the fairy-tale simplicity of Ivan's existence. After finding a "delightful little house, just the thing both he and his wife dreamt about," Ivan sets about decorating it: "Everything progressed, progressed [*Vse roslo, roslo,* literally, "grew, grew"] and approached the ideal he had set himself: even when things were only half completed they exceeded his expectations" (98, 3). A Russian reader would hear in this sentence the singsong cadence as well as the actual words from the well-known Russian fairy tale "The Fox-Wailer," a variant of the story of "Jack and the Beanstalk":

> There once lived an old man and an old woman and they had a little daughter. One day she was eating beans, and she let one fall on the ground. The **bean grew and grew, and grew** [*ros, ros, i vyros*] right up to the heaven. The old man climbed up to heaven, slipped in there, walked and walked, admired and admired, and said to himself, "I'll go and fetch the old woman; won't she just be delighted." [emphasis mine][28]

When the old man tries to carry his wife up the bean stalk, she falls to the ground and dies. In one variant of the fairy tale, called "The Fox-Physician," a fox-surgeon promises to bring the woman back to life, and performs his mysterious "surgery" behind closed doors. The old man enters the room, only to discover that the fox-surgeon has left the old woman's bones piled in the corner, and eaten up the pudding and butter he demanded as payment for his medical services. So, too, the self-important doctors who treat Ivan bewilder him with their scientific mumbo-jumbo, rob him of his dignity, and leave him more desperate than before. And like the old man in the fairy tale, Ivan is excited to think how the "charming" new home will impress his wife and daughter.

The fairy-tale motif running through the home-decorating passage also serves to underscore that Ivan's story is universal. As we survey the economic and personal wreckage left by the recent American home-buying frenzy, we recognize the continued relevance of the behavioral archetype. There was indeed something childlike in the way in which millions of Americans were lured by foxlike mortgage brokers and bankers into buying dream homes with borrowed money they didn't have; in some cases, that money didn't exist. We have learned once again the dangers of materialism, greed, and sheer naïveté—lessons so obvious and universal that they hardly seem worth rehashing, except perhaps to a child.

Figure 4   L. N. Tolstoy telling the story of the cucumber to his grandchildren, S. A. and I. A. Tolstoy. Kryokshino, Moscow province, 1909. Photo by V. G. Chertkov. Source: *Lev Tolstoy in Photographs by Contemporaries* (Moscow: Publishing House of the USSR, 1960). Courtesy of *Tolstoy Studies Journal*, online Tolstoy Image Gallery.

Yet human beings do repeat these behaviors, and just as the old woman falls from the bean stalk, so too Ivan falls from the ladder while showing the upholsterer where to hang the drapes. In both cases, the imagined heaven proves illusory. Like a fly lulled to its death by a beautiful light, Ivan is drawn in by the glitter of a familiar mediocrity: "In reality it is just what is usually seen in the houses of people of moderate means who want to appear rich, and therefore succeed only in resembling others like themselves: there were damasks, dark wood, plants, rugs, dull and polished bronzes—all the things people of a certain class [sort] have in order to resemble all other people of that class [sort]" (99, 3).

Here is a metaphor for Ivan's whole existence: an imitation of imitations, a blind attachment to external objects and symbols, and an absence of individual creative and spiritual will. In fact, this is an apt description of everyone in Ivan's social milieu, who embody what it meant to Tolstoy to simply "take life as it comes." This pejorative phrase, which he used in his 1895 letter to the journalist Mikhail Menshikov, captures the world of *Ivan:*

If there is no free activity of the reason [moral consciousness] to remove temptations in people, and thereby release in them the divine essence of their life—love; if every man is the product of the conditions surrounding him and the causes preceding him, then there is neither good nor evil, neither morality nor immorality, and there is no point in our thinking and talking and writing letters and articles, but we should *take life as it comes*, as the saying has it [italics in the original]. If my heredity and environment are bad, I shall be bad; if they are good, I shall be good. I don't think that is so. I think that every man possesses a free, creative divine power. (For as the Father hath life in himself, so hath he given to the Son to have life in himself—John 5:26). And this power is reason. The more this power increases, the more the essence of a man's life—love—is released within him, and the more closely is man united with other beings and with God.[29]

In a world of characters whom Tolstoy portrays as institutional appendages and pure products of their environment and biology, Gerasim, the peasant who supports Ivan's emaciated legs, stands out as an exemplar of spiritual vitality. While nearly everybody else keeps death at arm's length, only Gerasim holds the dying Ivan in his arms. Unlike his upper-class employers, this "peasant philosopher" does not deny death. "We'll all be there," he says to Pyotr Ivanovich at the funeral (89, 1). These simple, profound words, of course, will fall on deaf ears. But for Tolstoy Gerasim offers a lesson in courage and compassion that Ivan himself will learn in his last hours when he accepts his death and releases his family from the pain of watching him suffer. This is Ivan's first morally proactive decision, a singular expression of that "free, creative divine power" that Tolstoy believed resides in every human being.

A THIRD LIGHT

Tolstoy was certain that every person eventually manifests this power in his or her life, either painlessly and naturally, as does Gerasim, or after arduous spiritual cleansing, as in the case of Ivan. *The Death of Ivan Ilyich* becomes the first movement in a grand symphony of late prose works and tracts that would become a variation on this recurrent theme: only "by renouncing what is perishing and must perish—that is to say, our animal personality—can we obtain our true life which does not and cannot perish."[30] If we don't do this freely, "it is accomplished forcibly in each man at the bodily death of his animal personality, when under the weight of his sufferings he desires only one thing: to be freed from the painful consciousness of his perishing personality and pass over to another plane of existence."[31]

These words are from Tolstoy's lengthy essay *On Life* (1886–88), which he wrote while working on *The Death of Ivan Ilyich*. If the young Tolstoy could still believe in "a situation in which the satisfaction of the desire of the flesh does not contradict, but rather accords with desires of the spirit,"[32] then the later Tolstoy was far more extreme and dualistic in his thinking.[33] His attitude was closer to that of his hero the aristocrat turned monk Father Sergius, who begs God to explain: "'Why does the whole world, with its delights, exist if it is sinful and must be renounced? Why hast Thou created this temptation?'"[34]

The productive tension that had once existed in the writer's mind between spirit and flesh, heaven and earth, has become an untenable contradiction. Personality is a burden, ordinary consciousness a deception, and physical existence a mirage that must be overcome. Gratification of sexual desire, even in marriage, leads to evil, Tolstoy says in *The Kreutzer Sonata* (1889), a novella about a man who murders his wife after suspecting that she is sleeping with the violinist. Pursuit of financial gain is meaningless and leads us to suffering, Tolstoy insists in "Master and Man" (1895), a story about a merchant who dies in a snowstorm during a land-buying trip. "How much land does a man need?" Tolstoy rhetorically asks in the title of his short masterpiece about an acquisitive peasant who runs himself literally to death in pursuit of land. "Six feet from his head to his heels was all he needed," Tolstoy tells us in the story's final line.

From the vision of two equally illuminating lights—Levin's and Anna's—in *Anna Karenina* we have arrived at a battleground between light and darkness, goodness and evil, truth and falsehood. Now Tolstoy shows that the power of light and "the power of darkness," the title of his 1886 play about greed and temptation, are forever in battle in our world and our hearts. We must choose. "Walk in the Light While There is Light" (1886), Tolstoy enjoins readers in the title of a play by that name, written in the same year as *Ivan*, about a man who realizes in old age that he has wasted his life on worldly pursuits.

How tellingly ironic, then, that Ivan Ilyich was "attracted to people of high station as a fly is drawn to the light" (90, 2).[35] To Tolstoy this is the illusory lantern of egoism and worldly ambition guiding him towards doom. The important point is that this light is wholly external. The light he sees at the end is a private vision of salvation in the spiritual realm. Unfortunately, this moment also strikes many readers as artistically unconvincing. It is one thing to imagine what the process of dying feels like, quite another to describe what the actual "hour-of-death" experience looks like.

> "And death . . . where is it?"
> He looked for his former accustomed fear of death and did not find it. "Where is it? What death?" There was no fear because there was no death.
> In place of death there was light.
> "So that's what it is!" he suddenly exclaimed aloud. "What joy!"
> (128, 12)

Instead of infecting us with a visceral image of death we can see and touch and smell, as the artist does in earlier chapters, here the ideologue gives us a metaphor illustrating his idea of "true life," "exempt from time and space," that he described in On Life.[36] Many readers, myself included, have felt disappointment at Ivan's anticlimactic epiphany.[37] It seems an insufficiently riveting climax to one of the most blood-curdling death journeys in world literature. In the context of the work as a whole, the familiar image of the light appears so ordinary as to seem shockingly trite.[38] But upon reflection, I have realized that this might just be Tolstoy's intention. By frustrating our high expectations with such a commonplace image, he makes the extraordinary seem ordinary, challenging yet again familiar paradigms about what it means to die—and to live.

Do any of us really know what lies on the other side? What if there *is* a clear and simple light, a single ideal worth living for, a "truth that will destroy all evil in people, and give them great blessings?"[39] And what if It—that truth, that *pravda* (also a feminine noun in Russian)—has been staring at us the whole time? This is a possibility Tolstoy offers us as early as in War and Peace. That epic novel eschews moralizing and is anything but simplistic, yet even a dying Prince Andrei seems to be struck by the simple clarity of it all:

> "Yes, that was death. I died—I woke up. Yes, death is an awakening." Clarity suddenly came to his soul, and the curtain that until then had concealed the unknown was raised before his inner gaze. He felt the release of a force that previously had been as if bound in him and that strange lightness which from then on did not leave him.[40]

Despite the many obvious differences between Ivan and Andrei, their final moments are rendered with remarkable similarity. Prince Andrei shares with Ivan the unique status of having come as close as any of Tolstoy's characters to peering on the other side of death while still alive. Yet in *War and Peace,* despite the long description of how Andrei veers in and out of ordinary consciousness, the artist is not satisfied to leave readers for too long in the realm of the ethereal. Tolstoy brings us back down to the here-and-now, to what *we* are able to see and comprehend, by focusing our attention on the reaction of the onlookers to Andrei's death:

> "Is it over?!" said Princess Marya, after his body had already lain motionless before them for several minutes, growing cold. Natasha went up, looked into the dead eyes, and hastened to close them. She closed them and did not kiss them, but pressed her lips to that which was her nearest reminder of him.
>
> "Where has he gone? Where is he now? . . ."[41]

Those are questions Tolstoy does not try to answer in *War and Peace.* Interestingly, for all of his authorial heavy-handedness in *Ivan,* he does not try to answer them in the later work either. In the novella's final lines the great realist writer reasserts himself. After describing the mystical light Ivan sees, Tolstoy plants us firmly back on earth:

> To him all this happened in a single instance, and the meaning of that instant did not change. For those present his agony continued for another two hours. Something rattled in his throat, his emaciated body twitched, then the gasping and rattle became less and less frequent.
>
> "It is finished!" said someone near him.
>
> He heard these words and repeated them in his soul.
>
> "Death is finished," he said to himself. "It is no more!"
>
> He drew in a breath, stopped in the midst of a sigh, stretched out, and died. (128, 12)

We hear the rattling in Ivan's throat, watch his body twitch, and witness what the onlookers witness. Even Ivan's ethereal "'Death is finished . . .'" is an echo of the words he hears spoken near him in real time. The novella's final line is a stark, unidealized portrait of physical death. The Christian overtones in Ivan's stretching out, Christ-like, are strikingly this-worldly, stripped of all mysticism. Just as Christ died as a human being on a cross, so Ivan died as a man in a bed.[42]

Tolstoy thus ends the work where he began it: in our imperfect world. It is from within that finite perspective, the artist seems to concede, that we must grapple with the ultimate questions of life and death. He moves us, finally, not through a transcendent vision but by an earth-bound image we can immediately recognize: ourselves. He leaves us with a challenge: After we have traveled with Ivan on his agonizing odyssey, what does that emaciated, twitching, stretched-out body mean to us now? Does it prompt us to say with Pyotr Ivanovich and the other funeral-goers, "'Well, he's dead but I'm alive!'"? (84, 1). Or does that dead body make the truism "we are on this earth but briefly" come viscerally alive for us?

Tolstoy's best creative powers in *Ivan* go into his depiction of one man's agonizing confrontation with the ultimate existential truth, not so that readers would fear death, but so that they would embrace the possibilities of life. We need not stumble through our existence, like Ivan, Tolstoy tells us. We can make more positive, courageous choices about how we spend our time, treat others, and connect to the world around us. If this message is present at the end of *Ivan*, it will reverberate like a battle cry throughout Tolstoy's next novel, *Resurrection*.

twelve

COMING ALIVE

Dmitry Nekhliudov and *Resurrection*

Resurrection is Tolstoy's most didactic novel. He toiled over it on and off from 1889 through 1898, when he decided to finish it quickly in order to use the proceeds to aid the emigration of the Dukhobors, a persecuted Christian sect who were trying to emigrate to Canada. Theirs was one of Tolstoy's most public causes, but far from his only one. Throughout the 1890s the prophet and social critic railed against the privileged upper classes, merchants, lawyers, professors, artists, educators, preachers, and politicians, assailing nearly every modern institution with his indignant pen.

Tolstoy also hoped the novel would inspire readers with its positive message of redemption. He told his biographer, Pavel Biriukov, that he "wrote the whole novel *Resurrection* so that people would read the last chapter. If in my artistic works there is any worth, then it is only that they serve as an advertisement for the thoughts which appear there."[1] Readers are indeed struck by how many thoughts appear in this novel, and not only in the end, where the writer extensively quotes the Gospels, but throughout the work. We find authorial asides about characters' motivations and thought processes, angry social commentaries, and general philosophical reflections, often placed without quotation marks in the mind of Nekhliudov, the author's alter ego. At the heart of Tolstoy's thinking and teaching in this novel lies a radically simple idea, which he expressed over and over again in the last thirty years of his life, and puts into the mouth of his hero, Dmitry Nekhliudov: "[M]utual love is the fundamental law of human life" (450; II, 40).[2]

To a twenty-first-century reader, Tolstoy's didacticism might seem off-putting. Even in Tolstoy's time some Russian readers saw the work as preachy, and derisively referred to it as a "socio-moral pamphlet" and an "act of indictment."[3] *Resurrection* especially disturbed conservative thinkers and governmental authorities, who used the novel, which specifically indicts the Church, as occasion to expel the writer from that institution.[4] D. I. Ilovaisky, a prominent conservative professor of history at Moscow State University and editor of the progovernment weekly *The Kremlin*, spoke for most archconservatives when he recommended that the work be "relegated to oblivion."[5] As Soviet scholar Eduard Babaev later observed, Ilovaisky, attuned to the spirit of the times, must have sensed something "ominous and prophetic" in the novel: it all too accurately portended the downfall of the old order.[6]

Tolstoy's didacticism also bothered the writer Anton Chekhov, who eschewed moralizing in art. He found Tolstoy's portrait of corrupt officialdom penetrating but the novel's ending unconvincing. Chekhov's disapproval of the novel on aesthetic grounds has been echoed more recently by George Steiner and others.[7] But Edward Wasiolek breaks rank with the usual criticism of the novel, when he argues that Tolstoy's didacticism did "not mar *Resurrection*—at least as seriously as Steiner and others would have us believe."[8] The didactic essays, he argues, are "illustrative" and "generalizing" of Nekhliudov's "personal and seemingly exceptional" story, and both illustrate "the class nature of the evils that beset contemporary Russian life."[9] Wasiolek's emphasis on "the class nature of the evils" is perhaps too limiting, but his argument that there is an organic connection between the artistic and polemical elements of the novel provides an important corrective to those critics who have found the thinker and artist to be at cross purposes. If in *War and Peace* the polemical sections are reductive attempts to argue rationally what the novel shows artistically, and in *Anna Karenina* and *The Death of Ivan Ilyich* the author's ideological positions are more seamlessly integrated into the storyline, then in *Resurrection* the polemics *are* the storyline. The novel is one long argument, a massive social tract in images.

In Tolstoy's earlier novels we find a carefully balanced interchange between the real and the ideal. Tolstoy's beloved hero, Truth, is a union of both realms, the yin and the yang of his overarching vision of life. Even the ending of *Anna Karenina*, written when Tolstoy was set on finding

absolute theological solutions to life's challenges, honors the complex reality of Levin's ongoing evolution. In *Anna Karenina* there is a fuller human
portrait of the "negative" characters. We like Oblonsky, even as we find
him morally reprehensible. Not so the corrupt priest who leads the famous
prison service, or nearly any of the other characters Tolstoy mercilessly
lampoons in *Resurrection*. In this novel the writer tends to isolate specific
aspects of characters' behavior—such as the priest's having been brought
up wrongly, or his desire to send his children to an expensive school—and
these become the lens through which he explains their actions.

In *Resurrection,* which one British newspaper in 1899 appropriately
called "the most uncompromising book ever written," reality does not
unfold from moment to moment in a rich, subtle palette but is drawn
in stark, primary colors.[10] The novel's purpose is not to engage readers
vicariously in the hero's never-ending search, but to provide a persuasive
rationale for the ideals the novel intends to teach, and to provide a recognizable backdrop within which those lessons may be illustrated with maxi-
mal force. The psychological realist is in full service of the ideologue and
visionary.

In fact, it might be said that *Resurrection* is the first and one of the
most successful examples of the genre of social realism in Russian literature. According to socialist realist doctrine, which became dominant during the 1930s and 1940s in the Soviet Union, a work of art must present
a clear ideological position—which, in the Soviet context, meant the gospel of socialism. From the artistic standpoint, most socialist realist fiction
was mediocre at best—a fact that suggests the incommensurability of great
art and ideological agenda. However, as the Soviet critic Mikhail Bakhtin
pointed out, *Resurrection* represents a rare exception to this general rule.
He even recommended the novel as a model of effective socialist realism
for Soviet writers to emulate.[11]

Tolstoy presents his unifying idea and main argument in the novel's
famous opening paragraph:

> Though men in their hundreds of thousands had tried their hardest to
> disfigure that little corner of the earth where they had crowded them-
> selves together, paving the ground with stones so that nothing could
> grow, weeding out every blade of vegetation, filling the air with the
> fumes of coal and gas, cutting down the trees and driving away every
> beast and every bird—spring, however, was still spring, even in the
> town. The sun shone warm, the grass, wherever it had not been scraped
> away, revived and showed green not only on the narrow strips of lawn

on the boulevards but between the paving-stones as well, and birches, the poplars and the wild cherry-trees were unfolding their sticky, fragrant leaves, and the swelling buds were bursting on the lime-trees; the jackdaws, the sparrows and the pigeons were cheerfully getting their nests ready for the spring, and the flies, warmed by the sunshine, buzzed gaily along the walls. All were happy—plants, birds, insects, and children. But grown-up people—adult men and women—never left off deceiving and tormenting themselves and one another. It was not this spring morning which they considered sacred and important, not the beauty of God's world, given to all creatures to enjoy—a beauty which inclines the heart to peace, to harmony, and to love. No, what they considered sacred and important were their own devices for wielding power over each other. (19; I, 1)

No matter how thoroughly man degrades himself and defiles his world, Tolstoy tells us, no matter how far he strays from what is good in him, life's essential beauty and integrity—embodied in nature's transcendent truth—always renews itself. This optimistic view of humanity radiates throughout an otherwise mordant portrait of a Russian society awash in corruption and moral degradation. Everything in the novel springs directly from this idea. Just as the healing forces of spring return to the city, year after year, so the rejuvenating energies of the soul inevitably return to the fallen protagonists, Dmitry Nekhliudov and Katyusha Maslova, bringing them back to their authentic selves, to one another, and to the splendor of life. The narrator's commentaries and his artistic portrait of the physical and moral debasement of one human being by another point to the same objective truth: human beings mistreat one another simply because they do not see that every person is a particle of nature's indestructible beauty, indispensable to the all-encompassing "beauty of God's world."

The quotations from the Gospels found in the novel's epigraph and final part also derive from the novel's unifying truth: once we understand the nature of reality and the ultimate purpose of our lives, Tolstoy insists, then compassion, nonviolent resistance to evil, and a renunciation of all judgments of others—the lessons taught by Jesus in his Sermon on the Mount—become the only sensible ways of being in the world. Any other way of relating necessarily stems from a false perception of reality, and inevitably leads to suffering in ourselves and others.

"In Tolstoy's fiction," writes Richard Gustafson, "there is only one plot event: all works embody and reveal the way to love. . . . These narratives of human relatedness are emblematic stories of God's life coming to be."[12] This is perhaps an overstatement when applied to Tolstoy's earlier novels, but it is a helpful formulation of the worldview of *Resurrection*. If the earlier author gave us unflinching portraits of life as it is, then in *Resurrection* he offers an uncompromising vision of life as Tolstoy knows it *should* be.

And what should be is, in fact, coming to pass before our eyes, in the parablelike journey of the hero, Dmitry Nekhliudov, from sin to salvation. To reconnect with life's wonder, Nekhliudov need only free himself from his attachment to things and false symbols and external authorities, which prevent him from seeing the truth and hearing his authentic inner voice.

THE ISOLATED SEEKER

Nekhliudov, the last of the Tolstoyan seekers, is still asking the fundamental questions and fiercely examining the foundation upon which his life and society are built. His lonely journey proceeds without the support of family or friends or a nurturing community. This is a telling difference from the plight of earlier searchers. If Pierre, Andrei, Nikolai, and Levin eventually find a measure of personal fulfillment in family life on their estates, Nekhliudov does not. His ownership of land and participation in the institution of serfdom are a source of shame and a symbol of his "chronic selfishness."[13] Memories of his late mother, who condoned his sexual promiscuity and mocked his spiritual quest, now fill Nekhliudov with repulsion. His once close sister, Natalia, settled into a staid marriage with a morally stunted careerist, has become distant. Nikolenka Irtenev, Nekhliudov's childhood friend and moral inspiration, has died before the novel begins. His childhood friend Selenin, now a public prosecutor, has traded in his youthful dream of serving humanity for service to the State. That is why in adulthood he and Nekhliudov have become spiritual strangers, and Selenin's "eyes always looked sad" (366; II, 23).

Nekhliudov's isolation is presented not as one man's unhappy fate but as the universal condition of modern life. If he is, in John Bayley's words, "the kind of character who in Tolstoy is observed and not observing—a Tolstoyan object and not a Tolstoyan subject,"[14] then that is because, for the later Tolstoy, man's capacity for expansive awareness and stirring revelation has been diminished by the soul-numbing forces of modern life. "There was only one thing to do: not think about it," Nekhliudov decides after abandoning Katyusha (96; I, 18).

"Not thinking about it" has become the modus operandi of not only his life but that of nearly every other character. Spiritual sclerosis is a

Figure 5   L. N. Tolstoy on his way from Moscow to Yasnaya Polyana, 1886 or 1888. Original photo appeared in the St. Petersburg magazine *Kopecks*, 1910. Courtesy of L. N. Tolstoy State Museum, Moscow.

national epidemic. Nekhliudov knows that he has given up his youthful ideals, but what was he to do? "Now that he had become a great landed proprietor . . . [h]e did not want to go back into government service, and moreover, he had acquired luxurious habits which he felt unable to give up" (35; I, 3). The psychological realism here is devastatingly accurate— and familiar. Social power, financial success, and a comfortable lifestyle can be powerful deterrents to change, and can blind us to our authentic inner selves and needs.

In *Resurrection* Tolstoy gives this insight a distinctly Rousseauian col-oration—man is spiritually alive and morally aware, until the influences of modern society deaden him:

At first Nekhliudov made a fight for his principles but the struggle was too hard; since everything he had considered right when he put his faith in his own conscience was wrong according to other people, and vice versa, everything which he, believing himself, regarded as bad, was held to be good by all the people around him. And at last Nekhliudov gave in: that is, he let off believing in his own ideals and began to believe in those of other people. At first this renunciation of his true self was unpleasant but the disagreeable sensation lasted a very short while and very soon Nekhliudov, who in the meantime had begun to smoke and drink wine, forgot the uncomfortable feeling and even experienced great relief. (75; I, 13)

Nekhliudov's smoking, a detail emphasized throughout the novel, is, like Ivan's card-playing, an outward manifestation of his internal stupor. At least that is how Tolstoy probably viewed it. In the treatise "Why Do Men Stupefy Themselves?" published in 1890, when he was beginning work on *Resurrection,* Tolstoy wrote: "People drink and smoke, not casually, not from dullness, not to cheer themselves up, not because it is pleasant, but in order to drown the voice of conscience in themselves."[15] The healthy discomfort of Nekhliudov's once struggling conscience has been dulled by the narcotic of complacency. Falsehood and evil have become so embedded in the fabric of his ordinary, everyday life that he no longer recognizes them as false or evil. Gary Saul Morson, writing about Oblonsky, aptly describes Tolstoy's conception of evil: It is "right here, right now," and it "conquers by redirecting our attention from what we should do. It tempts us to negligence."[16]

Like an addict going through withdrawal, Nekhliudov will shed the comfortable numbness blinding him to the truth about himself and his world. Before he can answer the question "How should I live?" Nekhliudov must confront how he *has* lived. He must face with wounding clarity the falsehood, hypocrisy, and brutality within him—and around him. To appreciate why Tolstoy might have felt it necessary to put Nekhliudov through this crucible of questioning, it is helpful to understand something of the writer's personal connection with his hero.

Nekhliudov's story was inspired by an account Tolstoy heard in June 1887 from Anatoly Koni, a famous jurist who was visiting the writer at Yasnaya Polyana. Koni told the story of an agitated young man, an aristocrat (the future Nekhliudov), who had come to his office seeking assistance in conveying a letter to a girl recently sent to prison. The girl, Rozali Oni, a prostitute, had been sentenced for stealing money from a brothel guest. From his visitor Koni learned that Rozali Oni was the daughter of a Finnish widower, who was a tenant on a farmstead in one of the Finnish provinces. Upon discovering that he was fatally ill, the father turned to the owner of the farmstead, a wealthy Petersburg lady, and asked her to look after his daughter. While working as a servant on the lady's estate, the sixteen-year-old Rozali was seduced by the lady's relative, a young man in his late teens visiting for the summer; that relative was the man who appeared in Koni's office. After Rozali bore his child, she was sent away, and the young man abandoned her. She sent the child to a foster home, and slowly slipped into a life of prostitution.

Years later, she was sentenced to four months in prison for stealing a hundred rubles from a drunken brothel guest. As fate would have it, the man who seduced her was summoned to sit on the jury on the very day of her trial. Realizing that he was responsible for Rozali's fate, he resolved to make amends by marrying her. Although the marriage would have to be postponed because of Lent, her seducer frequently visited Rozali in prison, bringing her money and supplies. After Lent she contracted spotted fever and died. Koni never learned what happened to the young man after that.

Moved by this story, Tolstoy encouraged the talented Koni to write it up, and the jurist agreed. A year went by and nothing materialized, so Tolstoy asked Koni if he could use the story himself. Thus began Tolstoy's work on *Resurrection,* a novel that he continued to refer to as the "Koni story" in his private correspondence and diaries, even after he had settled on its final title. The Koni "story" probably made such a powerful impression on the writer because in his youth he had done something similar. He told Pavel Biriukov not long before his death:

> Here you're writing all good things about me. That's not true and incomplete. It's necessary to write about the bad, as well. In my youth I led a very debauched life, and two events from this life especially torment me to this day. And I will tell you, as my biographer, and request that you write this in my biography. These two events were: a liaison with a peasant woman in our village, before my marriage. There is a hint about this in my story, "The Devil." The second was a crime, which I committed with the chambermaid, Gasha, living in the home of my aunt. She was innocent, and I seduced her, abandoned her, and she died.[17]

This direct autobiographical link between the writer and his hero is underscored by the hero's name. Nekhliudov is the autobiographical hero of Tolstoy's early novella *A Landowner's Morning* (1856) and the short story "Lucerne" (1857), both about young men whose efforts at moral perfection are thwarted by social realities and personal egotism. In the early trilogy *Childhood, Boyhood, Youth* (1852–57), Nekhliudov is the friend of the narrator, Nikolenka Irtenev, and when he appears in *Boyhood* he inspires him with an "ideal of virtue and a firm belief that it was man's destiny to be constantly perfecting himself."[18] In *Resurrection* Nekhliudov and Nikolenka have changed positions. Nekhliudov has fallen, whereas Nikolenka Irtenev, as mentioned earlier, has died.

When *Resurrection* opens, Nekhliudov has long hidden his guilty conscience beneath a mountain of denial. His aunts, who have concluded that Katyusha was "a bad girl, and depraved by nature, just like her mother" (96; I, 18), made it easy for him to justify and forget his actions. Society, Tolstoy writes in his *Confession*, also made it easy for him to forget about his youthful sins by condoning and even encouraging his behavior. As the writer makes achingly clear in that work, only a complete transformation of values would lift him out of the swamp of lies. In creating the character of Nekhliudov and the story of his resurrection, Tolstoy recreated and relived the act of his personal salvation.

The writer makes clear from the outset that Nekhliudov embodies the habits of dehumanization that are rampant in all corners and classes of his society. Before we even meet him, we meet the woman he debased in his youth, Katyusha Maslova, a prostitute (based on Rozali Oni) who is facing trial for murder and who is being demeaned still further by her environment. The haggard-looking prison matron; the faceless, key-rattling prison warder, who fetches Maslova; the prison clerk, who hands Maslova and an official document reeking of tobacco over to the soldiers; and the nameless soldiers who escort her—all are blind functionaries. Themselves debased prisoners of the system they protect, they dehumanize their prisoner, while street spectators point fingers and make facile, self-deluding judgments. "'This is what evil conduct—conduct not like ours—leads to,'" think the onlookers (22; I, 1). The children "stared terror-stricken," but are relieved to see that the guards prevent the criminal from harming them. With biting irony, Tolstoy shows how the corrupting processes of socialization begin early, for the children's "protectors" uphold a social and legal machine that will condemn Maslova to hard labor in Siberia for a crime she did not commit.

As the pallid, beleaguered Katyusha in dirty prison garb is being taken to the courtroom, the twenty-eight-year-old Nekhliudov, a creature of habit and a prisoner of privilege, is having difficulty waking up, literally and metaphorically. He still lies "on his high crumpled bed with its springs and down mattress" (29; I, 3). His vacant eyes, staring into space, contrast with Maslova's "sparkling jet-black eyes" (21; I, 1), alive despite the dreariness of her circumstances. Nekhliudov's empty eyes also contrast with the plenitude of luxuriant objects comprising his morning toilette. He bathes his "muscular, plump white body" (30; I, 3), cleans his nails and teeth, and combs his hair—all with the finest, most expensive appurtenances—in a dressing-room reeking with the artificial aromas of elixirs, eau de Cologne, and perfumes. Then he puts on "clean freshly ironed linen and boots which shone like glass," and a necktie from his extensive collection (30; I, 3). The things that surround and adorn Nekhliudov are lively and clean, whereas the "dirt which had clogged his soul to the point of inaction," we later learn, has led nearly to "the total cessation" of his inner life (140; I, 28).

For Nekhliudov everything blurs together, as if questions about what to wear, whom to marry, and how to extricate himself from an irritating extramarital affair are all equally important. Having lost all ability to distinguish between the trivial and the significant, he thinks vaguely about marriage as a pleasant solution to "the irregularities of his sexual life" (37; I, 4) and a satisfactory antidote to the general emptiness of his life. But he is not ready to make any personal commitments. Concluding that he must first settle his affair with the Marshal of the Nobility's wife, Nekhliudov avoids Princess Missy Korchagina, a superficial gentlewoman who has just sent him a letter as part of her "skillful campaign" to lure him into marriage. He is relieved to step into his cab, and cheered that he is on his way to the courthouse, where he will now "fulfill a public duty in my usual conscientious way . . ." (38; I, 4). Public duty as an abstract category attracts him, as it does most characters in this novel, regardless of where they fit into the social hierarchy. Actual commitments of the heart are still beyond him.

An ordinary day in Nekhliudov's life turns extraordinary when, by some colossal coincidence, the hero discovers that the jury he has been summoned to sit on will decide the case of a certain Katyusha Maslova, accused of fatally poisoning and then robbing a merchant who had been a guest in her brothel. Nekhliudov recognizes Katyusha, whom he has not seen since abandoning her almost ten years ago, when she had been a young ward on his aunts' estate. The men who will decide her fate are, like Nekhliudov, philanderers and sybarites. The president of the court has a mistress, members of the jury steal furtive glances at the attractive Maslova during their breaks, and the assistant prosecutor has come to court tired, because of an evening of carousing that ended in the very brothel where Katyusha Maslova once worked. "Everybody drew a sigh of relief in the pleasant knowledge that now the trial had begun, and everything would be made clear and justice be satisfied" (60; I, 10). Tolstoy knows otherwise. His contempt for the charade of justice is undisguised.

Against the backdrop of the bogus courtroom proceedings Nekhliudov's inner drama unfolds. "Yes, it was she," the narrator indirectly reports his speech. "There was no mistaking that especial, mysterious individuality which distinguishes every face from all others, giving it something peculiar, all its own, and making it different from every other face" (55; I, 9). "Yes, it was Katyusha," the narrator reports Nekhliudov's thoughts again a few pages later (68; I, 12). During a flashback description of the young Nekhliudov's reunion with Katyusha after a three-year absence, the narrator repeats yet again: "It was she, Katyusha. The same Katyusha, only more enchanting than before" (79; I, 14). The shock of recognition is repeated three times; Nekhliudov's capacity to see the unique humanity of the girl he once loved may be dulled, but it is not defunct. So, too, his own soul might be badly bruised and besmirched, but is not wholly ruined.

"LOVE OF A STILL LOFTIER KIND"

By sandwiching the flashback in the middle of the description of the trial, Tolstoy achieves more than an obvious contrast between the cynical juror and the former idealist; he creates the impression of a spiritual continuity between the boy Nekhliudov was then and the man he has become. "The instant Katya entered the room, it was as if the sun had come out: everything seemed more interesting, gayer, and life held more meaning and was happier" (71; I, 12). Such is the teenage Nekhliudov's reaction to the young ward on his aunt's estate. In his innocent, all-embracing love, social distinctions disappeared, and thoughts of romantic conquest were nonexistent. His love for Katyusha "was simply one of the manifestations of the joys of life that filled his whole being and was shared by that sweet, light-hearted girl" (72; I, 12). Now, when he sees Katyusha entering a different kind of room under very different circumstances, something stirs again inside him. Even in prison garb her spirit shines through.

But he is a juror now, and she is a prisoner. He fears that at any moment his former relations with his aunts' ward will be discovered. Concerned with social appearances, he hides beneath his usual façade of moral superiority, deflecting judgment outward: He is "overwhelmed with horror at the thought of what Maslova, the innocent and charming girl he had known ten years ago, might have done" (60; I, 10). At some level he knows that he should he horrified at the thought of what he, the once innocent and charming boy, has done—not only to Katyusha, but to himself. Tolstoy compares his feelings to those of a hunter who wants to silence a wounded bird he has just shot, but the bird keeps fluttering in the game-bag. He cannot stifle the memory of what he did to the girl he loved.

As if to prolong not only Nekhliudov's discomfort but the reader's as well, Tolstoy lists with excruciating precision every gory detail of the coroner's report. The corpse of the boorish merchant—with "the serum oozing from the nostrils of the dead body, the eyes protruding from their sockets"—fills the courtroom with its stench and Nekhliudov with an "indefinable disgust" (100; I, 20). The decayed corpse reeks of too much truth, setting off alarms in the court of higher justice in session inside Nekhliudov's struggling conscience. Returning to the courtroom after a break, Nekhliudov is "panic-stricken, as though he were going, not to give a verdict but to be tried himself" (97; I, 19). He senses that the warning contained in the corpse and in Katyusha's strange reemergence in his life applies to him, though he would like to deny this inconvenient truth:

> He felt like a puppy when its master seizes it by the neck and rubs its nose in the mess it has made. The puppy squeals and draws back, trying to get as far away as possible from the effects of its misdeed and forget it; but the implacable master will not let it go. So Nekhliudov, now appreciating the baseness of what he had done, felt the mighty hand of the Master; but he still did not realize the significance of what he had done, or recognize the Master's hand. He did not want to believe that what he saw now was his doing. But the inexorable, invisible hand held him and he already had a presentiment that he would never wriggle free. (111; I, 22)

This strikingly earthy image injects an element of dark humor into an otherwise weighty situation. So skewed has Nekhliudov's moral perspective become that he cannot distinguish between a puppy who soils the carpet out of biological necessity and a young man who destroys a girl's life out of moral weakness. But in contrast to the puppy's offense, Nekhliudov's "ordinary" crime has had extraordinary consequences. So his puppylike fear and denial must be replaced by a more mature, human response. As occurs in some moments of epiphany in *War and Peace*— such as Andrei's lying on the battlefield of Austerlitz, or Pierre's watching the comet of 1812—the Master's "inexorable, invisible hand" guides Nekhliudov towards truth when he is not searching for it and least expects it. Nekhliudov has further to travel than the earlier characters, and he will have to work even harder than they do, and clear away more moral rot, in order to get to his destination. But Tolstoy's belief in a guiding higher truth has not changed.

Four times Nekhliudov thinks it a "strange," "extraordinary," "remarkable" "coincidence" that he happened to be sitting on the jury on that very day in that very case. The adjective Tolstoy uses each time is *"udivitel'-nyj"*—literally, "surprising." From Nekhliudov's perspective these uncanny coincidences and new insights are "surprising." From Tolstoy's godlike perspective, they are part of a larger, purposeful design. The capacity to sense that design, to be moved by a profound revelation, is returning to the character's slowly awakening consciousness.

Tolstoy intriguingly connects Nekhliudov's heightened awareness in the courtroom with his exalted perception of life in the years before he "gave in." Then life seemed to him a joyous gift, a continual surprise. He believed in the "endless perfectibility of himself and the whole universe" (68; I, 12). "God's world was a mystery, which with excitement he strove to penetrate. . . . [W]omen had seemed enchanting creatures—enchanting because of their very mystery" (73; I, 13). Human beings were not instruments for the gratification of his personal appetites, as they have since become, but vehicles through which Nekhliudov touched the transcendent. This is most powerfully communicated in the flashback description of an Easter service that Nekhliudov recalls during the court proceedings. Everybody is celebrating together—men, women, children, the gentry, the working classes, and the peasantry. Even Nekhliudov's horse "pricks its ears at the sight of the little lights round the church" (81; I, 15). Here is the embodiment of the ideal of community, the unity in the diversity of life, what in Russian Orthodoxy is call *sobornost'*. The inspired young idealist *"is surprised"* [my emphasis] that a subdeacon, who accidentally brushes up against the young Katyusha,

> did not understand that everything here—here, and in the whole wide world, too, existed solely for Katyusha, and that one might be careless about everything else in the world but not about her, because she was the center of the universe. For her glittered the gold of the iconostasis; for her burned all the candles in the candelabrum, and the candlestands; for her the joyful chant rang out: "The Passover of the Lord, Rejoice, O ye people!" All—all that was good on earth was for her. And

it seemed to him that Katyusha knew that it was all for her. So it seemed to Nekhliudov when he looked at her slender form in the white dress with the tucked bodice, and the happy rapt face whose expression told him that the song that his own heart was singing was echoed word-for-word in hers. (83–84; I, 15)

Everything we see and feel in this moment is through Nekhliudov's expanded consciousness, merging with that of the godlike narrator. Beginning with the impersonal Russian construction "Nekhliudov was surprised . . ." ("*Nekhliudovu zhe bylo udivitel'no,*" or, literally, "To Nekhliudov it was surprising"), the entire paragraph is built on either impersonal sentence constructions, or sentences whose subjects are the glittering gold of the iconostasis, the burning candles, and the candle-stands. These objects and Nekhliudov himself are the instruments through which the transcendent beauty of life is conveyed to the readers. Katyusha, in turn, is the vehicle through which they are communicated to him. "All—all that that was good on earth was for her." Distinctions between the animate and inanimate world, self and other, disappear for him, and they dissolve for the reader, as well. We see and hear the beauty of the service, because Nekhliudov sees and hears it. We hear the song in Katyusha's heart, because Nekhliudov hears it echoed in his own.

The imagery in this scene is not a metaphor for the divine. Here *is* the divine coming into being in this very moment.[19] The ceremonial objects are not symbols of something out there, but, when transformed by Nekhliudov's and the narrator's expanded perception, they glisten with meaning down here. The traditional Easter greeting "'Christ is risen!'" repeated over and over in this scene is a verbal expression of this idea. When Katyusha kisses the noseless beggar, she is Christ-like. When Nekhliudov listens to Matryona Pavlovna, the elderly maid of his aunts, pronounce the Easter greeting, he hears in her voice other words: "'On this night we are all equal'" (85; I, 15). Nekhliudov feels this unity, precisely because he feels the divine force within himself: "He knew she had that love in her because that night and morning he was conscious of it in himself, and conscious that in this love he became one with her" (86; I, 15).

The depiction of the Easter service contrasts sharply with Tolstoy's satirical presentation of religious symbolism elsewhere in the novel. The icons of Christ adorning the corrupt prisons and courthouses are presented as a travesty of Christ's teachings. The Eucharist ceremony in the prison, ending with the priest's going behind the partition and "drinking up all the blood left in the cup and eating all the remaining bits of God's body," is for Tolstoy a travesty of genuine Christian feeling (182; I, 39). The writer's message is clear: in order to rediscover the sort of love he experienced at the Easter service, Nekhliudov will have to see beyond all fake symbols, religious or otherwise, that have become substitutes for genuine human feeling and connection. In an interview with a Moscow newspaper, Tolstoy said that in *Resurrection,* "I tried to portray various forms of love: Exalted love, sensual love, and love of a still loftier kind, the love that ennobles man, and in this form of love lies resurrection."[20] What Nekhliudov experiences at the Easter service is "exalted love." Resurrection—that "still loftier kind of love"—is what he will experience during his journey back to himself, to Katyusha, and to the divine.

Temptations to abandon the voyage abound from the beginning. Katyusha is sentenced to penal servitude in Siberia, because of a juridical error (the jurors mistakenly omit the phrase "but without intent to take life" from the guilty verdict), providing Nekhliudov with just the out he needs: "The wounded bird would stop fluttering in the game-bag and would remind him of its existence no longer" (120; I, 23). But the Master's "invisible, inexorable" hand gently guides him forward.

One by one, old perceptions become shattered, as he begins to see his world through a new prism. He visits the Korchagins after the trial, and finds it "surprising" that "everything in the house jarred—everything, beginning with doorkeeper" (128; I, 26).[21] "'Shameful and disgusting, disgusting and shameful,'" becomes Nekhliudov's new catchphrase, which he repeats multiple times (136; I, 28). At home he sees his recently deceased mother in a new light. Framed in a tasteless portrait by a famous artist, her essence is laid bare before him, literally. Nekhliudov notices her heavily cleavaged bosom, naked shoulders and neck, and can still detect the "heavy sickening smell" of her decomposing body (138; I, 28). Significantly, he does not even notice her face, which, in Russian Orthodoxy, is a window into a human being's divine essence. A prisoner of her flesh, in death as in life, Nekhliudov's framed mother mirrors the empty egotism of his own life.

When Nekhliudov awakes the next morning, "he [knows] that something important and good [has] happened" to him (158; I, 33). And "by a surprising coincidence," that same morning a letter arrives from his lover, the Marshal of the Nobility's wife, who breaks off their relations and wishes him well, clearing the way for him to carry out his intention to "'shatter the lie which is binding me, and admit everything, and tell the truth to everybody'" (141; I, 28).

Critics have argued that the character's major spiritual transformation already has taken place by this point in the novel.[22] This is not quite the case. Even after he resolves to "'tell the truth to everybody,'" the spiritual being and the self-seeking egotist continue to battle inside of him. "'Haven't you tried before to improve and be better, and nothing came of it?' whispered the voice of the tempter within. 'So what is the use of trying any more? You are not the only one—everyone's the same—life is like that,' whispered the voice" (141; I, 28). That voice is familiar to those of us who have struggled, and failed, to overcome an addiction. It is the voice of rationalization for not doing something we know we should do or repairing something we know is broken in our lives. Tolstoy indicates that he had in mind just this universal dimension of Nekhliudov's inner struggle, when in an 1895 diary entry he "clarified something of importance" for the novel: "namely duality of intention—two people: one timid, lonely, striving to improve himself, a timid reformer; and the other a worshipper of tradition, living by inertia and poeticizing it."[23]

The man who lives by inertia grows increasingly delighted with himself for trying to reverse the technical error made by the jury. But, as Richard Gustafson astutely points out, Nekhliudov "begins with a flawed conception of sin as a past act, a single, individual violation of love he can correct."[24] The error in need of correction, Tolstoy makes clear, is not procedural but lies in the character's very way of being in the world. Nekhliudov's eyes fill with "good and bad tears: good because they were tears of joy at the awakening of the spiritual being within him, the being that had slumbered all these years; and bad tears of tender emotion at his own goodness" (142; I, 28). Tears come to his eyes again, and "an extraordinary feeling of elation seized him," when he contemplates telling Katyusha of his plan to atone for his sin by marrying her (162; I, 33). These are still the wrong kind of tears. Nekhliudov is crying over the exalted *idea* of expiation, and not because he has actually atoned or even fully understands yet what he must atone for.

The tears flow yet again when Nekhliudov awaits his first interview with Katyusha behind the wire netting at the prison. He congratulates himself for doing his duty: "'Yes, I am doing what I ought to do, I am showing that I'm sorry.'" He asks for her forgiveness "in a loud, expressionless voice, like a lesson learned by heart" (195; I, 43). Katyusha senses the false note, and remains unmoved. She treats Nekhliudov like one of those "well-dressed, well-groomed gentlemen" whom she has learned to make profitable use of (198; I, 43). She gives him "an alluring smile" and does what she would with any of her customers: She asks him for money—evoking, poignantly, their meeting years earlier, the day after the seduction, when Nekhliudov handed her "a sum of money—as much as he thought proper according to their respective stations" (95; I, 18). At that time, the shamed young woman tried to push the money away.

The connection between this moment in the prison and the earlier one goes deeper still. Shocked by the fallen woman with the "defiled and bloated face" before him, Nekhliudov is tempted simply to give Katyusha the money and leave, letting the wounded bird of his guilt die in the game-bag (199; I, 43). The "voice" of "the tempter," who suggests this expedient solution to him, reminds the reader of the egoist's voice that spoke to Nekhliudov on the night of the seduction: "Though feebly, the voice of his real love for her was still audible, speaking to him of her, of *her* feelings, *her* life. But another voice kept saying: 'Mind, or you'll miss the opportunity for *your* enjoyment, *your* happiness'" (89; I, 16).

When Nekhliudov visits Katyusha in prison, he is still thinking of his feelings, and the most superficial ones at that. At this very moment, however, he feels that his "inner life was, as it were, wavering in the balance, and that the slightest effort would tip the scale to one side or the other. And he made the effort, calling to God Whose presence he had felt in his soul the day before, and that God instantly responded" (199; I, 43). The egoistic shell finally does crack, and the scale tips in favor of spiritual awakening. For the first time since their relations nearly a decade earlier, Nekhliudov thinks of *Katyusha's* feelings, *Katyusha's* life: "All he wanted was that she should cease being what she was now, that she should awaken and become what she had been before" (200; I, 43).

The scale tips further during their next meeting, when Katyusha startles Nekhliudov with her searing insight into his moral posturing: "'You want to save yourself through me. . . . You had your pleasure from me in this world, and now you want to get your salvation through me in the world to come!'" (218–19; I, 48). The reader knows she is partly right, and so, it appears, does Nekhliudov. The extent of his crime and the falseness of his efforts to purchase redemption on the cheap are unmasked:

"So this is what it means—this," thought Nekhliudov as he left the prison, only now fully understanding his crime. Had he not tried to expiate, to atone for his guilt he would never have felt the extent of his crime; moreover, neither would she have become conscious of just how much she had been wronged. Only now was all the horror of it made plain. Only now did he see what he had done to the soul of this woman; only now did she see and realize what had been done to her. Up to now

Nekhliudov had been dallying with his feelings of remorse, delighting in himself: now he was quite simply filled with terror. To cast her off— that, he felt, he could never do now, and yet he could not imagine what would come of his relations with her. (220; I, 49)

In that vulnerable place, without the protective cover of past denials or the comforting clarity of how to proceed, Nekhliudov can begin the next stage of his redemption. He stands naked before the truth, stripped of his previous belief that he is "the splendid, noble, high-minded young fellow he considered himself to be" (95; I, 18). The puppy sees, in an immediate, personal way, that he has defiled not a parquet floor but a human soul.

Having acknowledged the rot within, Nekhliudov can see more clearly the pain and ugliness around him. His search for personal truth and quest for social justice now begin to merge, as they often do with Tolstoy's seeking characters. What happened between him and Katyusha becomes for Tolstoy a microcosm of what is wrong with the entire social order. What is now happening between them provides a glimpse of the path to redemption for all of Russian society. The writer takes his hero on a harrowing journey through his fallen society, revealing to him, and to his readers, just how monumental is the mess they have created. Tolstoy the teacher and prophet comes forward to tell them what they can and must do to fix it.

A THEOLOGY OF FORGIVENESS

As he makes his way through the massive Russian bureaucracy on behalf of Katyusha and the other prisoners he is helping, Nekhliudov comes to reject virtually all modern institutions, which, as he now perceives, under the guise of improving human life, degrade it further. Neither politicians nor preachers, conservatives nor liberals, have the right answers. They are not even asking the right questions, or, in most cases, any questions at all. Why, Nekhliudov wonders, is a drunken peasant who kills in a moment of passion sentenced to hard labor in the mines, while a drunken dandy who kills in a duel is set free and only becomes more interesting to society as a result of his crime? Why is the peasant Menshov, already humiliated by a legal system that permitted a corrupt local storekeeper to get away with raping Menshov's wife with impunity, being humiliated still further by sitting in prison for a crime he didn't commit? Why is a group of Christian sectarians, who meet secretly on Sundays to read the Bible, sitting in prison and awaiting deportation? In search of answers, Nekhliudov pores over studies on the court and criminal justice systems, only to find that science addresses "thousands of very subtle and ingenious questions touching criminal law," yet fails to answer the simplest and most important one of all: "Why and by what right does one class of people lock up, torture, exile, flog, and kill other people, when they themselves are no better than those whom they torture, flog, and kill?" (403; II, 30). A lawyer laughs aloud when Nekhliudov wonders at the injustice of the law courts and invites his younger companion to a Saturday soiree to discuss "'philosophy'" with scholars, writers, and painters. But these "'abstract problems,'" as the lawyer describes them, are urgent, personal questions to Nekhliudov (312; II, 11).

The revolutionaries he meets in prison and in Siberia are also asking questions, but their answers are often wrong, and their motivations confused. Nekhliudov pities the revolutionary Vera Bogodoukhovskaya, who, despite her good intentions, has wasted her life on self-sacrifice for a heroic cause that she herself cannot name. "[T]he manifest jumble that filled her mind" (240; I, 55) epitomizes the muddle Nekhliudov finds in all revolutionary efforts. Most dangerous of all is the famous, monomaniacal Novodvorov, whose desire for power appears to Nekhliudov to be "founded on nothing more than vanity, on a desire to be a leader among men" (512; III, 15). "'Isn't yours the same kind of despotism that produced the Inquisition and the executions of the French Revolution?'" challenges another young revolutionary, the consumptive Kryltsov, during a debate. "'They, too, knew, in the light of science, the one true path'" (511; III, 14). The tragedy of twentieth-century Russian history, when the Novodvorov type of revolutionaries ascended to totalitarian power, bears out the prescience of Kryltsov's remark.

This young revolutionary arouses Nekhliudov's sympathy far more than the charismatic, cynical Novodvorov. In his short life Kryltsov has witnessed human cruelty and injustice, including the hanging of two innocent teenage boys who were his cellmates in a former prison. In Siberia, Kryltsov dies of consumption. "'Why had he suffered? Why had he lived? Does he understand now what it's all for?'" Nekhliudov thinks, while looking at Kryltsov's dead body in a dimly lit cell with sacks, logs, and three other corpses, which is serving as a mortuary (561; III, 27). Tolstoy implicitly poses these same questions about the convicts whose corpses Nekhliudov witnesses after they died while being forced to march in the blistering sun. Just after this experience, Nekhliudov meets the old Prince Korchagin in a train station passenger lounge, but the prince isn't interested in philosophical reflection. He is enjoying a nice meal with a bottle of wine before departing to his wife's sister's estate. In that brief encounter the essential difference between Nekhliudov and nearly every other upper-class character is presented in stark colors. Even if Nekhliudov doubts the methods and motivations of the revolutionaries, he shares their outrage at the existing order. Unlike the Korchagins, he is fiercely challenging the moral foundation of his world.

Of all the forms of corruption Nekhliudov witnesses, cruelty in the guise of religious faith is the most pervasive and insidious. He is repulsed by the public preacher Kiesewetter, whose cloying rhetoric about salvation is all the rage in certain high-society circles. Then there is the old general who is more eager to listen to the spirit of Joan of Arc talk to him about life after death than to listen to Nekhliudov tell him about the suffering of mistreated prisoners. More sinister still is the cruel Toporov (from "*topor,*" or axe), who, as the secular head of the Russian Orthodox Church, oversees governmental policy on religion, yet "[a]t the bottom of his heart . . . really believed in nothing" (383; II, 27).

Toporov is modeled on an actual historical personage, Konstantin Pobedonostsev, who was Procurator of the Holy Synod under Alexander III, and who denounced Tolstoy when *Resurrection* was published. Tolstoy's darkly satirical portrayal of Toporov, as well as other scenes of open contempt for the Church, fueled Pobedonostsev's decision to excommunicate the writer in 1901. After meeting with Toporov, Nekhliudov reflects: "'Could it really be that all this talk about justice, goodness, law, religion, God and so on was nothing but so many words to conceal the grossest self-interest and cruelty?'" (387; II, 27). His answer, left unspoken, is amply clear to the reader: religion as practiced by the Church is a travesty of the Christian principle of compassion.

Capitalism and private ownership of land are no less noxious to Nekhliudov. So disgusted is he by "[t]he contrast between the abject poverty of the peasants in the country and this stupid waste in which he himself had once taken part" that he resolves to give away his land to his peasants, and his wealthy home to his sister (305–6; II, 10). In the city, where he has taken up modest lodging near the prison, he is struck, "as though he saw it for the first time," by the "clean, fat shopkeepers, obviously firmly convinced that their efforts to cheat the ignorant who knew nothing about the quality of their wares was a very useful occupation" (306; II, 10). Later, Nekhliudov lashes out when he sees the construction of a

"stupid, useless palace for a stupid useless person, one of the very people who rob and ruin [his workers]."

"Yes, it's an idiotic house," he said his thought aloud.

"What do you mean—an idiotic house?" the cabby protested in an offended tone. "Thanks to it the people get work. I don't call that idiotic."

"But it is such useless work."

"It can't be useless, or they wouldn't be buildin' it. It means food for the people," said the driver. (314; II, 12)

The conversation is cut off, not only by the clatter of wheels but also by the clash of worldviews. In response to Nekhliudov's (and his creator's) outright rejection of capitalism, an increasingly dominant theme in Tolstoy's writing in the 1880s onward, the cabby makes a valid point: the construction of the building provides jobs. Yet in the context of the larger novel the cabby's remark has another meaning. To Nekhliudov (and Tolstoy) it is further evidence of deep-seated corruption, in which the powerful take advantage of the poor, who blindly submit to the abuse. The cabby cannot see the injustice of which he is a victim, and those in positions of power, Nekhliudov now understands, have no incentive to bring it to his attention. In fact, they themselves are blind—or willfully blind themselves—to the evils in which they participate.

This revelation acquires a special poignancy for Nekhliudov during a visit to his sister, Natalia, just before his departure to Siberia with Katyusha. She tries to persuade him to abandon his idealistic intention of marrying that "dreadful woman" (406; II, 31):

"I hardly think you will be happy."

"It is not a question of my happiness."

"Of course not. But if she has a heart, she cannot be happy either; she cannot even wish for the marriage."

"She does not wish it."

"I understand, but life . . ."

"What about life?"

"Life requires other things from us."

"Life only requires us to do what is right," said Nekhliudov, looking into her face which was still beautiful in spite of the tiny wrinkles round the eyes and mouth.

"I don't understand," she said with a sigh. (408; II, 32)

With this "'I don't understand'" the conversation ends. The lack of communication between brother and sister is all the more heartbreaking because Nekhliudov remembers how his once spiritually vibrant older sister had shared his striving for moral perfection. Their paths have fundamentally diverged. The tiny wrinkles on Natalia's beautiful face are a touching reminder that life has indeed taken its toll on this mother of two and high-society wife of a brilliant lawyer. Family and social obligations, as well as financial and other life circumstances, have forced her to settle for lesser dreams, or, perhaps, no dreams at all. Nekhliudov's presence compels her, for a brief moment, to reexamine this path of compromise. Just as Nekhliudov's childhood friend Selenin "became painfully sad" after Nekhliudov exposed the distance between his present life and his former ideals, so Natalia secretly envies her brother's spiritual courage. It reminds her of how she used to be.

If the existing order is rotten, social reform ineffective, and revolution wrong-headed, what is the solution to this morass? Tolstoy gives his answer in the final Part Three:

Thus [Nekhliudov] realized quite clearly that the only sure means of salvation from the terrible wrongs which mankind endures is for every man to acknowledge himself a sinner before God and therefore unfitted either to punish or reform others. It now became clear to him that all the dreadful evil of which he had been a witness in prisons and halting-places, and the calm self-assurance of those who committed it, resulted from the attempt by men to perform the impossible: being evil themselves they presumed to correct evil. Vicious men undertook to reform other vicious men and thought they could do it by mechanical means. But the only thing that came of it all was that needy and covetous men, having made a profession of so-called punishment and correction, themselves became utterly corrupt, and continually corrupted their victims. Now he knew the cause of all the horrors he had seen, and what ought to be done to put an end to them. The answer he had been unable to find was the same that Christ gave to Peter: to forgive everyone always, forgive an endless number of times, because there were no people who were guiltless and therefore able to punish or reform. (564–65; III, 28)

Here Tolstoy seems to suggest through Nekhliudov that we are born evil—a view that would contradict the writer's lifelong adherence to Rousseau's belief that man is inherently good before society deforms him. This view also would seem inconsistent with the vision of the purity of Nekhliudov's and Katyusha's youth earlier in the novel. Does the author of *Resurrection*, horrified by what he has seen and agonizingly aware of his own imperfections, come to believe in original sin? This is a possibility, yet because there are no other passages in this novel and few other places in Tolstoy's corpus where he expresses this philosophy, it is more likely that the sinners he has in mind are precisely those society has corrupted—that is, almost everybody. In such a world total withdrawal is the only antidote. Tolstoy's most pugnacious novel ends, paradoxically, on a note of renunciation.

This is the answer that the prophet of nonviolent resistance to evil had been repeating in the last twenty years of his life. The only effective agent of social change, Tolstoy insisted, is the morally transformed individual, the person who has renounced all claims to worldly influence and power. Only that person has awakened to the divine force within and lives correctly. The old, illiterate tramp whom Nekhliudov meets in Siberia embodies this later Tolstoyan worldview. As he tells Nekhliudov, "'Many faiths there be, but the Spirit is one. In you, an' in me, an' in 'im. That means, if every man of us believe in the Spirit within 'im, us'll all be united. Let everyone be 'imself, and us'll all be as one'" (535; III, 21). Nekhliudov's task is neither to save Katyusha nor to redeem society but to renounce all judgments, all claims to moral superiority. His most important task is not external, but internal: to forgive completely, or, as Robert Donahoo puts it, "to renounce . . . his right not to forgive."[25] Thus, Tolstoy believed, Nekhliudov may become who he is once again: a manifestation of divine Spirit, an instrument of the Master's "inexorable" will and higher purpose.[26]

Katyusha flirts with a medical orderly in the prison hospital, where Nekhliudov helped secure her a job, and he is shocked at her ingratitude towards "a man of the world, whom any girl from high society would consider herself lucky to marry" (396; II, 29). This tit-for-tat thinking is still the voice of the egoist who wants to manipulate events to fit his narrow self-serving paradigm of reality. Only when he lets go of personal desire, and his limited view of how he thinks Katyusha's spiritual awakening should progress, does the right response come to him:

> "No, what has happened cannot alter my resolve—it can only strengthen it. . . . My business is to do what my conscience demands of me," he said to himself. The certainty that nothing Maslova might do could alter his love for her rejoiced and lifted him to heights unknown till now. Let her flirt with the medical orderly—that was her business: he loved her, not selfishly, but for her own sake and for God's. (393, 397; II, 29)

Nekhliudov's liberation comes not from doing what he wishes, or getting what he thinks he wants, but by doing what he must, what his conscience demands. This is not the same as when he fulfilled his "duty" by going to the courthouse, or when he worked to expiate his sin against Katyusha. Those were impersonal *shoulds,* implanted in him by the dictates of others. This is a deeply felt, incontrovertible *must.* While it is true, as Donna Orwin writes in a provocative article, that "[v]irtue—duty—has become Nexljudov's exclusive goal," his pursuit of that goal does not have quite the cold, philosophical overtones Orwin suggests.[27] Nekhliudov subordinates the needs of his ego to the callings of conscience not because he has reasoned his way to virtue but because he has glimpsed divine truth and is deeply moved by it. Just as he saw with harrowing clarity the mess he had made, so now he just as intimately has glimpsed and felt "'the Spirit within 'im.'"

In his late theological writings Tolstoy openly rejected the mystical elements of Christianity, including a belief in the divinity of Christ and the story of Jesus' miraculous resurrection. Tolstoy believed these to be esoteric distractions from the central message of compassion at the heart of Jesus' ethical teachings.[28] With this novel Tolstoy takes "resurrection" out of the realm of the supernatural and insists that it is a spiritual awakening achievable by imperfect human beings in this world. As early as 1855 Tolstoy dreamed of founding a "new religion" along similar lines: "the religion of Christ, but purged of beliefs and mysticism, a practical religion, not promising future bliss but giving bliss on earth."[29] The theological quest of Tolstoy's entire life was a striving towards just such a "practical religion" that would offer "bliss on earth." *Resurrection* is his boldest artistic expression of that quest.

In Tolstoy's own time as in ours, Tolstoy's views are bound to repulse more-traditional Christians. There are those in Russia today who are disturbed by the religious worldview he expressed in this novel. During a heated discussion in Moscow in the summer of 2008, a well-known scholar told me that "Tolstoy was a great artist but a bad Christian," echoing the official view of the writer promulgated by the Holy Synod at the end of his life. A heated debate flared up recently at the Tolstoy Museum and Estate over whether to publish a controversial article by a Western scholar about Tolstoy's religious views. Some members of the museum worried that the article would upset the Orthodox community, many of whom still consider Tolstoy an apostate, as he was declared to be by the Holy Synod in 1901. Even in our time dissemination of research that would add fuel to that fire is surreptitiously monitored.[30]

But if Tolstoy was no conventional Christian, neither was he a religious extremist, such as we have witnessed all too often at home and abroad in recent years. His radicalism is different from the hate-filled rhetoric of certain contemporary social and religious ideologues. His vision of human salvation is more spiritually and intellectually demanding than that offered today by high-profile TV evangelists and megapreachers, who spew feel-good religion to millions. Tolstoy's rage against the Church stems from a resolute, fundamentally humane conviction: "'If once we admit, be it for a single hour or in a single instance, that there can be anything more important than compassion for a fellow human being,' Nekhliudov thinks after witnessing the inhumane treatment of prisoners, 'then there is no crime against man that we cannot commit with an easy conscience'" (448; II, 40).

Twentieth-century history has borne out the wisdom of these words. Utopian social schemes in Russia, Eastern Europe, Germany, Italy, and elsewhere promised to create heaven on earth, yet ended up creating the exact opposite. Compassion became a negotiable value amid the demands of state-building and the pressures of ideological reeducation, leading to disastrous results. While many future Bolsheviks found inspiration in Tolstoy's social ideas, they failed to put into practice the principle of compassion at the core of his teachings and worldview.[31] For Tolstoy that principle was neither an ideology nor a creed, but the only reasonable, humane way of being in the world.

Yet Tolstoy's own biography amply illustrates how difficult it is to realize this ideal. How, after all, are we to reconcile the prophet of universal love and nonresistance with the man, who, while preaching these ideals, remained an egoist through and through? The writer famously tormented his wife and threatened to leave her—and in fact, did leave her on many occasions; in 1910, when she challenged the wisdom of some of his extreme moral positions, he made his final tragic flight. One of their highest-profile disputes was over Tolstoy's decision in 1891 to renounce the copyright to all his works published after 1881. Sofya Andreevna, distraught over her husband's decision, argued that he was depriving not only his children but future generations of an additional source of income.

Most ironically, the novel itself is a damning demonstration of just how difficult it was for the writer to follow Christ's injunction to Peter to forgive an endless number of times. The narrator of *Resurrection* is an angry God raging from his pedestal. Tolstoy mercilessly judges those who are blind to the truth and who fail to live up to his ideals—from the spiri-

tually stunted careerists to the well-meaning cabby, from the so-called protectors of justice in the courts and jails to the self-proclaimed prophets of
salvation in the Church. Mikhail Bakhtin does not exaggerate when he
summarizes Tolstoy's scathing indictment of modernity in *Resurrection*:
"Every activity in this world, whether it be conservative or revolutionary,
is equally false and evil and foreign to the true nature of man."[32] With this
novel Tolstoy helped pave the path to the Revolution of 1917, when the
institutions he abhorred actually *were* demolished—and with disastrous
human consequences.

Perhaps the further Tolstoy diverged from his ideals in his own life,
the more intolerant he became of "society," deflecting his self-judgment
outward, just as Nekhliudov does when he encounters Katyusha in the
courtroom early in the novel. Maybe the author's rage against the hyp-
ocritical proponents of compassion in the Church stemmed partly from
the fact that he sensed himself to be just such a hypocrite. Whatever the
explanation, ultimately the artist does not submit to the ideologue in this
novel. The psychological realist always lurks beneath the high tower of the
visionary's ideals.[33] When Katyusha announces her final decision to reject
Nekhliudov's offer of marriage and instead to marry the political prisoner
Simonson, Nekhliudov cannot escape familiar feelings of wounded pride.
"Plain jealousy entered into it also, perhaps: he had grown so used to her
loving him that he could not admit that she could love another" (519; III,
17). Nekhliudov is, after all, a human being—no more, no less.

That neither Tolstoy nor his hero could live up to his ideals may
explain why the writer grew tired of the novel and suddenly dropped it.
"It's not corrected," he wrote in 1899. "But it's pushed aside and doesn't
interest me anymore."[34] This rushed finish can be felt in the final pages, in
which Nekhliudov is transformed by his reading of the Gospels. If in the
second epilogue of *War and Peace* and the final part of *Anna Karenina* the
searching heroes continue their quest in a way that evolves organically out
of the rest of the novel, then the final paragraph of *Resurrection,* which
attempts to convey something similar, feels tacked on, unearned: "That
night an entirely new life began for Nekhliudov, not so much because he
had entered into new conditions of life but because everything that happened to him from that time on was endowed with an entirely different
meaning for him. How this new chapter of his life will end, the future will
show" (568; III, 28).

In 1904, five years after finishing *Resurrection,* Tolstoy envisioned a
second part of the novel that would tell the story of "Nekhliudov's Chris-

tian life." Not only did he fail to produce a single page of this second part, but it is not clear how firmly Tolstoy believed that such a "Christian life" was possible. *Resurrection,* Part Two was to focus not on the hero's piety but on his agricultural "work, tiredness, awakening gentry feelings, female temptation, his fall, mistake."[35] In that same year, Tolstoy finished *Hadji-Murat,* a distinctly un-Christian work that celebrates the eponymous hero's physical vigor, fierce individualism, and violent resistance of those who would destroy him. In fact, Tolstoy had begun working stealthily on *Hadji-Murat* in 1896, during the final stages of writing *Resurrection.*

thirteen

$\mathcal{H}$ADJI-MURAT

The Stubborn Thistle

Considered by Harold Bloom to be Tolstoy's greatest work, and by John Bayley to be a "parable without a point," *Hadji-Murat* has aroused a conspicuously small, yet highly divergent, range of critical responses.[1] One point on which most critics agree is that the novella is an unexpected departure in both form and content from the later Tolstoy's moralistic fiction and essays. There is, in one scholar's words, a "reassertion" of the "intuitive morality of the great artist over the systematic morality of the teacher and prophet."[2]

In this "summary epic" the writer in his seventies resurrects the epic spirit of his other great historical novel, *War and Peace*. The free-flowing exuberance of the earlier work is absent, but its broad, life-affirming vision is there, now compressed into fewer than two hundred pages and communicated through the so-called "peepshow" technique. In March 1898 Tolstoy wrote: "There is an English toy called the 'peepshow.' One thing and then another thing is shown beneath a glass. That's how I'd like to show Hadji-Murat: as a husband, a fanatic, etc."[3] Tolstoy was essentially returning to the narrative technique of *War and Peace,* in which the narrator, standing godlike above the fray, depicts events from multiple perspectives, allowing the reader to sense both the variety and the overarching unity of life. In *Hadji-Murat* the focus is on the complexity of the hero in his manifold interactions with the world. Appearing as he does in all but a few chapters, Hadji-Murat becomes a central presence. Continually changing yet consistently vital, he concentrates in his very being the philosophical gravitas and epic spirit of the entire work.

Yet, the author was not entirely comfortable with his new endeavor. In his correspondence, we can hear Tolstoy the moralist arguing with Tolstoy the artist. With Russia in the throes of revolution and repression, and the brutal grip of imperialism widening, Tolstoy felt ashamed to be spending his time on a work that seemed to him an artistic indulgence. "This is indulgence and foolishness, but it is begun and I'd like to finish it."[4] In September 1902 Alexei Petrovich Sergeenko, the secretary of Tolstoy's close friend and confidant Vladimir Chertkov, asked Tolstoy about the novella. "'Of course you are trying to say something through it?' Tolstoy responded: 'No, just imagine, I've been carried away by the purely artistic side.'"[5] Yet it is precisely by focusing on "the purely artistic side" that Tolstoy, in spite of himself, made a powerful statement about the dehumanizing effects of ideology and the corrosiveness of political power. "If art, in Tolstoy's concept, was to serve moral and spiritual regeneration," writes one critic, "then this is illustrated in Hadji-Murat, for here the underlying moral idea is precisely to arouse horror and indignation at man's behavior."[6]

At first glance, Hadji-Murat, written between 1896 and 1904 and published posthumously in 1912, appears to have little in common with Tolstoy's other, more philosophically oriented novels. Man's search for truth is not in the foreground of this work as it is in The Cossacks, War and Peace, Anna Karenina, The Death of Ivan Ilyich, and Resurrection. Of all the characters, only one, Butler, bears any resemblance to the earlier seekers. For, in Hadji-Murat, perhaps more than in any other work, the author himself becomes a character in the existential drama he has described throughout his artistic career. Self-critical but never self-mocking, Hadji-Murat is Tolstoy's personal swan song, revisiting the past and subsuming it into a wholly new vision. Like many of his characters, Tolstoy searches for a unifying order, combining elements from his earlier novels, his own biography, and the strong moral positions of his later years to create a whole that is greater than the sum of its parts.[7] The artist and the moralist are equally present, neither one trying to overcome the other. From the pages of this work of tendentious realism Tolstoy's beloved hero, Truth, radiates in all its dark beauty.

The gestation period for Hadji-Murat was roughly fifty years, longer than that of any other work by Tolstoy. His interest in the eponymous Chechen warrior goes back to his youthful days as a volunteer in the

Caucasus, where he spent two years fighting with the Russians in the war against the native mountain tribes. As early as 1851 Tolstoy announced in a letter to his brother that "Shamil's number two, a certain Hadji-Murat, went over to the Russian government the other day. He was the leading *dzhigit* (horseman) and brave in all of Chechnya, but it was a base thing to do."[8] Tolstoy's original intention in the novella was to focus on this betrayal. But the figure of Hadji-Murat expanded in his imagination and eventually came to embody an idea both more personal to Tolstoy and more universal: man's struggle for survival in a hostile world. In July 1896, Tolstoy would recall Hadji-Murat again while returning to Yasnaya Polyana through a ploughed field:

> Yesterday I walked through a black-earth, fallow field which had been ploughed up again. As far as the eye could see there was nothing but black earth—not one green blade of grass. And there on the edge of the dusty grey road was a Tatar thistle (burdock) with three shoots: one was broken, and a dirty white flower hung from it; the second was also broken and spattered with mud, black and with a cracked and dirty stem; the third shoot stuck out to the side, also black, but still alive and red in the middle. It reminded me of Hadji-Murat. I'd like to write about it. It fights for life till the end, alone in the middle of the whole field, somehow manages to win the fight.[9]

After months of chronic illness and creative lethargy, the sixty-nine-year-old author was inspired to return to work. Within a day he wrote a rough draft of the prologue. Its mood was positive and defiant, and the connection between the thistle and Hadji-Murat was explicit: "'Good for him!' I thought. And a certain feeling of buoyancy, energy, and strength seized me: 'That's the way! That's the way!' And I remembered a Caucasian story, the situation of a man was the same as that of the thistle, and that man was also a Tartar. This man was Hadji-Murat."[10]

During the next eight years Tolstoy would labor in fits and starts over the novella, returning to the image of the struggling thistle as one of his main inspirations. In the final version of the prologue, the connection between the thistle and Hadji-Murat is only implied, and the author removes the personal exclamation "'Good for him!'" The tone becomes more objective, transforming Tolstoy's personal reminiscences into a universal statement. The three interconnected themes from the diary entry—the beautiful wholeness of nature, the destructiveness of man, and the battle for life until the end—would remain at the core of his creative vision through all ten drafts. Here is how the final version of the prologue opens:

> I was returning home by the fields. It was midsummer, the hay harvest was over and they were just beginning to reap the rye. At that season of the year there is a delightful variety of flowers—red, white, and pink scented tufty clover; milk-white ox-eye daisies with their bright yellow centers and pleasant spicy smell; yellow honey-scented rape blossoms; tall campanulas with white and lilac bells, tulip-shaped; creeping vetch; yellow, red, and pink scabiosas; faintly scented, neatly arranged purple plantains with blossoms slightly tinged with pink; cornflowers, the newly opened blossoms bright blue in the sunshine but growing paler and redder towards evening or when growing old; and delicate almond-scented dodder flowers that withered quickly. (549, 1)[11]

In this vision, nature's beauty exists regardless of human perception or participation. Beauty simply *is*. But man is a selfish creature, incapable of enjoying what is without seeking to alter and destroy it for his own ends: "I gathered myself a large nosegay and was going home when I noticed in a ditch, in full bloom, a beautiful thistle plant" (549, 1). Tolstoy wants to include the thistle in the bouquet, but it proves difficult to uproot. After realizing that the thistle doesn't seem right among "the delicate blossoms," he throws it away, "feeling sorry to have vainly destroyed a flower that looked beautiful in its proper place" (550, 1).

The author returns home through a nobleman's black, ploughed field, where he discovers another Tatar thistle, this one mauled by a cartwheel, but still standing upright. Suddenly, his innocent uprooting of the thistle moments earlier takes on more universal implications: "'Ah, what a destructive creature is man. . . . How many different plant-lives he destroys to support his own existence! . . . What vitality!' I thought. 'Man has conquered everything and destroyed millions of plants, yet this one won't submit'" (550, 1). What began as a simple walk through the fields has grown into an allegory of Man, in which Tolstoy himself participates.

THE DEATH OF HADJI-MURAT

"How good it would be," Tolstoy wrote in 1898, "to write a work of art in which one could clearly express the shifting nature of man; the fact that one and the same man is now a villain, now an angel, now a wise man, now an idiot, now a strong man, now the most impotent of creatures."[12] Despite his tendency in later years to create one-dimensional characters who would illustrate his rigid moral ideals, the artist in Tolstoy never lost sight of man's fluid and multifaceted nature.[13]

The genuinely pious Hadji-Murat, who respects the variety of life as instinctively as the Russian commanders defile it, will kill without a moment's thought, if his or his family's survival depends on it. This self-possessed man with "Oriental Mohammedan dignity" (594, 10) slaps Councilor Kirillov on his bald pate when the "fat, unarmed little man dressed as a civilian" insults him (651, 22), demonstrating that even dignified Oriental indifference has its limits. Hadji-Murat, who wisely utters, "'its own customs seem good to each nation'" (642, 20), will not brook the custom of arrogance, routinely practiced by the Russian officials. When his pride is at stake, he strikes. And we admire him for it. He is proud, and has in abundance what most of the other characters—particularly all those in positions of power in the novella—have lost: a strong sense of innate worth, vitality, and individualism.

We first meet Hadji-Murat on a cold November evening. He has come to the village of Makhmet in preparation for his surrender to the Russians. Through messengers he informs Russian regiment commander, Prince Vorontsov, that he will help the Russians defeat the *imam* Shamil, Hadji-Murat's bitter enemy and now the de facto leader of the Caucasian resistance movement. In exchange, he asks for assistance in rescuing his mother, grandmother, and son, who are being held hostage by the *imam*.

Hadji-Murat's surrender becomes a cause célèbre in Russian circles. He is seen as a kind of exotic animal—something akin to how nineteenth-century Americans viewed the famous American Indian warrior Sitting Bull. The savage they must tame, Hadji-Murat is no ordinary rogue. Marya Dmitrievna, the major's wife, who takes a liking to Hadji-Murat during his stay with them, voices the author's admiration for him: "'It's a pity there aren't more Russian rogues of such a kind! . . . He has lived a week with us and we have seen nothing but good from him. He is courteous, wise, and just'" (645, 20).

Like Sitting Bull, who, after his surrender, toured with Buffalo Bill's Wild West Show, Hadji-Murat is paraded about Tiflis by his Russian hosts, who are certain he "could not help being pleased at what he saw" (595, 10). When the senior Vorontsov, Commander in Chief of the Russian forces and Hadji-Murat's primary host, asks him how he likes the brilliant evening party with "men in bright uniforms" and "half-naked" women (594–95, 10), he responds with indifference. He has other things on his mind. He wants to talk to the commander about his family, but "Vorontsov, pretending that he had not heard him, walked away, and Loris-Melikov [Vorontsov's young aide-de-camp] afterwards told Hadji-Murat that this was not the place to talk about business" (595, 10). Since this "business" is a matter of life and death to Hadji-Murat, he leaves.

News reaches him of Shamil's intentions to harm his family. What is he to do? Return to "that red liar?" Remain and "'conquer Caucasia for the Russian Tsar and earn renown, titles, riches? . . . That could be done,' thought he, recalling his interviews with Vorontsov and the flattering things the prince had said; 'but I must decide at once, or Shamil will destroy my family'" (652, 22). And he decides. Momentary temptation has passed, and questions of cultural loyalty vanish before the imperative to survive. Hadji-Murat is all action: "All he knew was that first of all he must escape from the Russians into the mountains; and he at once began to carry out his plan" (652, 23).

As he flees, Hadji-Murat is subsumed into the symphony of nature: "As soon as he entered the hall, the outer door of which stood open, he was at once enveloped by the dewy freshness of the moonlit night and his ears were filled by the whistling and trilling of several nightingales in the garden by the house" (652–53, 23). In the hours of preparation for flight his world becomes enmeshed with that of the nightingales. Their singing and the sound of impending battle are intertwined. When he enters the hall,

> [t]he songs of nightingales that had burst into ecstasy at dawn were now even louder and more incessant, while from his henchman's room, where the daggers were being sharpened, came the regular screech and rasp of iron against stone. . . . Then all was quiet again, except for the *tchuk, tchuk, tchuk, tchuk,* and whistling of the nightingales from the garden, and from behind the door the even grinding, and now and then the whiz, of iron sliding quickly along the whetstone. (653–54, 23)

In these musical flights Hadji-Murat's inner world is distancing itself from the here-and-now. His sense of time is compressing. Images of his youth flit though his mind. He remembers his grandfather, his son, and his mother, "not wrinkled, gray-haired, with gaps between her teeth, as he had lately left her, but young and handsome, and strong enough to carry him in a basket on her back across the mountains to her father's when he was a heavy five-year-old boy" (655, 23). Thoughts of his family and what Shamil will do to them agitate him. "He jumped up and went limping quickly to the door" (655, 23). He opens it. It is dawn and the night-ingales are still singing. Hadji-Murat is on the brink of night and day, life and death.

Metaphorically, he remains there for the rest of the tale. The reader almost misses the fact that in a few pages nearly a full day goes by from the moment of Hadji-Murat's escape with his *murids* (disciples) in the morning until his entrapment by the militiamen and last stand the next morning. This compression contrasts sharply with the sense of time created in the beginning of the novella, in which the events of a single day are spread out over the first eight chapters. Now time accelerates, heightening both the reader's sense of anticipation and our feeling that historical time is being replaced by epic time.

After trekking across a flooded rice field to dry ground, Hadji-Murat and his men decide to spend the night. Hadji-Murat stays awake, listening to the trilling of the nightingales, which remind him of Khanefi's prophetic song of the previous night. The song told of how the brave Hamzad and his men fought the Russians until the bitter end, and how, just before he died, Hamzad cried out to the flying birds to carry home the news of their impending death:

"Fly on, ye winged ones, fly to our homes!
Tell ye our mothers, tell ye our sisters,
Tell the white maidens, that fighting we died
For Ghazavat! Tell them our bodies
Never will lie and rest in a tomb!
Wolves will devour and tear them to pieces,
Ravens and vultures will pluck out our eyes." (654, 23)

Believing that he might at any moment find himself in Hamzad's position, Hadji-Murat's "soul became serious" (664, 25). He prays, and then, hearing the sounds of horses' feet splashing in the bog, knows that the enemy has surrounded him and that his fate is sealed. He entrenches himself in a ditch just as Hamzad had done in the song. Night turns to day, the commander of the militia troop tells Hadji-Murat to surrender, and "[i]n reply came the report of a rifle . . ." (665, 25). Sporadic shooting ensues for an hour. Two hundred mountaineers, who have come to join the Russian militia, charge the entrenchment. While managing to shoot down several with his carefully aimed bullets, Hadji-Murat is hit in the shoulder and plugs up the wound with cotton wool from the lining of his *beshmet*. In desperation, Hadji-Murat's *murid*, the young Eldar, charges the enemy.

After being struck with a bullet, he reels backwards onto Hadji-Murat's leg, his beautiful, ramlike eyes gazing up at his leader. "Hadji-Murat drew his leg away from under him and continued firing" (666, 25).

Another bullet hits Hadji-Murat, and he plugs it with more cotton. He knows that this wound is fatal and that he is dying. His mind is flooded with snapshots of his past. "All these images passed through his mind without evoking any feeling within him: neither pity nor anger nor any kind of desire; everything seemed so insignificant in comparison with what was beginning, or had already begun, within him" (667, 25). What is beginning within him is death. But "[l]ife asserts itself to the very end," Tolstoy wrote in 1896, referring to the stubborn thistle that reminded him of Hadji-Murat. That metaphor is now being realized.

The hero's last stand has a stoic, terrifying grandeur—a fitting end to his life of daring and battle. There are many unforgettable deaths in the works of Tolstoy, who was obsessed with the subject from the very first; yet this depiction is unique. There is no ecstatic illumination, as in the deaths of Prince Andrei and Ivan Ilyich, no extinguished "bright light," such as Anna Karenina experiences. Hadji-Murat's death is just one more battle in a lifetime of struggle. The passage describing it is worth quoting in full:

Gathering together his last strength, [Hadji-Murat] rose from behind the bank, fired his pistol at a man who was just running towards him, and hit him. The man fell. Then Hadji-Murat got out of the ditch, and limping heavily went dagger in hand straight at the foe.

Some shots cracked and he reeled and fell. Several militiamen with triumphant shrieks rushed towards the fallen body. But the body that seemed to be dead suddenly moved. First the uncovered, bleeding, shaven head rose; then the body with hands holding to the trunk of a tree. He seemed so terrible, that those who were running towards him stopped short. But suddenly a shudder passed through him, he staggered away from the tree and fell on his face, stretched out at full length, like a thistle that had been mown down, and he moved no more.

He did not move, but still he felt.

When Hadji Aga, who was the first to reach him, struck him on the head with a large dagger, it seemed to Hadji-Murat that someone was striking him with a hammer and he could not understand who was doing it or why. That was his last consciousness of any connection with his body. He felt nothing more and his enemies kicked and hacked at what had no longer anything in common with him.

Hadji Aga placed his foot on the back of the corpse and with two blows cut off the head, and carefully—not to soil his shoes with blood— rolled it away with his foot. Crimson blood spurted from the arteries of the neck, and black blood flowed from the head, soaking the grass. (667, 25)

In contrast to the death of nearly every other major Tolstoyan hero, Hadji-Murat's death is shown to us almost exclusively from the outside, in terms of horrific physical events. His experience of dying is depersonalized and reduced primarily to the physical sensations of the body. Yet, Tolstoy describes that body as "what had no longer anything in common with him," implying that his soul endures. When he falls to the ground on his face—the physical embodiment of one's spiritual essence in the Russian Orthodox tradition—and waters the soil with his blood, his spirit symbolically merges with nature. His face, belonging to the head which will be brought to the Russian fort in a bag, will bear "a kindly childlike expression" even in death (658, 24). That kindly countenance, which the major eerily kisses when the severed head is presented to him, becomes an iconic representation of Hadji-Murat's essential spiritual goodness, which transcends his bodily existence. Tolstoy thus shows us the meaning of death, which the officers who lightheartedly discuss the death of the general in Chapter Five, could not see. The narrator calls it "that most important moment of a life, its termination and return to the source from whence it sprung" (570–71, 5).

Hadji-Murat's heroic death becomes *the* event toward which the plot has been leading. Tolstoy creates a sense of its inevitability by showing us the hero's severed head in Chapter Twenty-Four before his final flight and death in Chapter Twenty-Five. The question then becomes not *whether* he will die but how. Like the mowed-down thistle from the prologue, the hero fights for life until the end. "'Man has conquered everything and destroyed millions of plants, yet this one won't submit.'" Both Hadji-Murat and the thistle will, of course, succumb to their "wounds." But they also both exhibit a stubborn, admirable life force. And Hadji-Murat exhibits something more. As he is dying, his thoughts are minimal and reflect a general incomprehension of what is happening. "[I]t seemed to Hadji-Murat that someone was striking him with a hammer and he could not understand who was doing it or why." Hadji-Murat is losing touch with his immediate, physical reality, but his confusion may also reflect an ethical inquiry, a budding moral consciousness.[14] Indeed, we wonder with him, why *is* his head being torn off? Why this senseless destruction of human life, this bestiality of man towards man? Today, over a century after Tolstoy wrote *Hadji-Murat,* foreign journalists are beheaded by radical Islamic militants, Muslim women are stoned to death by their communities for committing adultery, a Russian man is beaten to death by teenage hoodlums and thrown into the flame of a World War II Memorial, Georgian girls are raped by the soldiers of an invading Russian army, entire families and villages are being slaughtered in Darfur. Why? Hadji-Murat's incomprehension becomes a moral challenge to all of us.

Despite the hero's gruesome death, the novella, like all of Tolstoy's art, leaves the reader with a glimpse of a transcendent ideal. His conquerors see Hadji-Murat's death as nothing more than a military victory to be celebrated. But the nightingales, who have the penultimate word in the novella, sing of another truth. "The nightingales, that had hushed their songs while the firing lasted, now started their trills once more: first one quite close, then others in the distance" (668, 25). Just as the nightingales in Hamzad's prophetic song carry home the news of his violent death, so the nightingales at the end of *Hadji-Murat* carry to future generations of readers Tolstoy's tragic yet ennobling truth about the world. Military and natural "music" intertwine once again, as they did in the moments leading up to Hadji-Murat's flight, and we are reminded that bestiality, beauty, and the battle for survival always have been and will be inseparable aspects of human existence. Hadji-Murat's heroic life and tragic death are the very personification of this truth. His destiny becomes the destiny of Man.

The voices of the nightingales offer an unsentimental, yet life-affirming commentary on the meaning of Hadji-Murat's death. Yet theirs is not the final note; beyond them, in the novella's final sentence, we return to the world of the prologue: "It was of this death that I was reminded by the crushed thistle in the midst of the ploughed field" (668, 25). The work ends with an event, not in Hadji-Murat's story, but in that of Tolstoy, for whom the hero's death is a symbol of some higher truth: a celebration of the eternal cycles of life and death, of the indomitable life force, which continues despite the death of the individual.[15] Even in one of Tolstoy's most pessimistic works, the possibility for creative self-assertion still exists.

However we understand the hero's death, what is clear is that Tolstoy identified with Hadji-Murat's embattled life. In the final decade and a half of his life, he strove to remain strong in the face of increased illness and to hold to his high principles despite his inner conflict and hypocrisies. In the 1890s and early 1900s he fought actively—through stories, parables, essays, and political tracts—for the spiritual survival of a Russian society headed for revolution and self-annihilation. Yet, like his hero, Tolstoy painfully straddled two worlds. No longer the indulgent aristocrat who once insisted that "he who is happy is right!" he was not yet at home in his role of self-denying spiritual prophet. He had pledged himself to a life of abstinence and vegetarianism, yet he dined in luxury at Yasnaya Polyana at the large table set with European silverware and porcelain dishes. Tolstoy asked Sofya Andreevna to join him in willfully renouncing their property, but she found his idealism both insufferable and dangerous. Not only would such a decision confuse the children, she lamented, but "how could I, with my eight children . . . give up my usual life for the sake of an ideal, created not by me but forced upon me? . . . And so, the painful discord has ensued."[16] A distraught Sofya Andreevna tried unsuccessfully to commit suicide on multiple occasions in the final years of their marriage. She was a nagging reminder to Tolstoy of his family responsibilities, which often conflicted with his spiritual ideals.

On the night before his escape, as he lay awake, thinking, Hadji-Murat recalled a Tavlinian fable about a falcon. After living in captivity among humans, who put silver bells and jesses on him, the falcon returns home. But he is told to go back to where he came from. "'We have no bells and jesses,'" they tell him (652, 22). "The falcon did not want to leave his home and remained, but the other falcons . . . pecked him to death. 'And they would peck me to death in the same way,' thought Hadji-Murat" (652, 22). The image of the trapped falcon must have hit close to home for Tolstoy, as well. He and his character are pecked to death by their own—Hadji-Murat physically, Tolstoy spiritually and psychologically. In a desperate final quest for salvation, Tolstoy will abandon his home. Hadji-Murat will try to return to his. Both fighters die alone, Hadji-Murat in battle, Tolstoy in a train station.

"RETURN" TO A DIFFERENT CAUCASUS

If, in *Hadji-Marat,* Tolstoy embodies the dilemmas of his last years, he also returns to his literary beginnings, taking us back to the Caucasus of his youth—to that "wild land" with its thick forests and precipice-filled landscapes and native mountaineers, who work and celebrate and suffer and kill with Homeric vitality. Some passages in *Hadji-Murat* arouse feelings of *déjà vu,* recalling his first novel, *The Cossacks.* Here is the description of the Chechen *aoul* at the beginning of *Hadji-Murat:*

> On a cold November evening Hadji-Murat rode into Makhmet, a hostile Chechen *aoul* that lay some fifteen miles from the Russian territory and was filled with the scented smoke of burning *kizyak.* The strained

chant of the muezzin had just ceased, and through the clear mountain air, impregnated with *kizyak* smoke, above the lowing of the cattle and the bleating of the sheep that were dispersing among the *saklyas* (which were crowded together like the cells of honeycomb), could be clearly heard the guttural voices of disputing men, and sounds of women's and children's voices rising from near the fountain below. (550–51, 1)

The calm, orderly hum of nature and the melancholic drone of villagers going about their evening tasks is a bleak echo of the description of the Cossack village at the beginning of *The Cossacks*:

It was one of those wonderful evenings that occur only in the Caucasus. The sun had sunk behind the mountains but it was still light. . . . Talking merrily, the women who have been tying up the vines hurry away from the gardens before sunset. The vineyards, like all the surrounding district, are deserted, but the villages become very animated at that time of the evening. From all sides, walking, riding, or driving in their creaking carts, people move towards the village. Girls with their smocks tucked up and twigs in their hands run chatting merrily to the village gates to meet the cattle that are crowding together in a cloud of dust and mosquitoes which they bring with them from the steppe.[17]

In both works the village community, whether Cossack or Chechen, is a place where civilization and nature seem to merge. A sense of order reigns, shaped by the fierce communal loyalty forged in the struggles of everyday life. Despite these common elements, however, the joyfulness of the "wonderful evening" is totally lacking in the later description, which is dominated by cold, smoke, crowding, and disputation.

Tolstoy's vision has deepened. The tragic-comedic view of the young author of *The Cossacks* has expanded into the sublimely tragic vision of an author in his waning years. His emphasis is not on the rarefied philosophical search of a young Russian aristocrat but on the grim, immediate challenges of a Chechen brave, whose fate and that of his family depend on his ability to choose decisively among repugnant options. To Olenin the Caucasus represents the possibility of a brave, new world. To Hadji-Murat and the inhabitants of Makhmet, which the Russians have senselessly destroyed in a raid, the Caucasus is a physical home. The old men who set about restoring their razed village do not aspire à la Olenin to create something new and exciting for themselves. They try to recreate an actual world that once existed and that has been taken from them.

If, in *The Cossacks,* we see the Caucasus from the perspective of a Russian outsider living in a Cossack village on "this" side of the Terek, then in *Hadji-Murat* we experience the region from within. Just as the author of *The Cossacks* penetrated the inner landscape of the literary Caucasus as few Russian writers before him had done, so the author of *Hadji-Murat* tells the story of those who live on the other side of the river in a way it had not yet been told. He illuminates the drama of the conquered rather than that of the conquerors.

In *The Cossacks,* the Caucasus was still a place of refuge from the corrupting influence of modern society. In *Hadji-Murat* the region has become infiltrated by that very world: luxurious Russian forts now litter the Caucasian countryside. Through its pernicious blend of cultural sophistication, moral shallowness, and military force, the Russian empire has spread like a cancer, attempting to crush the "delightful variety" of life in the Caucasus into a black, uniform emptiness, as mangled as the ploughed field of the prologue. *The Cossacks,* originally subtitled "A Tale of 1852," and *Hadji-Murat,* which takes place from 1851 to 1852, offer two totally different visions of the almost identical era.

There are historical reasons for Tolstoy's shift in perspective. He worked on the novella at the turn of the century when impending revolution and violent government repression were in the air. After the author of the Great Reforms, Alexander II, was assassinated in 1881, his son, Alexander III, came to power, initiating the second most repressive regime in nineteenth-century Russia after that of his grandfather, Nicholas I. Believing that his father's death at the hands of a revolutionary terrorist was the result of too much liberalization, Alexander III was determined to stamp out revolution at its roots. He strengthened the long-standing principle of Autocracy-Orthodoxy-Nationality, which decreed that Russia was to be guided by one language, one nationality, one religion, and one government. To that end Alexander persecuted the Jews; destroyed Polish, Swedish, and German institutions in the provinces; and forcefully Russified and Christianized the non-Russian peoples in the Caucasus, a region the country had been trying to subjugate for over a century.

Alexander III must have reminded Tolstoy of the century's other notoriously repressive regime, that of Tsar Nicholas I, under whom Tolstoy grew up. In *Hadji-Murat,* set during the reign of Nicholas in the early 1850s, the tsar orders the execution of a Polish Roman Catholic student who, in a paroxysm of rage after failing his examinations, has attacked a professor with a penknife. The tsar's extreme punishment is motivated by his visceral hatred of all things Polish as well as his wish to set a terrifying example for the revolutionaries, whom he also despises. In Nicholas's threat, "'I will abolish this revolutionary spirit and will tear it up by the roots!'" Tolstoy's readers would have heard the voice of Alexander III, who tore up entire Russian and non-Russian communities in the name of Autocracy-Orthodoxy-Nationality (621, 15).

All forms of imperial aggression incensed Tolstoy. In his polemical writings and correspondence during the 1890s and early 1900s he spoke out against imperialism: Great Britain's subjugation of Egypt in 1882 and the Sudan in 1898, and its war on the Boers from 1899 to 1902, as well as Italian imperial ambitions in the Middle East. In his voluminous correspondence with Americans, documented in the recently published book *L. N. Tolstoi i S.Sh.A.: Perepiska* [L. N. Tolstoy and the U.S.A.: Correspondence], Tolstoy urged American artists and intellectuals to stand up to the forces of American jingoism under Theodore Roosevelt, and he decried the American aggression in the Spanish–American war over Cuba.[18] In his "Letter to the Italians" in 1896, Tolstoy diagnoses the disease of his era: "People from childhood are convinced that the best . . . nation is the Italian, the French, the German, the Austrian, the English, or the Russian. This deception is so stupid, that . . . you can only be surprised at how people fall for it. This can be explained only by the fact that this is instilled from earliest childhood, and in those conditions in which people are most susceptible to hypnotism—that is, en masse."[19]

Twentieth-century dictators—Stalin, Hitler, Mussolini, and Pol Pot—whose violent nationalistic agendas killed millions, confirm the prescience of Tolstoy's words. Have things changed in the twenty-first century? We have seen a brutal Russian invasion of Georgia, blood feuds in Chechnya and other regions of the Caucasus, genocide in Darfur, ethnic warfare in Iraq, and the ravaging of natural frontiers from Alaska to Lake Baikal for the sake of corporate profits. A worldwide financial crisis has made us all aware of the real and present dangers of unbridled economic ambition. The forces of militarism, nationalism, religious extremism, not to mention plain greed, continue to make a mockery of universal human values.

In *Hadji-Murat*, the specific political and social reality of Russian imperialism also becomes a microcosm of all those forces in the modern world that pervert humane values and desecrate the "delightful variety" of life, through killing, cant, ideology, or sheer egoism. Russian absolutism poisons the lives of almost every human being it touches, from the tsar and his circle of yes-men to the peasant soldier Avdeev, who dies in an unnecessary battle arranged by his company commander, Poltoratsky, so that his friend, Baron Freeze, may win a promotion. As we climb higher up the social ladder in the novella, moving from the simple soldiers in Chapter Two, to the regiment commander Vorontsov in Chapter Three, to his father, the Commander in Chief, in Chapter Nine, and finally to Tsar Nicholas in Chapter Fifteen, we descend deeper into human depravity.

Tolstoy's artistic restraint almost gives way in Chapter Fifteen: his repulsion for the fat, philandering tsar with an inflated sense of his own importance is the closest thing to a polemical tract we find in *Hadji-Murat*. The author "struggled" with that chapter, which he feared might be "disproportional" in tone and length. But he considered the depiction of Nicholas "very important, serving as the illustration of my understanding of power."[20] Moreover, Nicholas is depicted with such satirical sumptuousness that we almost feel sorry for this cruel, lifeless blob, whose entire existence is defined by deception and self-deception:

> Nicholas sat at the table in a black coat with shoulder-straps but no epaulets, his enormous body—with his overgrown stomach tightly laced in—was thrown back, and he gazed at the newcomers with fixed, lifeless eyes. His long pale face, with its enormous receding forehead between the tufts of hair which were brushed forward and skillfully joined to the wig that covered his bald patch, was specially cold and stony that day. His eyes, always dim, looked duller than usual, the compressed lips under his upturned moustaches, the high collar which supported his chin, and his fat freshly shaven cheeks on which the symmetrical sausages-shaped bits of whiskers had been left, gave his face a dissatisfied and even irate expression. (615, 15)

The higher a man stands on the political ladder in this novella, the more he is enslaved to his own power and the system from which it derives. Noble, humane instincts are superseded by political ones, which ultimately amount to blind submission to the will of Nicholas. Here is General Bibikov's reaction to the tsar's command to ruthlessly punish the mutinous peasants who would not accept the government-imposed Orthodox faith: "Not to agree with Nicholas's decisions would have meant the loss of that brilliant position which it had cost Bibikov forty years to attain and which he now enjoyed; and he therefore submissively bowed his dark head (already touched with grey) to indicate his submission and his readiness to fulfill the cruel, insensate, and dishonest supreme will" (622, 15). Submission has become a way of life for Bibikov, whose character is as flabby as Nicholas's waist. Bibikov is the norm, not the exception, among those in power. Like Prince Chernyshev, the Minister of War, and the Tsar's aide-de-camp, who in their manner and look are carbon copies of the lifeless Nicholas, Bibikov is a puppet of power, who lacks moral will and genuine individualism.

Russians are not the only guilty ones in *Hadji-Murat*. In 1903 Tolstoy told a friend that he was "concerned not only with Hadji-Murat and his tragic fate, but also with the extremely interesting parallelism between the two main adversaries of the period—Shamil and Nicholas—who represent together the two poles, as it were, of powerful absolutism—the Asiatic and the European."[21] If Russian autocracy creates flabby half-humans, then Asiatic absolutism, no less toxic, produces a different kind of beast. Hadji-Murat's disciple, Gamzalo, who wants "to slay and stab as many Russians as possible," is hardly a model of cultural tolerance (653, 23). But Shamil is the most terrifying example of violent religious extremism, as recognizable today as a century ago. When he calmly dictates a letter to Hadji-Murat through his son, who dutifully relays the intentions of his captor to put out his eyes or kill him if Hadji-Murat doesn't return, video images come to mind of the "last testament" read by Western hostages in the presence of their masked executors, or of Osama bin Laden explaining to the camera with an almost childlike innocence why his religious beliefs oblige him to eradicate us.

Against the spiritual bankruptcy of two forms of absolutism—Russian and Asiatic—Hadji-Murat's innate sense of right and wrong, as well as his personal daring, stand out in sharp relief. Even Shamil, for all his dreadful impressiveness, is something of a charlatan and a showman. The power he has over others stems more from calculated effect than from inner substance. By contrast, Hadji-Murat, the last of Tolstoy's "noble" heroes, is all substance and action, free of artifice and the trappings of ideology. He is one of the few fully alive characters in the novella.

AN ARTIST'S JOURNEY

In his encounters with two different Tartar thistles in the prologue, Tolstoy is retelling in miniature the story of his own personal and artistic journey. The narrator who innocently picks flowers for his bouquet is emblematic of the Tolstoy of the 1850s. This is the young author of *The Cossacks,* as well as the stories "The Raid" and "The Wood-felling," for whom the Russian South is a place of physical and spiritual plenitude and artistic exploration.[22] The Tolstoy who encounters the second Tartar thistle is the later ideologue—the moralist, pacifist, and preacher—who is painfully aware of the world's moral evils and of his participation in them. The depth of the prologue and of the entire work lies in the union of these two voices: the artist's joie de vivre in the midst of rich, sensuous nature and the moralist's pangs of guilt.

This is a more nuanced vision of the relationship between art and morality than the one Tolstoy develops in his treatise "What is Art?" published in 1897 and written while he was working on *Hadji-Murat*. In that essay the author makes a rigid distinction between two different kinds of art. "True" art happens when the artist achieves total communion with his surroundings, unconsciously infecting his audience with the same feelings of universal love that he carries within himself. "False" art is produced by the artist who strives for a titillating effect, who creates from the selfish needs of the ego rather than from the Christian ideal of purity, compassion, and love.

If, as Tolstoy claimed, the art of Homer, Dante, Shakespeare, Michelangelo, and Beethoven, as well as his own *War and Peace* and *Anna Karenina*, fail to qualify as "true" art, then so would Tolstoy's bouquet of flowers, which he creates out of an impulse to gather up the world and rearrange it according to his selfish designs. The author of "What is Art?" denounces this sort of "false" artist, but the author of *Hadji-Murat* asks us merely to reflect on the implications of his actions, for to denounce him would be to repudiate the egoism that is an inevitable part of our nature, and without which Tolstoy's greatest works would never have been written. The selfish artist and the guilt-ridden moralist are both fully present, subsumed into a unifying vision that celebrates what is vital in human nature, censures what is destructive, and embraces life in its totality.

Vitality and destruction go hand in hand in *Hadji-Murat*. Take, for example, the description of the burnt bees and beehives and the destroyed apiary in the razed Chechen village, which recalls a small but significant detail from the prologue: "I climbed down into the ditch, and after driving away a velvety humble-bee that had penetrated deep into one of the flowers and had there fallen sweetly asleep, I set to work to pluck the flower" (549, 1). Tolstoy's tiny, innocent disruption of nature becomes a microcosm of what the Russian imperial system does to a Chechen village, a region of the world, on a grand, tragic scale. In both cases natural processes are disturbed, organic relationships (in both the human and natural worlds) are severed, and life itself is defiled and destroyed. Suddenly Tolstoy's moment of innocent ebullience is complicit in the pernicious forces of imperialism. When, in the prologue, Tolstoy writes that he felt "sorry to have vainly destroyed a flower that looked beautiful in its proper place," he is metaphorically expressing the deeper regret of a privileged aristocrat and artist, whose lifelong creativity and vitality, he now knows, have been purchased at such high cost.

These confessional overtones can be heard even more distinctly in the figure of Butler, the young, handsome officer of the guards who has come to the Caucasus with the same romantic hopes that Olenin once had. Significantly, Butler, who "forgot that he was ruined, and forgot his unpaid debts" (628, 16), is the Olenin of the very earliest drafts of *The Cossacks*—a ne'er-do-well who goes south to escape his failed career and gambling debts. The Olenin of the final version is a seeker. Butler is no searcher, and he has none of Olenin's expansive inner life. If Olenin strives, albeit unsuccessfully, to penetrate the mysteries of Cossack life, Butler will-fully hides behind his romantic illusions, with sinister consequences: "War presented itself to him as consisting only in exposing himself to danger and to possible death, thereby gaining the respect of his comrades here, as well as of his friends in Russia. Strange to say, his imagination never pictured the other aspect of war: the death and wounds of the soldiers, officers, and mountaineers" (627, 16).

The "other aspect of war," which Butler cannot—will not—see is depicted with such revolting specificity in the next chapter that the censors eliminated almost all of it from the first Russian publication in 1912.[23] We watch, horror-stricken, as the "handsome bright-eyed boy who had gazed with such ecstasy at Hadji-Murat, was brought dead to the mosque on a horse covered with a *burka* [felt cape]: he had been stabbed in the back with a bayonet" (629, 17). His mother, in a torn smock that exposes her withered breasts, stands wailing over her son's dead body, digging her nails into her face until it bleeds, while the boy's father digs his son's grave with a pickaxe. We are told of the destroyed apiary and of the burnt bees and beehives, the broken and scorched apricot and cherry trees. We hear

> [t]he wailing of the women and the little children, who cried with their mothers, mingled with the lowing of the hungry cattle for whom there was no food. The bigger children, instead of playing, followed their elders with frightened eyes. The fountain was polluted, evidently on purpose, so that the water could not be used. The mosque was polluted in the same way, and the Mullah and his assistants were cleaning it out. (629, 17)

Nowhere else in Tolstoy's fiction is war presented in such gruesome detail. Nowhere are the romance of adventure and the innocence of youth so directly complicit in the treachery of Russian imperial power. In the paragraph immediately following the description of the razed village, Butler looks at the majestic mountains, "inhaling deep breaths and rejoicing that he was alive, that it was just he that was alive, and that he lived in this beautiful place" (630, 18). In an early draft of *Hadji-Murat,* subtitled "Reminiscences of an Old Soldier," these exact words are spoken in first person by Tolstoy himself. By the time he completed the work, the sixty-nine-year-old author, unlike Butler, understands the ramifications of his actions.

Yet, despite the moral distances that separate them, both Butler, who kills with blithe innocence, and the narrator, who destroys the wildflowers for his bouquet, are as integral to life's "labyrinth of linkages" as the thistle uprooted by Tolstoy, or Hadji-Murat, who fights for survival until the end. Every individual—from the peasant, Avdeev, who serves against his will and dies tragically, to Tsar Nicholas I, who guides the imperial engine with his predatory bestiality—plays his or her necessary role in the circle of life.

Why does the handsome, curly-headed Butler fall "into a sound, dreamless, and unbroken sleep" (629, 16) after the raid on the Chechen village, while the bright-eyed Chechen boy, whose name we never learn, is buried by his parents? Why does the humble peasant soldier, Avdeev, die tragically and unnecessarily? The narrator does not pretend to know the answers to these questions. Avdeev's mother has perhaps the wisest response of all. When the news of her son's death reaches her, she "wept for as long as she could spare time, and then set to work again" (585, 8). That is also Tolstoy's answer: to keep working, keep fighting. "No matter how old or how sick you are, how much or little you have done," the sixty-two-year-old Tolstoy wrote to his secretary, Vladimir Chertkov: "your business in life not only isn't finished, but hasn't yet received its final, decisive meaning until your very last breath. That's happy, invigorating."[24] This "happy, invigorating" worldview is the hopeful undercurrent running through an otherwise disturbing portrait of the world. Tolstoy's entire journey as a man and artist reflects this life-affirming spirit.[25]

"I'm not afraid of objections," he wrote in his diary in 1874. "I am a seeker. I don't belong to any camp. And I ask my readers not to."[26] These words encapsulate the lifelong quest of an artist and thinker, who never settled for long into any single vision or paradigm. Tolstoy was that rare bird in nineteenth-century Russia: a free artist and independent thinker. He created at least one movement, Tolstoyism, and contributed to many others: Christian anarchism, nonviolent resistance to evil, and Russian socialism. Yet he didn't belong to any of them.

Just as his searching characters create, reject, and resurrect truths about themselves and their world, so, throughout his lifetime, Tolstoy continually creates and destroys and recreates his own artistic visions. His rejection of his artistic past, which begins with *Confession* and finds its fullest expression in "What is Art?" is a position that he would overcome when he created *Hadji-Murat* in the last decade of his life. Nothing repeats in Tolstoy's fluid world. The oak tree has already changed when Prince Andrei sees it for the second time. *Hadji-Murat* is less a reassertion than a reimagining. In a final letter to his children, written while he lay dying in the train station at Astapovo, Tolstoy implored his son, Seryezha, to "think about your own life, who you are, what you are, what is the meaning of a man's life and how every reasonable man should live it."[27] Tolstoy's final diaries and correspondence reveal that he had enormous difficulty following his own advice. In his last hours he kept repeating the phrase "I do not understand what it is I am supposed to do."[28] Hadji-Murat had his moment of doubt, as well. Each one makes a courageous, irreversible decision. Hadji-Murat refuses to go down without a fight. Tolstoy refuses to go home. Both return to the source from which they came, and escape into eternity.

epilogue

$\mathscr{T}$HE LITTLE GREEN STICK REDISCOVERED

I was returning to my hotel in the hot July sun by the fields of Yasnaya Polyana. A light evening breeze brushed my face, carrying with it a wonderful variety of sweet, spicy scents from the linden, birch, and maple trees filling the forest on the edge of the field, as well as from the wildflowers dotting the landscape with colorful bouquets. The field stretched in front of me, like a green tapestry, accented here and there with the soft white and yellow of lantanas and summer sunflowers, the milky-white and light-blue campanulas, the purple-leaved stems of creeping vetch, stately purple plantains, and bright-blue, newly blossomed cornflowers.

I was far from my hotel, far from the center of the estate, in the remote reaches of Yasnaya Polyana, where Tolstoy loved to get lost. In this luxuriant expanse of nature, without paths or borders, he sought to connect with that inexhaustible essence of life, which his searching characters seek and sense in rare, fleeting moments. Here, in nature, Tolstoy found, in Richard Gustafson's well-chosen words, "the emblem of God's life in this world."[1] But the great poet of nature's beauty was also one of the great transcribers of life's uglier sides. The inexhaustible beauty that often brought Tolstoy to tears of joy did so in proportion to the baseness and brutishness he saw all around him.

Lying in the middle of one of the flowerbeds, crushing the sunflower petals and breaking the fragile stems of the daisies, was a broken beer bottle. Who threw it there and why? I wondered. Even Yasnaya Polyana, one of the few remaining cultural and spiritual centers in a Russian society now awash in corruption, is not immune to the human impulse to carelessly desecrate beauty. Looking at the discarded bottle, I found the words from the prologue of *Hadji-Murat* come to mind: "'Ah, what a destructive creature is man. How many plant-lives he destroys to support his own existence!'"[2]

It was not lost upon me that I was walking through the very meadow where Tolstoy himself stood in July of 1896 and was inspired to create *Hadji-Murat*. I, too, was looking at the "delightful variety of flowers" that he describes in the prologue. I, too, was witness to man's baseness, evident in the discarded bottle, a sight so familiar I often overlook it.

Tolstoy has taught me to see that every detail, every action—no matter how seemingly insignificant—has its repercussions. It is no wonder that he particularly liked the words of Father Zossima in *The Brothers Karamazov*: "Everything, like an ocean, everything flows and comes into contact—you touch in one place, and at the other end of the world it reverberates."[3]

This applies to all of us who "innocently" enjoy the comforts of modern civilization and the privileges of power. How easy it once was to travel to other countries as an American, admired and respected, instinctively confident in our greatness as a nation, secure in the knowledge of our economic and political power, sanctimonious in our belief that we killed only for necessary and noble causes. That age of innocence is past. The specter of war looms large, our economic might is in question, and our complicity in the world's pain is undeniable.

I first saw my own role in events several years ago when I was taking a summer seminar for professors of Russian at the Pushkin Russian Language Institute in Moscow. During a heated discussion of world affairs, Raheem, an Iraqi in his late twenties, stood up and announced to the hundred and fifty participants from twenty countries that "America is the number one exporter of evil and imperialism the world over." Furious at his ingratitude, I defended my country's good intentions and justified its actions in the world and in his country, in particular. Rationally, perhaps, I was right, and I argued my point of view convincingly, like a well-trained academic.

Yet in doing so, I was avoiding another, more all-encompassing truth, which was staring me in the face: I am the beneficiary of privileges and freedoms, in whose name human lives are being destroyed every day. What could I say to a man whose home was being torn apart in the name of democracy-building, and whose uncle was killed in the mayhem? I listened to Raheem, tried to *hear* him, and understood that I, too, unwittingly have had a part in his pain.

We are all enmeshed in a tightly woven web of circumstances, decisions, events. Nobody is completely guilty. Nobody is completely innocent. Our every action, our very existence, is integral to the world's "labyrinth of linkages." This great truth, illuminated by Tolstoy's fiction, is sobering; yet it can also be ennobling. Guy de Maupassant once said that the goal of realist art is "to force us to think, to understand the profound and hidden meaning of events."[4] Tolstoy's art does just that. The writer invites his readers to think not only *about* him but *with* him, to engage their world with the same brimming attention with which he engages his. In Tolstoy's age of insidious, often internalized lies, this was one of the most courageous and difficult things a writer could do. The same is true of our own age. I offer my own, seemingly "insignificant," experience as illustration.

During that same visit to Yasnaya Polyana, I went to Tolstoy's gravesite to take pictures for a public presentation I was about to give. When I had visited his tomb the previous summer, it was adorned with "a bouquet of freshly picked wildflowers," as I describe in the first chapter. This time, however, there were only three flowers wrapped in a thick, plastic flower holder—a skimpy offering of store-bought flowers that clearly wouldn't work for my presentation! I temporarily removed the bouquet, replaced it with wildflowers that I had picked myself, and proceeded to shoot my pictures. This petty crime weighed on my conscience for some time. I felt sorry to have removed somebody else's delicately placed flowers. I had falsified the reality of the moment in order to make it fit the reality I required for my own purposes. A distinctly un-Tolstoyan act, by one who had been listening to Tolstoy's voice all his adult life.

In today's world, when we are constantly bombarded by the thoughts of others and seduced by striking semblances of truth and simulacra of reality, hearing Tolstoy's calm, truthful voice is a feat. Yet, by listening to his voice we begin to hear our own a little more distinctly. By penetrating his humane, all-encompassing vision of life, we begin to see, as if for the first time, not only who we are but who we might become.

notes

INTRODUCTION

1. I have borrowed this formulation from Anthony T. Kronman, *Education's End: Why Our Colleges and Universities Have Given Up on the Meaning of Life* (New Haven, CT, and London: Yale University Press, 2007), pp. 9–35.

2. *Polnoe sobranie sochinenii L. N. Tolstogo* [The Complete Collected Works of L. N. Tolstoy], 90 vols. (Moscow, 1928–58), vol. 5, p. 262.

3. Andrew Wachtel, *The Battle for Childhood: Creation of a Russian Myth* (Palo Alto, CA: Stanford University Press, 1990).

CHAPTER 1

1. *Polnoe sobranie sochinenii L. N. Tolstogo* [The Complete Collected Works of L. N. Tolstoy], 90 vols. (Moscow, 1928–58), vol. 5, p. 262, published by the Russian Academy of Sciences. Hereafter cited as *PSS* volume number, page number. Unless otherwise stated, translations are mine. When I use other translations, I make modifications as necessary.

2. From Babel's essay "O tvorcheskom puti pisatelia" ["About the Artistic Path of a Writer"], *Sochineniia v dvukh tomakh* (Moscow: Terra, 1996), p. 450.

3. Quoted in Ernest J. Simmons, *Leo Tolstoy* (Boston: Little, Brown and Company, 1946), pp. 21–22.

4. Entry from January 1855. In R. F. Christian, ed. and trans., *Tolstoy's Diaries, vol. 1, 1847–1894* (London: The Athlone Press, 1985), p. 100.

5. Ibid.

6. Entry from May 1853. Ibid., p. 67.

7. Entry from August 1857. Ibid., p. 141.
8. Entry from April 1855. Ibid., p. 104.
9. Entry from November 1853. Ibid., pp. 76–77.
10. Entry from June 1855. Ibid., p. 105.
11. Entry from July 1853. Ibid., p. 88.
12. Entry from April 1847. Ibid., p. 11.
13. Entry from August 1857. Ibid., p. 141.
14. Entry from July 1853. Ibid., p. 88.
15. Entry from July 1860. Ibid., p. 157.
16. Entry from May 1860. Ibid., p. 156.
17. Entry from May 1862. Ibid., p. 164.
18. Leo Tolstoy, *Confession*, trans. David Patterson (New York: W. W. Norton, 1983), pt. 3, p. 23.
19. Ibid., pt. 3, p. 26.
20. Ibid., pt. 5, pp. 34–35.
21. Ibid., pt. 15, p. 85.
22. Ibid., pt. 8, p. 55.
23. Ibid., pt. 2, p. 18.
24. Ibid., pt. 2, pp. 18, 20.
25. Ibid., pt. 3, p. 25.
26. Ibid., pt. 11, p. 70.
27. Simmons, *Leo Tolstoy*, p. 326.

CHAPTER 2

1. V. V. Rozanov, *O pisatel'stve i pisateliakh* (Moscow, 1995), p. 31.
2. Pyotor Vasilievich Palievsky of the Gorky Institute of World Literature in Moscow first suggested this idea to me during a private conversation.
3. From the short story "Sevastopol in May" (1855). In Michael R. Katz, ed. *Tolstoy's Short Fiction* (New York: W. W. Norton, 1991), p. 43.
4. Annenkov's article, called "Notes on the Latest Works of I. S. Turgenev and L. N. Tolstoy," appeared in *The Contemporary* in 1855. Selections of the article are reprinted in V. A. Knowles, ed., *Tolstoy: The Critical Heritage* (London, Henley, and Boston: Routledge and Kegan Paul, 1978), pp. 50–53.
5. From *Le roman russe*, first published in 1886. Quoted in Isaiah Berlin, *The Hedgehog and the Fox: An Essay on Tolstoy's View of History* (Chicago: Ivan R. Dee, 1993), p. 1.
6. Lidiia Ginzburg, *O psikhologicheskoi proze* (Leningrad: Khudozhestvennaia literatura, 1977).
7. The contemporary Russian scholar P. V. Palievsky coined the phrase in his book *Literatura i teoriia,* 2nd ed. (Moscow, 1978), p. 7.
8. Harold Bloom, *The Western Canon: The Books and School of the Ages* (New York: Riverhead Books, 1994), p. 315.
9. A. A. Donskov, ed., *L. N. Tolstoy and N. N. Strakhov: Complete Correspondence*, 2 vols. (Ottawa, Canada: Slavic Research Group at the University of Ottawa and State L. N. Tolstoy Museum, 2003), vol. 1, p. 268. Also quoted in *Lev Tolstoi ob iskusstve i literature* (Moscow: Sovetskii pisatel,' 1958), p. 517.

10. Quoted in John Bayley, *Tolstoy and the Novel* (London: Chatto and Windus, 1966), p. 13.

11. The voluminous correspondence between Tolstoy and Strakhov was initiated by Tolstoy in 1870, the year in which Strakhov's third article about *War and Peace* appeared, and lasted until the month of Strakhov's death on January 24, 1896. The intensity of their personal and intellectual relationship, as well as the extent of their personal correspondence, is documented in Donskov, *L. N. Tolstoy and N. N. Strakhov: Complete Correspondence.*

12. Quoted in Leo Tolstoy, *War and Peace,* 2nd ed. (New York: W. W. Norton, 1996), p. 1114.

13. Ibid., p. 1084.

14. In Jeff Love's recent reading of *War and Peace,* cognitive limitation and human finitude become the novel's highest wisdom, its source of artistic power and structural unity. But the novel also transmutes intellectual paradox into an exquisite, confident vision of artistic order. See Jeff Love, *The Overcoming of History in* War and Peace, Studies in Slavic Literature and Poetics 42 (Amsterdam; New York: Rodopi, 2004).

15. Leo Tolstoy, *Confession,* trans. David Patterson (New York: W. W. Norton, 1983), pt. 5, pp. 34–35. For a fascinating study of Tolstoy's "conversion" in the context of the intellectual and religious culture of his time, see Inessa Medzhibovskaya, *Tolstoy and the Religious Culture of His Time: A Biography of a Long Conversation, 1845–1887* (Lanham, MD, and Plymouth, UK: Lexington Books, 2008).

16. Quoted in George Steiner, *Tolstoy or Dostoevsky: An Essay in the Old Criticism* (New York: Alfred A. Knopf, 1959), p. 6.

17. Diary entry from 15 September 1858. Quoted in R. F. Christian, ed. and trans., *Tolstoy's Diaries, vol. 1, 1847–1894* (London: The Athlone Press, 1985), p. 152.

18. From Strakhov's 1870 essay about *War and Peace,* republished in Nikolai Strakhov, *Kriticheskie stat'i ob I. S. Turgeneve i L. N. Tolstom (1862–1885),* vol. 1, 4th ed. (Kiev: Izdanie I. P. Matchenko, 1901 [Reprint: The Hague, Paris: Mouton, 1968]), p. 277.

19. Diary entry from 19 October 1852. Ibid., p. 61.

20. Diary entry from 5 June 1852. Ibid., p. 54.

21. Leo Tolstoy, *Resurrection,* trans. Rosemary Edmunds (New York and London: Penguin Books, 1966). pp. 252–53.

22. Leo Tolstoy, *War and Peace,* p. 1084.

CHAPTER 3

1. L. N. Tolstoi, *Polnoe sobranie sochinenii,* 90 vols. (Moscow, 1928–58), vol. 47, p. 10.

2. I. S. Turgenev, *Polnoe sobranie sochinenii i pisem* (Moscow and Leningrad, 1961–68), vol. 10, p. 207.

3. Scholar Anthony Anemone seems to concur when he intriguingly argues that *The Cossacks* artistically attempts to transcend the mystification-demystification dialectic altogether: "The contradictory presentation of Rousseauian motifs in *The Cossacks* should not be seen either as the sign of the author's artistic or philosophical immaturity, or of the unresolved struggle in Tolstoy's early works between Romanticism and Realism. Rather, it should be read as Tolstoy's heroic attempt to think through, and even to transcend, the limitations of the philosophical and linguistic culture into which he was born."

Anthony Anemone, "Gender, Genre, and the Discourse of Imperialism in Tolstoy's *The Cossacks," Tolstoy Studies Journal*, 6 (1993): 61.

4. Among recent scholarship on the novel, only an article by Philip Rogers focuses on the existential dimension of Olenin's quest. See Philip Rogers, "The Sufferings of Young Olenin: Tolstoy's Werther," *Tolstoy Studies Journal*, 17 (2005): 59–70. Other recent scholarship of the novel has been of the "cultural criticism" type. In these approaches, Olenin's search for meaning is treated primarily as a means for Tolstoy to explore the complexities of Russian national identity, rather than as the expression of a universal human quest for existential meaning. See, for instance, Katya Hokanson, *Writing at Russia's Border* (Toronto: University of Toronto Press, 2008), pp. 198–223; Susan Layton, *Russian Literature and Empire: Conquest of the Caucasus from Pushkin to Tolstoy* (New York: Cambridge University Press, 1994), pp. 233–51; Judith Kornblatt, *The Cossack Hero in Russian Literature: A Study in Cultural Mythology* (Madison: University of Wisconsin Press, 1992), pp. 91–96. For a representative collection of essays about Russian literature and Orientalism see Monika Greenleaf and Stephen Moeller-Sally, eds., *Russian Subjects: Empire, Nation, and the Culture of the Golden Age* (Evanston, IL: Northwestern University Press, 1998).

5. Donna Orwin's work on Tolstoy has demonstrated the depth and richness of Tolstoy's thinking in his fiction. See Donna Tussing Orwin, *Tolstoy's Art and Thought, 1847–1880* (Princeton, NJ: Princeton University Press, 1993).

6. A. Herzen. "The Russian People and Socialism. A Letter to Michelet" (1851) in *The Memoirs of Alexander Herzen*, vol. 4. (London: Chatto and Windus, 1968), p. 1649.

7. Quoted in Boris Eikhenbaum, *Tolstoi in the Sixties*, trans. Duffield White (Ann Arbor, MI: Ardis, 1982), p. 89.

8. See "Part I: Tolstoi Outside of Literature," in Eikhenbaum, *Tolstoi in the Sixties*, pp. 3–62. [In Russian: *Lev Tolstoi. 60-e gody.* Leningrad-Moscow: Goslitizdat, 1931.]

9. The page number refers to the English translation in *Great Short Works of Leo Tolstoy*, trans. Louise and Aylmer Maude (New York: Harper and Row Publishers, 1967). My citations are based on the Maude translation, but I make changes when necessary. For the benefit of readers using other editions of *The Cossacks*, I also include the chapter number after the page number.

10. Robert L. Jackson, "The Archetypal Journey: Aesthetic and Ethical Imperative in the Art of Tolstoj," *Russian Literature*, 11 (1982): 410. John Hagan argues that Olenin "feels the pull of an ethic of love and self sacrifice as fully as he feels the pull of an amoral freedom from such an ethic. Should he yield to the natural impulse or resist it?" Hagan argues that in *The Cossacks* Tolstoy never resolves this dilemma. See John Hagan, "Ambivalence in Tolstoy's *The Cossacks," Novel: A Forum on Fiction*, 3 (1969): 44.

11. In August 1857 Tolstoy goes into ecstasies over his reading of the *Iliad*: "Read the *Iliad*. That's the thing! Wonderful! Wrote to Ryabinin. I must revise the whole of the Caucasian tale [*The Cossacks*]" (Quoted in R. F. Christian, ed., *Tolstoy's Diaries* [London: The Athlone Press, 1985], *vol. 1, 1847–1894*, p. 141). Two days later Tolstoy repeats this thought: "*The Iliad* is making me completely rethink *The Fugitive* [*The Cossacks*]" (Ibid.). Less than two weeks later, Tolstoy writes in his diary: "Finished reading the *unbelievably delightful* ending of the *Iliad*. [emphasis in the original] Read the *Gospels*, which I haven't done for a long time. After the *Iliad*. How could Homer not have known that goodness is love! It's a revelation! There is no better explanation" (Ibid., p. 142). It is rather paradoxical that Tolstoy, who is ecstatic over Homer, also feels that he missed the point. Tolstoy never resolved this paradox in his novel; instead, it becomes one of the central tensions underlying the work.

12. Interestingly, the only other work in his career that caused Tolstoy such an extended period of creative torment (nearly a decade) was *Hadji-Murat*, the author's last novella, which embodies a Homeric ethic, and thus directly challenges the Christian morality Tolstoy had been preaching during his later years as he was working on that novella.

13. Both the twentieth-century Russian literary scholar and linguist Mikhail Bakhtin and the nineteenth-century Russian existentialist philosopher Lev Shestov seem to have misunderstood this paradoxical aspect of Tolstoy's artistic universe. Focusing on Tolstoy's poetics, Bakhtin argues that the essence of Tolstoy's poetics is "monologism," which implies a totalizing authorial perspective on the world:

> A second autonomous voice (alongside the author's voice) does not appear in Tolstoy's world. For that reason, there is no problem of linking voices, and no problem of a special positioning for the author's point of view. Tolstoy's discourse and his monologically naive point of view permeate everywhere, into all the corners of the world and the soul, subjugating everything to its unity. (Mikhail Bakhtin, *Problems of Dostoevsky's Poetics,* ed. and trans. Caryl Emerson [Minneapolis: University of Minnesota Press, 1984], p. 56)

In fact, there is a substantial amount of dialogue between the narrator and his hero in *The Cossacks*. This dialogic relationship serves the purpose of "opening" up the artistic universe in the novel, allowing for a playful interaction between narrator and hero. This is precisely the sort of relationship that Bakhtin sees as the essence of Dostoevsky's art but as absent in Tolstoy's. Bakhtin is not entirely correct about Tolstoy. Lev Shestov also mistakenly sees in Tolstoy's art a purely deterministic universe. Discussing Tolstoy from a philosophical point of view, Shestov argues that the writer does not sympathize with his characters in the way that Zola, Turgenev, and Dickens do. Readers

> therefore reproach him for his coldness, insensitivity, and hardness. . . . To many readers this attitude appears so incomprehensible and revolting that they are even inclined to deny Tolstoy's genius. . . . And, from their point of view, these readers are only too right . . . [because] Tolstoy, who manifests no humane feelings, frightens such people. (Lev Shestov, "The Good in the Teaching of Tolstoy and Nietzsche: Philosophy and Preaching," in *Dostoevsky, Tolstoy, and Nietzsche,* ed. Spencer Roberts and Bernard Martin [Athens: Ohio University Press, 1969], pp. 20–21)

Contrary to Shestov's interpretation of Tolstoy's art, I argue that in *The Cossacks* the spirit of philosophical determinism coexists with a sense of artistic play and a recognition of the possibility for positive moral choice in the world. For a provocative, theoretically rich discussion of the strengths and limitations of Bakhtin's understanding of Tolstoy, see Caryl Emerson, "The Tolstoy Connection in Bakhtin," *PMLA* 100, no. 1 (January 1985): 68–80.

14. Donna Orwin also believes this synthetic imagination to be at the core of all of Tolstoy's art. Tolstoy's "major theme," she writes, "was not, as it seemed to a post-Victorian like Merezhkovsky, a celebration of the body; rather, it was the struggle to accommodate the body and soul, earth and sky, real and ideal in the life of the individual." Orwin, *Tolstoy's Art and Thought,* p. 12.

15. Soviet criticism of the novel emphasized this point, although in a Marxist context. According to this reading, Olenin is an example of an "unenlightened" Rousseauian ide-

alist, who does not understand that he cannot change his character by an act of personal will, since his character is necessarily determined by his class and the economic forces of his age. See, for example, L. D. Opul'skaia, "Povest' L. N. Tolstogo Kazaki" in L. N. Tolstoi, *Kazaki*, Moscow, *Akademiia Nauk*, 1963, pp. 341–51.

16. Nikolai Chernyshevsky, in an 1856 article on Tolstoy, was the first critic to use the phrase "*dialektika dushi*" ("dialectic of the soul"), to refer to a characteristic aspect of Tolstoy's representation of the inner world of his characters, and "*vnutrennii monolog*" ("interior monologue"), to describe the artistic technique used by Tolstoy to describe that inner world. See N. G. Chernyshevsky, "Detstvo i otrochestvo. Voennye rasskazy," in *L. N. Tolstoi v russkoi kritike* (Moscow: Gosudarstvennoe izdatel'stvo khudozhestvennoi literatury, 1952.)

17. In Tolstoy's 1852 story "The Raid," the purifying power of nature can be felt even more explicitly than in *The Cossacks*. Take, for instance, the narrator's comment shortly after his description of battle: "Can it be that there is not room for all men on this beautiful earth under those immeasurable starry heavens? Can it be possible that in the midst of this entrancing Nature feelings of hatred, vengeance, or the desire to exterminate their fellows, can endure in the souls of men? All that is unkind in the hearts of men should, one would think, vanish at contact with Nature—that most direct expression of beauty and goodness" (*PSS* 3, 29). Translation taken from Leo Tolstoy, *The Raid and Other Stories,* trans. Louise and Aylmer Maude (Oxford, New York: Oxford University Press, 1982), p. 16.

18. In the Maude translation the ellipsis comes before the phrase "*a gory*" each time, whereas in the original the ellipsis *follows* the repeated phrase. An anonymous reviewer from *Slavic and East European Review* of an earlier version of this chapter has rightly pointed out that "the position of the ellipsis is more effective in the original since it invites the reader to fill in the omission and so draws him into Olenin's mind and into participating in the narration." In my citation of this passage I have modified the Maude translation by placing the ellipsis where it appears each time in the original.

19. In *Tolstoy as Man and Artist,* Dmitry Merezhkovsky writes of Daddy Eroshka's philosophy: "This primitive philosophy is incarnate in the real hero of the story, the old Cossack, Uncle Yeroshka, one of the finest and most perfect creations of Tolstoy, a character who enables us to see into the darkest and most secret depth of the author's being; a depth which perhaps was never laid bare to his own consciousness." Dmitry Merezhkovsky, *Tolstoy as Man and Artist* (New York: Knickerbocker Press, 1902), p. 13.

20. The eponymous hero of Cooper's novel, Natty Bumppo, also called the Pathfinder, is, like Daddy Eroshka, a skillful hunter and a shrewd survivor in a harsh natural environment. He also possesses an innate moral sense, which makes him, like Daddy Eroshka, an edifying force in the lives of others. Cooper describes the Pathfinder in this way:

> His feelings appeared to possess the freshness and nature of the forests in which he passed so much of his time, and no casuist could have made clearer decisions in matters relating to right and wrong; and yet, he was not without his prejudices, which, though few and coloured by the character and usages of the individual, were deep-rooted, and had almost got to form a part of his nature. But the most striking feature about the moral organization of Pathfinder was his beautiful and unerring sense of justice. This noble trait, and without it no man can be truly great, with it no

man other than respectable, probably had its unseen influence on all who associated with him, for the common, rude and unprincipled brawler of the camp had been known to return from an expedition made in his company, rebuked by his sentiments, softened by his language and improved by his example. (James Fenimore Cooper, *The Pathfinder, Or the Inland Sea,* ed. Richard Dilworth Rust [Albany: State University of New York Press, 1981], p. 134)

The Pathfinder is also something of a spiritual loner, which makes him similar to both Eroshka and Olenin. And like Olenin, Bumppo moved from the civilized world to settle on the frontier; however, Bumppo lives there permanently and becomes a full member of that community, counting native Indians among his closest friends. Other settlers, inexperienced in the ways of frontier life, rely on Bumppo as their trusted guide through that wild region—a feature that also distinguishes him from Olenin, who is always the student, never the guide.

21. Robert Jackson makes a similar point, although he does not specifically trace the development of the underlying archetype of the Garden of Eden in the novel: "The metaphorical character of Olenin's journey is clear. He is not simply walking into a forest in search of an animal's lair; he is going backwards into man's mythic past, and his search for the stag (*olen'*) is, of course, a search for himself, 'Olenin,' a search for his inmost organic being, for primeval man. The journey, then, is not only in space but time. And the forest is not only an area stretching out beyond a Cossack village in the middle of the nineteenth century, but the primeval forest" (Jackson, "The Archetypal Journey," p. 396.)

22. For a discussion of this and other matters related to the composition of the novel, see A. E. Gruzinskii, "Istoriia pisaniia i pechataniia Kazakov," in *PSS* 6, 271–93. For a thorough analysis of the many generic forms Tolstoy considered using for the work, see C. J. G. Turner, "Tolstoy's *The Cossacks:* The Question of Genre," *The Modern Language Review* 73 (July 1978): 563–72.

23. Paul Friedrich pointed out to me yet another layer of meaning. In Russian peasant culture the gatepost of a loose girl would be smeared with tar. The deeper psychological implication is clear: Olenin is the symbolic tar that smothers Maryanka, pressuring her into illicit behavior for which she senses that she will be punished.

24. Hugh McLean has pointed out to me that Tolstoy is also mocking Vanyusha's pseudoculture with his use of French words spelled in Cyrillic letters to indicate mispronunciation (e.g., La fil' for La fille).

25. In a superb analysis of the poetics of *The Cossacks,* Paul Friedrich observes how Tolstoy builds the novel on a chiasmic structure, or series of parallel reversals. See Paul Friedrich, "Tolstoy, Homer, and Genotypical Influence," *Comparative Literature* 56, no. 4 (Autumn 2004): 283–99. Friedrich claims that there are seventy-five chiasmic parallels in the work. One of the most prominent "is illustrated near the very end, as if the author were teasing us: 'Then as now a three-horse conveyance was standing at the porch.' However, now (in Chapter 42), in contrast to then (in Chapter 1), Olenin is not promising himself a new life. A deeper strand shared by the two chapters is the breakup of a courtship: in Chapter 1, Olenin is leaving a young woman whom he has compromised; in Chapter 42, Olenin is spurned by a young woman who has lured him on" (Friedrich, pp. 288–89). This major parallel reversal, as well as the chiasmic structure of the entire work, enhances the impression of both internal dialogue and overarching unity in the novel.

CHAPTER 4

1. Quoted in Leo Tolstoy, *War and Peace*, ed. George Gibian (New York; London: W. W. Norton, 1996), p. 1089.

2. Sergei Bocharov discusses the far-reaching implications of *"mir,"* the word translated as "peace" in the novel's title. As Bocharov points out, in Russian, *mir* also means "world," or "cosmos," or "totality of human life," but does not necessarily imply metaphysical order: "The word *mir* in *War and Peace* suggests not only the peacefulness of an epic and the simplicity of a chronicle, but also what K. Leont'iev called in the book 'a contemporary agitated complexity' [*sovremennoj vzvolnovannoj slozhnost'iu*]" (from S. G. Bocharov, *O khudozhestvennykh mirakh* [Moscow: Sovetskaia rossiia, 1985], p. 230). I argue that the novel ultimately subsumes life's complexity and angst into a vision of metaphysical order. In a footnote to his review essay in *Tolstoy Studies Journal*, Hugh McLean points out that in the old orthography used by Tolstoy the different meanings of the word *mir* were indicated by different spellings. When spelled with the Russian vowel *"и,"* *mir* meant the absence of war, agreement, calm, or peace. However, when it was spelled with the Latin vowel "i," *mir* meant cosmos, world. In Tolstoy's time the word in the title of *War and Peace* always was written with the и vowel spelling (suggesting peace, the absence of war). But throughout the novel Tolstoy often uses the other spelling, thus evoking rich interplay among the word's various connotations. See Hugh McLean, "Review Article: *War and Peace*, Original Version," *Tolstoy Studies Journal*, 20 (2009): 87.

3. Lukacs writes:

> The really great novelists are in this respect always true-born sons of Homer. True, the world of objects and the relationship between them and men has changed, has become more intricate, less spontaneously poetic. But the art of the great novelists manifests itself precisely in the ability to overcome the unpoetic nature of their world, through sharing and experiencing the life and evolution of the society they lived in. . . . [The] pictures of Tolstoy are never mere scenery, never merely pictures and descriptions, never merely contributions to the "totality of objects. . . ." Such a presentation of the "totality of objects" dispenses Tolstoy—like every truly great epic poet—from giving dry and tedious descriptions of a setting, the connection between which and individual destinies is always general and abstract and hence always remains coincidental. The "totality of objects" in Tolstoy always expresses, in immediate, spontaneous and palpable form, the close bond between individual destinies and the surrounding world. (Georg Lukacs, "Tolstoy and the Development of Realism," in *Tolstoy: A Collection of Critical Essays,* ed. Ralph E. Matlaw [Englewood Cliffs, NJ: Prentice-Hall, Inc., 1967], p. 78)

George Steiner develops Lukacs's thesis further. Tolstoy and Dostoevsky, Steiner argues, are the sole torchbearers in modern literature of the great ancient philosophical tradition of attempting to see the world whole. Tolstoy is the bearer of the epic tradition of Homer, and Dostoevsky is the inheritor of the dramatic vision of Shakespeare. George Steiner, *Tolstoy or Dostoevsky: An Essay in the Old Criticism* (New Haven, CT: Yale University Press; 2nd ed., 1996).

4. Kathryn Feuer gives a provocative account of Tolstoy's rejection of the arguments

in favor of reform in the 1850s. See "Chapter 7: Tolstoy's Rejection of the Spirit of 1856" in Kathryn B. Feuer, *Tolstoy and the Genesis of* War and Peace, ed. Robin Feuer Miller and Donna Tussing Orwin (Ithaca, NY, and London: Cornell University Press, 1996), pp. 135–67.

5. See Feuer, *Tolstoy and the Genesis of* War and Peace.

6. Donna Orwin makes a similar point when she writes of the novel's sense of "the whole, which subsumes everything, all those opposites that comprise the world, within it. And a dynamic view of nature includes even the history of individuals and nations within it. Nature in *War and Peace* is ruled by harmonic reason, which operates through the metaphysics of opposites." Donna Orwin, *Tolstoy's Art and Thought, 1847–1880* (Princeton, NJ: Princeton University Press, 1993), p. 107.

7. The Soviet Formalist scholar Viktor Shklovsky goes so far as to argue that Tolstoy distorts historical facts in order to further his ideological agenda. A prominent example of this for Shklovsky is the author's suppression of the real reason that Princess Marya's peasants at Bogucharovo rebel in Volume Three, Part Two, when she offers to take them with her to Bald Hills: because they believed that, by staying at Bogucharova, they would be freed by Napoleon. "Of course, Tolstoy, who was very interested in questions of labor," Shklovksy writes, "could have explained to the reader the peasants' behavior, but then the uprising would not have appeared senseness, and the question would have arisen that only in this instance the peasants were mistaken [about the heartfelt intentions of their baroness]" (Viktor Shklovskii, *Mater'ial i stil' v romane "Voina i mir."* [Moscow: Izdatel'stvo "Federatsiia" (Reprint: University of Michigan Press, 1967, p. 84]). Agreeing with Shklovsky, Kathryn Feuer points out that in the novel's final version Tolstoy had removed a sentence, appearing in the first draft, that explains that the peasants "were prepared to receive Napoleon who was freeing them" (Feuer, *Tolstoy and the Genesis of* War and Peace, p. 149). Still, the thrust of Feuer's analysis is to show how Tolstoy's original ideological intention is superseded by the demands of artistic truth. On the other hand, Shklovsky, who is writing in the highly politicized 1920s in the Soviet Union, views *War and Peace* as a brilliant web of self-serving artistic illusions.

8. "The great chain of being," an idea at the core of world religious, philosophical, and artistic thought from ancient through modern times, posits that there is an inherent design to the universe, in which every animate and inanimate object has its proper place. The "great chain of being" is defined by the principles of "plenitude," "continuity," and "graduation," thus implying a kind of providentially ordained hierarchy of existence. The idea applies, in part, to the later Tolstoy's notions about the universal brotherhood of man. But it applies equally—and perhaps even more so—to the much more pantheistic holism of *War and Peace,* in which life's plenitude and continuity can coexist with social hierarchy, something the later Tolstoy could not accept. For the definitive study of "the great chain of being," see Arthur Lovejoy, *The Great Chain of Being: The Study of the History of an Idea,* 2nd ed. (Cambridge, MA: Harvard University Press, 2005).

9. The question of revolution was crucial to Tolstoy's earliest conception of the novel, which grew out of *The Decembrists,* an unfinished novel about a Russian Decembrist returning from Siberian exile. As Tolstoy worked he realized that in order to describe his hero he would first need to understand his formative years during the Napoleonic wars. A lasting trace of this original conception is the character of Pierre Bezukhov, the Decembrist hero of the original novel (under the name Pyotr Labazov) and the future Decembrist-in-the-making at the end of *War and Peace.*

10. Leo Tolstoy, *War and Peace,* trans. Richard Pevear and Larissa Volokhonsky (New York: Alfred A. Knopf, 2007). All English citations from *War and Peace* are from

this edition with modifications when necessary. For the benefit of readers using other editions, after the page number I also give the volume, part, and chapter number in that order, based on the definitive original version of the novel in *Polnoe sobranie sochinenii,* or *The Complete Collected Works of L. N. Tolstoy,* 90 vols.

11. From "Neskol'ko slov po povodu knigi 'Voina i mira'" ("Some Words about *War and Peace*"), published in 1868 (*PSS* 16, 8). Quoted in Leo Tolstoy, *War and Peace,* ed. George Gibian, p. 1090.

12. John Bayley, *Tolstoy and the Novel* (London: Chatto and Windus, 1966), p. 101.

13. From "Some Words about *War and Peace.*"

14. Tolstoy, *War and Peace,* ed. George Gibian, p. 1091.

15. Another example of this sort of sociologically oriented literary criticism is, of course, Pisarev's article about *War and Peace,* "The Old Gentry" (*Staroe barstvo*), which I discuss later in this chapter.

16. Notebook, 5 April 1870. *PSS* 48, 125–26.

17. Ibid., p. 125.

18. Notebook, 13 March 1870. Ibid., p. 118.

19. The book was written by Dr. P. S. Alexéyev, brother-in-law of Aylmer Maude, the author's friend and favorite translator of his works into English.

20. Leo Tolstoy, "Why Do Men Stupefy Themselves?" in *Recollections and Essays,* trans. Aylmer Maude (London, 1937; reprint ed., 1961), p. 81.

21. This quotation originally appeared in Charles Johnston, "How Count Tolstoy Writes," *The Arena* (Boston), 21 (1899): 269–72. It has been reprinted in Peter Serkirin, ed., *Americans in Conversation with Tolstoy: Selected Accounts, 1887–1923* (Jefferson, NC: McFarland and Co., 2006), pp. 57–58.

22. V. A. Zelinskii, ed., *Russkaia kriticheskaiia literatura o proizvedenniiakh L. N. Tolstogo: khronologicheskii sbornik kritiko-bibliograficheskikh statei,* 8 vols. (Ann Arbor, MI: University Microfilms reprint, 1966), vol. 3, p. 3.

23. Ibid., p. 29.

24. Ibid., pp. 72, 71.

25. Ibid., pp. 143–44.

26. A. V. Knowles, ed., *Tolstoy: The Critical Heritage* (London, Henley, and Boston: Routledge and Kegan Paul, 1978), p. 182.

27. Ibid., p. 216.

28. Quoted in Tolstoy, *War and Peace,* ed. George Gibian, p. 1114. For a historical survey of the critical responses that emphasize the novel's formal peculiarities, see "Formal Peculiarities of 'War and Peace'" and "Solving the Puzzle of 'War and Peace'" in Gary Saul Morson, *Hidden in Plain View: Narrative and Creative Potentials in* War and Peace (Palo Alto, CA: Stanford University Press, 1987), pp. 38–80.

29. Tolstoy valued in Strakhov the same qualities he valued above all in an artist: clear thinking, moral-spiritual commitment, and strength, balanced by a tender compassion for people: "Under the clarity and brevity of the exposition is a softness, coupled with strength: you do not rip with teeth, but with soft, strong paws." Quoted in "Roundtable Discussion from IMLI: *The Complete Correspondence of Leo Tolstoy and Nikolai Strakhov,*" *Tolstoy Studies Journal,* 18 (2006): 90.

30. From Strakhov's 1870 essay about *War and Peace,* republished in Nikolai Strakhov, *Kriticheskie stat'i ob I. S. Turgeneve i L. N. Tolstom (1862–1885),* vol. 1, 4th ed. (Kiev: Izdanie I. P. Matchenko, 1901 [Reprint: The Hague, Paris: Mouton, 1968], p. 277).

31. Ibid., p. 278.

32. The critics who made these comments were, respectively, Nikolai Shelgunov and S. Navalikhin, both radical social critics. Navalikhin's article originally appeared in *Delo* (*Affair*) in June 1868, and was provocatively called "Iziashchnyi romanist i ego isiashchnye kritiki" ("An Elegant Novelist and His Elegant Critics"). Linda Gerstein points out that S. Navalikhin, who was in exile at the time, was the pen name of F. Flerovsky, author of the influential *The Position of the Working Class in Russia*. See Linda Gerstein, *Nikolai Strakhov* (Cambridge, MA: Harvard University Press, 1971), p. 82.

33. Strakhov, *Kriticheskie stat'i*, pp. 278–79.

34. D. I. Pisarev, *Literaturnaya kritika v trex tomax* (Leningrad: Khudozhestvennaya literatura, 1981), vol 3, p. 245.

35. Ibid.

36. Ibid., p. 261. We should keep in mind that Pisarev had only seen the first three volumes of the novel. The epilogue, in which Nikolai takes up agriculture, had not yet come out.

37. Ibid.

38. Ibid.

39. Ibid., p. 246.

40. This is the same strategy that Pisarev used in his 1862 essay "Bazarov" [*Bazarov*]. In that essay Pisarev holds up Turgenev's hero, Bazarov, of *Fathers and Sons*, as the embodiment of the admirable traits of egoism and self-affirmation, qualities towards which Pisarev believed contemporary Russians should strive. In speaking of Bazarov as if he were a real person in society, rather than a literary hero, the critic reveals his tendency—also characteristic among the so-called social critics of the day—to read Turgenev's novel as if it were a social document, rather than a work of art. In so doing, Pisarev's discussion overlooks, among other things, the artistic and human complexities of the work, not least Turgenev's deep ambivalence about Bazarov. Edward J. Brown discusses Pisarev's "transformation" of "art" into "non-art": "Pisarev's treatment of Turgenev and Dostoevsky is a special case of translation, or paraphrase, or transformation, as I have called it. Here he appropriates two verbal objects that he acknowledges as art and transforms each into non-art, into social meanings. In Kenneth Burke's phrase, he transforms a complexity into a simplicity." Edward J. Brown, "Pisarev and the Transformation of Two Novels," in *Literature and Society in Imperial Russia, 1800–1914*, ed. William Mills Todd III (Palo Alto, CA: Stanford University Press, 1978), pp. 151–72.

41. Pisarev, p. 246.

42. From Strakhov's 1869 article about *War and Peace*. Strakhov, p. 194. Charles Moser also quotes these lines from Strakhov's article, and in his book he places them in the context of the larger contemporary debate on the extent to which art should depict the real, or aspire to create an ideal. See Charles A. Moser, *Esthetics as Nightmare: Russian Literary Theory, 1855–1870* (Princeton, NJ: Princeton University Press, 1989), pp. 153–54.

43. Strakhov, p. 194.

44. Among the most prominent of this group of minor novelists, who are sometimes called "the plebeian novelists of the sixties" (*belletristy-raznochintsy*), were Nikolai Uspensky, Reshetnikov, and Pomyalovsky. Uspensky and Reshetnikov became popular for their unadorned portrayal of ugly truths of peasant life. Pomyalovsky was best known for his novel *Molotov* (1861), which describes the frustrations of a typical young idealist of the 1860s. These novelists drew on the form of the physiological sketch, practiced by Turgenev and Gogol before them, in order to expose the ills of the contemporary

social order. For more on the physiological sketch in Russia, see Joachim T. Baer, "The 'Physiological Sketch' in Russian Literature," in *Mnemozina: Studia litteraria russica in honorem Vsevolod Setchkarev,* ed. Joachim T. Baer and Norman W. Ingham (Munich: Wilhelm Fink Verlag, 1974), pp. 1–12.

45. Strakhov, p. 202.

46. Ibid., p. 208.

47. Ibid., p. 208.

48. Ibid., p. 205.

49. These are phrases that Strakhov himself uses in the article: "What is an ordinary man in comparison with the hero? What is the private man in relation to history? In a more general form this is just the question that has long since been worked out by our artistic realism: what is the ordinary, everyday reality in comparison with the ideal, the wonderful life? [*chto takoe obyknovennaia, budnichnaia deistvitel'nost' v sravnenii s idealom, s prekrasnoiu zhizniu?*]" (Strakhov, p. 197).

50. Ibid., p. 261.

51. Ibid., p. 196.

52. Ibid., pp. 296–97.

53. For the best analysis in English of Tolstoy's and Strakhov's extensive dialogue, particularly on matters of faith and science, see Irina Paperno, "Lev Tolstoy's Correspondence with Nikolai Strakhov: The Dialogue on Faith," in Donna Tussing Orwin, ed., *Anniversary Essays on Tolstoy* (Cambridge: Cambridge University Press, 2010), pp. 96–119.

54. Tolstoy scholars continue to debate about which edition of *War and Peace* is the definitive one. In the past few years this argument became so heated, in fact, that an editor of *The Complete Collected Works of L. N. Tolstoy in 100 Volumes,* currently being published by the Russian Academy of Sciences, quit her post over disagreements about which edition of the novel should be used for the new publication.

55. Jeff Love, *The Overcoming of History in* War and Peace (Amsterdam; New York: Rodopi, 2004), p. 96.

56. During a private conversation in Moscow, Sergei Bocharov first called my attention to Eikhenbaum's phrase.

57. Quoted in Boris Sorokin, *Tolstoy in Prerevolutionary Russian Criticism* (Columbus: The Ohio State University Press for Miami University, 1979), p. 156.

58. Isaiah Berlin, *The Hedgehog and the Fox: An Essay on Tolstoy's View of History* (Chicago: Ivan R. Dee, 1993), p. 3.

59. George R. Clay, *Tolstoy's Phoenix: From Method to Meaning in* War and Peace, Studies in Russian Literature and Theory (Evanston, IL: Northwestern University Press, 1998.)

60. Sergei Bocharov, *Roman L. N. Tolstogo "Voina i mir"* (Moscow: "Khudozhestvennaia literatura," 1987).

61. Love, *The Overcoming of History in* War and Peace.

CHAPTER 5

1. By analyzing Tolstoy's use of repetition (of words, images, motifs) in the novel, Natasha Sankovitch comes to a similar conclusion. Yet in her analysis, repetition is seen more as a rhetorical strategy for constructing absent meaning than as the expression of the writer's fundamental belief in higher truth:

Just as characters must work to connect the details or parts of their experience in order to achieve an understanding of their lives as wholes that are never quite whole, readers, too, as co-creators of the literary text, must work to make sense of the continuously developing whole of the text. . . . Repetition for both characters and readers brings order into something which may in immediate experience be largely disordered.

Consistent with her poststructuralist theoretical framework, a still dominant paradigm in American Slavic studies, Sankovitch doesn't believe that either Tolstoy or his characters ultimately discover the unifying order they seek. See Natasha Sankovitch, *Repetition in Tolstoy: Creating and Recovering Experience* (Palo Alto, CA: Stanford University Press, 1998), p. 33.

2. My use of the oak tree image to describe the architectonics of *War and Peace* is similar to the description by the Soviet critic O. V. Slivitskaia, who, expanding on the work of V. D. Dneprov, describes the structure of *War and Peace* with the term *"federativnost'"*, or, literally, "federality." (The root of the word, *"feder,"* is related to the Latin word for "league," as in the Russian word, *federatsiia*, or "federation.") In Slivitskaya's interpretation, *War and Peace* becomes a kind of artistic counterpart to the political concept of "federation": "The word *federativnost'* . . . signifies the dialectical mutuality of each component's dependence on and independence from all the 'linkages' of the book. Each artistic component is at once both an element of the whole system and possesses inherent value in itself; it both gravitates towards the artistic center and is independent of it" (translation mine). See O. V. Slivitskaia, *"Voina i mir" L. N. Tolstogo: Problemy chelovecheskogo obshcheniia* (Leningrad: Izdatel'stvo Leningradskogo universiteta, 1988), p. 14.

3. Leo Tolstoy, *War and Peace,* trans. Richard Pevear and Larissa Volokhonsky (New York: Alfred A. Knopf, 2007), p. 177.

4. Kutuzov's sleeping in this scene is often read as an indication of his general disregard for strategic planning, and particularly for the kind of tedious planning combined with politicking that takes place during war councils. Michael Denner goes even further in suggesting that Kutuzov's behavior is, in fact, an early exemplar of Tolstoy's philosophy of nonaction that will resurface years later in his doctrine of non-violent resistance to evil. See Michael A. Denner, "Tolstoyan Nonaction: The Advantage of Doing Nothing," *Tolstoy Studies Journal,* vol. XIII (2001). But Hugh McLean concurs with Russian scholar Alexander Skaftymov, who has offered an intriguing alternative interpretation: Kutuzov's advice not to fight a battle at Austerlitz was already rejected by the highest authority, the young autocrat Alexander I. "Kutuzov had the ingrained habits of a lifetime soldier: when you are overruled by a higher authority, you shut down your mind, assume an air of compliance, and 'go to sleep.'" Quoted in Hugh McLean, *In Quest of Tolstoy* (Brighton, MA: Academic Studies Press, 2008), p. 219.

5. Natasha Sankovitch points out that Prince Andrei repeats the phrase "Here it is! It's beginning" three times before the Battle of Schöngrabern, as well. See Sankovitch, *Creating and Recovering Experience: Repetition in Tolstoy,* p. 196.

6. Ibid., p. 196.

7. Sergei Bocharov, *Roman L. N. Tolstogo "Voina i mir,"* 4th ed. (Moscow: Khudozhestvennaia literatura, 1987), p. 68.

8. George R. Clay sees a similar evolution in Nikolai from folly to wisdom: "One by one, Nicholas recognizes the indivisibility of values he once considered absolute opposites. From Telyanin, he learns that truth can be harmful; at Enns Bridge and Schöngra-

bern, that it may sometimes be right to run from the enemy; at Ostravna, that it may be wrong to kill or even wound the enemy; in every battle, that fear is part of courage; while harmonizing with Natasha after his huge gambling losses to Dolokhov, that 'one might kill and rob and yet be happy'; from Princess Mary, that plainness can be beautiful and spirituality seductive." See George R. Clay, *Tolstoy's Phoenix: From Method to Meaning in* War and Peace (Evanston, IL: Northwestern University Press, 1998), p. 69.

9. We must distinguish Tolstoy's artistic transformation of life from Nietzsche's conception of art, described in *The Birth of Tragedy,* as transcendence and a "justification" of life: "Only as an aesthetic phenomenon is the world justified" (quoted in Walter Kaufmann, *Nietzsche: Philosopher, Psychologist, Antichrist,* 4th ed. [Princeton, NJ: Princeton University Press, 1975], p. 323). For Nietzsche, artistic transcendence is a way of imparting meaning to a fundamentally meaningless existence, a way of giving purpose to the essential tragedy of human existence. For Tolstoy, the transcendent capacity of art lies in its ability to celebrate the harmonies and beauty of life that already exist but are frequently hidden from characters' ordinary consciousness.

10. See David Sloane, "The Poetry in *War and Peace,*" *Slavic and East European Journal* 40, no. 1 (Spring 1988): 63–84.

11. There is evidence from Tolstoy's own writings that he viewed prose and poetry as closely related forms of artistic expression. In 1851 the author notes in his diary: "Where the border is between prose and poetry I will never understand; although there is a question about this subject in the study of verbal arts. But it's impossible to understand the answer. Poetry is verse. Prose is not verse. Or: poetry is everything excluding business papers and text books." Quoted in *Lev Tolstoi ob iskusstvo i literature* (Moscow: Sovetskii pisatel', 1958), vol. 1, p. 71.

12. Christian credits another scholar, J. M. Meijer, for coining the term "situation rhyme" in connection with Dostoevsky, but to my knowledge Christian is the first to have applied it to Tolstoy. See R. F. Christian, *Tolstoy's* War and Peace: *A Study* (Oxford: Clarendon Press, 1962), pp. 131–35.

13. The optimism inherent in Tolstoy's art explains why Lionel Trilling saw an absence of any "imagination of disaster" in Tolstoy, and why the Russian scholar Pytor Palievsky more recently has written of the "indispensable cheerfulness and clarity of [Tolstoy's] spirit": "[Tolstoy] simply shows us the meaning that others have lost and that has become invisible from the various dead ends, from which the voices of despair resound. In his optimism there is nothing artificial or forced. And he can show that in the so-called tragic element of existence there is more of our own weakness, than truth." See P. V. Palievsky, *Russkie Klassiki: Opyt obshchej kharakteristiki* (Moscow: Khudozhestvennia literatura, 1987), p. 130.

Palievsky's insight touches on one of my overarching theses: namely, that in order to appreciate Tolstoy's worldview in *War and Peace,* we must strive to understand the work's totality, its "labyrinth of linkages." Many individual moments in the novel are tragic, such as the sudden death of Petya Rostov, the execution of prisoners witnessed by Pierre, and the killing of Vereshchagin by the mob. However, by viewing these scenes in the context of the entire work, we recognize that tragedy is always subsumed into a larger, ultimately consoling, picture of life.

14. Nicholas O. Warner has come to a similar conclusion through his analysis of the novel's depiction of time. What I call "the ongoing processes of human consciousness" Warner refers to as "the inner perspectives and emotions of individual characters." Tolstoy, he writes, "depicts time as a complex phenomenon, dealing not only with objective, chronological time, but also with subjective time, which depends on the inner perspectives and emotions of individual characters, rather than on the rigid delineations of clock

and calendar." See Nicholas O. Warner, "The Texture of Time in *War and Peace*," *The Slavic and East European Journal* 28, no. 2 (Summer 1984): 193.

15. George Clay coined the apt phrase "Tolstoy's perpetual present." See "Chapter Two: Tolstoy's Perpetual Present," in Clay, *Tolstoy's Phoenix: From Method to Meaning in* War and Peace, pp. 20–32. This is significantly different from Nietzsche's notion of "eternal recurrence," which posits that each moment should be lived as if it were to recur eternally, for, in a universe devoid of transcendent meaning, we are condemned to live forever with the choices we make and the meanings we create in every instance. In the world of *War and Peace*, though, the "perpetual present" suggests patterns of human experience in a universe with an overarching design. Happiness comes to Tolstoy's characters in *War and Peace* when they begin to apprehend this hidden inner truth, and not when they try to impose their own individual truths on the world.

16. My idea of the trivial suddenly becoming significant is crucially different from Gary Saul Morson's notion that in *War and Peace* "the unnecessary is necessary, the radically insignificant is radically significant" (see Gary Saul Morson, *Hidden in Plain View: Narrative and Creative Potentials in* War and Peace [Palo Alto, CA: Stanford University Press, 1987], p. 147). According to Morson, seemingly random details are important in the novel, because they reveal the fundamental randomness of life. "History is a fabric of lost thread, and so is much of *War and Peace*," Morson argues (p. 148). But as I have shown, the seemingly random detail "Titus, don't bite us!" is significant, precisely because it *is* essential to illuminating recurrent patterns of human experience. Through the repetition of this detail the narrator deftly weaves Andrei's and Nikolai's individual stories during the Battle of Austerlitz into a coherent artistic whole, in which every human experience and aspiration—no matter how seemingly small—is a vital element in the world's overarching design.

17. Brian Turner, *Here, Bullet* (Farmington, ME: Alice James Books, 2005).

CHAPTER 6

1. Although today the spelling is the same in Russian for both senses of the word, in Tolstoy's day these different connotations were indicated by slightly different spellings. See note 2 in chapter 4 for a more detailed explanation.

2. Why is the "dead, reproachful face of his wife" one of Andrei's "best moments"? It is likely because that moment coincides with the one in which he realizes "the joyful meaning of [the baby's] cry," in other words, that his son has just been born (327; II, 1, 9). That Andrei would remember the moment in terms of the loss of his wife rather than the gain of his son is probably because in him feelings of joy are often inextricably tied to feelings of guilt.

3. Another way of seeing this moment, in purely aesthetic terms, is that the oak is the "objective correlative," T. S. Eliot's term for the external equivalent, of Andrei's inner change.

4. Originally, Tolstoy had intended to have Captain Tushin, a battery captain at the Battle of Schöngrabern, ride into Bogucharovo to save Princess Marya. That the author changed his mind, and has Nikolai save her instead, reflects the importance to him of creating a heightened Romantic atmosphere, in which destiny seems to be the driving force.

5. Mikhail Lermontov, *A Hero of Our Time*, trans. Marian Schwartz (New York: The Modern Library, 2004), p. 114.

6. This moment will be echoed faintly by Tolstoy years later in the final scene in Book Seven of *Anna Karenina*, in which Anna, having thrown herself in front of the

train, has a sudden pang of regret for what she is doing. "'Where am I? What am I doing? Why?' She wanted to rise, to throw herself back, but something huge and implacable pushed at her head and dragged over her." Even Anna, a tragic heroine in a fundamentally tragic novel, has an attachment to life in her most despairing moment. It seems that no matter how hopeless things become for Tolstoy's characters, they always exhibit some mysterious attraction to life and an impulse for self-assertion. The implacable forces of nature and history never squelch the inner voice of Tolstoy's characters. That voice can always be heard bubbling quietly just beneath the surface.

7. Gary Saul Morson has made a similar point: "Each of Prince Andrei's renewals of belief in something ends with a recognition that what he has recently respected is in fact worthless, another self-enclosed game with no real meaning." See Gary Saul Morson, *Hidden in Plain View: Narrative and Creative Potentials in* War and Peace (Palo Alto, CA: Stanford University Press, 1987), p. 264. But as I suggest below, it is Andrei's nature—his fundamental inability to heed his heart and trust his instincts, and not his immersion in the games of life—that prevents him from sustaining his moments of renewal.

8. This is a rare instance in which I disagree with Pevear's and Volokhonsky's translation. They translate Andrei's "*Stydno, gospodin ofitser*" as "Shame on you, officer." But in the original Russian, "on you" is intentionally left out and not necessarily implied, as Pevear and Volokhonsky render it. The "shame" Andrei refers to here is something more general and universal.

9. George Steiner points to several instances in *War and Peace,* such as this one, in which Tolstoy "conveyed a psychological truth through a rhetorical, external statement, or by putting in the minds of his characters a train of thought which impresses one as prematurely didactic." This, according to Steiner, is the result of a "thinness of [Tolstoy's] metaphysics," of his inability to penetrate the psychospiritual dimensions of human experience as deeply as Dostoevsky. See George Steiner, *Tolstoy or Dostoevsky: An Essay in the Old Criticism* (New York: Alfred A. Knopf, 1959), p. 274. As a result, Steiner argues, Tolstoy's metaphysics overpowers his poetics so that his representation of the realm of the mystical and spiritual comes across as abstract and general in his art. But in this scene the sudden movement from emotional spontaneity to philosophical abstraction is Andrei's, not the narrator's.

10. Quoted in R. F. Christian, *Tolstoy's* War and Peace: *A Study* (Oxford: Clarendon Press, 1962), p. 17.

11. Neither could have happened had Andrei lived, since he was already engaged to be married to Natasha, and Russian law forbade a man (Nikolai) to marry his sister-in-law (Princess Marya).

12. Though Prince Andrei is the novel's one tragic hero, he has a strong, attractive spiritual side, which is most fully illuminated in death. In fact, the contradiction between his spiritual striving and his comprehension of imperfect earthly reality is the very source of his tragic status. I therefore cannot agree with Patricia Carden's assessment of Andrei as a "fatal man," who makes "death . . . [a] career" ("The Expressive Self in War and Peace," *Canadian-American Slavic Studies* 12, no. 4 [(Winter 1978]: 530–33); or with Edward Wasiolek, when he writes that "Andrew goes to his death without finding the truth he had searched for for so long," (*Tolstoy's Major Fiction* [Chicago: University of Chicago Press, 1978], p. 82); or with George Clay, who insists that Andrei "dramatizes, in . . . emphatic terms, an individual's failure to develop from folly towards wisdom" (*Tolstoy's Phoenix: From Method to Meaning in* War and Peace [Evanston, IL: Northwestern University Press, 1998], p. 78).

13. In a letter dated May 1, 1858, Tolstoy replied to his relative, Countess A. A. Tolstaya, who took exception to the author's contrast between the tormented death of the Christian noblewoman in the first part and the more serene death of the brute peasant in the second part. Tolstoy's response reveals his belief in the close connection between the spiritual quality of a person's life and his or her experience of death:

> Une brute, you say; but how can une brute be bad? Une brute is happiness and beauty, and harmony with the whole world, and not discord as in the case of the lady. The tree dies peacefully, honestly and beautifully. Beautifully—because it doesn't lie, doesn't put on airs, isn't afraid, and has no regrets. There you have my idea, and of course you don't agree with it; but it can't be disputed—it is in my soul, and in yours too. (Quoted in R. F. Christian, ed. and trans., *Tolstoy's Letters, vol. 1, 1828–1879* [New York: Charles Scribner's Sons, 1978], p. 122)

Tolstoy's description of the more tranquil death of the peasant and of the tree in the third part of the story is similar to Prince Andrei's death in *War and Peace*. In Tolstoy's metaphysics, then, Prince Andrei's life comes closer to embodying the ideal of the noble savage, or even of nature, than to that of the self-involved, tormented Christian noblewoman.

CHAPTER 7

1. For example, Russian Old Believers crossed themselves and returned home when they encountered a dog. In Slavic mythology dogs and wolves were often interchangeable as symbols of greed and carnal desire. In Alexander Blok's famous poem *The Twelve*, which nervously celebrates the impending Russian revolution, Christ leads the caravan of imagined followers toward the glorious socialist future, but, significantly, "a hungry, mangy dog / Hobbles in the rear." Blok sensed that the revolution, however inspired, also stirred up the doglike avarice and reckless passions of the masses.

2. A. A. Saburov, *"Voina i mir" L. N. Tolstogo: Problematika poetiki* (Moscow: Izdatel'stvo Moskovskogo universiteta, 1959), pp. 176, 181.

3. Quoted in Leo Tolstoy, *War and Peace,* ed. George Gibian, 2nd ed. (New York: W. W. Norton, 1996), p. 1088.

4. Diary entry from 3 March 1863. In R. F. Christian, ed. and trans., *Tolstoy's Diaries, vol. 1, 1847–1894* (London: The Athlone Press, 1985), p. 177.

5. Pierre represents, in the words of Kathryn Feuer, the value of "withdrawal, a spiritual rather than a political attitude towards moral questions." Kathryn B. Feuer, *Tolstoy and the Genesis of* War and Peace, ed. Robin Feuer Miller and Donna Tussing Orwin (Ithaca, NY, and London: Cornell University Press, 1996), pp. 45–46.

6. Pierre is an example of the kind of "thinker" that the Soviet critic V. V. Vinogradov saw in all the great Russian writers: "Our great writers did not hold to any single and exclusive system of realistic depiction. Turgenev wrote to L. N. Tolstoy (in a letter of 3/15 January 1857): 'Systems are valued only by those who can't get a grip on the whole truth and try to grab it by the tail; a system is like the tail of the truth, but the truth is like a lizard; it leaves the tail in your hand and escapes, knowing that it will soon grow another.'" V. V. Vinogradov, *O iazyke khudozhestvenoi literatury* (Moscow, 1959), p. 506.

7. The word "intoxication" (*op'ianenie*) will appear twice more in *War and Peace,* in connection with Natasha's feelings of exhilaration and disorientation, when she is at the opera, where Anatole Kuragin will seduce her. Just as Pierre "decided . . . that this had necessarily to be so" (76; I, 1, 19), so Natasha will think: "That must be how it's supposed to be!" (561, II, 5, 9). But Pierre's "decision" and Natasha's "supposition" are both examples of futile attempts at rational understanding, of the mind's game of chess continuing to be played while the inevitable forces of life go on.

8. "With my estate I wanted to achieve perfection and forgot that first of all it's necessary to correct all the imperfections, of which there are too many." Entry from July 1853. In Christian, *Tolstoy's Diaries, vol. 1, 1847–1894,* p. 88.

9. Pierre may be linked to this tradition of the nineteenth-century Russian intelligentsia, who, according to Philip Pomper, "are distinguishable from both intellectual workers and pure intellectuals, from the former by their concern with ultimate questions, and from the latter by their active commitment to human self-fulfillment." See Philip Pomper, *The Russian Revolutionary Intelligentsia* (Arlington Heights, IL: Harlan Davidson, 1970), p. 1.

10. The twentieth-century dissident writer Andrei Sinyavsky, himself a victim of Soviet repression, convincingly argued that in its efforts to create heaven on earth, the Soviet state succeeded only in creating its opposite. He describes the cultural processes that led to this in his fascinating *Soviet Civilization: A Cultural History,* trans. Joanne Turnbull (New York: Arcade Publishing, 1991).

11. Though he lacks the savvy of Andrei, who successfully executes on his estate the kinds of reforms that Pierre only dreams about, Pierre is nevertheless more of a visionary figure than his best friend. His spirit now bruised, Prince Andrei carries out his "successful" reforms with almost a mechanical glumness when he returns to Bogucharovo after his disillusionment at Austerlitz. In contrast, for Pierre the reforms are an expression of the profound utopian striving that lies at the very center of his being—and at the core of Russian national consciousness. His actions stem from a genuine belief in the brotherhood of man and in the possibility of universal happiness—beliefs that Tolstoy held throughout his lifetime. Pierre's life thus becomes a prophetic manifestation of currents that run deep in the Russian national psyche.

12. Diary entry from March 1852. Cited in Christian, *Tolstoy's Diaries, vol. 1, 1847–1894,* p. 47.

13. Daniel Rancour-Laferriere, *Tolstoy's Pierre Bezukhov: A Psychoanalytic Study* (London: Bristol Classical Press, 1993), p. 5.

14. We might also mention that, in contrast to Prince Andrei, Pierre is totally inexperienced in warfare. Yet this does not make his perceptions any less accurate than Andrei's. In fact, it might be argued that Pierre sees more accurately, since he recognizes the limits of his ability to rationally understand what is happening.

15. Victor Shklovsky underestimates the importance of this, when he insists that Karataev is a schematic image, "purified, as it were, cleaned up and generalized" (Victor Shklovsky, *Lev Tolstoy,* trans. Olga Shartse [Moscow: Raduga Publishers, 1988], p. 329). Robert L. Jackson rightly emphasizes the concrete sensory quality of Pierre's rebirth (Robert L. Jackson, "The Second Rebirth of Pierre Bezukhov," *Canadian-American Slavic Studies* 12, no. 4 [(Winter 1978)]: 335–42).

16. Laura Olson has linked the recurrence of the roundness motif with the specifically "feminine" qualities of Karataev and Russia in the novel. See Laura J. Olson, "Russianness, Femininity, and Romantic Aesthetics in *War and Peace,*" *Russian Review* 56, no. 4 (October 1997): 515–31.

CHAPTER 8

1. "Some Words about *War and Peace*," originally published in *Russkij Arkhiv* (Russian Archive) in 1868. Translation published in Leo Tolstoy, *War and Peace*, ed. George Gibian (New York: W. W. Norton, 1996), p. 1090.

2. Letter to P. D. Boborykin, July or August 1865, published in Tolstoy, *War and Peace*, ed. George Gibian, p. 1084.

3. From the same diary entry, quoted in an earlier chapter, in which Tolstoy wrote: "The mind's chess game goes on independently of life and life of it" (3 March 1863). Quoted in R. F. Christian, ed. and trans., *Tolstoy's Diaries, vol. 1, 1847–1894* (London: The Athlone Press, 1985), p. 177.

4. It was personally important for Tolstoy to make that distinction, for were he unable to do so, he could not affirm his own vital nature as healthy and good. He needed to integrate the truth he knew so well from personal experience—that human behavior is driven by the needs of the ego—into his larger philosophical worldview.

5. It is significant that both Natasha and Pierre—two of the novel's most vital characters—are seduced by the Kuragin siblings. There is, paradoxically, something of Kuragin-like egotism in both of them. In the novel's earliest drafts, in fact, Tolstoy had intended the future Pierre to contain elements of the future Anatole Kuragin. But Pierre continued to grow in stature in Tolstoy's imagination during the writing process, while Anatole remained what he was from his earliest conception: a narrow egotist.

6. During the final stage of working on *War and Peace*, Tolstoy read Schopenhauer's *The World as Will and Representation*. In a letter written in August 1869 to poet and friend A. A. Fet, he wrote: "Do you know what this summer has meant for me? Constant raptures over Schopenhauer and a whole series of spiritual delights which I've never experienced before." Quoted in R. F. Christian, ed. and trans., *Tolstoy's Letters, vol. 1, 1828–1879* (New York: Charles Scribner's Sons, 1978), p. 221.

7. History is most emphatically not reduced to purely biological forces in the epilogue, as one recent feminist scholar has argued: "Here, people's lives—that is, history—are no longer to be defined as a series of distinct, individual, and significant events, but as a cyclical repetition of births, marriages, and deaths. History is biology." Tolstoy vehemently opposed such a vulgar materialist worldview throughout his lifetime. As we've seen repeatedly, his realism moves beyond coarse naturalism and affirms the importance of spiritual no less than biological evolution in characters' lives. See Laura J. Olson, "Russianness, Femininity, and Romantic Aesthetics in *War and Peace*," *Russian Review* 56, no. 4 (October 1997): 531.

8. The image of Arakcheev in Nikolenka's dream comes from a conversation the boy overhead earlier that day. Nikolai Rostov and "Uncle Pierre" were arguing about the state of affairs in Russia, when Rostov assured Pierre that, although they were the best of friends, he would nevertheless not hesitate to cut Pierre and his antigovernment society down, were he ordered to do so by Arakcheev.

9. Nikolenka is his father's son. His words here echo those of Prince Andrei before the Battle of Austerlitz: "[I]f I want this—want glory, want to be known to people, want to be loved by them, it's not my fault that I want it, that it's the only thing I want, the only thing I live for" (264–65; I, 3, 12).

10. In particular, Sinyavsky discusses the "power of the idea" as one of the motivating forces of the Russian Revolution. See Andrei Sinyavsky, *Soviet Civilization: A Cultural History*, trans. Joanne Turnbull (New York: Arcade Publishing, 1990), pp. 28–34.

CHAPTER 9

1. The number refers to the page number in Leo Tolstoy, *Anna Karenina*, trans. Richard Pevear and Larissa Volokhonsky (New York: Penguin Books, 2004). When necessary I modify citations for accuracy. For the benefit of readers using other editions of the novel, I have included the part number and chapter numbers after the page number in each citation.

2. Near the completion of *Anna Karenina*, Tolstoy wrote in his diary: "I can see my idea clearly now. For a work to be good one must love the main, basic idea in it. So in *Anna Karenina* I love the *family* idea" (3 March 1877). The centrality of family to Tolstoy's conception of the world also can be seen in the fact that almost every major moment, event, and decision in Levin's life happens in the context of family. By contrast, two of the most important events in Anna's life—the birth of her child with Vronsky and her suicide—take place either in the presence of her artificially created family with Vronsky or in complete isolation.

3. Nikolai Strakhov was one of the few prominent intellectuals at the time who shared Tolstoy's views. In 1870 he wrote a response to John Stuart Mill's book *On the Subjection of Women,* published in Russia in 1869. He criticized the author for treating male–female relations in purely legalistic fashion, and for failing to take into consideration their deeper spiritual and emotional dimension, which he calls "the most essential aspect of the phenomenon under investigation." Strakhov writes: "The relation between the sexes—these mysterious and significant relations, the source of the greatest joy and the greatest sufferings, the embodiment of every charm and of every infamy, the real knot of life on which essentially depend its beauty and its ugliness—these relations are overlooked by Mill and not introduced into the question of women's rights." Cited in Boris Eikhenbaum, *Tolstoi in the Seventies,* trans. Albert Kaspin (Ann Arbor, MI: Ardis, 1982), p. 98. Tolstoy, who had not yet met Strakhov, was so moved by the article that he wrote Strakhov a letter, in which he said that "I subscribe to its conclusions with both hands." Cited in A. A. Donskov, ed., *L. N. Tolstoy and N. N. Strakhov: Complete Correspondence,* 2 vols. (Ottawa, Canada: Slavic Research Group at the University of Ottawa and State L. N. Tolstoy Museum, 2003), p. 1.

4. Cited in Leo Tolstoy, *Anna Karenina* (W. W. Norton, Critical Edition, 1993), p. 764.

5. One vitriolic liberal critic and revolutionary, P. N. Tkachov (1844–85), having read the first installments of the novel, was repulsed by Tolstoy's conservatism, and spoke of Levin's "self-satisfied and limited egoism." To drive home his point the critic jokingly predicted that the land-loving Levin would fall in love with his cow, Pava, and that there would ensue a passionate love triangle, in which Kitty and the cow would battle for Levin's affection. Cited in A. V. Knowles, ed., *Tolstoy: The Critical Heritage* (London, Henley, and Boston: Routledge and Kegan Paul, 1978), p. 260. For a succinct overview of all of the contemporary Russian critical responses to the novel, see also A. V. Knowles, "Russian Views of *Anna Karenina,* 1875–1878," *The Slavic and East European Journal* 22, no. 3 (Autumn 1978): 301–12.

6. The author of these lines was Vsevolod Solvyov (1849–1903), brother of the well-known symbolist philosopher Vladimir, and a popular but mediocre historical novelist. Cited in Knowles, *Tolstoy,* pp. 244–45.

7. Gary Saul Morson, Anna Karenina *in Our Time: Seeing More Wisely* (New Haven, CT: Yale University Press, 2007), p. 38. Marina Ledkovsky also sees Dolly as

a central hero in the novel: Marina Ledkovsky, "Dolly Oblonskaia as Structural Device in *Anna Karenina*," *Canadian-American Slavic Studies* 12, no. 4 (Winter 1978—special issue on Tolstoy edited by Richard Gustafson): 543–48.

8. Gary Saul Morson, "Prosaics and *Anna Karenina*," *Tolstoy Studies Journal*, 1 (1988): 1–12. Morson expounds on his theory of "prosaics" in his *Hidden in Plain View: Narrative and Creative Potentials in* War and Peace (Palo Alto, CA: Stanford University Press, 1988) and in Gary Saul Morson and Caryl Emerson, *Mikhail Bakhtin: Creation of a Prosaics* (Palo Alto, CA: Stanford University Press, 1991).

9. Leo Tolstoy, *Anna Karenina* (W. W. Norton, Critical Edition, 1993), p. 751. Nabokov also singled out this birth scene as a remarkable description of the pain and mystery associated with the birthing experience. See Vladimir Nabokov, *Lectures on Russian Literature*, ed. Fredson Bowers (New York and London: Harcourt Brace Jovanovich, 1981), p. 163.

10. April 1876. Cited in R. F. Christian, ed. and trans., *Tolstoy's Diaries, vol. 1, 1847–1894* (London: The Athlone Press, 1985), p. 298.

11. This is one of many examples of characters' failure to communicate with one another in *Anna Karenina*. One scholar, Malcolm Jones, has argued that such failure of communication is endemic to all of the relationships in the novel, and it points to Tolstoy's basic insight into the challenges of mutual understanding in the modern world. See Malcolm V. Jones, "Problems of Communication in *Anna Karenina*," in *New Essays on Tolstoy*, ed. Malcolm Jones (New York: Cambridge University Press, 1979), pp. 85–107.

12. Allan Bloom, *Love and Friendship* (New York: Simon and Schuster, 1993), p. 237.

13. Hence the far-ranging connotations of the word "mir"—"peace"—in the title *War and Peace*, discussed in a previous chapter.

14. Pevear and Volokhonsky translate Kitty's last name as Shcherbatsky, thus transporting it from the feminine form (Shcherbatskaya) to the masculine form. Formerly this was the usual approach to handling last names of females, but I have chosen to preserve the feminine ending -aya, because this has become the more common practice in the recent past.

15. For example, Prince Shcherbatsky is the first one to see through the artificiality of the Pietist, Madame Stahl, whom Kitty meets at the German spa. He rightly senses that Madame Stahl's Christian humility is a cover for her personal deficiencies and her political ambitions.

16. Eikhenbaum, *Tolstoi in the Seventies*, p. 76.

17. Herein lies the basic problem with Gary Saul Morson's "193 Tolstoyan Conclusions" in his Anna Karenina *in Our Time: Seeing More Wisely*. Taken separately, each one of those conclusions is compelling and interesting, and there is evidence from Tolstoy's extraliterary writings that he held many of the views Morson ascribes to him. But to extract a Tolstoyan "conclusion" from the world of the novel is to misread *Anna Karenina* as a polemical treatise rather than a work of art. Vladimir Alexandrov's excellent book explains why such "message"-oriented readings, or readings that attempt to look at the novel from the perspective of any single theoretical paradigm, are bound to be reductive. Vladimir Alexandrov, *Limits to Interpretation: The Meanings of* Anna Karenina (Madison: University of Wisconsin Press, 2004).

18. For example, in his search for a more effective way of doing business, Tom Chappell, founder of Tom's of Maine, enrolled in divinity school. Inspired there by the world's religious traditions, he decided to recreate his company from the ground up, transform-

ing the workplace into a community of people with a renewed sense of dedication to one another, to their customers, and to society at large. The once overly bureaucratic corporate headquarters evolved into an environment that now fed people not only materially but spiritually. He describes this process in *The Soul of a Business: Managing for Profit and the Common Good* (New York: Bantam, 1996), a book that has much in common with the one Levin is writing.

19. Tolstoy's carefully chosen word, "lovely," *prelestnyj*, transports us back to the night on the haystack before Levin sees Kitty at dawn. "How lovely [*prelestno*] everything is on this lovely [*prelestnyj*] night!" he thought to himself then, thus creating a subliminal association in the reader's mind between that moment and this one. The loveliness of that night and now of Kitty's eyes form a "labyrinth of linkages" united by the extraordinary power of love.

20. This detail might well reflect Tolstoy's own honeymoon experience, during which sexual initiation proved troubling for the newly married couple.

21. Fyodor Dostoevsky, *A Writer's Diary, vol. 1, 1873–1876,* trans. Kenneth Lantz (Evanston, IL: Northwestern University Press, 1994), p. 876.

22. Upon reading these pages of my manuscript, Hugh McLean observed: "The thought occurred to me as I read this page that Kaufman consistently treats fiction as if it were life itself, without any recognition of its artificiality. Maybe this is a credit to Tolstoy's realism." Other contemporary readers are likely to have a similar reaction to my book, and perhaps respond less charitably than does Professor McLean. In anticipation of this criticism, I ask readers to understand that my "naïve" approach to Tolstoy's fiction is intentional, and reflective of the larger purpose of my book, which I describe in the prologue: to reconstruct, rather than deconstruct, Tolstoy's artistic universe. I have tried to enter as deeply as possible into Tolstoy's world, and to recreate it by "retelling" the characters' stories just as they unfold in Tolstoy imagination, not mine. Tolstoy's truth, not the critic's demystifying ingenuity, is the hero of my tale.

CHAPTER 10

1. Quoted in Leo Tolstoy, *Anna Karenina,* ed. George Gibian, 2nd ed. (New York: W. W. Norton, 1995), pp. 754–55.

2. Letter from January 1878, quoted in R. F. Christian, ed., *Tolstoy's Letters, vol. 1, 1828–1879* (New York: Charles Scribner's Sons, 1978), p. 311.

3. Page number refers to Leo Tolstoy, *Anna Karenina,* trans. Richard Pevear and Larissa Volokhonsky (New York: Penguin Books, 2004). On occasion I have made slight modifications when I felt the original meaning was not clear. For the benefit of readers using other editions of the novel, I have included the part number and chapter number after the page number in each citation.

4. Quoted in Donna Orwin, *Tolstoy's Art and Thought, 1847–1880* (Princeton, NJ: Princeton University Press, 1993), p. 177.

5. This perception of division is all the more striking given that Wasiolek is one of a handful of modern Tolstoy scholars sensitive to the writer's artistic and philosophical holism. See Edward Wasiolek, *Tolstoy's Major Fiction* (Chicago, London: University of Chicago Press, 1978), p. 129. However, Donna Orwin has identified the link between Levin and Anna. She sees these two characters as "spiritually akin." They both have "physical grace." They both are highly changeable "even to the point of seeming illogical." They both feel "natural flux," yet they "cannot simply go with the flow. . . . Both

live morally: one chooses evil and dies, while the other chooses good and lives." As I show later, it is highly debatable that Anna "chooses evil." See Orwin, *Tolstoy's Art and Thought*, p. 177.

6. Gary R. Jahn, "The Crisis in Tolstoy and in *Anna Karenina*," in Liza Knapp and Amy Mandelker, eds., *Approaches to Teaching Tolstoy's* Anna Karenina (New York: The Modern Language Association, 2003), p. 70.

7. See Helena Goscilo, "Motif-Mesh as Matrix: Body, Sexuality, Adultery, and the Woman Question," in Knapp and Mandelker, *Approaches to Teaching Tolstoy's* Anna Karenina, pp. 88–89.

8. *PSS* 20, 562.

9. See Boris Eikhenbaum, *Tolstoi in the Seventies*, trans. Albert Kaspin (Ann Arbor, MI: Ardis, 1982), p. 146; and Gary Jahn, "The Unity of *Anna Karenina*," *Russian Review* 41, no. 2 (April 1982): 152.

10. Boris Eikhenbaum has described Tolstoy's more general participation in the heated debates of his time about the "woman question." See Eikhenbaum, *Tolstoi in the Seventies*, pp. 94–106.

11. In her very good feminist reading, Amy Mandelker tries to resurrect the novel from damning, reductivist readings that insist on seeing the work as fundamentally misogynist. A feminist herself, Mandelker nonetheless argues that the novel is more profeminist than misogynist, in that it expresses "the necessity for freeing a woman's beauty from its economic and sexual entrapment and for pursuing instead a sublime involvement with humanity." See Amy Mandelker, *Framing* Anna Karenina: *Tolstoy, The Woman Question, and the Victorian Novel* (Columbus: The Ohio State University Press, 1993), p. 181.

12. Fyodor Dostoevsky, *A Writer's Diary, vol. 1, 1873–1876*, trans. Kenneth Lanz (Evanston, IL: Northwestern University Press, 2009), p. 1071.

13. As Robert Jackson has pointed out in one of the best articles about the novel, the very first words Anna speaks, "'I still don't agree with you'" (62; I, 18), though seemingly insignificant social repartee, also typify an essential rebelliousness of her nature. Vronsky, who overhears Anna from behind the door, "knew it was the voice of the lady he had met at the entrance" (61; I, 18). Anna's enigmatic lure, which emanates first from her physical being, now from her voice, immediately draws him in, as it will Levin later in the novel. See Robert L. Jackson, "Chance and Design in *Anna Karenina*" in *The Discipline of Criticism: Essays in Literary Theory, Interpretation, and History*, ed. Peter Demetz, Thomas Greene, and Lowry Nelson Jr. (New Haven, CT: Yale University Press, 1968), p. 317.

14. Quoted in Introduction to Leo Tolstoy's *Anna Karenina*, trans. Richard Pevear and Larissa Volokhonsky (New York: Penguin Books, 2004), xv.

15. Vadimir Nabokov, *Lectures on Russian Literature*, ed. Fredson Bowers (New York and London: Harcourt Brace Jovanovich, 1981), p. 145.

16. If *Anna Karenina* were a juridical document, or an analytical "argument," as many contemporary literary scholars take literature to be, then perhaps we could speak of something like "allowable passions." But the phrase makes little sense when referring to a work of art such as *Anna Karenina*, in which passion, like pain and joy, is neither "allowable" nor forbidden but belongs to a mysterious order of things. See David Herman, "Allowable Passions in *Anna Karenina*," *Tolstoy Studies Journal* 8 (1995–1996): 5–32. By analyzing the meaning of the novel's epigraph, "Vengeance is mine; I will repay," in the context of Tolstoy's reading of Schopenhauer, Boris Eikhenbaum has also come to the conclusion that the novel is neither a legal argument nor a cautionary tale

but presents readers with "a problem of higher ethics." See Eikhenbaum, *Tolstoi in the Seventies*, p. 146.

17. According to Morson, Tolstoy emphasizes over and again that fatalism is a motif introduced by Anna and always seen from her perspective. Fatalism is part and parcel of Anna's "belief in romance, her extremism, and above all, her cultivated habits of contrived misperception." Gary Saul Morson, Anna Karenina *in Our Time: Seeing More Wisely* (New Haven, CT, and London: Yale University Press, 2007), p. 139. Yet as I have shown, fatalism is more than a fiction created by characters. It figures prominently into Tolstoy's artistic universe, and readers rightly feel its presence.

18. Gustafson has made a similar point in Richard Gustafson, *Leo Tolstoy: Resident and Stranger: A Study in Fiction and Theology* (Princeton, NJ: Princeton University Press, 2006), pp. 118–32, 303–9.

19. Tolstoy's ideal of human togetherness in this scene is by no means what Janko Lavrin calls a "community of meek and selfless men united in that static pre-individual love in which alone [Tolstoy] saw a guarantee for peace and happiness." Levin and his peasants are a community of powerful, healthy, vital men, who come into contact with their truer, nobler individual selves, precisely because they are connected to one another and to a larger whole. Janko Lavrin, "Tolstoy and Nietzsche," in *Tolstoy: An Approach* (New York: The MacMillan Company, 1946), p. 158.

20. Critics agree that Anna's journey to Petersburg is, in Robert Jackson's words, "one of the great transitional moments in her drama." See Robert Louis Jackson, "The Night Journey: Anna Karenina's Return to Saint Petersburg," in Knapp and Mandelker, *Approaches to Teaching Tolstoy's* Anna Karenina, p. 150.

21. In this image we hear the screeching sound of a violin being tuned to a high pitch, or a train coming to an abrupt stop on the iron rails, after rolling over Anna's body. The eerie metaphor is realized several sentences later: "something screeched and banged terribly, as if someone was being torn to pieces; then a red fire blinded her eyes, and then everything was hidden by a wall" (101; I, 29).

22. The image of the train is obviously central to the novel and has been mentioned by most scholars who write about *Anna Karenina*. Some have analyzed the image in detail. For example, Gary Jahn has written an article about the railroad as a symbol of "the concept of the social," with which the individual must come to terms if he is to find happiness. See "The Image of the Railroad in *Anna Karenina*," *The Slavic and East European Journal* 25, no. 2 (Summer 1981): 1–10. Elizabeth Stenbock-Fermor sees the image as central to the architecture of the book. She argues that the novel's design comprises a series of "arches" supported by "columns," which are key chapters linked in various ways to the image of the railroad. Elizabeth Stenbock-Fermor, *The Architecture of* Anna Karenina (Lisse, Netherlands: Peter de Ridder Press, 1975).

23. In *Escape from Freedom* Erich Fromm has shown how Soviet Communism and German and Italian Fascism were inspired by precisely such a desire for self-transcendence. This desire to give oneself over to a power greater than oneself, and to abdicate moral responsibility, stemmed, Fromm argues, from the anxieties produced by life in the modern world: there is "no more pressing need than the one to find someone to whom he can surrender, as quickly as possible, that gift of freedom which he, the unfortunate creature, was born with." Erich Fromm, *Escape from Freedom* (New York: Avon Books, 1969), p. 173. Herein lay the seductiveness that authoritarian systems of governance had for their subjects.

24. *PSS* 54, 121.

25. This is different from the role "suddenness" often plays in *War and Peace*. Sud-

den revelations and the intense emotional explosions that accompany them—such as Pierre's realization that he is in love with Natasha when he sees the comet of 1812—have about them a quality of wholesome authenticity. Pierre has grown to love Natasha over time; it is only his recognition of this fact that comes suddenly.

26. For example, Judith Armstrong insists that Anna "becomes an active principle, a woman who wills her own destiny." Judith Armstrong, "*Anna Karenina* and the Novel of Adultery," in Knapp and Mandelker, *Approaches to Teaching* Anna Karenina, p. 122. See also her psychoanalytical, feminist reading of the novel: Judith Armstrong, *The Unsaid* Anna Karenina (New York: Saint Martin's Press, 1988). Another recent scholar, critical of moralistic readings of the novel, insists that "[i]n heroes, values are nice, but vitality is better." Bob Blaisdell, Review of Anna Karenina *in Our Time: Seeing More Wisely*, by Gary Saul Morson, *Tolstoy Studies Journal* 19 (2007): 124. These celebratory readings of Anna have a long tradition, beginning with the nineteenth-century philosopher Lev Shestov, who misread *Anna Karenina* as a kind of Nietzschean amorality tale. The philosopher believed that Tolstoy prefers the vital "Superman" to the dead man of morals. That, he argues, is why we are moved by characters, such as Anna, who take risks and defy social morality, but are rather bored by Levin's ethical quest, or by the pious "faded flower," Varenka, whom Kitty meets in Germany. Lev Shestov, "The Good in the Teaching of Tolstoy and Nietzsche: Philosophy and Preaching," in *Dostoevsky, Tolstoy, and Nietzsche*, ed. Spencer Roberts and Bernard Martin (Athens: The Ohio University Press, 1978), pp. 1–140.

27. Judith Armstrong makes a similar point: "Family structures were for Tolstoy not merely a social glue but also a means of containing the horror of rampant sexuality that obsessed him, less out of concern for society than because of his own sexual urges, which he strove to repudiate." See Armstrong, "*Anna Karenina* and the Novel of Adultery," p. 122.

28. Gary Jahn writes: "Thus Levin ultimately accepts his dilemma, rather than capitulating to it as do Stiva and Karenin in varying degrees, or defying it in the manner of Anna . . . Anna, on the contrary, lacks the ability to live in and out of society simultaneously. She insists upon the outward (social) realization of her inner ideals, even if this means that she must throw down the gauntlet to her society." See Jahn, "The Unity of *Anna Karenina*," p. 157.

29. In his *Confession*, Tolstoy describes his famous spiritual crisis, which eventually led him to the verge of suicide. "And there I was, a fortunate man, carrying a rope from my room, where I was alone every night as I undressed, so that I would not hang myself from the beam between the closets. And I quit going hunting with a gun, so that I would not be too easily tempted to rid myself of life." Leo Tolstoy, *Confession*, trans. David Patterson (New York and London: W. W. Norton, 1983), p. 28.

30. Orwin writes that "Levin escapes his suicidal despair only when he realizes that what he seeks is inaccessible to his intellect but visible in a life well lived." The "true philosopher," in Tolstoy's definition, approaches life in a similar fashion: "Rather than apply abstract categories to explain behavior, the true philosopher arrives at them through the analysis of experience and constantly returns to that experience to check the truth of his conclusions against it." See Donna Orwin, "Tolstoy's Antiphilosophical Philosophy in *Anna Karenina*" in Knapp and Mandelker, *Approaches to Teaching* Anna Karenina, p. 99.

31. Gary Saul Morson writes that "*Levin comes to learn the complexity of things, and Anna the simplicity*" (italics in original). Morson, Anna Karenina *in Our Time*, p. 133. Morson's and my formulation are complementary: Levin's view of complexity

embraces the principle of both-and; Anna's vision of "simplicity" is more maximalist. It insists on the principle of either-or.

32. The allusion to Darwin's theory of natural selection is not coincidental. *The Origin of Species* first appeared in Russia in translation in 1864, and would be hotly discussed in all the major journals throughout the 1860s and 1870s. In fact, Levin, who had studied natural science in college, overhears a discussion in Part One about the animal nature of man between Koznyshev and a well-known philosophy professor. Yet he is frustrated, because he cannot find a connection between their theoretical discussion and his own pressing existential questions. The best discussion in English of the Tolstoy–Darwin connection is "Claws on the Behind: Tolstoy and Darwin," in Hugh McLean, *In Quest of Tolstoy* (Brighton, MA: Academic Studies Press, 2008), 159–80.

33. Barbara Lönnqvist, "*Anna Karenina*," in *The Cambridge Companion to Tolstoy*, ed. Donna Tussing Orwin (Cambridge: Cambridge University Press, 2002), p. 88.

34. Quoted in *The New Criterion*, 26 (January 2008): 1.

35. David Benatar, *Better Never to Have Been: The Harm of Coming into Existence* (New York: Oxford University Press, 2006), p. 1.

36. Morson writes that "Fyodor's words are not the answer but the catalyst . . . for Levin's process of discovering the answer." Morson, Anna Karenina *in Our Time*, p. 210.

CHAPTER 11

1. Letter of September 1869, in R. F. Christian, ed. and trans., *Tolstoy's Letters, vol. 1, 1828–1879* (New York: Charles Scribner's Sons, 1978), p. 222.

2. In 1884 Tolstoy transformed the Arzamas experience into the autobiographical, unfinished short story "Notes of a Madman." He would return to the story again in 1896.

3. Letter of December 1885, in Christian, *Letters, vol. 1*, p. 391.

4. Leo Tolstoy, *Confession*, trans. David Patterson (New York: W. W. Norton, 1983), pt. 5, pp. 34–35.

5. Page number refers to the English translation of the novella in Michael Katz, ed. and trans., *Tolstoy's Short Fiction* (New York and London: W. W. Norton, 2008). On occasion I make slight modifications when I feel Tolstoy's original meaning is not clear. For the benefit of readers using other editions of the novella I include the chapter number after the page number in each citation.

6. Quoted in L. P. Grossman, "Smert' Ivan Il'icha: Istoriia pisanie i pechatanie," in *PSS* 26, 81.

7. The best analysis I know of the genesis of the novella is V. A. Zhdanov, *Ot "Anny Kareninoj" k "Voskresen'iu"* (Moscow: Izdatel'stvo "Kniga," 1968), pp. 82–122. For an interesting and clear discussion of the ways in which Tolstoy exploits the individual-universal opposition throughout the work, see Robert Russell, "From Individual to Universal: Tolstoy's 'Smert' Ivana Il'icha,'" *The Modern Language Review*, 76, no. 3 (July 1981): 629–42.

8. There are obvious religious allusions in Ivan's first name, John, and patronymic, Ilya—Ely, or Elias. His first name recalls John the Baptist, who figures prominently in the New Testament as the prophet who proclaimed the arrival of Jesus. This was likely intended by Tolstoy, who had recently studied the Gospels and who was increasingly interested in the teachings of Jesus as a model for ethical behavior. In fact, nearly six

years before publishing *The Death of Ivan Ilyich*, Tolstoy had written his *Harmonization and Translation of the Four Gospels* (1880–81). Regarding Ivan's patronymic, Ilya, this is a likely allusion to the prophet Elias, or Elijah, of the Old Testament. Furthermore, in Matthew 11:14 Jesus is quoted as saying, "and if you are willing to accept it, he [John] is the Elijah who was to come" (New International Version, 2011). The religious overtones in the novella are many and complex, and have been discussed in depth by scholars Robert Duncan, George Gutsche, and Gary Jahn. See note 39 in this chapter.

9. For a sampling of some recent approaches, see Gary Jahn, ed., *Tolstoy's "The Death of Ivan Il'ich": A Critical Companion* (Evanston, IL: Northwestern, 1999).

10. Quoted in Mark Shcheglov, *Literaturnaia kritika* (Moscow: Izdatel'stvo "Khudozhestvennaia literatura," 1971), p. 10.

11. Ibid., p. 11. It should be pointed out that not all of Tolstoy's contemporary readers were enamored of the work. For example, the populist critic Nikolai Mikhailovsky thought that *Ivan was* "not of the first rank in artistic beauty, in strength or clarity of thought, or finally in the fearless realism of the writing" (quoted in Gary R. Jahn, *"The Death of Ivan Il'ich": An Interpretation* [New York: Twayne Publishers, 1993], p. 10). Tolstoy's own brother sardonically remarked, "They're praising you for having discovered that people die" (quoted from Tolstoy's 1886 letter to an acquaintance in *PSS* 63, 357).

12. *PSS* 26, 687. More recently, Y. J. Dayananda called the work "an extraordinary contribution to the literature of death and dying," and details the clinical accuracy of Ivan's confrontation with death. Quoted in *Tolstoy's Short Fiction*, p. 415. The original article appeared as Y. J. Dayananda, *"The Death of Ivan Ilyich*: A Psychological Study on Death and Dying," *Literature and Psychology*, 22 (1972): 191–98.

13. *PSS* 26, 684.

14. In other words, through Pyotr Ivanovich's eyes we are tourists, whereas later we become more like voyeurs. My thinking about this distinction was partly inspired by Gary Saul Morson's important article on *The Sevastopol Tales*. See Gary Saul Morson, "The Reader as Voyeur: Tolstoi and the Poetics of Didactic Fiction," *Canadian-American Slavic Studies* 12, no. 4 (Winter 1978): 465–80.

15. For a clinical analysis of the five stages of Ivan's dying, see Dayananda, *"The Death of Ivan Ilych*: A Psychological Study on Death and Dying."

16. Zhdanov writes: "Tolstoy chose a crafty method of juxtaposing the legal process with medicine. He is not interested in science per se, but wanted to show that in two seemingly mutually exclusive spheres—punishment and healing—the general principle is the same. This is the most severe indictment of medicine." Zhdanov, p. 99.

17. Leo Tolstoy, *War and Peace*, trans. Richard Pevear and Larissa Volokhonsky (New York: Alfred A. Knopf, 2007), p. 982; IV, 1, 16.

18. The formulation belongs to the Russian philosopher Lev Shestov, whose article "The Last Judgement: Tolstoy's Last Works," is still the most penetrating existentialist reading of the novella. See Lev Shestov, "The Last Judgement: Tolstoy's Last Works," in Leo Shestov, *Job's Balances: On the Sources of the Eternal Truths*, trans. Camilla Coventry and C. A. Macartney (Athens: Ohio University Press, 1957), pt. 1, p. 85.

19. Gary Comstock explains why neither the naïve nor the deconstructionist interpretation of "*It*" quite hits the mark: "If the naïve reader makes a mistake by thinking of *It* too quickly as death, the deconstructor makes a mistake by passing over the incontrovertible identification that Ivan finally confronts face to face." Gary Comstock, "Face to Face with *IT*: The Naïve Reader's Moral Response to *Ivan Ilych*," *Neophilologus* 70, no. 3 (July 1986): 331.

20. The torment he goes through is indeed one of the terrible "consequences of consciousness," to borrow Donna Orwin's apt phrase. But given that *The Death of Ivan Ilyich* is Tolstoy's most direct exploration of both the limits and pain of consciousness, it is surprising that Orwin only mentions the work once. See Donna Tussing Orwin, *Consequences of Consciousness: Turgenev, Dostoevsky, and Tolstoy* (Palo Alto, CA: Stanford University Press, 2007).

21. Akira Kurosawa's 1952 classic movie *Ikiru*, which was inspired by *The Death of Ivan Ilyich*, beautifully captures this quality of the hero's life. Only when he realizes that he is dying does Kanji Watanabe, the bureaucrat based on Ivan, begin to live. In Japanese "Ikiru" means "to live."

22. Anthony Daniels, "Chekov [*sic*] and Tolstoy," *The New Criterion* 23, no. 8 (April 2005): 33.

23. Edward Wasiolek, *Tolstoy's Major Fiction* (Chicago and London: The University of Chicago Press, 1978), p. 175.

24. Quoted in Aleksei Zver'ev and Vladimir Tunimanov, *Lev Tolstoi* (Moscow: Molodaia gvardiia, 2006), p. 420.

25. Some students giggle or tune out during the exercise. Others say what they think someone with six months to live would or should say. For most this remains a purely hypothetical exercise. In one iteration of the course I had a student who was told in high school that she might have a malignant tumor. Even in her case little had changed. She explained how she went to school, watched TV, did her homework, ate dinner with her family, and went to bed as usual. Death was not a constant presence in her life.

26. In response to readers who dismiss the work's moral message on the grounds that Tolstoy is too intrusive and manipulative, Edward Wasiolek argues for a more sympathetic reading of the author on his own terms: "Tolstoy was able to do what is perhaps most distinctive of Russian fiction, to trace out the extreme, but logically possible, reaches of a human characteristic. We do not have character represented in *The Death of Ivan Ilyich* as it presents itself phenomenologically, but as it is theoretically possible in the human condition." Edward Wasiolek, "Tolstoy's *The Death of Ivan Ilyich* and Jamesian Fictional Imperatives," *Modern Fiction Studies* 6, no. 4 (Winter 1960/1961): 321.

27. This might be a reason that one of Tolstoy's contemporaries observed that, in contrast to many of the writer's other late didactic works, *Ivan* "stands out sharply" as "something harmoniously whole and unusually complete." Quoted in Shcheglov, *Literaturnaia kritika*, p. 10. Shcheglov himself believes that *The Death of Ivan Ilyich* is an illustration of the capacity of great literature to represent "artistic form not as something important in and of itself, but as the complete *crystallization of content*" (11).

28. From "Lisa-Placheya" ["The Fox-Wailer"], quoted in A. N. Afanas'ev, *Narodnye Russkie Skazki*, pt. 1 (Moscow: Gosudarstvennoe izdatel'stvo khudozhestvennoi literatury, 1957), p. 33. Translation mine.

29. Letter from September 1895. In R. F. Christian, ed. and trans., *Tolstoy's Letters, vol. 2, 1880–1910* (New York: Charles Scribner's Sons, 1978), p. 521.

30. Lev Tolstoi, *On Life* and *Essays on Religion*, Aylmer Maude, trans. (London: Oxford University Press, 1934), p. 72.

31. Ibid., p. 70.

32. From diary entry of March 1855. In R. F. Christian, ed. and trans., *Tolstoy's Diaries, vol. 1, 1847–1894* (London: The Athlone Press, 1985), p. 102.

33. The most thorough philosophical treatment of Tolstoy's dualism is to be found in G. W. Spence, *Tolstoy the Ascetic* (London: Oliver and Boyd, 1967). In an interesting

recent article about Tolstoy's artistic treatment of "the feeling and the poetry of life," scholar V. I. Fatiushchenko divides Tolstoy's *oeuvre* into three different stages:

> [t]he stage, when the feeling of life and the poetry of life are dominant in his art, when "life" remained whole and wonderful; the stage, when Tolstoy doubted this feeling, when life's happiness was perceived as a "charm," as a temptation; the stage, when thoughts about life, the search for its meaning trumped spontaneous apprehension of life. Theoretically, intuitively he sensed the worth of life, but already differently: He discovered for himself the stages (the spheres, the "dwelling-places") of life, the search for the "passage" to a different life. In those years an original Tolstoyan theology took root—a religion of life in the fullest sense.

The Death of Ivan Ilyich would belong to the third stage in V. I. Fatiushchenko's delineation. See V. I. Fatiushchenko, "Chustvo zhizni i poeziia zhizni v tvorchestve L. N. Tolstogo (1850-e—1860-kh. godov)," in *Tolstoi i o Tolstom: Materialy issledovania*, Vypusk 3 (Moscow: IMLI, 2009), p. 21.

34. *Tolstoy's Short Fiction*, p. 247.

35. In his article analyzing the use of light and dark imagery in the novella, David Danaher concludes that "the figurative motif made up of light and dark imagery serves as an iconic embodiment of Ivan's journey toward the truth." See David Danaher, "Tolstoy's Use of Light and Dark Imagery in *The Death of Ivan Il'ic*," *Slavic and East European Journal* 39, no. 2 (1995): 237. This sentence quoted from the novella is one of several examples of Tolstoy's use of comic devices, especially in the pages describing Ivan's "simple," "ordinary," and "terrible" life. An in-depth, if wrong-headed, analysis of this aspect of the novella can be found in James L. Rice, "Comic Devices in *The Death of Ivan Ilich*," *Slavic and East European Journal* 47, no. 1 (2003): 77–95. Rice rightly detects the presence of a comic impulse in the novella, but he misunderstands the function of that impulse, and he greatly overemphasizes its frequency. In his reading, *Ivan* becomes less a work by Tolstoy and more like a work by George Bernard Shaw, whose droll reading of the novella in his article "Tolstoy: Tragedian or Comedian" appears to have inspired Rice. The comic element in the story is subdued, and it is always in the service of Tolstoy's larger moral purpose: to expose the emptiness of Ivan's "ordinary" life. It does not, as Rice argues, represent "a compromise between the author's exacerbated moral seekings" and his desire to engage in the sheer joy of verbal play (93).

36. *On Life*, Aylmer Maude, trans., pp. 63, 55. For a good discussion of the specific connections between *On Life* and *The Death of Ivan Ilyich*, see Jahn, The Death of Ivan Ilich: *An Interpretation*, pp. 93–102.

37. John Bayley goes further than I do in arguing that the entire novella is filled with many such unreal moments: "[T]he author's metaphors and figures of speech have the property of removing the individuality of what is happening. Perhaps apprehending this, Tolstoy usually distrusts them, as one feels he would have distrusted Turgenev's graphic metaphor in *On the Eve*.

> Death is like a fisherman who has caught a fish in his net and leaves it for a time in the water. The fish still swims about, but the net surrounds it, and the fisherman will take it when it wishes.
>
> How many of us, as individuals, actually feel ourselves in this position?

And it is as individuals, and not as metaphors, that we die. (John Bayley, *Tolstoy and the Novel* [London: Chatto and Windus, 1966], p. 89)

38. Daniel Rancour-Laferriere has captured the somewhat deflationary quality of the depiction of Ivan's sudden transformation, when he writes: "When Ivan Il'ich thinks 'Death is finished,' he is terribly mistaken. Death is in fact about to occur. It is not finished, and Ivan I'lich is jumping the gun. *It* is not over until it is over." See Daniel Rancour-Laferriere, "Narcissism, Masochism, and Denial in *The Death of Ivan Il'ich*," in Gary R. Jahn, ed., *Tolstoy's "The Death of Ivan Il'ich": A Critical Companion* (Evanston: Northwestern University Press, 1999)p. 130.

39. Quoted in N. N. Apostolov, *Zhivoi Tolstoi* (Moscow, 1928), p. 18.

40. Leo Tolstoy, *War and Peace*, trans. Richard Pevear and Larissa Volokhonsky (New York: Alfred A. Knopf, 2007), Volume IV, Part 1, Chapter 16, p. 985.

41. Ibid., p. 986; IV, 1, 16.

42. In one of the best articles on Tolstoy's theological vision in the novella, George Gutsche shows the ways in which *Ivan* illustrates major differences between "conventional Christian ethos and Tolstoy's Christianity." George Gutsche, "Moral Fiction: Tolstoy's *The Death of Ivan Il'ich*," in Gary R. Jahn, ed., *Tolstoy's "The Death of Ivan Il'ich": A Critical Companion*, p. 77. On this topic see also Robert Duncan, "Ivan Ilych's Death: Secular or Religious?" *University of Dayton Review* 15 (1981): 99–106; and on the specific connections between Ivan's death and Jesus' Crucifixion, see Gary R. Jahn, "A Note on the Miracle Motifs in the Later Works of Lev Tolstoi," in *The Supernatural in Slavic and Baltic Literatures: Essays in Honor of Victor Terras* (Columbus, OH: Slavica, 1988), pp. 191–99.

CHAPTER 12

1. Quoted in Aleksei Zver'ev and Vladimir Tunimanov, *Lev Tolstoi* (Moscow: Molodaia gvardiia, 2006), p. 552.

2. Page numbers in parentheses refer to L. N. Tolstoy, *Resurrection,* trans. Rosemary Edmonds (New York and London: Penguin Books, 1966). All translations from the novel are taken from this edition, with my modifications where necessary. For the benefit of readers using other editions of the novel, I include the part and the chapter number after the page number in each citation.

3. Quoted in K. N. Lomunov's article "Lev Tolstoi o romane 'Voskresenie,'" in *Roman L. N. Tolstogo "Voskresenie": Istoriko-funktsional'noe issledovanie* (Moscow: "Nauka," 1991), pp. 8–9. By contrast, Ernest Crosby, one of the foremost proponents of Tolstoy's ideas in America at the end of the nineteenth century, welcomed Tolstoy's social critique, which he thought would have a positive impact on his contemporary American society. In a personal letter to Tolstoy, written in October 1899, Crosby told the writer that "I am sure [*Resurrection*] will do more good than a mere treatise. The description of Nekhludoff's [sic] gradual awakening to the character of the society he believed in, the professions of his official friends and the useless life of the rich must touch many minds that have never before thought of it." N. Velikanova and R. Whittaker, eds., *L. N. Tolstoi i S.Sh.A.: Perepiska* [L. N. Tolstoy and the U.S.A.: Correspondence] (Moscow: Gorky Institute of World Literature of the Russian Academy of Sciences, 2004), p. 567.

4. Though it is often asserted that Tolstoy was "excommunicated" from the Church, scholars still debate what actually happened. There is a growing consensus that Tolstoy

was not officially excommunicated, but rather denounced by the Church, and invited to return. The word the Church used to describe Tolstoy's status was "*otpadenie*," or "defection," thus leaving open the possibility that the writer would recant his ideas and embrace the Church anew. Tolstoy never did. For the sake of consistency, I will use the word "excommunicate" elsewhere in this chapter, although, as I've indicated, the situation was more complex than that. For a fascinating, detailed account of Tolstoy's final days and the public response to it, see William Nickell, *The Death of Tolstoy: Russia on the Eve, Astapovo Station, 1910* (Ithaca, NY: Cornell University Press, 2010).

5. L. D. Opul'skaia, *Lev Nikolaevich Tolstoi: Materialy k biografii s 1892 po 1899 god* (Moscow: IMLI, 1998), p. 364.

6. Babaev read between the lines: "The historian Ilovaisky knew and understood much more than the publicist Ilovaisky could permit himself to express in the pages of the newspaper, 'The Kremlin.' Maybe, for precisely that reason he was concerned and preoccupied by the novel *Resurrection,* in which he found confirmation of several of his own secret fears regarding the future, and which he wanted to dispel and forget, like a bad dream, more real than actual reality." Eduard Babaev's article, "Sud'ba 'Voskreseniia' (pervye otkliki gazetnoj i zhurnal'noj kritiki v Rossii)," in Lomunov, *Roman L. N. Tolstogo,* p. 17.

7. Steiner writes: "When Tolstoy came to write *Resurrection,* the teacher and prophet in him did violence to the artist. The sense of equilibrium and design which had previously controlled his invention was sacrificed to the urgencies of rhetoric. In this novel the juxtaposition of two ways of life and the theme of the pilgrimage from falsehood to salvation are set forth with the nakedness of a tract." See George Steiner, *Tolstoy or Dostoevsky* (New York: Knopf, 1957), p. 92.

8. Edward Wasiolek, *Tolstoy's Major Fiction* (Chicago and London: The University of Chicago Press, 1978), p. 192.

9. Ibid.

10. The article in *Clarion* was published June 19, 1899. Reverse translation from the Russian, quoted in Opul'skaia, p. 364.

11. See M. N. Bakhtin, *Literaturno-kriticheskie stat'i* (Moscow: Khudozhestvennaia literatura, 1986), pp. 100–20.

12. Richard Gustafson, *Leo Tolstoy: Resident and Stranger: A Study in Fiction and Theology* (Princeton, NJ: Princeton University Press, 1986), p. 205.

13. Tolstoy repeatedly berated himself and his family in the later years about their selfish lifestyles. In 1894 Tolstoy tried to convince his daughter, Tatyana L'vovna, to transfer land over to the peasants on her estate, according to the model of the single tax system created by the American economist Henry George, whose ideas Tolstoy deeply admired. Nekhliudov's attempts to implement similar reforms are met with resistance.

14. John Bayley, *Tolstoy and the Novel* (London: Chatto and Windus, 1966), pp. 248–49.

15. *Essays and Letters by Lev Tolstoy,* trans. Aylmer Maude (New York: Oxford University Press, 1911), p. 31.

16. Gary Saul Morson, Anna Karenina *in Our Time: Seeing More Wisely* (New Haven, CT: Yale University Press, 2007), p. 49.

17. Quoted in N. K. Gudzi, "Istoriia pisaniia i pechataniia 'Voskresenia,'" in *PSS* 33, 334

18. Leo Tolstoy, *Childhood, Boyhood, Youth,* trans. Michael Scammel (New York: The Modern Library, 2002), p. 223.

19. As Richard Gustafson has noted, "Tolstoy's God of Life and Love is an Eastern

Christian God. The concept of God as an abstract idea of absolute being has been replaced by a God who dwells in the world of change even as He transcends it." Gustafson, *Leo Tolstoy: Resident and Stranger,* p. 108.

20. Quoted from "Introduction" (p. 16) in Leo Tolstoy, *Resurrection,* trans. Rosemary Edmonds.

21. As an interesting side note, one of the characters Nekhliudov meets at Korchagins, Ivan Ivanovich Kolossov, "a former Marshal of the Nobility, now a bank director, Korchagin's friend and a liberal," was in an early draft named Ivan Ilyich. This suggests a connection in Tolstoy's imagination between the spiritually numb hero of the earlier work and the equally empty socialites of *Resurrection.* Both are products of their social environment.

22. See, for example, E. N. Kuprejanova, *Estetika L. N. Tolstogo* (Moscow, Leningrad: Nauka, 1966), p. 298; and G. Ia. Galagan, "Geroi i siuzhet v poslednem romane L. N. Tolstogo," in *Problemy realizma russkoj literatury XIXogo veka,* ed. B. I Bursov and I. S. Serman (Moscow; Leningrad: Nauka, 1961), pp. 238–62. One of Tolstoy's contemporaries, the critic Platon Nikolaevich Krasnov (1866–1908?), speaks for many readers when he declares that "Nekhliudov remains little motivated and unexplained" (quoted in Opul'skaia, p. 363). Yet as an illustration of Tolstoy's spiritual and social ideals, Krasnov conceded, Nekhliudov is powerfully conceived.

23. Entry of 4 June 1895. Quoted in R. F. Christian, ed., *Tolstoy's Diaries, vol. 2, 1895–1910* (London: The Athlone Press, 1985), p. 410.

24. Gustafson continues: "Through life the sinner learns that in order for his soul to keep on growing, he must participate in the redemption of this unjust world . . . by clearing himself of his judgments so that he can right now help to create human relatedness." Gustafson, *Leo Tolstoy: Resident and Stranger,* p. 175.

25. Robert Donahoo, "Toward a Definition of *Resurrection:* Tolstoy's Novel as Theology and Art," *Literature and Belief,* 11 (1992): 11. Donahoo's article is a response to those critics who have dismissed *Resurrection* as marred because of its religious ideology. On the contrary, Donahoo argues, the union of theology and art is one source of the novel's power: "The field of *Resurrection* is the field of the spiritual self, the field of evoking dramatic images for theological ideas, the field of meditation" (p. 11).

26. David Patterson has broadened this to a general principle in the later Tolstoy's worldview: The "task of Tolstoy's lived theology," Patterson writes, is "[t]o become who I am, a human being and thus an expression of divine being." See David Patterson, "The Theological Dimension of Tolstoy's *Resurrection,*" *Christianity and Literature* 40, no. 2 (Winter 1991): 131.

27. For example, Orwin writes: "Although he still feels its allure, [Nekhliudov] rejects personal happiness as impossible . . ." (p. 477); and "Self-control and ultimately self-sacrifice must arise in order to counter full-blown passions. This they can do only through reason: the self-control of Nexljudov replaces the expansive nature of Pierre [of *War and Peace*] or Nikolen'ka [of *Childhood, Boyhood, Youth*]" (p. 478). On the contrary, Tolstoy emphasizes the unreasoning joy Nekhliudov experiences when he does his duty and heeds his conscience: "The certainty that nothing Maslova might do could alter his love for her rejoiced and lifted him to heights unknown till now . . ." (397). See Donna Orwin, "The Riddle of Prince Nexljudov," *The Slavic and East European Journal* 30, no. 4 (Winter 1986): 473–86.

28. The best article in English on this subject is Hugh McLean, "Tolstoy and Jesus," in *Christianity and Eastern Slavs,* vol. 2, *Russian Culture in Modern Times,* ed. Robert P. Hughes and Irina Paperno (Berkeley: University of California Press, 1994), pp. 103–23.

29. Entry from March 1855. In R. F. Christian, ed. and trans., *Tolstoy's Diaries, vol. 1, 1847–1894* (London: The Athlone Press, 1985), p. 101.

30. I learned about the controversy at the Tolstoy Museum and Estate during a private conversation with a scholar who works at the museum. This scholar, who spoke to me on the condition of anonymity, also mentioned other cases in which scholarly material was either rejected or published with significant revisions because of concerns over the reaction of the Orthodox community. The article in question was ultimately published, but only after the author was asked to make revisions.

31. Hence, the emergence of a cultlike figure, Felix Dzerzhinsky (1877–1926), founder of the Bolshevik secret police, the Cheka, widely admired for his willingness to kill for the sake of revolution. He did so, Andrei Sinyavsky put it, "in the name of a Heavenly Kingdom on earth. So that in Soviet iconography, the Crucified Lord is replaced by a Holy Executioner." See Andrei Synyavsky, *Soviet Civilization: A Cultural History,* trans. Joanne Turnbull (New York: Arcade Publishing, 1990), p. 126.

32. Bakhtin, p. 113. But as Michael Denner has shown in a penetrating recent essay, future generations of Soviet readers would battle to assimilate Tolstoy's moral authority to their own ideological agendas, even if those agendas were at odds with Tolstoy's stated positions. See Michael A. Denner, "The 'proletarian lord': Leo Tolstoy's Image during the Russian Revolutionary Periods," in Donna Tussing Orwin, ed., *Anniversary Essays on Tolstoy* (Cambridge: Cambridge University Press, 2010), pp. 219–44.

33. Donna Orwin intriguingly suggests that while Tolstoy's idealism might be a weakness in his critical thought, it does not necessarily undermine his artistic realism. In fact, his idealism, Orwin argues, is *necessary* for the success of his fiction: "[W]hile Tolstoy's hopefulness can be a defect in his thought, which can expect too much of human beings and sweep too much of human history under the carpet, in his fiction it is yet another element of his unsurpassed realism, which would be less true and less complete without it." Donna Tussing Orwin, ed., *Anniversary Essays on Tolstoy* (Cambridge: Cambridge University Press, 2010), p. 5.

34. Quoted in Opul'skaia, p. 356.

35. Ibid., pp. 368–69.

CHAPTER 13

1. See Harold Bloom, "Tolstoy and Heroism," in *The Western Canon: The Books and School of the Ages* (New York: Riverhead Trade, 1994), p. 336; and John Bayley, *Tolstoy and the Novel* (London: Chatto and Windus, 1966), p. 192.

2. In Cain's formulation, Tolstoy's essay "What is Art?" may be presumed to be included in the category of systematic moralizing, which Tolstoy is said to have overcome in his final novel (T. G. S. Cain, *Tolstoy* [London: Paul Elek, 1977], p. 187). Other critics have also remarked on the presence of ostensibly "un-Tolstoyan" ideas and its unexpected appearance at a time when Tolstoy seemed to be exclusively concerned with moralistic writings. David Kvitko, for instance, thinks it "surprising" that "'Hadji-Murat' recalls in style and theme [Tolstoy's] very first manner of writing; it is a beautiful novel in which Tolstoy forgot almost completely to moralize" (David Kvitko, *A Philosophic Study of Tolstoy* [New York, 1927], p. 103). L. D. Opul'skaia has gone so far as to suggest that there is hardly a modicum of religious/ethical thought in the novel (L. D. Opul'skaia, "O iubeleinom sobranii sochinenii Tolstogo," *Literaturnoe nasledstvo,* 69, no. 2 (1961): 522.]

3. L. N. Tolstoi, *PSS* 53,188.

4. L. N. Tolstoi, *PSS* 35, 598.

5. Ibid., p. 609.

6. Edmund Heier, "*Hadji-Murat* in Light of Tolstoy's Moral and Aesthetic Theories," *Revue Canadienne des Slavistes* 21, no. 2 (February 1979): 335.

7. Monika Greenleaf, from Stanford University, first suggested to me the idea of *Hadji-Murat* as a kind of literary "pastiche." "Pastiche," however, suggests literary parody, and Tolstoy's purpose in his final novella is not to playfully deconstruct his earlier artistic visions, but to reconstruct them along different lines in the service of a serious moral vision.

8. Letter to Count Sergei Nikolaevich Tolstoy and Maria Mikhailovna Shishkina, December 1851. Quoted in R. F. Christian, *Tolstoy's Letters, vol. 1, 1828–1879* (New York: Charles Scribner's Sons, 1978), p. 17.

9. Quoted in R. F. Christian, ed., *Tolstoy's Diaries, vol. 2, 1895–1910* (London: The Athlon Press, 1985), p. 429.

10. L. N. Tolstoi, *PSS* 35,286.

11. Page numbers in parentheses refer to the Maude translation of *Hadji-Murat* in Leo Tolstoy, *Great Short Works of Leo Tolstoy*, trans. Louise and Aylmer Maude (New York: Harper and Row Publishers; Perennial Classics edition, 2004).

12. Christian, *Tolstoy's Diaries, vol. 2, 1895–1910*, p. 457.

13. In *Resurrection* Tolstoy wrote: "Human beings are like rivers: the water is one and the same in all of them but every river is narrow in some places, flows swifter in others; here it is broad, there still, or clear, or cold, or muddy or warm. It is the same with men. Every man bears within him the germs of every human quality, and now manifests one, now another, and frequently is unlike himself, while still remaining the same man" (Leo Tolstoy, *Resurrection*, trans. Rosemary Edmunds [New York and London: Penguin Books, 1966], pp. 252–53; I, 59).

14. This might be an instance of Tolstoy's replacing "nature" with "rational consciousness" as the final arbiter of morality, as Donna Orwin argues he does in *Hadji-Murat*. See Donna Orwin, "Nature and the Narrator in *Chadži-Murat*," *Russian Literature* 28, no. 1 (July 1990): 125–44.

15. In an important article about the poetics in *Hadji-Murat*, Donald Fanger has made a similar point: "Nature as the vital theater of this drama—cruel, beautiful and subsisting. Its beauty is the same that led Turgenev either to sentimentalism (the epilogue to *Fathers and Sons*) or to stoical despair (the prose poem *Razgovor*), but Tolstoi seems to regard it here with something like relief from the demands of his religious anthropocentrism, extending to its variety that same *amor intellectualialis*—that knowledge founded on acceptance and love—which embraces all the characters (save one) in the clear-eyed, tough-minded, deeply poetic swan song which may well be his sketch for *la ficcion de la totalidad*." See Donald Fanger, "Nazarov's Mother: On the Poetics of Tolstoi's Late Epic," *Canadian-American Slavic Studies* 12, no. 4 (Winter 1978): 579.

16. Quoted in Alexandra Popoff, *Sophia Tolstoy: A Biography* (New York: Free Press, 2010), p. 106. Popoff's is the best biography of Sofya Andreevna in English. It provides a fascinating, detailed, and honest account of the Tolstoy marriage from the perspective of Tolstoy's wife.

17. Quoted in Tolstoy, *Great Short Works of Leo Tolstoy*, trans. Louise and Aylmer Maude, pp. 101–2, 5.

18. These are among the many criticisms of and observations about American society contained in the book. Unfortunately, the book's introduction, its brief biographical sketches of Tolstoy's American correspondents, and the footnotes are all in Russian,

but the letters themselves are translated into English and make fascinating reading, particularly for an American audience. N. Velikanova and R. Wittaker, eds., *L. N. Tolstoi i S.Sh.A.: Perepiska* [L. N. Tolstoy and the U.S.A.: Correspondence] (Moscow: Gorky Institute of World Literature of the Russian Academy of Sciences, 2004).

19. L. N. Tolstoi, *PSS* 31, 196.

20. A. P. Sergeenko, *Khadzhi-Murat L'va Tolstogo: Istoriia sozdaniia povesti* (Moscow: Sovremennik, 1983), p. 98.

21. L. N. Tolstoi, *PSS* 35, 622.

22. The renowned Russian graphic artist Evgeny Lanseray, in his beautiful illustrations of *Hadji-Murat,* published in multiple editions in the Soviet Union in the 1920s and 1930s, also sensed this connection. He painted the narrator walking through the fields as the young Tolstoy.

23. One wonders whether, in doing so, the censors had an inkling that they, like Butler, were participants in that very imperial structure with its labyrinth of lies and mechanisms of destruction, which brought so much suffering into the lives of so many.

24. Letter to V. G. Chertkov, Feburary 1890. L. N. Tolstoi, *PSS* 87, 10.

25. In his seminal article about *Hadji-Murat,* the Soviet scholar V. A. Tunimanov also concludes that the work ultimately offers "an optimistic philosophy of life." See V. A. Tunimanov, "Istoriia-iskusstvo" v povesti L.N. Tolstogo 'Hadji-Murat,' *Russkaia literatura: Istorika-literaturnyj zhurnal,* 1 (1984): 34. In a more recent article, American Tolstoy scholar David Herman sees the novella as an embodiment of Tolstoy's search for a divine truth he could never find, and his fundamental skepticism about the capacity of words to do anything more than point to the absence of such a truth. But this pessimistic, fragmented worldview is Herman's, not Tolstoy's. See David Herman, "Khadzhi-Murat's Silence," *Slavic Review* 64, no. 1 (Spring 2005): 1–23.

26. R. F. Christian, *Tolstoy's Diaries, vol. 1, 1847–1894* (London: The Athlone Press, 1985), p. 191.

27. R. F. Christian, *Tolstoy's Letters, vol. 2, 1880–1901* (New York: Charles Scribner's Sons, 1978), p. 716.

28. Aylmer Maude, *The Life of Tolstoy: Later Years* (London: Constable and Co. Limited, 1911), p. 669.

EPILOGUE

1. Richard Gustafson, *Leo Tolstoy: Resident and Stranger: A Study in Fiction and Theology* (Princeton, NJ: Princeton University Press, 1986), p. 212.

2. Leo Tolstoy, *Great Short Works of Leo Tolstoy,* trans. Louise and Aylmer Maude (New York: Harper and Row Publishers; Perennial Classics edition, 2004), p. 550.

3. F. M. Dostoevskii, *Polnoe sobranie sochinenii,* 30 vols. (Leningrad, 1976), vol. 14, p. 290.

4. Guy de Maupassant, "Le Roman," Preface to *Pierre et Jean* (Paris: Louis Conrad, 1909), p. xii.

bibliography

Afanas'ev, A. N. "Lisa-Plac heya." In *Narodnyie russkie skazki.* Pt. 1. Moskva: Gosu-darstvennoe izdatel'stvo khudozhestvennoi literatury, 1957.

Alexandrov, Vladimir. *Limits to Interpretation: The Meanings of* Anna Karenina. Madison: University of Wisconsin Press, 2004.

Anemone, Anthony. "Gender, Genre, and the Discourse of Imperialism in Tolstoy's 'The Cossacks.'" *Tolstoy Studies Journal,* 6 (1993): 47–63.

Apostolov, N. N. *Zhivoi Tolstoi.* Moscow, 1928.

Armstrong, Judith. "*Anna Karenina* and the Novel of Adultery." In Knapp and Mandelker, *Approaches to Teaching Tolstoy's* Anna Karenina. 117–23.

———. *The Unsaid* Anna Karenina. New York: Saint Martin's Press, 1988.

Babel, Isaak. "O tvorcheskom puti pisatelia" ["About the Artistic Path of a Writer"]. In *Sochineniia v dvukh tomakh.* Vol. 2. Moscow: Terra, 1996. 448–58.

Baer, Joachim T. "The 'Physiological Sketch' in Russian Literature." In *Mnemozina: Studia litteraria russica in honorem Vsevolod Setchkarev,* ed. Joachim T. Baer and Norman W. Ingham. Munich: Wilhelm Fink Verlag, 1974. 1–12.

Bakhtin, M. N. *Literaturno-kriticheskie stat'i.* Moscow: Khudozhestvennaia literatura, 1986.

———. *Problems of Dostoevsky's Poetics.* Ed. and trans. Caryl Emerson. Minneapolis: University of Minnesota Press, 1984.

Bayley, John. *Tolstoy and the Novel.* London: Chatto and Windus, 1966.

Benatar, David. *Better Never to Have Been: The Harm of Coming into Existence.* New York: Oxford University Press, 2006.

Berlin, Isaiah. *The Hedgehog and the Fox: An Essay on Tolstoy's View of History.* Chicago: Ivan R. Dee, 1993.

Blaisdell, Bob. Review of Anna Karenina *in Our Time: Seeing More Wisely,* by Gary Saul Morson. *Tolstoy Studies Journal* 19 (2007): 123–26.

Bloom, Allan. *Love and Friendship*. New York: Simon and Schuster, 1993.

Bloom, Harold. "Tolstoy and Heroism." In *The Western Canon: The Books and School of the Ages*. New York: Riverhead Trade, 1994. 310–25.

———. *The Western Canon: The Books and School of the Ages*. New York: Riverhead Trade, 1994.

Bocharov, S. G. *O khudozhestvennykh mirakh*. Moscow: Sovetskaia rossiia, 1985.

———. *Roman L. N. Tolstogo "Voina i mir."* 4th ed. Moscow: Khudozhestvennaia literatura, 1987.

Brown, Edward J. "Pisarev and the Transformation of Two Novels." In *Literature and Society in Imperial Russia, 1800–1914*, ed. William Mills Todd III. Palo Alto, CA: Stanford University Press, 1978. 151–72.

Cain, T. G. S. *Tolstoy*. London: Paul Elek, 1977.

Carden, Patricia. "The Expressive Self in *War and Peace*." *Canadian-American Slavic Studies* 12, no. 4 (Winter 1978): 519–34.

Chernyshevsky, N. G. "Detstvo i otrochestvo. Voennye rasskazy." In *L. N. Tolstoi v russkoi kritike*. Moscow: Gosudarstvennoe izdatel'stvo khudozhestvennoi literatury, 1952.

Christian, R. F., ed. and trans. *Tolstoy's Diaries, Vol. 1, 1847–1894*. London: The Athlone Press, 1985.

———. *Tolstoy's Diaries, Vol. 2, 1895–1910*. London: The Athlone Press, 1985.

———. *Tolstoy's Letters, Vol. 1, 1828–1879*. New York: Charles Scribner's Sons, 1978.

———. *Tolstoy's Letters, Vol. 2, 1880–1910*. New York: Charles Scribner's Sons, 1978.

———. *Tolstoy's* War and Peace: *A Study*. Oxford: Clarendon Press, 1962.

Clay, George R. *Tolstoy's Phoenix: From Method to Meaning in* War and Peace. Studies in Russian Literature and Theory. Evanston, IL: Northwestern University Press, 1998.

Comstock, Gary. "Face to Face with IT: The Naïve Reader's Moral Response to 'Ivan Ilych.'" *Neophilologus* 70, no. 3 (1986): 321–33.

Cooper, James Fenimore. *The Pathfinder, Or the Inland Sea*. Ed. Richard Dilworth Rust. Albany: State University of New York Press, 1981.

Danaher, David. "Tolstoy's Use of Light and Dark Imagery in 'The Death of Ivan Il'ych.'" *Slavic and East European Journal* 39, no. 2 (1995): 227–40.

Daniels, Anthony. "Chekhov and Tolstoy." *The New Criterion* 23, no. 8 (April 2005): 31–36.

Dayananda, Y. J. "'The Death of Ivan Ilych': A Psychological Study on Death and Dying." *Literature and Psychology*, 22 (1972): 191–98.

de Maupassant, Guy. *Pierre et Jean*. Paris: Louis Conrad, 1909.

Michael A. Denner. "The 'proletarian lord': Leo Tolstoy's Image during the Russian Revolutionary Period." In Donna Tussing Orwin, ed., *Anniversary Essays on Tolstoy*. Cambridge: Cambridge University Press, 2010. 219–244.

———. "Tolstoyan Nonaction: The Advantage of Doing Nothing." *Tolstoy Studies Journal* XIII (2001): 8–22.

Donahoo, Robert. "Toward a Definition of Resurrection: Tolstoy's Novel as Theology and Art." *Literature and Belief*, 11 (1991): 1–12.

Donskov, A. A. *L. N. Tolstoy and N. N. Strakhov: Complete Correspondence*, 2 vols. Ottawa, Canada: Slavic Research Group at the University of Ottawa and State L. N. Tolstoy Museum, 2003.

Dostoevskii, F. M. *Polnoe sobranie sochinenii*. 30 vols., vol. 14. Leningrad, 1976.

Dostoevsky, Fyodor. *A Writer's Diary, Vol. 1, 1873–1876*. Trans. Kenneth Lanz. Evanston, IL: Northwestern University Press, 1994; 2009.

Duncan, Robert. "Ivan Ilych's Death: Secular or Religious?" *University of Dayton Review* 15 (1981): 99–106.

Eikhenbaum, Boris. *Tolstoi in the Seventies*. Trans. Albert Kaspin. Ann Arbor, MI: Ardis, 1982.

———. *Tolstoi in the Sixties*. Trans. Duffield White. Ann Arbor, MI: Ardis, 1982. [In Russian: *Lev Tolstoi. 60-e gody.* Leningrad-Moscow: *Goslitizdat*, 1931.]

Emerson, Caryl. "The Tolstoy Connection in Bakhtin." *PMLA* 100, no. 1 (January 1985): 68–80.

Fanger, Donald. "Nazarov's Mother: On the Poetics of Tolstoi's Late Epic." *Canadia–American Slavic Studies* 12, no. 4 (Winter 1978): 571–82.

Fatiushchenko, V. I. "Chustvo zhizni i poeziia zhizni v tvorchestve L. N. Tolstogo (1850-e—1860-kh. Godov)." In *Tolstoi i o Tolstom: Materiialy issledovaniia, Vypusk 3.* Moscow: IMLI, 2009.

Feuer, Kathryn B. *Tolstoy and the Genesis of* War and Peace. Ed. Robin Feuer Miller and Donna Tussing Orwin. Ithaca, NY, and London: Cornell University Press, 1996.

Friedrich, Paul. "Tolstoy, Homer, and Genotypical Influence." *Comparative Literature* 56, no. 4 (Autumn 2004): 283–99.

Fromm, Erich. *Escape from Freedom.* New York: Avon Books, 1969.

Galagan, Ia. "Geroi i siuzhet v poslednem romane L. N. Tolstogo." In *Problemy realizma russkoj literatury XIXogo veka*, ed. B. I. Bursov and I. S. Serman. Moscow; Leningrad: Nauka, 1961.

Gerstein, Linda. *Nikolai Strakhov.* Cambridge, MA: Harvard University Press, 1971.

Ginzburg, Lidiia. *O psikhologicheskoi proze.* Leningrad: Khudozhestvennaia literatura, 1977.

Goscilo, Helena. "Motif-Mesh as Matrix: Body, Sexuality, Adultery, and the Woman Question." In Knapp and Mandelker, *Approaches to Teaching Tolstoy's* Anna Karenina, 83–89.

Greenleaf, Monika and Stephen Moeller-Sally, eds. *Russian Subjects: Empire, Nation, and the Culture of the Golden Age.* Evanston, IL: Northwestern University Press, 1998.

Grossman, L. P. "Smert' Ivan Il'icha: Istoriia pisaniia i pechataniia." In Tolstoy, *Polnoe sobranie sochinenii L. N. Tolstogo.* Vol. 26. Moscow, 1936. 679–91.

Gudzi, N. K. "Istoriia pisaniia i pechataniia 'Voskreseniia.'" In Tolstoy, *Polnoe sobranie sochinenii L. N. Tolstogo.* Vol. 33. Moscow, 1935. 329–22.

Gutsche, George. "Moral Fiction: Tolstoy's *The Death of Ivan Il'ich*." In *Tolstoy's "The Death of Ivan Il'ich": A Critical Companion*, ed. Gary R. Jahn. Evanston, IL: Northwestern University Press, 1999.

Gustafson, Richard. *Leo Tolstoy: Resident and Stranger: A Study in Fiction and Theology.* Princeton, NJ: Princeton University Press, 1986; 2006.

Hagan, John. "Ambivalence in Tolstoy's *The Cossacks*." *Novel: A Forum on Fiction* 3, no. 1 (1969): 28–47.

Heier, Edmund. "*Hadji-Murat* in Light of Tolstoy's Moral and Aesthetic Theories." *Revue Canadienne des Slavistes* 21, no. 2 (February 1979): 324–35.

Herman, David. "Allowable Passions in *Anna Karenina*." *Tolstoy Studies Journal*, 8 (1995–96): 5–32.

———. "Khadzhi-Murat's Silence." *Slavic Review* 64, no. 1 (Spring 2005): 1–23.

Herzen. A. "The Russian People and Socialism. A Letter to Michelet" (1851). In *The Memoirs of Alexander Herzen.* Vol 4. London: Chatto and Windus, 1968.

Hokanson, Katya. *Writing at Russia's Border.* Toronto: University of Toronto Press, 2008.

Ikiru. Director Akira Kurosawa. Japan, 1952.

Jackson, Robert L. "The Archetypal Journey: Aesthetic and Ethical Imperative in the Art of Tolstoy." *Russian Literature* 11 (1982): 389–410.

———. "Chance and Design in *Anna Karenina*." In *The Disciplines of Criticism: Essays in Literary Theory, Interpretation, and History,* ed. Peter Demetz, Thomas Greene, and Lowry Nelson, Jr. New Haven, CT: Yale University Press, 1968.

———. "The Night Journey: Anna Karenina's Return to Saint Petersburg." In Knapp and Mandelker, *Approaches to Teaching Tolstoy's* Anna Karenina, 150–60.

———. "The Second Rebirth of Pierre Bezukhov." *Canadian-American Slavic Studies* 12, no. 4 (Winter 1978): 335–42.

Jahn, Gary. "The Crisis in Tolstoy and in *Anna Karenina*." In Knapp and Mandelker, *Approaches to Teaching Tolstoy's* Anna Karenina, 67–73.

———. *"The Death of Ivan Ilich": An Interpretation.* New York: Twayne Publishers, 1993.

———. "The Image of the Railroad in *Anna Karenina*." *The Slavic and East European Journal* 25, no. 2 (Summer 1981): 1–10.

———. "A Note on the Miracle Motifs in the Later Works of Lev Tolstoi." In *The Supernatural in Slavic and Baltic Literatures: Essays in Honor of Victor Terras.* Columbus, OH: Slavica, 1988. 191–99.

———, ed. *Tolstoy's "The Death of Ivan Il'Ich": A Critical Companion.* Evanston, IL: Northwestern University Press, 1999.

———. "The Unity of *Anna Karenina*." *Russian Review* 41, no. 2 (April 1982): 144–58.

Jones, Malcolm V. "Problems of Communication in *Anna Karenina*." In *New Essays on Tolstoy,* ed. Malcolm Jones. New York: Cambridge University Press, 1979.

Kaufman, Andrew. "Existential Quest and Artistic Possibility in Tolstoy's *The Cossacks*." *Slavonic and East European Review* 83, no. 2 (April 2005): 208–33.

———. "Tolstoi i Strakhov: Labirinty tvorcheskikh stseplenii." In *Tolstoi i o Tolstom: Materiialy issledovaniia, Vypusk 3.* Moscow: IMLI, 2009. 240–53

———. "Microcosm and Macrocosm in *War and Peace*: The Interrelationship of Poetics and Metaphysics." *Slavic and East European Journal* 43, no. 3 (Autumn 1999): 495–510.

Kaufmann, Walter. *Nietzsche: Philosopher, Psychologist, Antichrist.* 4th ed. Princeton, NJ: Princeton University Press, 1975.

Knapp, Liza, and Amy Mandelker, eds. *Approaches to Teaching Tolstoy's* Anna Karenina. New York: The Modern Language Association, 2003.

Knowles, A. V. "Russian Views of *Anna Karenina,* 1875–1878." *The Slavic and East European Journal* 22, no. 3 (Autumn 1978): 301–12.

———., ed. *Tolstoy: The Critical Heritage.* London, Henley, and Boston: Routledge and Kegan Paul, 1978.

Kornblatt, Judith. *The Cossack Hero in Russian Literature: A Study in Cultural Mythology.* Madison: University of Wisconsin Press, 1992.

Kronman, Anthony T. *Education's End: Why Our Colleges and Universities Have Given Up on the Meaning of Life.* New Haven, CT, and London: Yale University Press, 2007.

Kvitko, David. *A Philosophic Study of Tolstoy.* New York, 1927.

Kuprejanova, E. N. *Estetika L. N. Tolstogo.* Moscow, Leningrad: Nauka, 1966.

Lavrin, Janko. "Tolstoy and Nietzsche." In *Tolstoy: An Approach.* New York: The Macmillan Company, 1946. 153–61.

Layton, Susan. *Russian Literature and Empire: Conquest of the Caucasus from Pushkin to Tolstoy*. New York: Cambridge University Press, 1994.

Ledkovsky, Marina. "Dolly Oblonskaia as Structural Device in *Anna Karenina*." *Canadian-American Slavic Studies* 12, no. 4 (Winter 1978—special issue on Tolstoy edited by Richard Gustafson): 543–48.

Lermontov, Mikhail. *A Hero of Our Time*. Trans. Marian Schwartz. New York: The Modern Library, 2004.

Lomunov, K. N., ed. "Lev Tolstoi o romane 'Voskresenie.'" In *Roman L. N. Tolstogo "Voskresenie": Istoriko-funtsional'noe issledovanie*. Moscow: "Nauka," 1991. 8–12.

———. "Sud'ba 'Voskreseniia' (pervye otkliki gazetnoj i zhurnal'noj kritiki v Rossii)." In *Roman L. N . Tolstogo "Voskresenie": Istoriko-funtsional'noe issledovanie*. Moscow: Nauka 1991. 13–50.

Lönnqvist, Barbara. "*Anna Karenina*." In *The Cambridge Companion to Tolstoy*, ed. Donna Tussing Orwin. Cambridge: Cambridge University Press, 2002. 80–95.

Love, Jeff. *The Overcoming of History in* War and Peace. Studies in Slavic Literature and Poetics 42. Amsterdam; New York: Rodopi, 2004.

Lovejoy, Arthur. *The Great Chain of Being: The Study of the History of an Idea*. 2nd ed. Cambridge, MA: Harvard University Press, 2005.

Lukacs, Georg. "Tolstoy and the Development of Realism." In *Tolstoy: A Collection of Critical Essays*, ed. Ralph E. Matlaw. Englewood Cliffs, NJ: Prentice-Hall, Inc., 1967. 78–94.

Mandelker, Amy. *Framing* Anna Karenina: *Tolstoy, the Woman Question, and the Victorian Novel*. Columbus: The Ohio State University Press, 1993.

Maude, Aylmer. *The Life of Tolstoy: Later Years*. London: Constable and Co. Limited, 1911.

McLean, Hugh. *In Quest of Tolstoy*. Brighton, MA: Academic Studies Press, 2008.

———."Review Article: *War and Peace*, Original Version." *Tolstoy Studies Journal* 20 (2009).

———. "Tolstoy and Jesus." *Christianity and Eastern Slavs*. Vol. 2, *Russian Culture in Modern Times*, ed. Robert P. Hughes and Irina Paperno. Berkeley: University of California Press, 1994.

Medzhibovskaya, Inessa. *Tolstoy and the Religious Culture of His Time: A Biography of a Long Conversation, 1845–1887*. Lanham, MD, and Plymouth, UK: Lexington Books, 2008.

Merezhkovsky, Dmitry. *Tolstoy as Man and Artist*. New York: Knickerbocker Press, 1902.

Morson, Gary Saul. Anna Karenina *in Our Time: Seeing More Wisely*. New Haven, CT, and London: Yale University Press, 1997.

———. *Hidden in Plain View: Narrative and Creative Potentials in* War and Peace. Palo Alto, CA: Stanford University Press, 1987.

———. "Prosaics and *Anna Karenina*." *Tolstoy Studies Journal*, 1 (1988): 1–12.

———. "The Reader as Voyeur: Tolstoy and the Poetics of Didactic Fiction." *Canadian-American Slavic Studies* 12, no. 4 (Winter 1978): 465–80.

Moser, Charles A. *Esthetics as Nightmare: Russian Literary Theory, 1855–1870*. Princeton, NJ: Princeton University Press, 1989.

Nabokov, Vladimir. *Lectures on Russian Literature*. Ed. Fredson Bowers. New York and London: Harcourt Brace Jovanovich, 1981.

Nickell, William. *The Death of Tolstoy: Russia on the Eve, Astapovo Station, 1910*. Ithaca, NY: Cornell University Press, 2010.

Olson, Laura J. "Russianness, Femininity, and Romantic Aesthetics in *War and Peace*." *Russian Review* 56, no. 4 (October 1997): 515–31.

Opul'skaia, L. D. *Lev Nikolaevich Tolstoi: Materialy k biografii s 1892 po 1899 god.* Moscow: IMLI, 1998.

———. "O iubeleinom sobranii sochinenii Tolstogo." *Literaturnoe nasledstvo* 69, no. 2 (1961): 522.

———. "Povest' L. N. Tolstogo Kazaki." In *L. N. Tolstoi, Kazaki.* Moscow: Akademiia nauk, 1963. 341–51.

Orwin, Donna Tussing, ed. *Anniversary Essays on Tolstoy.* Cambridge: Cambridge University Press, 2010.

———. *Consequences of Consciousness: Turgenev, Dostoevsky, and Tolstoy.* Palo Alto, CA: Stanford University Press, 2007.

———. "Nature and the Narrator in 'Chadži-Murat.'" *Russian Literature* 28, no. 1 (July 1990): 125–44.

———. "The Riddle of Prince Nexljudov." *The Slavic and East European Journal* 30, no. 4 (Winter 1986): 473–86.

———. "Tolstoy's Antiphilosophical Philosophy in *Anna Karenina.*" In Knapp and Mandelker, *Approaches to Teaching Tolstoy's* Anna Karenina, 95–103.

———. *Tolstoy's Art and Thought, 1847–1880.* Princeton, NJ: Princeton University Press, 1993.

Palievsky, P. V. *Literatura i teoriia.* 2nd ed. Moscow, 1978.

———. *Russkie Klassiki: Opyt obshchej kharakteristiki.* Moscow: Khudozhestvennaia literatura, 1987.

Patterson, David. "The Theological Dimension of Tolstoy's *Resurrection.*" *Christianity and Literature* 40, no. 2 (Winter 1991): 123–36.

Pisarev, D. I. *Literaturnaya kritika v trex tomax.* 3 vols. Leningrad: Khudozhestvennaia literatura, 1981.

Pomper, Philip. *The Russian Revolutionary Intelligentsia.* Arlington Heights, IL: Harlan Davidson, 1970.

Popoff, Alexandra. *Sophia Tolstoy: A Biography.* New York: Free Press, 2010.

Rancour-Laferriere, Daniel. "Narcissism, Masochism, and Denial in *The Death of Ivan Il'ich.*" In *Tolstoy's "The Death of Ivan Il'ich": A Critical Companion,* ed. Gary R. Jahn. Evanston, IL: Northwestern University Press, 1999.

———. *Tolstoy's Pierre Bezukhov: A Psychoanalytic Study.* London: Bristol Classical Press, 1993.

Rice, James L. "Comic Devices in *The Death of Ivan Ilych.*" *Slavic and East European Journal* 47 no. 1 (2003): 77–95.

Rogers, Philip. "The Sufferings of Young Olenin: Tolstoy's Werther." *Tolstoy Studies Journal,* 17 (2005): 59–70.

Rozanov, V. V. *O pisatel'stve i pisateliakh* (Moscow, 1995).

Russell, Robert. "From Individual to Universal: Tolstoy's 'Smert' Ivana Il'icha.'" *The Modern Language Review* 76, no. 3 (July 1981): 629–42.

Saburov, A. A. *"Voina i mir" L. N. Tolstogo: Problematika poetiki.* Moscow: Izdatel'stvo Moskovskogo universiteta, 1959.

Sankovitch, Natasha. *Repetition in Tolstoy: Creating and Recovering Experience.* Palo Alto, CA: Stanford University Press, 1998.

Sergeenko, A. P. *Khadzhi-Murat L'va Tolstogo: Istoriia sozdaniia povesti.* Moscow: Sovremennik, 1983.

Serkirin, Peter, ed. *Americans in Conversation with Tolstoy: Selected Accounts, 1887–1923.* Jefferson, NC: McFarland and Co., 2006.

Shcheglov, Mark. *Literaturnaia kritika.* Moscow: Izdatel'stvo "khudozhestnvennaia literatura," 1971.

Shestov, Lev. "The Good in the Teaching of Tolstoy and Nietzsche: Philosophy and Preaching." In *Dostoevsky, Tolstoy, and Nietzsche,* ed. Spencer Roberts and Bernard Martin. Athens: Ohio University Press, 1978; 1969. 1–140.

———. *Job's Balances: On the Sources of the Eternal Truths.* Trans. Camilla Coventry and C. A. Macartney. Athens: Ohio University Press, 1957.

Shklovsky, Victor. *Lev Tolstoy.* Trans. Olga Shartse. Moscow: Raduga Publishers, 1988.

———. *Mater'ial i stil' v romane "Voina i mir."* Moscow: Izdatel'stvo "Federatsiia." Reprint: University of Michigan, 1967.

Simmons, Ernest J. *Leo Tolstoy,* Boston: Little, Brown and Company, 1946.

Sinyavsky, Andrei. *Soviet Civilization: A Cultural History.* Trans. Joanne Turnbull. New York: Arcade Publishing, 1990.

Slivitskaia, O. V. *"Voina i mir" L. N. Tolstogo: Problemy chelovecheskogo obshcheniia.* Leningrad: Izdatel'stvo Leningradskogo universiteta, 1988.

Sloane, David. "The Poetry in *War and Peace.*" *The Slavic and East European Journal* 40, no. 1 (Spring 1988): 63–84.

Sorokin, Boris. *Tolstoy in Prerevolutionary Russian Criticism.* Columbus: The Ohio State University Press for Miami University, 1979.

Spence, G. W. *Tolstoy the Ascetic.* London: Oliver and Boyd, 1967.

Steiner, George. *Tolstoy or Dostoevsky.* New York: Knopf, 1959.

———. *Tolstoy or Dostoevsky: An Essay in the Old Criticism.* 2nd ed. New Haven, CT: Yale University Press, 1996.

———. *Tolstoy or Dostoevsky: An Essay in the Old Criticism.* New York: Alfred A. Knopf, 1959.

Stenbock-Fermor, Elisabeth. *The Architecture of* Anna Karenina. Lisse, The Netherlands: Peter de Ridder Press, 1975.

Strakhov, Nikolai. *Kriticheskie stat'i ob I. S. Turgeneve i L. N. Tolstom (1862–1885).* Vol. 1, 4th ed. Kiev: Izdaniie I. P. Matchenko, 1901 [Reprint: The Hague; Paris: Mouton, 1968].

Tolstoy, Leo. *Anna Karenina.* New York: W. W. Norton and Co., Ltd., Critical Edition, 1993.

———. *Anna Karenina.* Ed. George Gibian. 2nd. ed. New York: W. W. Norton and Company, 1995.

———. *Anna Karenina.* Trans. Richard Pevear and Larissa Volokhonsky. New York: Penguin Books, 2004.

———. *Childhood, Boyhood, Youth.* Trans. Michael Scammel. New York: The Modern Library, 2002.

———. *Confession.* Trans. David Patterson. New York and London: W. W. Norton and Company, 1983 (first published in 1884).

———. "The Death of Ivan Ilych." In *Tolstoy's Short Fiction,* ed. Michael R. Katz. New York and London: W. W. Norton and Company, 2008. 83–128.

———. *Essays and Letters by Lev Tolstoy.* Trans. Aylmer Maude. New York: Oxford University Press, 1911.

———. *Great Short Works of Leo Tolstoy.* Trans. Louise and Aylmer Maude. New York: Harper and Row Publishers, 1967.

———. *Great Short Works of Leo Tolstoy.* Trans. Louise and Aylmer Maude. New York: Harper and Row Publishers; Perennial Classics edition, 2004.

———. *Lev Tolstoi ob iskusstve i literature.* Moscow: Sovetskii pisatel,' 1958.

———. *On Life and Essays on Religion.* Trans. Aylmer Maude. London: Oxford University Press, 193.

————. *Polnoe sobranie sochinenii L. N. Tolstogo* [*The Complete Collected Works of L. N. Tolstoy*]. 90 vols. Moscow, 1928–58.

————. "Roundtable Discussion from IMLI: The Complete Correspondence of Leo Tolstoy and Nikolai Strakhov." *Tolstoy Studies Journal,* 18 (2006): 90.

————. *The Raid and Other Stories.* Trans. Louise and Aylmer Maude. Oxford; New York: Oxford University Press, 1982.

————. *Resurrection.* Trans. Rosemary Edmonds. New York and London: Penguin Books, 1966.

————. "Sevastopol in May" (1855). In *Tolstoy's Short Fiction,* ed. Michael R. Katz. New York: W. W. Norton and Company, 2008. 14–45.

————. *Tolstoy's Major Fiction.* Chicago and London: The University of Chicago Press, 1978.

————. *War and Peace.* Ed. George Gibian. 2nd ed. New York: W. W. Norton, 1996.

————. *War and Peace.* Trans. Richard Pevear and Larissa Volokhonsky. New York: Alfred A. Knopf, 2007.

————. "Why Do Men Stupefy Themselves?" In *Recollections and Essays,* trans. Aylmer Maude. London, 1937; Reprint, 1961.

Tunimanov, V. A. "Istoriia-iskusstvo" v povesti L.N. Tolstogo 'Hadji-Murat.'" *Russkaia literatura: Istorika-literaturnyj zhurnal,* 1 (1984): 14–34.

Turgenev, I. S. *Polnoe sobranie sochinenii i pisem.* Vol. 10. Moscow and Leningrad, 1961–68.

Turner, Brian. *Here, Bullet.* Farmington, ME: Alice James Books, 2005.

Turner, C. J. G. "Tolstoy's *The Cossacks:* The Question of Genre." *The Modern Language Review* 73 (July 1978): 563–72.

Velikanova, N., and R. Whittaker, eds. *L. N. Tolstoi i S.Sh.A.: Perepiska* [L. N. Tolstoy and the U.S.A.: Correspondence]. Moscow: Gorky Institute of World Literature of the Russian Academy of Sciences, 2004.

Vernelli, Toni. Interview. *The New Criterion,* 26 (January 2008): 1. Print.

Vinogradov, V. V. *O iazyke khudozhestvenoi literatury.* Moscow, 1959.

Wachtel, Andrew. *The Battle for Childhood: Creation of a Russian Myth.* Palo Alto, CA: Stanford University Press, 1990.

Warner, Nicholas O. "The Texture of Time in *War and Peace.*" *The Slavic and East European Journal* 28, no. 2 (Summer 1984): 192–204.

Wasiolek, Edward. "Tolstoy's *The Death of Ivan Ilyich* and Jamesian Fictional Imperatives." *Modern Fiction Studies* 6, no. 4 (Winter 1960/1961): 314–24.

————. *Tolstoy's Major Fiction.* Chicago: University of Chicago Press, 1978.

Zelinsky, V. A., ed. *Russkaia kriticheskaiia literatura o proizvedenniiakh L. N. Tolstogo: khronologicheskii sbornik kritiko-bibliograficheskikh statei.* 8 vols. Ann Arbor, MI: University Microfilms reprint, 1966.

Zhdanov, V. A. *Ot 'Anny Kareninoi' k 'Voskresen'iu'* Moscow: Izdatel'stvo "Kniga," 1968.

Zver'ev, Aleksei, and Vladimir Tunimanov. *Lev Tolstoi.* Moscow: Molodaia gvardiia, 2006.

index